D0373420

¡Pobre Raza!

F. ARTURO ROSALES

¡POBRE RAZA!

Violence, Justice,
and Mobilization
among México
Lindo Immigrants,
1900–1936

UNIVERSITY OF TEXAS PRESS ⟨⟩ AUSTIN

Copyright © 1999 by the University of Texas Press
All rights reserved
Printed in the United States of America

First edition, 1999

Requests for permission to reproduce material from this work
should be sent to Permissions, University of Texas Press, Box 7819,
Austin, TX 78713-7819.

⊗The paper used in this publication meets the minimum
requirements of American National Standard for Information
Sciences—Permanence of Paper for Printed Library Materials,
ANSI Z39.48-1984.

Library of Congress Cataloging-in-Publication Data

Rosales, Francisco A. (Francisco Arturo)
    Pobre raza! : violence, justice, and mobilization among México
Lindo immigrants, 1900–1936 / F. Arturo Rosales. — 1st ed.
        p.   cm.
    Includes bibliographical references (p.   ) and index.
    ISBN 0-292-77094-4
    ISBN 0-292-77095-2 (pbk.)
    1. Mexicans—Civil rights—United States.   2. Mexicans—
Crimes against—United States—History—20th century.
3. Immigrants—Civil rights—United States.   4. Criminal
justice, Administration of—United States—History—20th century.   5. Discrimination in criminal justice administration—
United States—History—20th century.   I. Title.
E184.M5 R637   1999
323.1'16872073—dc21   98-58049

Paperback cover photos reprinted by permission from the Joseph
and Grace Alexander Collection, Arizona Collection, Arizona State
University Libraries (top), and the Arizona Historical Foundation,
Hayden Library, Arizona State University (bottom).

Judging by their garb, they were simply poor peasants, very unlikely to give the police a hard time. They came here to work. Why were they shot? ¡pobre raza!

—*EL COSMOPOLITA* (KANSAS CITY), MAY 4, 1918
   (TRANSLATED BY AUTHOR)

Dedicado a la memoria de Papa Beto y Papa Igo, y también a George "Chochi" Dalton, mis padres.

Contents

Acknowledgments   xi

Introduction   1

1   The Mexican Revolution, Border Mexicans, and
     Anglos   9

2   México Lindo Mobilization   22

3   The Consuls and México Lindo   34

4   Mexican Criminals in the United States   49

5   Police Treatment of Mexican Immigrants   75

6   Civilian Violence against Mexican Immigrants   99

7   Mexicans and Justice in the Courtroom   122

8   Capital Punishment and Mexicans in the United
     States   136

9   Doing Time for Mexicans in the United States   156

10   Extradition between Mexico and the United States   177

Conclusion   193

Appendix A. White and Black Civilian Violence against
     Mexicans   203

Appendix B. Mexican-on-Mexican Violence in Texas and
     the Chicago Area   213

Notes   219

Bibliography   255

Index   271

ILLUSTRATIONS

1   Villistas posing and relaxing, about 1915   18

2   Carrancistas and the Cruz Blanca nursing brigade   19

3   Jesús Franco, civil rights activist   31

4   Venustiano Carranza   41

5   D. Eduardo Ruíz, consul general in San Francisco   43

6   Double wedding in Phoenix of Rosales brothers and García sisters   56

7   Newspaper clippings of police killings in Houston   83

8   A group of Arizona Rangers   92

9   Five Mexicans condemned to die at Florence, Arizona   138

10   Pedro Sánchez with priest   146

11   Guards and Mexican prisoners at Arizona State Prison at Florence   159

12   Clipping about Blue Ridge Farm   160

13   William H. "Wenceslao" Laustauneau's mug shot   175

14   The young and charismatic Lucio Blanco   182

15   Bernardo Roa's mug shot   185

16   James Price's mug shot   192

TABLES

1   Arrest Rates for Mexicans in Proportion to the Mexican
Population for Selected Regions, 1929   51

2   Percentage of Mexicans Who Immigrated after 1920 for
Most Recent to Oldest Colonias   52

3   Ratio of Mexican Men to Women for Selected Cities,
1930   57

4   Natives of Mexico by State, 1930   58

5   Percentage of Mexicans between the Ages of Eighteen
and Thirty-five in Five Cities, 1930   59

6   Mexican-on-Mexican Violence, 1900–1935 ($N = 62$)   64

7   Homicides in Chicago by Ethnic-Racial Group,
1922–1927   65

8   Incidents of Civilian Violence toward Mexicans,
1900–1936   100

9   Executions in Arizona, California, New Mexico, and
Texas, 1901–1935   137

10   Mexicans in Folsom Prison by Crime, September 1929   163

Acknowledgments

IN THE GATHERING of the data for this book, many individuals and institutions have been of great support. Indeed, I acquired my first important pieces as early as the 1970s when I wrote my dissertation on Mexican immigration to East Chicago, Indiana. I uncovered the final documents for the work in 1996 in Chicago and Springfield, Illinois; Mexico City; and, in 1997, in Houston. If I could list all of the sources of support, they would date back to my years as a graduate student at Indiana University, as a faculty member at the University of Houston, and, most recently, as a member of the Arizona State University (ASU)community. I am particularly grateful for the Arts, Sciences, and Humanities Grant I received from the Office of Research at ASU when I first started writing. Also, travel awards from the Center for Latin American Studies and the College of Liberal Arts and Sciences at ASU have allowed me to continue my research in various parts of Mexico and the United States.

I must thank Barbara Metcalf, who, as chair of the department of history at the University of California, Davis, was so kind to me and my wife when I taught there during the 1992–1993 academic year. She did not burden me with any work other than my teaching duties, which were relatively light. It was during my year at Davis that I finished the first draft and was also able to spend a great deal of time at the Bancroft Library and the California State Library at Sacramento doing further research. In addition, during 1992 and 1993, two consecutive Recovering the Hispanic Literary Past grants from the University of Houston allowed me to visit archives at UCLA and the Huntington Library where, although my mission was for another project, I collected more information for this book.

To those individuals at the various archives who often helped beyond the call of duty, I will be eternally grateful. The folks at the Illinois State Library at Springfield and at the Secretaría de Relaciones Exteriores in Mexico City, where I spent the lion's share of my research time, were particularly helpful. Because of the archival support staff wherever I worked, I was able to home in quickly on the items necessary for this study.

I would like to thank John Wunder who plowed through the first painfully long draft and provided essential ideas or reorganization. I am also grateful to Harvey Rice, Ed Escobar, Oscar Martínez, Arnoldo De León, Clare "Bud" McKanna, Roberto Alvarez, Daniel Arreola, Si Fullinwider, Arnold Bauer, and the anonymous referees for the University of Texas Press who read all or significant portions of my manuscript and made important criticisms and suggestions. My colleague and *compañero* Brian Gratton also has helped me shape my ideas on race and class, agreeing with me on some and challenging me on others.

Nicolás Kanellos, John Aguilar, and Miguel Tinker Salas not only made important suggestions on this work but also have supported me as friends during some very trying times in my career, much of which has spanned the creation of this study. I also owe a special debt to Christine Marín, who was always there for me next door at the Chicano Collection. To Al French, my student, who shared Jesús Franco's documents and long-forgotten book on Las Comisiones Honoríficas Mexicanas, I hope that the memory of your grandfather will live on in my book.

The members of my extended family, my mother, Refugio Dalton, my *tía*, Mercedes Rosales; my father, Jorge Dalton; and my *tíos* Roberto and Rodrigo Rosales, who are not with me anymore, all remembered the era on which I wrote. It is from them that I first learned about Aurelio Pompa, Alfredo Grijalva, the *hermanos* Hernández, the *hermanos* León, and other characters who loom large in my book. In Chicago, my friends Eduardo Peralta and José Anguiano served a similar purpose—*que en paz descancen.* To them the long forgotten prison escape stories of Bernardo Roa and his mates and life in the "Roaring Twenties" were vivid memories when I interviewed them in the 1970s.

Finally, I owe a great deal of gratitude to my wife, Graciela. In the five years we have been married she tolerated my periodic immersions into my work and patiently listened to my ruminations and theories, even, I suspect, when the conversation was not terribly interesting.

Note: All translations are by the author.

¡Pobre Raza!

INTRODUCTION

IN THE UNITED STATES, large-scale outbursts against immigration began in the nineteenth century when Anglo Americans reacted first to the influx of Catholic Irish and German newcomers and then to Asians and southern and eastern Europeans, but in this century, Mexicans have been the main recipients of such antipathy.[1] Americans are again angry over immigration, especially the influx from south of the border. This latest anti-immigrant trend, however, is mild when compared with the most severe reaction to Mexicans in U.S. history during the first decades of this century, the era of the story covered in this book.

Perhaps the most startling discovery in preparing this study is the aplomb these immigrants displayed for interacting with American officials and politicians of all types to combat abuse, all the while desiring to return to Mexico. That the Mexican government aided the immigrants does not in any way reduce their own contribution. The account of how Mexican immigrants combated this abuse is presented mainly within the framework of the U.S. justice system, violence within that system, and the immigrants' reaction to the Anglo hostility that emerged during massive Mexican immigration from the 1890s to the 1930s.

In the early phase of Chicano studies, nationalistic young scholars searched intently for examples of victimization to demonstrate the thorough oppression of Mexicans in the United States.[2] Now many scholars believe it is time to move on beyond the search for oppression because the pantheon of Chicano research is replete with sufficient examples of victimization, and some critics even believe that the experience of Mexicans is no different than that of other immigrants, especially those who came to the United States in the late nineteenth century.[3]

But in the rush to judgment, the significant themes of oppression have not been adequately developed, and, in many cases, they are caricatures in the mold of what Alex Saragoza called "we versus them" historiography. Recognizing the need to transcend simplistic racism or victimization models in explaining the history of Mexicans in the United States does not nullify oppression as a major defining ingredient. So rather than setting aside the abuses and moving on to more agency oriented issues, I believe oppression and racism still require closer analysis and reinterpretation, but not just to indulgently parade before readers a stream of demonized Anglo American acts.

In looking at other studies on immigration in this era, including some of my own work, it is obvious that immigrants and the Mexican government viewed inequities in the justice system and civilian mistreatment as perhaps the most severe form of repression. They quickly mobilized politically around the issue because it could not be put on hold; the abuse provoked too much pain, both physical and psychological.

Before the beginning of massive Mexican immigration of the 1890s, the relationship between native Southwest Mexicans and Anglos had evolved within a competitive milieu that pitted the two ethnic groups in trade, mining, and land tenure. Anglo control of Mexican labor, although not having the priority of later years, also propelled discord. During the late nineteenth century, both Mexicans and Anglos engaged in border smuggling and banditry, but Mexican outlaws provoked the greatest indignation. Vigilante committees administered summary justice to all criminals regardless of race or ethnic background, but a disproportionate number of Mexicans received this treatment. Racially motivated lynchings proved to be particularly galling to Mexicans. Moreover, in the nineteenth century few Mexicans served on juries, they were unevenly sentenced to jail, and were given longer sentences than Anglos. A major justice issue for southwestern Hispanics was their inability to understand court proceedings conducted in English because of a lack of Spanish-speaking lawyers or interpreters.[4]

Nonetheless, most of the time Anglos accepted, even if grudgingly, that Mexicans in areas acquired by the United States had a right to remain, and upper-class Mexicans in the Southwest were acceptable for socializing and for marriage. In the nineteenth century, contrary to the images portrayed in Hollywood westerns, many lawmen and municipal court officials in the West were Mexicans, a factor that allowed for more egalitarian treatment than has been previously believed.[5]

Unfortunately, this "live and let live" arrangement between Mexicans and Anglos eroded in the twentieth century after industrialization and modernization reduced the jobs available to Mexican immigrants to the lowest types of manual labor. Instability caused by the Mexican Revolution and its aftermath dislocated hundreds of thousands of Mexicans. They crossed the border and had to contend with poor housing and malnutrition, which made them vulnerable to disease and to brushes with the legal system. Generally, the only Americans who wanted immigrants in the country were employers who tolerated Mexicans because they were low-wage laborers who could be manipulated and persuaded to return to their homeland when their labor became unnecessary. "Greenhorn" immigrants encountered more difficulty in dealing with police and the courts than their settled southwestern brethren. The immigrants adjusted, but during the painful process of adapting, they remained extremely vulnerable.[6]

Middle-class Americans perceived the massive influx of labor as threatening to the social and cultural order, while the white and black working classes feared them as competitors who lowered wages and took jobs they felt belonged to them. Certainly, poor eastern and southern Europeans ("new" immigrants) who immigrated during this period shared this burden, but Americans saw Mexicans as less racially acceptable than the "new" immigrants. Although negative attitudes toward other groups emerged because of conditions contemporaneous to the period of their immigration, Anglos had despised Mexicans as a mixed breed since early in the nineteenth century, before massive immigration. Indeed, proponents of Manifest Destiny rationalized encroachment into Mexican territory by demonizing a mongrelized Mexican culture—a stigma that endured.[7]

When the first major immigration wave occurred early in the century, Mexicans were experiencing the most violent political upheaval in their history. Because the part of the upheaval that took place on the northern border had anti-American overtones, often manifested by threats against American property, border raids, and angry anti-"Gringo" rhetoric, many Americans took out their frustrations on immigrant workers who were not involved in any of this activity in a hysteria that historian Ricardo Romo has dubbed the "Brown Scare" (fear of Mexicans during the Mexican Revolution).[8] Even after the militant phases of the Revolution ended, border problems persisted—the smuggling of liquor, drugs, and large numbers of "illegal" immigrants—and continued as sources of resentment toward Mexico and its people.

The flood of Mexican immigration caught Anglo Americans and their institutions off guard. To government officials, social workers, educators, and scholars this became known as the "Mexican Problem." The rapport with southwestern Hispanics forged in the nineteenth century proved inadequate for interacting with landless laborers from Mexico who engulfed southwestern barrios. To Americans it became clear that the Jim Crow laws employed for blacks could be applied to the new foreigners. Even though new codes did not avowedly target Mexicans, laws regarding vagrancy, weapon control, alcohol and drug use, and smuggling were partially designed to control Mexican immigrant behavior. In addition, education policy, private-sector housing, and labor segmentation combined with the judicial web to keep Mexicans powerless and easier to control.

The newcomers were not only extremely poor but also mainly illiterate, and Americans perceived them to be more of Indian than old Hispanic stock. A November 1926 editorial in the *New York Times* warning about dangers stemming from unregulated immigration captures this sentiment. There were two kinds of Mexicans in the United States, the *Times* proclaimed—the old stock with more Spanish blood, thus desirable by American standards, and newer immigrants, more visibly Indian. Fortunately, said the *Times* editorial, "For the most part they return to their old homes as soon as laced by a few hundred dollars." [9]

Among the many foibles that Americans attributed to Mexicans was an innate propensity to crime. An assessment in the social-work magazine *Charities and the Commons* during 1907 gave three reasons why 60 percent of those convicted of felonies in Arizona were Mexicans: one, it acknowledged prejudice in the court system; two, that among the immigrants came "fugitives from justice in Sonora and Chihuahua"; and, three, that "many are of mixed Indian and renegade American blood." [10] Much of this perception had to do with negative media publicity. Arrest rates and even conviction rates did not necessarily measure comparative *offense rates* (the real rate of crime). More often they reflected *differential application of the law.* [11] Essentially, this means that law officials expected Mexicans to be criminally prone, so they dogged them and caught them in the act or considered them guilty even if they were only suspects. [12] As a consequence, American institutions that dealt out justice became the first to encounter the Mexican immigrants and a sour relationship developed from the outset.

Mexican expatriates, in turn, immediately identified police brutality, prejudice in the courtroom, disproportionate arrest and conviction rates, uneven application of the death sentence, and unpunished violence from white civilians (bosses and workers) as the most onerous conditions they had to endure. This realization was beaten into their everyday lives, regardless of whether they were poor working people or economically comfortable.

Feeling unwelcome and rejected, the subordinated immigrants adopted an intense expatriate nationalism that revered "México Lindo" (Beautiful Mexico), as their *colonias* (Mexican immigrant communities) swelled. This conviction served as a source of empowerment by providing them with identity and a sense of unity. The mainly nostalgic ideology incorporated Spanish language preservation; *indigenismo* (pride in Indian background); celebration of the *fiestas patrias* (Mexican patriotic holidays); reverence for patriots like Miguel Hidalgo y Costilla and Benito Juárez; Catholicism, specifically as manifested by Our Lady of Guadalupe; and an ambivalent form of anti-Americanism.[13] The Mexican consuls who acted as brokers in the struggles and encouraged mobilization provided the movement with an infrastructure and mechanism to spread nationwide.

Kerby Miller, in a marvelous study of Irish emigration to the United States, evokes a similar concept. He argues that while immigrants from the Emerald Isle certainly left for a better life in the United States, they chose to see their sojourn as a product of victimization by the British. Therefore, they saw their stay in the United States as a temporary exile, even when they entered American politics. In fact, numerous symbols evoking a nostalgic and romantic notion of their homeland, and hate for their British victimizers, sustained much of the legendary political activity of the Irish Americans.[14]

The México Lindo identity came earlier to communities like Tucson and San Antonio where immigration first appeared on a large scale. As early as the 1880s, for example, a writer for Tucson's *El Fronterizo*, Francisco Dávila, encouraged Mexicans to return to Mexico by projecting idealized notions of the mother country. By the late 1910s, as immigrants and their children in these older immigrant *colonias* settled into a more permanent place, such fervor waned. *El Tucsonense*, Tucson's premier Spanish-language daily in this era, for example, contained few allusions to Mexico's pre-Columbian heritage, a staple of identity for new arrivals. The same is true of writers for San Antonio's *El Imparcial de Texas* and *La Prensa* who turned their attention to extolling the virtues of Mexicans who fought in World War I for the United States and to encouraging Mexicans to become U.S. citizens and vote.[15]

By the 1920s, communities with large numbers of recently arrived immigrants promoted México Lindo ideology more forcefully. In Chicago during the 1920s, immigrants from Jalisco or Guanajuato encountered *paisanos* who had themselves only recently arrived; few had political influence or knew the proverbial ropes. In addition to the city's bone-chilling winters, a painful contrast to the warmer latitudes of Central Mexico, Mexicans had to adjust to schools, neighborhoods, and a justice system far different from anything they had known. Rapid coalescing proved essential to recreating an ethnic space in this strange terrain. In 1926, an editorial in one of Chicago's first Spanish language publications, *El Correo,* proclaimed that upon arriving in Chicago, Mexicans immediately sought each other out: "Our Mexicanness is rooted to the degree of fanaticism. Celebrating our patriotic festivals, where we honor glorious historical heroes in a cooperative and zealous spirit, is a divine mandate." [16] Regardless of the area, leaders evoked an immigrant nationalism when confronting abuse.

But those leading the campaigns did not see their compatriots as simply innocent victims. Aware of the violence and crime that existed in their communities, including Mexican-on-Mexican crime, they often launched moralistic diatribes against deviant behavior among their own people. Yet they protested vehemently when compatriots were unjustly treated at the hands of the law. Although there is no doubt that some Mexicans required policing, what is obvious in this historical study is that policemen habitually overreacted, sometimes because they feared Mexicans, or on other occasions because it allowed certain neurotic policemen to empower themselves at the expense of the powerless. Just as tragic is that a legal system designed to protect individuals from violence all too often left Mexicans with little or no protection against vindictive American civilians.

Nonetheless, this book demonstrates that the Mexican experience with the law of the United States varied region by region. The time of immigration, regional origins, social conditions in Mexico, and the configuration of host communities all contributed to shaping the character and frequency of Mexican immigrant crime. For example, those who concentrated in industrial areas and who were new to the United States had the highest arrest and conviction rates. This had much to do with the complex process of establishing roots, family networks, and immigrant institutions. Although arrest rates, capital punishment, police violence, and white civilian hostility toward Mexicans increased and de-

creased in well-defined patterns, antipathy, or at least its physical manifestations, never reached the white-heat intensity evident when border
violence during the Mexican Revolution and immigration converged.

Within a few short years of their arrival, however, Mexican immigrants from this period experienced considerable relief from these oppressive conditions. Two structural theories help explain this change.
One is that Anglo intolerance decreased as chronological distance separated extreme border hostility generated during the Mexican Revolution
from continuing Mexican immigration in later years. The second, more
complex and drawn out within the context of various themes throughout the book, concerns the role of labor competition and the aging and
stabilization of the immigrant community.

The issues discussed above are treated in thematic fashion throughout this book. The first chapter addresses how border raids into the
United States and anti-Americanism during the Mexican Revolution
exacerbated prejudices already held against Mexicans. Chapters 2 and 3
trace the process by which both immigrants and the Mexican government established a system to defend against the violation of civil rights.
Chapter 4 examines the extent of Mexican criminal behavior, especially
internecine violence, and determines to what degree it merited the treatment Mexicans received at the hands of the law. The phenomenon of
police consistently violating the civil rights of Mexicans is treated in
Chapter 5. Brutality that white, and to a lesser degree black, civilians
inflicted on Mexicans, is treated in Chapter 6. Chapter 7 assesses the
courts, which played a crucial role in the destiny of Mexicans caught
in the snare of the U.S. justice system. Capital punishment, the worst
nightmare for Mexicans who got into trouble with the law, is assessed
in Chapter 8. The life of incarcerated Mexicans and their release from
prison is treated in Chapter 9. The final chapter of this book portrays Mexicans seeking asylum in their homeland when U.S. authorities
sought to imprison them.

TERMS OF REFERENCE FOR
MEXICANS IN THE UNITED STATES

Throughout the book I use the word *Mexican* to denote those born in
Mexico and *Mexican American* for persons who are ethnically Mexican
but born in the United States. The term *ethnic Mexicans* is applied at
times to people born on either side of the border who have a connection
to the *mestizo* culture and race forged in Mexico after the arrival of

Spaniards. At times the word *Hispanic* or *Hispano* appears, usually to portray natives of the Southwest during the nineteenth century who did not have a very strong link to the emerging political entity known as Mexico, especially after the United States annexed the Southwest. The term mainly serves the utilitarian purpose of making the distinction more easily understandable for the reader.

1 | THE MEXICAN REVOLUTION, BORDER MEXICANS, AND ANGLOS

THE "BLACK LEGEND" is an early source of Anglo American antipathy toward Hispanics. According to this interpretation, sixteenth-century English propagandists translated Bartolomé de las Casas' critical writings on Spanish colonization of the Caribbean and Mexico to discredit the reputation of the Spaniards. Consequently, Anglo Americans held negative views about Mexicans even before confronting them on New Spain's frontiers, where the encounter deepened prejudices and provided at least one important rationale for Manifest Destiny. The violence of the Texas Rebellion and the Mexican-American War intensified the antipathy. Then during the late nineteenth century, Mexican border smuggling and banditry created a perception that the region was lawless. Although many Anglos along the border engaged in illicit activity, white Americans reserved their resentment for Mexican outlaws.

As the Southwest acquired greater economic importance, Anglo Americans attempted to tighten control of the border by repressing Mexican culture through enforcement of smuggling and immigration laws and by cracking down on Mexican lawbreakers. However, just as the Americanization of the Southwest seemed to be succeeding, the Mexican Revolution, which began in 1910 and lasted in varying degrees into the 1920s, unexpectedly demonstrated that the idea of a border was more fragile than Anglos had previously imagined. The turmoil of the insurrection, which also affected Anglos along the border in Mexico, received extensive coverage in the media. The resulting indignation served American private interests by convincing U.S. politicians to intervene in Mexico to protect Anglo investments there. Unfortunately, these dynamics affected relationships between Anglos and U.S. Mexicans who were neither involved in political intrigue nor in revolutionary activity.[1]

Even before the first shots of the Revolution, plots by Mexican *revoltosos* on U.S. soil rankled Americans. United States authorities zealously pursued the Flores Magón brothers and other members of the Partido Liberal Mexicano (PLM) exiled by President Porfirio Díaz. Eventually, U.S. officials jailed PLM members for violating U.S. neutrality laws, a process the press followed closely.[2] Americans living in Mexico reported their mistreatment to relatives, to their government, or to newspapers in the United States, provoking a flurry of complaints; however, stories reaching the United States were exaggerated. Of central concern to expatriate Americans was the Mexican government's interference in their economic affairs. Most foreigners in Mexico were offered few if any special considerations during the Porfiriato. Mexican officials played investors against each other, including Americans, and at times even betrayed them. Local power groups often conspired, with official help, to defraud Americans. More often, Americans who had engaged in unsuccessful ventures returned home with anti-Mexican sentiment.[3]

In the late Porfiriato, Americans resented rising Mexican economic nationalism. After some successful Mexican campaigns to quell Yaqui uprisings in Sonora during May 1908, the Nogales, Arizona, *Vidette* greeted the news cheerily, saying U.S. investments were safe: "Watch the state of Sonora grow. Millions of American dollars are invested in our sister state, the best in the United States of Mexico, and hundreds of people will rush into the rich mining and agricultural sections just as soon as the news of peace with the Indians is learned throughout the country." But Mexican nationalism soured these hopes. In August the newspaper augured, "Readers of English should read in the *Mexican Herald* of July 19 the translation of *La Patria* newspaper's [anti-Díaz in Mexico City] fiery article under the caption 'Pro Patria.' It defines the policy of 'Mexico for Mexicans,' warns the foreigners that they must not ask too much."[4]

Mexican judicial treatment of Americans also provoked disgruntlement. What Americans feared most were the extreme privations in jails and the inefficiency and lack of common-law principles in legal proceedings. A sense of Anglo superiority incensed suspects' families and friends in the United States who felt loved ones should be above Mexican law, which some saw as inherently unjust.[5]

Indignation over anti-American acts during the revolution created the mood for the "Brown Scare."[6] But even before fighting began in Mexico, Americans dwelling on the border, aware that Mexican exiles operated on the U.S. side, associated revolutionaries with border banditry. Mexican outlaws crossed at San Benito in July 1910, attacking and killing numerous Texas Rangers, and as posses pursued them into Mexico, the press depicted the band as revolutionary. Many Americans blamed Francisco I. Madero, exiled in Texas during 1910 before beginning the revolution that year, for any signs of border unrest.[7] Signs of increasing antiforeign sentiment in Mexico also alarmed Americans who had previously felt safe in their enclaves.

According to rumors, an uprising against all foreigners was scheduled to began in Tampico on the centennial anniversary of Mexico's independence. Indeed, on September 14 a heavy downpour and three hundred soldiers liberally bayoneting the participants quelled an outbreak against Spanish merchants.[8] That same month, a report from San Luis Potosí warned that anti-American feeling was such that "even sober-minded Americans of long residence stated that a rabid leader provided with a few barrels of native liquors could at any time put in peril the lives and property of Americans."[9]

Rioting in Mexico, in response to a Texas lynching, intensified Anglo fear along the border. On November 2, 1910, enraged townspeople in Rock Springs burned Antonio Rodríguez at the stake for killing a white woman named Mrs. Clem Anderson. Widely publicized in the Mexican press, the outrage provoked violent anti-American demonstrations in Mexico City and in Guadalajara. In the melee, rioters roughed up Americans and damaged their property. The events, misreported in the American press or exaggerated by Ambassador Henry Lane Wilson, provoked a heated backlash against Mexicans in the United States, especially those living in Texas.[10]

FEAR IN THE MADERO YEARS

American backlash to the riots only signaled the beginning of a negative response to border provocations during the Mexican Revolution. As called for in El Plan de San Luis Potosí, the call for an uprising against Díaz' rule, Madero entered Mexico on November 20, 1910, but returned to Texas when the uprising miscarried. Madero enjoyed support from influential Texas Anglos disenchanted with Díaz, but average Americans resented Mexicans hatching plots on U.S. soil. In February 1911, Texas governor Oscar B. Colquitt became so concerned that he asked President William H. Taft for help in enforcing neutrality laws.[11] That month *maderista* insurgents alarmed Arizonans by attacking the Sonoran border town of Algodones after traveling on American trains from Yuma, Arizona. As one account has it, "After this incident . . . the entire Yuma

County was placed on alert and many local citizens were cleaning their firearms in case the insurgents decided to attack Yuma." [12]

During the months between Madero's victory over Díaz in May 1911 and his assumption of the presidency, anti-American activity in Mexico escalated. In Piedras Negras, for example, Mexican crowds stoned Anglo American businesses during Independence Day celebrations on September 16, 1911. In the meantime in El Paso and San Antonio, Reyistas, followers of the exiled Porfirista General Bernardo Reyes, openly plotted against Madero, infuriating many Anglo Texans. On November 20, 1911, Governor Colquitt ordered all Mexican rebels to leave Texas within forty-eight hours and sent Texas Rangers to the border. Then Pascual Orozco, a player in Díaz' ouster, turned against Madero in February 1912 and his forces lay siege to Ciudad Juárez. As a result, El Paso residents demanded protection, prompting Governor Colquitt to again deploy Texas Rangers. Meanwhile, President Taft threatened to invade Ciudad Juárez and police the city. In the spring of 1912, Orozco's anti-U.S. posture resulted in attacks against American properties throughout northern Mexico, forcing hundreds of Americans to flee their ranches. In Arizona during August, Anglos in Bisbee pledged to cross into Nacozari, El Tigre, and Cananea if they were threatened by rebels. Eventually an uneasy American public pressured the Taft administration to impose an arms embargo on Mexico. [13]

Although General Victoriano Huerta defeated Orozco's forces at Ciudad Juárez in August 1912, small groups of followers continued raids into Texas—excursions the press quickly exaggerated. During October 1912, Governor Colquitt committed more ranger forces to the border and asked the State Department to allow pursuit of marauders into Mexico, a request that was denied. [14] Conditions worsened, and by year's end Colquitt asked for federal assistance in keeping peace along the border, indicating that Texas could not sustain the expense. Meanwhile, New Mexico senator Albert Bacon Fall, concerned about American investments in Mexico, clamored for a U.S.-engineered ouster. Responding to protection pleas from Texans, the War Department assured that the four thousand troops already stationed along the border could maintain order. [15]

WOODROW WILSON STEPS UP INTERVENTION

In February 1913, Huerta ousted Madero and had him shot. Woodrow Wilson, inaugurated as U.S. president the same month, recalled Ambassador Wilson, who had also been involved in the ouster. President

Wilson refused to recognize Huerta's government, prompting the general to orchestrate a wave of anti-American agitation played up by the press in both countries.[16] During the July 4 celebration, Anglo American revelers tore down the Mexican flag at the Tucson consulate, a deed replicated during Mexican Independence Day celebrations elsewhere in Arizona and Texas. Mexico demanded an official apology, but American newspapers disapproved, indicating it would be tantamount to recognizing Huerta.[17]

In this atmosphere of mistrust El Paso customs agents in September shot to death Lieutenant Francisco G. Acosta, a member of a troop contingent commanded by Huertista General José Inés Salazar. The mounted but drunken Acosta, with two bandoleers strapped across his chest, charged across the international bridge, firing a 30-30 Winchester and screaming that he wanted to kill a gringo. Anglo El Pasoans became alarmed when more than one thousand angry Ciudad Juárez residents, some from General Salazar's forces, gathered menacingly on the Mexican side of the bridge. In response, two squadrons of the Thirteenth Cavalry arrived at El Paso and all the troops at Fort Bliss were put on alert.[18] Anti-American agitation increased when agents of Venustiano Carranza recruited adherents to his anti-Huerta movement activity, resulting in their arrest for violating neutrality laws. The Carrancista operation did not gain steam, however, until Francisco Villa formed the División del Norte and confiscated Chihuahua assets belonging to Americans and the landed oligarchy.[19]

Because of the resurgence of insurrection along the border in 1913, Mexican immigrants continued to be objects of Anglo American antagonism and fear. In Texas, Huertista mass meetings denouncing President Wilson unnerved Anglos in Laredo and other border cities, and they asked for military protection. The gatherings also made them apprehensive about Mexican American loyalty, an attitude which led to severe retaliation against immigrants.[20] In November, the San Antonio consul general, J. A. Fernández, reported to the Foreign Ministry that "With relations between the U.S. and Mexico worsening, Mexican workers in the U.S. suffer privations and persecution and violations of their rights." In his letter, Fernández listed a series of violations that included mobs violently evicting immigrants from homes and the arbitrary treatment of Mexicans in the U.S. justice system.[21]

California experienced border tension as well. In November 1913 when rumors had anti-Huerta rebel Rudolfo Gallegos poised to attack Mexicali, the *Los Angeles Times* reported that federal agents had discovered weapons caches in border towns stored by Mexicans angry about President Wilson's opposition to Huerta. Ironically, the *Times* noted, instead of Wilson's posture heartening anti-Huerta rebels, it

> engendered in them a hatred that is likely to burst forth
> in terrible acts at any moment. . . . The plunder motive
> is strong with border Mexicans just now. Looking across
> the geographic line called the 'border,' the plunder bund
> of Mexicans sees rich valleys, wealthy cities, immense
> ranches well worked and well tilled, prosperous houses,
> banks with real money . . . in contrast with those in
> Northern Mexico . . .[22]

A few months later, in March 1914, Mexican bandits killed Tecate postmaster Frank V. Johnston after he refused to open a safe, then burned down the building that served both as a customs station and post office. At first it was thought the killers were Mexican federal soldiers stationed at the international line. Later, a Fort Rosencrans investigator announced that three Mexican laborers from a camp a few miles from town had shot Johnston. In reporting this incident, the *New York Times* indicated that "a lot of hostility existed towards Mexicans in the area." [23]

On April 21, purportedly to end political chaos, President Wilson directed U.S. troops to occupy Veracruz. American law officials were alerted that angry Mexicans and Mexican Americans might launch reprisals. The invasion put El Paso Anglos in such an ugly mood that city officials warned Mexicans not to create a disturbance. In Austin on April 25, intimidated Mexicans assured Governor Colquitt they would not cause any commotion. So alarmed was the governor, however, that he personally prepared war plans.[24]

Even after Huerta's ouster in July 1914, border tension and suspicions remained high. In August, the *Arizona Republican* revealed a plot brewing in the Salt River Valley. Nine conspirators were jailed after Maricopa County officers tracked them for two months. The incredible-sounding conspiracy

> had for its object the capture of the city of Phoenix by
> hordes of banditti, the rifling of the stores and banks and
> the gradual spread of conditions of anarchy into other
> portions of the state, together with an armed attempt by
> a combined force of Indians and Mexicans against the
> government of the United States starting in this section.[25]

The foray was allegedly a Villista plot to yield munitions, money, and supplies to conduct a revolution in Mexico and in the United States. Besides Mexicans, Yaquis from Guadalupe (who three years prior were implicated in another conspiracy) and Pimas from the Sacatón reservation were to join. The plotters appealed to the Indians in terms of avenging wrongs done by Anglos. Five of the alleged conspirators received two-year sentences in a trial held shortly after their arrest.[26]

Retaliation for the Texas-based Plan de San Diego in 1915 is unparalleled in its degree of anti-Mexican violence by Anglos. The declaration, scheduled for February 20, called for a multiracial uprising of Mexicans, Indians, Japanese, and Blacks. It was irreverently designed to coincide with George Washington's birthday. Violence against Mexicans, which is detailed further in Chapter 5, began as soon as Texas officials released news of the proposed insurrection after Basilio Ramos, Antonio González, and Manuel Flores were caught smuggling the document across the border in January 1915, and the violence lasted until the spring of 1916.[27]

VILLISTA PROBLEMS

Early in 1915, with his forces in Ciudad Juárez, Pancho Villa curried favor with Americans hoping, with U.S. help, to prevail in the struggle against Carranza. The American press still romanticized Villa's image at this point, but events in the ensuing months led to his being demonized as the most villainous enemy of Americans. Villa began to turn against the United States after President Wilson, in October, extended de facto recognition of Carranza. The following month his dwindling army was almost destroyed in an attack on Agua Prieta, Sonora, a town of strategic importance for Villistas. Villa became extremely hostile toward Wilson because Carranza, with U.S. permission, transported his soldiers from Chihuahua through New Mexico and Arizona on American railroads to fortify Agua Prieta. The populist leader then embarked on a campaign with a two-fold purpose: to retaliate against the United States and to create such a chaotic climate that Carranza would not be able to rule effectively. On November 25, 1915, Villistas in Nogales, Sonora, goaded Twelfth Infantry Negro soldiers and members of the Arizona National Guard into firing across the border, just as Carrancistas entered town. Ten thousand well-armed U.S. troops amassed in the border town, vastly outnumbering the Carrancistas. In the ensuing firefight, one American soldier perished and five were wounded. U.S. soldiers killed sixty Mexicans and wounded several others. In January 1916, Villistas dragged eighteen American mining engineers from a train at Santa

Ysabel, Chihuahua, and killed them. The bodies were brought back from Chihuahua through El Paso in coffins draped with American flags. The killings whipped Anglos into a frenzy of revenge and they went on a rampage, attacking every Mexican man they encountered.[28]

Villistas also staged border raids into American territory. The most infamous was the March 9, 1916, pre-dawn raid on Columbus, New Mexico. Eighteen American soldiers and civilians died and many others were wounded while Villa's forces suffered more than two hundred casualties. The reaction was swift as U.S. troops led by General John Pershing pursued Villa into Chihuahua in the foray known as the "Punitive Expedition." Concurrently, Mexicans suspected of subversion suffered indignities at the hands of hostile Americans. On March 10 and 11 in El Paso, for example, officials rounded up two hundred Mexicans accused of being Villistas, deported them, and continued to arrest anyone showing anti-American feelings.[29]

During May 1916, a number of violent incidents, mainly in the Texas Big Bend area, shook American sensibilities. On May 7 about sixty Villistas crossed the border at Alpine and attacked a U.S. Army garrison near Glenn Springs. According to the *El Paso Times,* nine soldiers barricaded inside an adobe store attempted to fend off sixty Mexicans who screamed, "Death to the Gringos!" The marauders set fire to the thatched roof, smoked out the soldiers, killed three, and captured the rest. They proceeded to Boquillas, robbed a general store, and seized the owner and his assistant. As they crossed to Chihuahua, the looters attacked the International Mining Company; robbed the company store; and kidnapped the superintendent, the company physician, and five employees. The bandits also reportedly kidnapped and killed a ten-year-old deaf-mute American boy because he did not answer their questions.[30] Anger over this atrocity was still smoldering when United States army patrols were instructed to double their vigilance."[31]

Rumors persisted that raids would continue. Plan de San Diego leader Luis de la Rosa planned an invasion of Texas sometime between May 10 and 15, said U.S. officials. On May 11 authorities arrested a number of Mexicans in Corpus Christi on charges of involvement in the conspiracy. According to the *Houston Chronicle,* the uprising included New Mexico and Arizona. The most prominent of the plotters were Colonel Morín, a former Villista; Euralio Velásquez, a newspaper editor; and Victoria Ponce, a merchant. Authorities released most of the thirty or so Mexicans arrested in the plot, but the ringleaders were turned over to Texas Rangers and disappeared.[32] Early on the morning of May 16, the Sunset Central passenger train bound from El Paso to San Antonio derailed. Only three passengers suffered injuries, but investigators blamed Mexican terrorists.[33]

As Villa had expected, the border incursions corroded U.S.-Carranza relationships. Carrancistas even considered invading Texas to force Pershing's troops out of Mexico, a strategy canceled at the last moment.[34] Nonetheless, Carranza still maintained pressure on the United States through small-scale raids. On June 11, a day after the invasion was called off, a small group of Carrancistas burned a railroad trestle and cut telegraph wires near Laredo—some perished and others were captured. In resulting clashes, U.S. troops killed one raider and wounded a second. The following day near Laredo, sixty Mexicans, led by Plan de San Diego adherent Isabel de los Santos, crossed the river and attacked the U.S. Army barracks at San Ignacio. In the ensuing firefight, soldiers slew a number of infiltrators and captured several others. The raiders, in turn, killed a number of American soldiers. U.S. officials threatened to invade and occupy Matamoros until Carranza officials put a stop to the incursions.[35] Hostility came to a head on June 21 when Carrancistas inflicted heavy casualties on a Pershing patrol at Carrizal—fourteen U.S. troops died. Such turmoil prompted President Wilson to launch an arms embargo that forced Carrancistas to smuggle supplies from Texas, promoting even more border violence. In the end, diplomacy won out and on February 5, 1917, Pershing's army vacated Mexico. Throughout the rest of the year, however, troops shot at each other continuously across the river.[36]

After a series of May 1917 border raids, rumors circulated that Texas Mexicans were participants. Anglos living on isolated ranches and in small villages in the Big Bend area sought refuge in Marfa, Alpine, and Marathon. On June 18, President Wilson activated the Arizona, New Mexico, and Texas National Guards to bolster federal troops on the border. Initially, Americans welcomed this, but as skirmishes produced casualties, sacrificing U.S. soldiers to Mexican chaos dampened enthusiasm. Border forces of the United States totaled 110,957 in the summer of 1917. During August of 1917, José Antonio Arce, Vicente Lira, Jesús María Cerda, and Paulino Martínez were tried for participating in the 1916 attack on the U.S. Army barracks at San Ignacio. Lira and Cerda received death sentences. Arce, only sixteen years old, and Martínez, who was tried while lying on a stretcher, were sentenced to life imprisonment. The Mexican government unsuccessfully argued that the group be treated as war prisoners, but an appeals court overturned the convictions the following year, and they returned to Mexico.[37]

In 1917, most raids were still Villista inspired. Villa took advantage

FIGURE 1. VILLISTAS IN OJINAGA, CHIHUAHUA, RELAXING AND POSING
FOR PHOTOGRAPH, CIRCA 1915. FROM AUTHOR'S PRIVATE FILE.

of Pershing's withdrawal to regain strategic positions in Chihuahua, and
by October his men controlled areas around Ojinaga, which became a
headquarters. U.S. soldiers stationed at nearby Presidio pursued bandits
after every raid with unprecedented zeal. In December, a frustrated
Governor William P. Hobby turned to Francisco Chapa, publisher of *El
Imparcial de Texas,* to arrange a meeting with Nuevo León governor
Nicéforo Zamorano to see if both governments could end the violence.[38]
After the meeting, a Christmas Day raid outraged Anglo Americans to
a degree not seen since the 1916 incursions. Pillagers, allegedly Villistas,
crossed near Marfa, raided the Brite Ranch and general store, and took
about two thousand dollars. Guests coming to a party given by ranch
foreman Van Neill were warned off or allowed to proceed to the house
unharmed. But bandits fired on postman Mitchell Welch as he approached in a hackney and killed two Mexican passengers. They hanged
the mailman when he tried to prevent the taking of his mules.[39]

Big Bend vigilantes, taking matters into their own hands, disarmed
all Mexicans living in Brewster, Presidio, Jeff Davis, Culberson, and
Hudspeth Counties. Then on January 18, 1918, vigilantes and Texas
Rangers, with U.S. Army troops lying in wait, executed fifteen Mexican immigrants in the town of Porvenir as retaliation for the previous

FIGURE 2. CARRANCISTAS AND THE CRUZ BLANCA NURSING BRIGADE IN CHARCAS, MEXICO. REPRINTED, BY PERMISSION, FROM RECOVERING THE U.S. HISPANIC LITERARY PROJECT/ARTE PÚBLICO PRESS.

month's attack on Brite Ranch.[40] Meanwhile, shooting between soldiers continued. On January 24, two Mexicans were killed after they shot at U.S. soldiers at the "Island" near Fabens, Texas. During March in another peace meeting, Carrancista representative Andrés García discussed with U.S. Army officers how to prevent further shootings. At the same time, General James Harley of the Texas Militia recruited extensively to beef up border vigilance.[41] In mid-March, Mexicans avenging the Porvenir massacre raided Ed Neville's ranch near Marfa, killing his son. A U.S. Army patrol chasing the suspects skirmished with fifteen Mexicans near El Polvo Ranch in Chihuahua. After the clash, six Mexicans lay wounded or dead and one American officer was injured.[42]

This incessant border violence created tensions that by 1919 again brought the two nations close to war. Americans, doubting Carranza's loyalty in World War I and tired of his resisting U.S. efforts to influence Mexico's economy, supported his onetime partisan and now political challenger, Alvaro Obregón. Senator Albert Bacon Fall, allying with reactionary Felicistas (followers of Félix Díaz), clamored for intervention and held congressional hearings to investigate the inability of "wild Bolshevists" to stabilize Mexico. President Wilson rebuked him, but the widely publicized proceedings reinforced the notion of a Mexico plagued by a violent and unstable socialism.[43]

THE GERMAN QUESTION

World War I–induced xenophobia increased the fear of Mexicans and caused more doubt about the loyalty of those living in the United States. Moreover, Mexican leaders Huerta and Carranza were suspected of having pro-German sympathies. The 1914 Yripanga incident, in which the U.S. Navy confiscated German arms bound for Huerta, convinced many of his German leanings. After being ousted during 1914, Huerta languished in Spanish exile until 1915, planning a return to power. As an accomplice, he chose former enemy Pascual Orozco—both colluded with the Germans.[44] Americans saw German intrigue in another scheme. During January 1917, U.S. officials arrested New York consul Juan T. Burns for arranging for German arms to be sent to Mexico in contravention of the embargo. A few days after his arrest, the Zimmerman telegram convinced more Americans of Carranza's duplicity. The fear of a Mexico allying with Axis powers heightened after the United States entered the war in April.[45]

A dramatic skirmish took place between Mexican and American troops at the Nogales border on August 28, 1918. It started when a Mexican crossing the international line was threatened by a U.S. sentry. A Mexican customs guard came to the Mexican's defense, and the incident soon escalated into a battle requiring four companies of Negro cavalry hurriedly brought in from Fort Huachuca. The clash lasted long into the night and ended only after high-ranking officers from both sides, including General Plutarco Elías Calles, who came from Hermosillo, negotiated a truce. A U.S. Army official in Nogales attributed the battle to German agitation and preparations. By his account, Germans trained the Mexicans for the battle, including giving lessons in trench warfare.

At El Paso, U.S. Army Major E. Lowry Humes, in January 1919, announced that Hipólito Villa, Pancho's brother, accepted half a million dollars in war supplies for the Villista cause from the German agent F. A. Somerfield. The announcement confirmed Mexican collaboration in the minds of many Americans who, no longer burdened with the European war, clamored for an invasion of Mexico.[46] Rumors were so rife that José Luis Velasco and Luis R. Alvarez were arrested in mid-July in El Paso for publishing a story claiming the United States planned an invasion of Mexico. They even divulged U.S. military war plans probably leaked to them by Carrancista spies.[47]

It is within this context of mistrust and border violence that the largest immigration influx from Mexico began, as shall be seen, with tremendous repercussions for the non-involved immigrant who came to the United States mainly to work or to escape the violence of the upheaval.

2| MÉXICO LINDO MOBILIZATION

THE 1890S MARK the beginning of a large-scale immigration from Mexico that has continued almost unabated into the present. As U.S.-built railroads penetrated south into West-Central Mexico's Bajío and Lerma River Basin, they induced the migration of landlocked Mexicans that swelled U.S. *colonias* made up primarily of *norteños* (Mexican northerners) and native southwestern Hispanics. The new *colonias* that sprang up along railway lines in agricultural towns and mining districts expanded the settlement of Hispanic people beyond the older centers. A concurrent arrival of Anglos who mainly filled the positions of power pushed most Mexicans into labor reserves through a repressive and demeaning process.[1] But as indicated in the introduction, immigrants coalesced to defend their interests mainly by relying on a México Lindo orientation. This immigrant nationalism gave them stamina and encouraged them to forge campaigns to protect themselves and to deter defamation of things Mexican.

IMMIGRANT POLITICS OF PROTEST

Violations of Mexico's sovereignty unleashed vociferous protest campaigns and even elicited talk of armed insurrection among U.S. Mexican immigrants. After the 1914 invasion of Vera Cruz, the Los Angeles *Record* led off with the front-page headline, "Mexicans in Los Angeles patriotically cry 'Viva Mexico!'" All those interviewed supported Mexico, and a U.S.-born Mexican American even volunteered to fight for Mexico if war broke out.[2] In 1927, Andrés Avila, a Tucson resident, remembered how Mexicans prepared for war against the United States during the invasion: "Yes, if the Americans had advanced a little more the 'raza' here would have risen up in arms."[3] During the invasion, El Paso authorities cordoned off the premises of *México Libre* for publishing anti-American propaganda and threatened to close down the *El Imparcial*, another publication in the same city.[4] As Mexico and the United States verged on war in 1919, Mexican officials and immigrants reacted furiously to a congressional speech by U.S. Senator Henry Ashurst of Arizona, who proposed annexing Baja California. E. Medina, president of La Asamblea General in Bisbee, Arizona, sent Ashurst a resolution calling his proposition imperialistic and circulated copies to Spanish-language newspapers throughout the United States.[5] Mexican immigrant nationalism existed almost in direct proportion to antipathy toward the United States. David Villaseñor, a Tucson shoe repair shop owner from Guadalajara, said in 1927 that someday Mexicans would recover the lost territories taken from Mexico. The Spaniards were in Mexico four hundred years, by his reckoning, and "yet we kicked them out."[6]

Mexican immigrant leaders quickly denounced defamation in the public media. Prominent in this was Francisco Chapa, publisher of *El Imparcial de Texas*. Born into a prestigious Matamoros family, Chapa studied pharmacy at Tulane University before building a thriving drug store business in San Antonio during the 1890s. Chapa served as a member of San Antonio's Board of Education in 1906 and in 1911 assumed a post on the board of directors of the prestigious International Club. He integrated himself into Texas political life by becoming an advisor to Governor Oscar Colquitt and Governor James E. Ferguson. In 1918, Chapa led a delegation to ask Governor W. P. Hobby to ban the screening of denigrating films in Texas, a request to which the governor agreed.[7] The following year in April, Tucson's *El Mosquito* protested the screening of films with anti-Mexican overtones at the Tucson Opera House because "Respectable Mexican families found them offensive."[8] In 1928, *La Opinión* endorsed a move by the Mexican government to prohibit the denigrating films in Mexico.[9]

Immigrant leaders routinely objected to racist literature and negative journalism as well. In November 1920, former Texas governor James E. Ferguson proclaimed in his personal broadside, the *Ferguson Forum*, that Mexicans were inferior to Negroes and that Mexico had contributed nothing to civilization.[10] Alonso L. Perales, a political activist and World War I veteran, wrote Ferguson denouncing his diatribe, saying he defended Texas Mexicans and immigrants alike. *El Imparcial de Texas* published Perales' letter, adding, "The majority of Mexicans living in Texas are law abiding, thus Ferguson's propaganda will fall on deaf ears."[11]

Mexican leaders also countered slurs by invoking a proud pre-Columbian heritage. Dr. Benjamin Goldberg, a physician, wrote an

article published in the *Chicago Tribune* during 1928 proclaiming undesirable Mexican immigrants as a "menace to the health of the American
people." Chicago's *México*, responded that "Such writings inspired by
hate and malice . . . jeopardize the good relations between Mexican and
American people." The newspaper reminded readers of Mexico's proud
history and recounted achievements of the Aztecs, the Toltecs, and the
Mayas, which "were powerful races in their time." [12]

Mexicans were particularly sensitive to being cast as undesirables.
During the recession of 1926, a period rife with anti-Mexican sentiment,
the Los Angeles City Council considered banning Mexicans from city
contract jobs. *La Opinión* accused labor leaders of lobbying for this law
then quoted G. Figueroa del Valle, an official at the Bank of Italy, who
stated that employers and Californians in general appreciated the Mexican workers' contributions to the state's prosperity. The negative stereotypes of Mexicans as criminal, violent, and unruly, perpetuated by
border unrest, particularly concerned expatriates. In 1926, Comisiones
Honoríficas Mexicanas sponsored speeches in the United States given by
Elaine Ramírez, an official at the Mexican Ministry of Education. She
lamented that banditry along the border projected an unfair impression
of Mexico. [13]

Immigrant leaders promoted the positive aspects of *colonia* life to
counter negative stereotypes. During 1928, *La Opinión* columnist Rodolfo Uranga announced that Ignacio Castañeda, a Detroit automobile
worker, saved a woman from drowning in the Rio Grande as he crossed
at El Paso from his native Jalisco. He then wrote:

We have heroes here in the United States. Anglo Americans have no right to criticize our crime and banditry in
Mexico. They have crime galore here. Look at the situation in Chicago. It is not just to brand 'inferior' Mexicans as uniquely imbued with criminal tendencies. [14]

MOBILIZATION

When mobilizing for any purpose, immigrant identification with "*lo
mexicano*" ("Mexican-ness") helped bridge *patria chica* (small father-
land) allegiance to the home village and class divisions. For example,
nationalism encouraged immigrants to aid compatriot victims of natural
disasters. In 1919, *colonias* in the U.S. raised $46,539 to aid flood victims
in the Veracruz-Puebla region. Immigrants in Miami, Arizona, alone
raised two thousand dollars. Mexicans in East Chicago, Indiana, re-

sponded enthusiastically to *El Amigo del Hogar*'s fund-raising in 1926 when floods devastated regions of Nayarit. In March 1928, numerous immigrant organizations joined to help survivors when a dam broke at Santa Paula, California, drowning over one hundred Mexican farm-workers.[15]

Mexican immigrants also challenged school segregation both in the courts and through direct confrontation with school officials. The longer immigrants lived in the United States, the more they expected a quality education and the less they accepted teaching their children English as a reason for segregating them. But desegregation efforts required stability and permanency, a process that took time.[16]

The first successful desegregation court battle took place in Tempe, Arizona, in 1925. Mexican families whose ancestors helped to found the city in the 1870s successfully challenged an eleven-year-old segregation policy. Unfortunately, the effort succeeded in integrating mainly the off-spring of established families. Children who had recently arrived and were from poorer families continued to be separated until the 1940s.[17] Mexican parents in Argentine, Kansas, most of them natives of Guana-juato who had been in the community for more than ten years, became defiant when white parents petitioned the school board not to allow Mexican students into the town's only high school. The protest proved only mildly successful. The superintendent of schools guaranteed high school admission to Mexican children, but segregation continued in ele-mentary schools. In 1929, students, parents, and the Mexican govern-ment objected to efforts by the San Bernardino, California, school board to segregate Mexicans with blacks at the De Olivera Elementary School. The Superintendent of Public Instruction, Ida Collins, responded with the explanation that separation was necessary to teach children English. The most encompassing court victory in this era occurred in Lemon Grove, California, during 1930 when parents, most from tight-knit fami-lies with origins in Baja California, won a court battle to keep their chil-dren in a school designated for whites only.[18]

Mexicans opposed segregation in public places as well because sepa-rate facilities were inferior and because the practice reduced them to the level of blacks from whom they sought to distinguish themselves. Dur-ing August 1919, *Hispano América* and Consul Gerónimo S. Seguín pro-tested that 113 Mexicans had to live in the Negro section of San Francisco and that they were segregated in public buildings. The newspaper again complained in 1923 that the Ku Klux Klan led a campaign to segregate Mexicans in Richmond, California. Mexicans in Modesto, California, objected during 1928 when the Catholic cemetery denied Tranquilino Zavala a burial because of a "whites only" policy. In Chicago during 1936, *El Nacional* inveighed against Mexicans being forced to use Negro undertakers. The newspaper reasoned that sharing a cemetery with blacks demeaned Mexicans in the eyes of white Americans.

Mexicans objected to being segregated with blacks in hospitals and jails. San Antonio Consul Rafael Aveleyra requested that Mexicans be taken out of "Negro" wards at the county hospital after a patient complained to Mexican president Portes Gil during 1929.[19]

Defense against Legal Abuses

Mexican immigrants defending themselves against abuses in the justice system became one of the most pressing issues. Resistance occurred informally, but it inspired Mexican immigrants to withhold information or to be uncooperative with the police. Mexicans resorted to direct intervention to block the arrest of countrymen or to protect them from whites. Two Mexican men in 1908 beat Los Angeles police officers to thwart the arrest of a drunken female compatriot. In May 1914, one hundred Mexicans rioted in the Los Angeles plaza to foil a compatriot's arrest. In December of the same year, one hundred fifty Mexicans reportedly attacked the Oakville, Texas, jail upon learning that whites threatened to hang two Mexicans accused of killing a jailer. In March 1925, after a white mob gathered in Elko, Nevada, to lynch Guadalupe Acosta, who had confessed to killing a local policeman, seventy-five armed Mexicans surrounded the jail to protect him.[20] Mexicans spontaneously helped in small ways as well. During 1913 in Taylor, Texas, local Mexicans collected $21.50 to defend a transient Mexican couple jailed for theft whom they believed the sheriff had framed. In Kansas City during 1916, Bernardo López, a successful merchant, personally obtained the release of a group of compatriots held as material witnesses without being charged.[21]

During the revolution, Mexicans found it difficult to depend on consuls, so societies oriented toward mutual aid, patriotism, and recreation stepped into the breach. Some groups organized to defend immigrant rights from the outset. This formation for legal defense began earlier in Texas, which by 1910 had more than 65 percent of all Mexican immigrants. Native Tejanos, or Texans of Mexican ancestry, had acquired some self-determination in the nineteenth century, but this characteristic either weakened considerably during the period of heavy immigration or else it failed to accrue to the immigrants. The inability to counter such abuses as lynchings sadly demonstrated this lack of leverage. Fourteen-year-old Antonio Gómez was lynched in June 1911 after stabbing a German American to death. A number of Mexican organizations, led by the Orden Caballeros de Honor, protested but became bitterly disappointed when local authorities failed to investigate.[22]

Such failures in the justice system only served to intensify mobilization efforts. Mexicans in San Antonio started La Agrupación Protectora Mexicana in 1911 to provide "legal protection for its members whenever they faced Anglo perpetuated violence or illegal dispossession of their property."[23] In Houston, schoolteacher J. J. Mercado started a chapter that worked with recent immigrants through the Mexican consul to ameliorate such employment grievances as lack of compensation for accidents at work.[24] In 1911 in Laredo, Nicasio Idar, editor of *La Crónica,* organized El Primer Congreso Mexicanista, a civil rights association, the main objective of which was to end school segregation, lynchings, and police brutality and to urge Mexicans not to sell land. The Congreso declined quickly because of Anglo Texans' violent opposition, but it was a building block for future mobilization.[25]

Mobilization also appeared early in Arizona because, like Texas, the state absorbed initial immigration waves; more Mexicans lived there in 1900 than in California. During the late nineteenth century, new railroads facilitated mining and agriculture, which employed thousands of Mexican immigrants as laborers. In the 1880s, Carlos Velasco, editor of *El Fronterizo,* attempted to start El Centro Radical Mexicano in Tucson to address problems Mexicans faced with the Tucson police. In 1894, La Alianza Hispano Americana began as a mutual aid society and protective organization. By the 1920s, the group could point to some success in protecting civil rights and stood in the forefront of efforts to save Mexicans condemned to the gallows. In Phoenix, La Liga Protectora Latina began during 1914 to deal with civil rights violations and labor abuse. Averting a May 1915 hanging of five Mexicans for unrelated crimes became the first major legal issue La Liga tackled (see Chapter 8). In the ensuing years, the group led protests against proposed legislation to prohibit non-English speakers from working in Arizona mines.[26]

Self-defense groups proliferated during the 1920s in larger urban areas as more Mexican immigrants arrived. In Houston, where the Mexican population increased fivefold from 1910 to the mid-twenties, businessmen led by Fernando Salas and Frank Gibler, a former U.S.

consul married to a Mexican, formed the Asamblea Mexicana in 1924. The organization forced the suspension of a police sergeant in 1928 for jailing, without medical attention, a young Mexican injured in an auto accident. That same year Asamblea member Frank Gibler's facility with English helped get an earlier release from the Houston jail for at least five Mexicans. Gibler also protested to Governor Dan Moody the abuse of Mexicans in Texas penitentiaries.[27]

In Los Angeles, where the Mexican population increased more rapidly than in other cities in the 1920s, La Liga Protectora Latina, originally formed in Arizona, and La Confederación de Sociedades Mexicanas included in their budget funds for hiring attorneys to protect legal rights.[28] When the Los Angeles City Council considered excluding city contractors who hired noncitizens during the 1926 recession, Arturo Chacel, "Supreme Organizer" of La Liga Protectora Latina, warned that Liga lawyers would sue if the code passed. During the 1920s, at least one Protestant organization, Los Angeles' Plaza Methodist-Episcopal Social Service Center, headed by Mexican-born Dr. E. M. Seen, provided legal aid as well.[29]

Emerging Mexican communities in the Midwest during the 1910s became more susceptible to judicial abuse than in the Southwest. Newly arrived from Central Mexico, the majority of immigrants in *colonias* in Kansas and Missouri lacked experienced leadership. This resulted in a belated appearance of immigrant institutions, which as late as 1920 had barely begun to acquire the maturity already evident in Texas and Arizona.[30] Large-scale immigration came last to Chicago and Detroit, so defense organizations in those cities did not emerge until the mid-1920s. Eventually in Chicago, where the Mexican arrest rate was higher than in southwestern communities, organizations with emphasis on the protection of legal rights emerged. La Confederación de Sociedades Mexicanas de los Estados Unidos de América, founded in Chicago on March 30, 1925, served as an umbrella organization for thirty-five Chicago mutual aid societies. Its objectives included assistance to new immigrants with jobs and loans, assistance to combat racism, and fund-raising "to provide defense funds to help Mexicans before the courts."[31]

The life span of most groups was short. Many times lack of cohesion, mismanagement, and the community's poverty forced organizations to fold. Generally, whenever one group failed another took its place, but Mexican societies declined throughout the United States in the depression of the 1930s. Increased poverty in the *colonias* and the repatriation of unemployed Mexicans crippled the ability of organizations to sustain themselves. Moreover, a distinct ideological thrust of Mexicans born in the United States (Mexican Americans), reflecting the changing demographic character of the *colonias,* became more dominant.

DEFENSE OF POLITICAL REFUGEES

Immigrants frequently mobilized to defend Mexicans arrested by U.S. officials for violating neutrality laws, for border banditry, for smuggling arms into Mexico, or for union activity. The most persecuted activists were PLM members whom authorities pursued even before the revolution. When federal agents in Los Angeles jailed PLM organizer Manuel Sarabia in January 1908 for neutrality act violations, immigrant sympathizers across the country clamored for his release. For years Texas governors were pressured to release *los mártires de Texas,* PLM members led by Jesús Rangel who were jailed after killing a Tejano deputy sheriff as they crossed the border in 1913 to join Zapatistas.[32] The pressure came mainly from immigrant sympathizers but included a rare diplomatic foray by Emiliano Zapata, who, through the Brazilian Embassy, pleaded for Rangel's release because "he is an honorable man and friend of the Revolution."[33] It was not until 1926 that Governor Miriam "Ma" Ferguson acceded to the pressure and freed *los mártires.*

Helping political prisoners provided experience in defending against other kinds of judicial aggression. In the spring of 1912, Dr. J. B. Ruffo, a surgeon in President Madero's army, defected to Pascual Orozco's rebellion, but in the fall, with Orozco in decline, Ruffo fled to Arizona. When Phoenix consul Francisco Olivares persuaded U.S. officials to arrest Ruffo in Tucson, sympathizers in Phoenix, led by Pedro de la Lama, founded La Liga Protectora de Refugiados. Two years later the group devolved into La Liga Protectora Latina, which addressed more general civil rights issues. In 1927, Francisco García y Alva, publisher of *México* in Los Angeles, joined *Hispano América* editor Julio Arce in San Francisco and Dr. José I. Trejo of Oakland to help free General Enrique Roque Estrada, a former Mexican cabinet member in Alavaro Obregón's administration. Federal officials arrested him in San Diego during September 1926 when he was recruiting supporters for the Cristeros (Catholic rebels). Other refugee organizations had loftier goals. During 1918, La Alianza Liberal Mexicana in San Antonio, a group comprising conservative political refugees such as General Francisco Coss and Emilio Madero, put forth its objectives: to work for peace and unity in Mexico so that they could return home.[34]

ACTIVISM OF JOURNALISTS

Because of the language barrier, Spanish-language newspapers could not effectively sway Anglo public opinion. Instead, they attempted to mobilize the community or to publicize progress in campaigns to protect compatriots. As members of the Congress of the Latin American Press, these newspapers borrowed articles or editorials from each other on a variety of concerns. Local issues achieved national and even international prominence through informal links publishers maintained throughout the United States and Mexico. Discussions of legal matters in these newspapers were usually mundane. The publications mainly explained immigration law or warned readers against violating vagrancy laws, carrying weapons, or using alcohol during prohibition. *El Imparcial de Texas* featured a regular column from La Liga Protectora Mexicana that offered legal counsel.[35]

But journalists also encouraged readers to join campaigns to obtain clemency for condemned compatriots. In Los Angeles, Juan de Heras, editor of *El Heraldo de México,* the first Spanish-language daily in California, consistently supported celebrated such cases as those of Aurelio Pompa and Juan Reyna (see Chapters 8 and 9). The Lozano family owned newspapers in the two largest Mexican communities—*La Prensa* of San Antonio and *La Opinión* of Los Angeles.[36] Francisco Chapa, the editor of *El Imparcial de Texas,* became one of the most effective defenders of civil rights because he successfully cultivated Anglo connections. Through his help, for example, at least three Mexicans condemned to the gallows received clemency.

FIGHTING CAPITAL PUNISHMENT

Because so many compatriots were executed in prisons throughout the United States, the Mexican immigrant intelligentsia, mostly journalists, articulated compelling arguments against capital punishment. Jesús Franco, publisher of Phoenix' *El Sol* in the 1930s, served as the Arizona correspondent for El Paso's *La Patria* in the 1920s. As a journalist and a member of numerous Mexican organizations in Phoenix, he crusaded on behalf of Mexicans accused of crimes.[37] Another Arizona journalist-crusader, Pedro de la Lama, helped to found La Liga Protectora Latina and published various newspapers in Phoenix, such as *Justicia.* He came to Arizona from Veracruz during the late nineteenth century, and by his own account opposition to the war with Spain almost led to his lynching in 1898.[38]

Julio Arce, also known by his pen name, Jorge Ulica, became one of

FIGURE 3. JESÚS FRANCO, A CIVIL RIGHTS ACTIVIST AND A COMISIÓN HONORÍFICA MEXICANA ORGANIZER IN TEXAS AND ARIZONA WHO BECAME THE PUBLISHER OF THE NEWSPAPER *EL SOL* IN PHOENIX. REPRINTED, BY PERMISSION OF MARY JO FRENCH, DAUGHTER OF JESÚS FRANCO, FROM JESÚS FRANCO, *EL ALMA DE LA RAZA,* PRIVATE PRINTING IN FRENCH'S FILES.

the most persistent critics of capital punishment. As editor of two Guadalajara dailies he had to flee his native Jalisco for San Francisco in 1915 after railing against both Madero and his usurper, Huerta. A prolific writer, Arce often satirized American culture and its effects on Mexican immigrants, but he also directed his pen at criticizing the justice system's effect on Mexican immigrants.[39] Arce believed Mexicans were often framed for capital murder because police, anxious to convict, manipulated evidence-gathering procedures. He also upbraided authorities for not providing competent interpreters for immigrants unable to understand English in court proceedings. His ultimate explanation for mistreatment was racism. He wrote:

Prejudice against our race is tremendous and the anti-
Mexican campaign waged by the cinema and the press

has branded us with a reputation for irrepressible criminality. . . . In the trial the most base racial prejudices
overshadow any ability for the courts to provide Mexicans justice.[40]

There were other crusading journalists. Daniel Venegas—a Los
Angeles columnist, businessman, and novelist—launched, as president
of La Confederación de Sociedades Mexicanas, a number of campaigns
to defend Mexicans whom he believed were unjustly treated by the
legal system. Antonio Redondo, the Los Angeles correspondent for *El
Tucsonense,* moved by record executions of Mexicans at San Quentin in
the 1920s, employed classic eighteenth- and nineteenth-century European rationales against taking a human life. In his daily column, "Glo-
sario del Día," Rodolfo Arango, brother of one of Los Angeles' most
active playwrights, wrote on the plight of Mexicans in prisons and the
need to defend them on death row. "Las crónicas de Loreley," penned
by María Ester Garza for *La Prensa* of San Antonio, also called for compassion toward condemned Mexicans. There were so many efforts in
the 1920s to save Mexicans from execution that anthropologist Thomas
Sheridan has dubbed this era in Arizona the "clemency movement"
period.[41]

SELF-HELP

Mexicans also recognized that immigrant behavior, especially Mexican-
on-Mexican violence, provoked trouble with the police. In Chicago, for
example, *colonia* leaders admitted that drinking and fighting contributed to high arrest rates, but they attributed this problem to alcohol
abuse and alienation rather than inherent deficiencies—a view common
in mainstream Chicago.[42] Nonetheless, middle-class immigrants often
looked at the foibles of their poorer *paisanos* (countrymen) with disdain.
According to one historian, Mexican elites in Kansas City condemned
the carousing of compatriots because the behavior went against "their
desire to promote the idea that Mexicans were an educated, cultured,
and civilized people[;] the group condemned the actions which belied
that image and diminished their own stature in the eyes of the Anglo
majority." [43]

Mexican leaders also appealed to miscreants through shaming and
rebukes. Newspapers reported crimes didactically and implored readers
to eschew drunkenness and attendant vices by promoting good Mexican
values. In Kansas City, publishers of *El Cosmopolita* chastised Mexi-

cans for "wasting their time and money in pool halls, cantinas and other centers of vice."[44] *La Gaceta Mexicana* in Houston regularly advised its young readers to send their money home instead of engaging in riotous living. In a 1926 article called "The Victim," Chicago's *México* told of a young Mexican immigrant couple who profited materially by making and selling bootleg liquor but who soon came to perdition; she became a prostitute and he an alcoholic.[45] In April 1927, Indiana Harbor's *El Amigo del Hogar* linked carrying guns to immoral behavior and counseled against the practice. Similarly the Kansas City consul, through *El Cosmopolita,* conducted a campaign to warn Mexicans about harsh consequences resulting from arrests on weapons charges.[46]

Some leaders, mostly Protestant, went beyond words and became warriors against vice. In 1931, Dr. Eliud García Treviño, a Mexican physician, founded the Committee Against Alcohol in conjunction with the Mexican consul, the Youth Baptist Union of South Chicago, and six Mexican organizations.[47] In San Pedro, California, Baptist minister Miguel Padilla would visit Mexicans jailed for alcohol-related crimes and would try to lure them away from drink through a mission that had baths, a kindergarten, and a library with books in both Spanish and English.[48] A Baptist minister in St. Louis, converted in his native Durango, typifies the motives of these religious campaigners. In his words:

I wanted to help my countrymen in every way and I did
not lose any opportunity to do so. I secured work for
them, served as an interpreter, got them out of jail. . . .
I did this social work first because they were my countrymen, secondly because it was my duty and also with the
end of converting them to the Baptist church.[49]

Ultimately, most other immigrants came to support their *paisanos* who had problems with the law in spite of misgivings they might have about their behavior. In 1916, the Sociedad Mutualista Benito Juárez in Kansas City balked at helping a Mexican who killed another compatriot because he was a "common criminal." The Mexican consul finally convinced the group that it was more important to make the U.S. justice system own up to its egalitarian claims than to condemn the deviant behavior of a compatriot. Besides, members of the club knew that encounters with the law did not respect class boundaries and just being Mexican in the United States invited police repression.

3 | THE CONSULS AND MÉXICO LINDO

CONSULS PROMOTED México Lindo patriotism among immigrants by supporting the already deeply felt desire to strengthen their Mexican identity in the expatriate community. In the process consuls hoped to assure immigrant loyalty to the home government by appropriating *lo mexicano* ("Mexican-ness") and denying this claim to exiled subversives. In the 1860s, for example, the San Francisco consul promoted *juntas patrióticas* (patriotic organizations) to support Benito Juárez' Republicanism at a time when Mexican conservatives and French invaders forced his government from Mexico City. To bring economic and political unity to Mexico, Porfirian officials enhanced nationalism and exported it to the expatriates in the United States.[1] For example, in Phoenix, Arizona, during July 1898, newly arrived immigrants organized La Junta Patriótica Mexicana in cooperation with Consul León Navarro to celebrate the eighty-eighth anniversary of Mexico's declaration of independence. In November, the same immigrants started El Club Social Mexicano in order to include women, choosing as their logo the Mexican eagle on a nopal cactus.[2]

Promoting immigrant loyalty was not just a lofty patriotic endeavor, it was a corollary to using the consulates as spy centers. As early as 1869, Servando Canales led an unsuccessful attack on Camargo, Tamaulipas, from Río Grande City "for the Constitution of 1857 and against the dictatorship which dishonors us." Arrested for violating U.S. neutrality laws, he claimed that Benito Juárez' agents colluded with American authorities to hamper his efforts.[3] The need to win the loyalty of neutral immigrants became more apparent to Porfirian policymakers whose repressive tactics forced hundreds of dangerous dissidents to flee to the United States. Among the better-known efforts to thwart saboteurs in the United States are the manipulations against the Tejano Catarino Garza, who, like Canales, attempted to invade Mexico, and the Flores Magón brothers, fomenters of unrest among Mexican workers on both sides of the border. Tucson consul Arturo Elías, for example, virtually limited himself to keeping watch on Magonistas. The radicals, in turn, retaliated by exposing consular ineptness through their organ, *Regeneración.*[4]

Irrespective of Porfirista agents' spying, Francisco I. Madero, from his Texas exile, successfully organized an effort to overthrow Díaz in 1911. Madero also used the diplomatic service for his own political ends. For example, in February 1912, Abraham Molina, Madero's El Paso emissary, allegedly led the police to arrest Industrial Workers of the World activist F. Martínez Palomares, screaming, "Look out for that fellow! He is the principal leader and a very dangerous man!"[5] Victoriano Huerta also ousted Madero in 1913 with the help of dissidents who plotted insurrection on U.S. soil. It was then Huerta's turn to seek support in the United States through the consuls, but like Madero and Díaz, he failed. In the last months of his dictatorship, desperate Huertista consuls turned all their energies to propagandizing and spying.[6]

Venustiano Carranza, who orchestrated Huerta's downfall in 1914, tried using the consular corps for political purposes by ordering them to diffuse the influence exiled subversives had on other immigrants. Many consuls were actually placed by Rafael Zuburán Capmany, Carranza's cunning, confidential agent in Washington, even before the United States recognized the rebel government in October 1915.[7] A year earlier, for example, Kansas City partisans led by Dr. D. F. Osorio and two brothers, M. A. and J. A. Urbina, ousted Huertista consul Eduardo Velarde. Osorio became consul and the Urbinas began publishing the Carrancista-subsidized *El Cosmopolita.* In 1915, an Anglo American supporter of the rebels from New Mexico, Jack Dancinger, replaced Osorio and took over the propagandistic newspaper.[8] The following year in October, Julio Arce, with the support of San Francisco consul Ramón P. de Negri, requested from the Foreign Ministry a monthly stipend to support his newspaper *Mefistófeles,* "to offset the propaganda put out by enemies of the revolution through cartoons and editorials which is negative for Mexico."[9] Arce enhanced the appeal by reminding the Foreign Ministry that the influential *La Crónica* of San Francisco, "after the purging of one of the owners," was now run by antirevolutionaries; *científicos* (scientists) and Villistas passing off as legalists." His newspaper, added Arce, would counter the turncoat *Crónica,* which was capable of swaying the gullible *vulgo* (lower class).[10] In December, de Negri sent to Mexico the first copies of *Mefistófeles* portraying the Carrancistas working diligently to bring about a Constitutional Convention and the Constitutionalist Army routing Villistas in Chihuahua. By June 1917, the newspaper received a subsidy of five hundred pesos a month.[11] In February of 1918, de Negri asked his superiors to increase the allotment because the newspaper is

> the only organ in this region that defends with unbridled
> enthusiasm, our institutions. Without *Mefistófeles,* we
> would not be able to offset the damage done by our ene-
> mies and provide the people with the truth.[12]

The Mexican Foreign Ministry during 1918 stepped up efforts to gather immigrant support by establishing *juntas patrióticas* "wherever ten or more Mexicans live to foster support for the true and revolutionary government of Mexico."[13] The campaign included aggressive attempts to discredit opponents in the United States, a move that provoked vitriolic denouncements from exiles. As Mexican agents attempted to establish the *juntas* in Arizona during June, Amado Cota Robles, a leading member of Tucson's Mexican expatriate community, opposed the effort in a series of articles published in *El Tucsonense.* Tucson consul Raúl R. Rodríguez then accused the newspaper of being "dominated by Catholic clergy."[14] In November, the Carranza consul in San Diego managed to have the philosopher José Vasconcelos arrested for violating neutrality laws. Vasconcelos had been in the cabinet of the failed Conventionalist Government of Eulalio Gutiérrez established after the fall of Huerta. Pancho Villa had supported the regime, but Carranza spurned it from the beginning. Eventually the Conventionalist Government lost support from all factions, forcing its officials to flee Mexico.[15]

Carranza's government also worried over the effect that Mexican Americanization could have on immigrants. The concern probably had more to do with security reasons than with a lofty desire to inject expatriates with a love for *lo mexicano.* During 1919, as Mexico pursued rhetorical warfare with the United States, Reginald del Valle, a descendent of an old *californio* family, and J. J. Uriburu started the American Latin League in Los Angeles, ostensibly to help Mexican workers obtain better treatment, housing, and wages. Nonetheless, the Los Angeles consul heard rumors that the league's purpose was Americanization, an allegation both Uriburu and Del Valle vehemently denied.[16] The following year, Kansas City's *El Cosmopolita* denounced naturalization. "Why would Mexicans want to renounce their nationality and become citizens of a country where every day their rights and dignity are trampled upon?" admonished the newspaper.[17]

CONSULAR PROTECTION DURING THE PORFIRIATO

Besides engaging in political intrigue, the consuls also put much energy into protecting immigrants for whom life in the United States presented constant challenges. A protection policy is evident as early as 1848. Because of mistreatment of Mexicans who remained in the territory ceded after the Mexican War, Mexico put aside two hundred thousand dollars from the U.S. payments it had received to repatriate these people into Mexico. Then in 1850 during the California Gold Rush, when Congress passed the Foreign Miners Tax to keep Latin Americans out of gold fields, the Mexican consul in San Francisco protested through the Foreign Ministry.[18]

At the end of the century, increased emigration to the United States required a more defined expatriate policy.[19] During the 1907–1908 depression, Los Angeles and San Francisco consuls induced the more fortunate immigrants to provide housing and food for thousands of their unemployed compatriots. San Francisco alone had close to one thousand destitute Mexicans who could not find food or shelter. The Mexican government appropriated one hundred thousand pesos to repatriate stranded workers and paid for train fare through El Paso from various points in California.[20] The Porfirian corps also helped immigrants caught in the U.S. justice system. As early as 1903 the Mexican consulate in Los Angeles had a special fund to help Mexican expatriates with legal problems.[21]

During the uprising that resulted in Díaz' overthrow, consular protection deteriorated. When thirteen-year-old Antonio Gómez was lynched in Thorndale, Texas, during the spring of 1911, the activist Nicasio Idar, editor of Laredo's *La Crónica,* charged Mexico with neglecting the issue so as not to jeopardize diplomatic relations with the United States. The editor then asked sarcastically if consuls were going to behave as they did in the November 1910 Antonio Rodríguez lynching in Rock Springs, where Texan officials never charged the guilty parties in spite of repeated Mexican government requests. Preoccupied with saving his teetering dictatorship, Díaz failed to apply more diplomatic pressure, although Rodríguez' family in Coahuila received an undisclosed indemnification.[22] After Díaz' ouster in May 1911, Francisco León de la Barra's caretaker government reorganized the consulate system and reassessed governance policy, adding the office of Visitador General. The Foreign Ministry also committed to raising salaries, upholding seniority, and requiring that consuls be Mexican citizens with higher educational qualifications. They were also prohibited from practicing other professions.[23]

Consul Protection and Post-Díaz Regimes

When Madero became president in December 1911, consular protection for immigrants weakened even more according to his critics. In January 1913, Texas Rangers gunned down Juan Reyes as they arrested him for highway robbery and murder even though he only vaguely fitted the description of the killer. After casting doubts on consular effectiveness, San Antonio's *La Prensa* demanded, "Let us hope that the Mexican consul in El Paso can look into this matter." [24] From the time Madero assumed the presidency in October 1911 to his bloody ouster in February 1913, endless plots to overthrow him were hatched both in and out of Mexico, dynamics that forced the consuls to expend their energy thwarting these activities. [25]

It is difficult to say if Victoriano Huerta's consuls improved protection efforts. In November 1913, J. A. Fernández, the consul general in San Antonio, reported thirty cases of Mexicans being treated arbitrarily by legal authorities; he asked for additional funds to pay consular lawyer Fred N. Cowen and gave assurances that Cowen was dealing effectively with the problem. [26] A poignant report from the Galveston consul during October of 1913 reveals a deeply felt compassion:

They have neither abandoned their hope of returning
to Mexico nor have they decided to become naturalized
Americans. I want to distinguish with this name, many
of our compatriots who in great numbers abandon their
national territory coming here in search of work and
where they suffer as true "martyrs." [27]

But when a man named Moore murdered Refugio Lucas in September 1913, a frustrated *La Prensa* scolded that a consul's duty was to protect Mexicans "killed in this country, which calls itself civilized, at the hands of prejudiced individuals." [28]

The prestige of Mexican consulates in the United States sank to a new low during the Huerta era. When Anglo American celebrants tore down Mexico's flag flying above the Tucson consulate and trampled it during the 1913 Fourth of July festivities, city officials simply advised Consul Ainelle to hoist an American flag over the Mexican flag. [29] Because Mexico's relations with the United States ceased during Huerta's administration, in April 1914, the Spanish ambassador represented Mexico in an unsuccessful bid to save León Cárdenas Martínez, a teenager sentenced to die for the murder of a white woman. [30] Huerta's solution to immigrant abuse was to hinder emigration. The Foreign Ministry, in October 1913, considered restricting emigration by imposing a fine on labor recruiters but retracted the effort because of public opposition.[31]

The Veracruz invasion weakened Huerta's hold and led to his ouster in August 1914. When the United States gave recognition to Carranza's government in October 1915, Eliseo Arredondo traveled to Washington as confidential agent. By December 1915, Arredondo's status rose to ambassador and a new consular group loyal to Carranza was ensconced.[32] Regardless of intentions, it proved difficult for Mexican diplomats to succeed in this turbulent era. Carranza's diplomats embarked on an equally fruitless quest to save four Mexicans hanged in Arizona between December 1915 and July 1916 (see Chapter 8).

Under Carranza, the corps, which had fallen into a muddle since the fall of Díaz, did not immediately improve. Many posts, announced ceremoniously as a slate at the beginning of 1916, were vacated with dizzying regularity. Because of the breach in diplomatic relations following the 1916 cross-border raids by Pancho Villa and Pershing's punitive foray, near paralysis plagued the corps. With the Pershing expedition deep inside of Chihuahua in June, Kansas City consul Jack Dancinger resigned and the French consul Emile S. Bius assumed his duties. As an American, Dancinger could not serve in this period of binational tension, which proved detrimental to immigrant protection.[33] In November 1916, Foreign Ministry circulars ordered consuls to work with local authorities to help immigrants with justice problems. The directives, which simply codified duties in effect since the Porfiriato, in themselves could not repair the fragile consular system.[34]

Some limited successes did take place, however. With U.S. entry into World War I, stringent laws in May 1917 required draft registration for males over the age of nineteen. Military service was required only of U.S. citizens, but noncitizens had to register and prove foreign origin or go to prison. Draft boards conscripted immigrants they suspected of being Mexican Americans, provoking a brief but massive return to Mexico. After intensive diplomatic work, authorities resolved the problem and the influx from south of the border resumed. By January 1918, consuls organized meetings to explain draft rules and assisted in the registration process. The emissaries also went to great lengths to obtain the release of immigrants jailed for not registering and to secure discharges for those mistakenly drafted.[35] When labor strife involved Mexican immigrants, consuls monitored procedures to prevent rights violations. During the 1917 copper mine strikes in Arizona, when Cochise County officials detained four thousand Mexican strikers, Douglas consul Ives Levelier helped to get hundreds of them released.[36]

Consuls also protested objectionable working conditions. Vice Consul Gustavo G. Hernández in Globe, Arizona, wrote the State Federation and Governor George W. P. Hunt in May 1918 asking for an investigation into conditions causing the dreaded black lung disease among miners. He also dogged management to comply with state regulations that required ventilation of mining shafts.[37]

The 1917 Constitution solidified Carranza's legitimacy, but tense relations with the United States and threats from exiles continued. Consequently, diplomatic posts went to loyal but untested emissaries.[38] Charges of cronyism and incompetence finally persuaded Carranza to promote an image of professionalism. The Foreign Ministry reorganized the consular corps during the spring of 1918 and issued directives recognizing the importance of experience rather than revolutionary loyalty. Nonetheless, by 1918 the service was disorganized and short of funds. An unprecedented number of immigrants lived in the United States, yet the Foreign Ministry decided to enforce a policy in which Mexicans who lived in the United States for more than ten years without registering with a consulate lost protection eligibility. Reinstatement required returning to Mexico, a hardship for cash-strapped immigrants needing immediate assistance.[39]

Ignacio Bonilla's rise—first to ambassador to the United States, then to head of the Foreign Ministry in 1919—demonstrated Carranza's continued need to have unquestioned loyalty. Bonilla, a *sonorense* (Sonoran), had stood with Carranza through thick and thin since he joined revolutionary efforts earlier in the decade. Such a strategy did little to ameliorate the problems in the consular service engendered by the years of instability, however. When Lino B. Rochín replaced José Garza Zertuche in Los Angeles during 1920, he became the fifteenth consul to serve in that capacity since 1918.[40]

When World War I ended, Americans suspected Mexico of having considered an alliance with Germany. Carranza resented President Wilson's meddling, and Washington criticized Carranza's inability to control border raids. Relations became so strained that the United States made plans to invade Mexico in 1919. Consuls throughout the Southwest then asked expatriates to support Mexico in case of war.[41] As Carranza's diplomatic effectiveness diminished in his last years, expatriates criticized the consuls even more. During the Clifton, Arizona, strike of 1918, Mexican strikers became so destitute that Consul C. Emilio Martínez

FIGURE 4. VENUSTIANO CARRANZA. REPRINTED, BY PERMISSION, FROM
RECOVERING THE U.S. HISPANIC LITERARY PROJECT/ARTE PÚBLICO
PRESS.

Preciat attempted to repatriate them to northern Mexico. Strike leaders,
however, accused him of attempting to provide labor to Sonoran and
Chihuahuan mines, which were as exploitative as U.S. mines.[42]

There can be no doubt, however, that consular protection during
Carranza's presidency improved tremendously from the Madero and
Huerta years. Carranza's nationalism also extended to a sincere concern
for compatriots in the United States and genuine efforts to ameliorate
their problems. He always reserved room in his criticism of U.S. foreign policy for a condemnation of the abusive treatment immigrants
received.[43]

THE NEW ERA: THE 1920S

After Carranza's violent ouster in 1920, new diplomatic challenges confronted his successor Alvaro Obregón. U.S. insistence on pegging recognition of his regime to assurances that foreign-owned oil properties
would not be expropriated became the most thorny demand. Mexico

was represented in Washington by Manuel Téllez, who served only as special emissary, a status with limited diplomatic powers. Major immigrant problems also greeted Obregón's government. Particularly vexing were the large numbers of Mexicans on death row and police brutality. The El Paso consul, in 1920, documented the indiscriminate killing, mainly by police, of 391 compatriots during a ten-year period. In addition, the 1921 depression threw hundreds of thousands of Americans out of work and provoked anti-Mexican riots, some extremely violent (see Chapter 5). But only fifty-one consulates existed throughout the United States in 1920 to serve the hundreds of thousands of Mexicans who immigrated during the decade. Although consular offices did not increase by much afterward—62 existed in 1928—the Foreign Ministry did add personnel and funds. In July, the Mexican government formed a cabinet-level agency within the labor ministry with a three-fold purpose: to investigate migration causes, to prevent immigration, and to deal with repressive treatment in the United States.[44]

Immigrant difficulties during the 1921 depression also prompted the founding of Comisiones Honoríficas Mexicanas after consuls met in San Antonio during April at a conference organized by the San Francisco consul general D. Eduardo Ruíz. According to Jesús Franco, a Comisión organizer who attended the San Antonio meeting, after the conference adjourned "all of the consuls that attended, except for three . . . arrived at San Marcos [Texas] to witness the simple ceremony that inaugurated the first Comisión Honorífica Mexicana in the United States."[45]

After a high consular official met with Texas governor Pat Neff in April 1921 to discuss immigrant unemployment and repression, the Foreign Ministry established *comisiones* in San Antonio, Dallas, and Austin to repatriate jobless workers and to address justice issues. During the decade, numerous chapters were founded throughout the United States.[46] The *comisiones* promoted nationalism by organizing *fiestas patrias* (patriotic festivals) and supporting schools to teach Mexican history and "proper" Spanish. The consuls also countered attempts to dilute Mexican identity. In Phoenix, Consul M. G. Prieto offered Spanish literacy lessons during 1923 to offset Americanization efforts by the Friendly Settlement House.[47]

Government introspection spawned new and innovative ideas. A 1922 internal report to President Obregón suggested that Mexico imitate techniques used by the Italian government to foster solidarity among its nationals in the United States. The plan required close contact with immigrants, controlled emigration, and an aggressive policy of protection.

FIGURE 5. D. EDUARDO RUÍZ, CONSUL GENERAL IN SAN FRANCISCO AT
THE TIME, ORGANIZED MEETINGS IN SAN ANTONIO DURING 1921 THAT
LED TO THE FOUNDING OF THE COMISIONES HONORÍFICAS MEXICANAS.
REPRINTED, BY PERMISSION OF MARY JO FRENCH, DAUGHTER OF JESÚS
FRANCO, FROM JESÚS FRANCO, *EL ALMA DE LA RAZA,* PRIVATE PRINTING
IN FRENCH'S FILES.

According to the document, Italy encouraged remittances from immigrants to Italian banks, which, in turn, sparked industrialization. That
year the Foreign Ministry codified consular duties, and in keeping with
previous goals, the rights of Mexican nationals in the United States took
priority. The United States recognized Obregón's government after Mexico concurred in the 1923 Bucareli Agreement that foreign oil properties
would not be confiscated. Téllez' status rose to ambassador and he
announced that conditions had ameliorated for Mexicans in the United
States.[48]

Early in 1926, the Foreign Ministry, looking back at almost three
years of improving treatment of expatriates, insisted again that hostility
toward Mexican immigrants had "diminished considerably."[49] But no
sooner was the pronouncement made than economic downturns racked

the Southwest, provoking anti-Mexican atrocities and increased deportations. Further, in 1926 when President Plutarco Elías Calles reconsidered the subsoil rights of foreign oil companies, Secretary of State Frank Kellogg and his ambassador in Mexico, James Sheffield, responded by publicly bashing Calles and denouncing him as a Bolshevik. Immigration foe, Texas congressman John C. Box, took advantage of the antipathy to try to create a climate favorable to passing restrictions on immigration from Mexico.[50] The year also marked the beginning of the Cristero Rebellion, a violent reaction to Calles' crude attempt at enforcing anti-Catholic constitutional provisions. In the United States, influential Church leaders and Catholic politicians, sympathizing with their Mexican counterparts, joined the anti-Calles campaign. During the crisis, Mexican consuls spied on militant Catholic exiles, especially in San Antonio, which was a hotbed of anti-Calles subversion. General Francisco Coss, who at a Catholic refugee banquet announced his intention of sabotaging relations between the United States and Mexico, became a primary target.[51]

The new sub-secretary of education under Calles, Moisés Sáenz, initiated a campaign to deter Americanization of immigrants, an effort coinciding with a campaign in Mexico to combat rural "superstition and backwardness" allegedly fostered by the Catholic Church.[52] Margarita Robles y Mendoza from the Mexican Education Ministry toured the United States in January 1928 to promote this peculiar form of Mexicanization among immigrants. That month the Edendale, California, consul opened a lyceum to educate children. The Escuela Morelos (Morelos School) was started in Burbank during February with former Michoacán teacher Josefina Venegas in charge. By May, seven schools were fending off Americanization in Los Angeles because of Robles y Mendoza's efforts. A Mexican Chamber of Deputies member from Oaxaca, Alfonso Ramírez, touring *colonias* in the United States in February, assured immigrants that their U.S.-born children were still Mexican citizens and urged parents to discourage Americanization.[53] Opposition to the schools cropped up in the likely circles of exiled Mexican Catholics and their American supporters who saw in the concept a "plan to introduce Soviet teachings into the United States."[54]

The consuls also took an active role in desegregation efforts. In 1931, the Education Ministry conducted a study using American education experts on the debilitating effects that segregated schools had on Mexican children. The year the report was issued, the Foreign Ministry provided travel funds so that lawyers for the League of United Latin American Citizens could travel to Washington to argue a Del Rio, Texas, desegregation case pending before the Supreme Court.[55]

In the 1930s, however, the Mexican government was still concerned about the possibility of subversives abroad. In 1930, Consul Rafael de la Colina placed an agent to serve as the chauffeur of a prominent Mexican family in Los Angeles that supported the exiled Archbishop of Guadalajara, Francisco Orozco y Jiménez. The Mexican government believed that the prelate conspired to raise arms for a revolt in Mexico.[56] In 1936, the head of the Foreign Ministry, Eduardo Hay, warned consuls

that we have to deter alienation of Mexicans in the United States towards their motherland, otherwise a cadre of "White Mexicans" will appear just as there are "White Russians." One of the latest examples of this is a prize offered by *La Prensa* of San Antonio to the composer of the best national hymn of "el México de afuera." For Mexicans anywhere there should only be one flag and one hymn.[57]

IMMIGRANT ASSESSMENT OF CONSULS: THE 1920s

What did immigrants think of consuls? Often expatriates did not know that consuls faced certain limitations. In 1924, after Mexicans killed a Chicago off-duty policeman during a speakeasy holdup, police indiscriminately arrested scores of Mexicans. Spanish-language newspapers and Consul Lorenzo Lupián protested but the community became angry at the official because his protests went unheeded.[58] During the Cristero Rebellion, the consuls again shifted to espionage priorities at the expense of protecting immigrants, said critics. In June 1926, so many pro-Catholic articles appeared in San Antonio's *La Prensa* that officials banned the newspaper from circulating in Mexico.[59] Rodolfo Arango, a columnist for *La Opinión* in Los Angeles, accused all the consuls in the United States of not representing Mexico and of being Calles' henchmen.[60]

But in successful consular efforts, immigrants expressed gratitude. In 1927, Chihuahua native Nivardo del Río, a former revolutionary turned miner in Miami, Arizona, told of how the Phoenix consul and a lawyer were taken to jail for parking their car illegally when they came to Miami to discuss police brutality problems. Del Río said he was proud of the way the consul complained "about the treatment which the police give to Mexicans, so it seems that they were dealing with thieves rather than working people."[61]

At times, critics who opposed consuls for political reasons some-times relented and singled out exceptions. *El Amigo del Hogar,* published in Indiana by conservative Catholic exiles from Jalisco, became critical of the Mexican government after the Cristero struggle broke out. But in December 1925, an article had lauded the Chicago consul for promoting patriotic festivities. "Such support from the home government," said the newspaper, "reinforces efforts by the publishers to promote correct Mexican behavior."[62]

Even New Orleans Consul Arturo Elías, who as a consul for Díaz' government spent most of his time spying on Magonistas, succeeded in helping immigrants. During and after the Revolution, the veteran consul was called an opportunist because he managed to stay in the diplomatic corps regardless of who was in power. But in 1921, after a long-drawn-out contest with Louisiana officials, Elías obtained the re-lease of three illegally jailed Mexicans in Monroe for the robbery-murder of a white couple operating a grocery store.[63] In 1928, Los Angeles Vice Consul Joel Quiñones pestered the Police Commission to intervene after the Los Angeles Police Vagrancy Squad repeatedly arrested unemployed Mexican workers who gathered downtown. He claimed that officials jailed and released vagrancy suspects without pre-ferring charges. Police officials often ignored consular complaints, but this time Los Angeles mayor George Cryer asked the Los Angeles Police Department (LAPD) to change its procedures.[64]

In September 1927, four young Mexicans—Julián del Hoyo, Jesús Silva, Victor Fern, and José Cristóbal Roa—were charged in a Brooklyn courthouse bombing, an apparent protest against the execution of Ital-ian immigrant anarchists Nicola Sacco and Bartolomeo Vanzetti, whose trial had symbolized the plight of foreign workers.[65] The police also jailed Mario Medreno, a Puerto Rican, and Eugenio Fernández, a Cu-ban. The six worked as waiters and dishwashers in New York City restau-rants, but they also made dolls in their spare time, a process requiring lead and wire, materials that could be used in bombs. *El Universal* of Mexico City angrily accused U.S. authorities of seeking scapegoats but added that the Mexican government hired "one of the best firms of local lawyers at the service of the prisoners. For the prestige of our race and for humanity's sake . . ."[66]

Interim Ambassador J. Willis Cook cautioned that the *El Universal* piece "is likely to create anti-American sentiment, especially if followed by similar articles."[67] Ambassador Sheffield had just been recalled for his clumsy treatment of President Calles and American officials did not want the questionable New York arrests to mar the diplomatic repairs being undertaken by the new ambassador, Dwight Morrow. But it took the FBI, under the zealous J. Edgar Hoover, two months to determine that no link existed between the bombing and the young Mexicans.[68]

On at least one occasion, Mexican government mediation left a lasting legacy of protection for expatriates. In October 1923, the Mexican Embassy and California consulates engaged in a long-drawn-out effort to show that California Law 263, passed to deny foreigners the right to own arms, was unconstitutional. The embassy reacted when the Los Angeles consul reported a police raid in 1923 in Santa Paula, a town notorious for poor police-Mexican relations. The raid was one of many civil rights violations induced by Law 263; consequently, the Mexican government lent its support to a California campaign that led to the code being declared unconstitutional.[69]

At times, however, consuls ignored cases that the community did not consider deserving. During the spring of 1931, Alberto Velasco killed Juvenciano Horta in a fight over a "gay Polish woman" in Chicago. The newspaper, *El Nacional,* reported the crime as a Mexican-against-Mexican murder over a woman of questionable virtue. Consequently, little sympathy appeared for Velasco, who received a life sentence. First-degree murder cases, Vice Consul Adolfo Domínguez erroneously informed Velasco when he sought help, were outside his jurisdiction. Chicago consulate officials were probably distracted because hundreds of destitute families were deluging their offices during the terrible Great Depression of the 1930s.[70]

Mexican emissaries themselves also suffered indignities. In March 1926, the University of Texas invited José Puig Casauranc, Mexican minister of the Education Ministry, to deliver a lecture in Austin. At the behest of Webb County district attorney John Valls, who harbored an undying hatred for the Calles administration, police arrested Puig Casauranc for libel at San Benito, Texas, a charge that stemmed back to the 1922 assassination of the revolutionary Lucio Blanco in Laredo (see Chapter 10). Puig posted bond and continued his American tour, then exited via California.[71] Such disregard by U.S. officials for diplomatic privilege was made clear in numerous other incidents. More drastic, in 1931 Vice Consul Adolfo Domínguez was jailed briefly by a Chicago judge who became tired of the envoy's zealous courtroom advocacy on behalf of immigrants, an incident discussed at more length in Chapter 7.

In the massive repatriation of the 1930s, young single males, the most prone to get into trouble with the law, returned to Mexico first and, consequently, the number of problems immigrants brought before consuls declined. In the 1930s, consuls still intervened in labor disputes, mainly in California, but in most cases Mexican workers were not as dependent on consuls as in previous decades. But Mexicans still criticized the consular service. Retired general Raúl Aguirre Manjarrez, in a 1936 letter to President Lázaro Cárdenas, identified a number of failings in the consular efforts to protect immigrants. Cárdenas then embarked on a renewed campaign to protect immigrants.[72]

4| Mexican Criminals in the United States

The few contemporary studies that discuss Mexican criminality in the United States during the late nineteenth and early twentieth centuries consider it within a social banditry framework or as the outcome of racism and poverty. Academicians, social workers, clergymen, and government officials from that period had more varied assessments. They depicted Mexicans as being unfairly stereotyped, resorting to crime because of poverty and discrimination, or being inherently villainous. Dr. Edith Abbott, director of the 1930 Wickersham Commission on crime and the foreign born, wrote:

> In attempting to attribute criminality to any particular
> group, it is important to remember that there has been
> in this country in each period of our history much reck-
> less and prejudiced criticism of one or another of our
> immigrant groups. At the present time it is the Mexican,
> recently the Italian has been bitterly attacked, but during
> the period preceding and immediately following the Civil
> War such criticism was visited upon the Irish.[1]

Lower-class ignorance—not knowing what constituted infractions—also figured as a reason for high arrest rates according to period analysts.[2]

In the 1920s, perceptions of Mexican criminality differed regionally. Anglos in areas with long-standing Mexican populations saw Mexicans as less threatening. A law officer in Texas told Taylor that "the average Mexican is peaceable and gives less trouble than among whites."[3] Paul Warnshius, another Commission researcher, found that attitudes held by most officials whom he interviewed in Chicago provided a contrast. One Chicago desk sergeant asserted that Mexicans "were born criminals" because of their admixture of Indian and Negro blood.[4] Significantly, in Chicago the Mexican *colonias* were relatively new.[5]

Mexican officials in turn defended the behavior of their compatriots across the board. In 1928, Oaxaca Mexican deputy Alfonso Ramírez, who traveled to Los Angeles to investigate Mexican unemployment, observed the LAPD arresting hundreds of jobless Mexicans for vagrancy. Before he returned to Mexico, he lamented to *La Opinión* that his countrymen were "victims caught in an economic situation beyond their control for which they are not prepared."[6]

Among the Anglo American public, notions of Mexican criminal behavior reflected a popular dichotomy. On one side stood the bandido, cruel and cunning, who masked a cowardly nature with false bravado. For Americans who had never seen Mexicans, the emerging movie industry cultivated this romantic, albeit negative, image.[7] The peon— a docile, harmless, hat-wringing creature, satisfied with little, and who did not look the *patrón* in the eye—composed the other side of the dichotomy.

The perception of border officers who oversaw smuggling prevention was overwhelmed by the belief that all Mexicans were criminals. In a 1929 report, U.S. customs agent Frank Buckley put it this way:

San Antonio, El Paso, Del Rio, Brownsville, and Laredo— all American cities, but Mexican in population, atmosphere and morals. Law-enforcement conditions in most such places reflect the moral laxity of Latins: liquor, narcotics, gambling, and prostitution all flourish—openly in some places, under cover in others—but flourishing nevertheless. It is a fact . . . so far as the moral texture of Texas border communities is concerned, that the annual immigration tide from the southern Republic leaves upon our doorsteps a horde of low-caste Mexicans— ignorant, immoral and unassimilable.[8]

Accounts creating an image of uncontrolled Mexican crime that reflected more an Anglo American ethnocentrism than the behavior of Mexicans are embedded in back issues of English-language newspapers in U.S. regions where Mexicans lived. According to historian Sarah Deutsch, for example, Colorado newspapers fed the belief that Mexican coal miners in Weld County accounted for two-thirds of all criminal cases. But a 1924 investigation found Mexicans represented no more than 10 percent of the Justice of the Peace cases, which was equal to their proportion in the county's population.[9]

**TABLE 1. ARREST RATES FOR MEXICANS IN PROPORTION TO
THE MEXICAN POPULATION FOR SELECTED REGIONS, 1929**

COMMUNITY OR COUNTY	% OF MEXI-CAN POPULA-TION IN COMMUNITY/ COUNTY	% OF MEXI-CANS IN ARREST POOL
CHICAGO	0.006	0.015
LOS ANGELES	7	11
SAN FRANCISCO	0.8	1.4
SAN ANTONIO	35	30
NUECES COUNTY, TEX.	45	34
IMPERIAL COUNTY, CALIF.	36	30
DIMMIT COUNTY, TEX.	75	50

NOTE: BOTH COLUMNS INCLUDE NATIVES OF MEXICO AND MEXICAN AMERICANS (ETHNIC MEXICANS BORN IN THE UNITED STATES).

SOURCE: DERIVED FROM THREE CHAPTERS IN *REPORT ON CRIME AND CRIMINAL JUSTICE IN RELATION TO THE FOREIGN BORN, FOR THE NATIONAL COMMISSION ON LAW OBSERVANCE AND ENFORCEMENT*, NO. 10, ED. EDITH ABBOTT; PAUL LIVINGSTON WARNSHIUS, "CRIME AND CRIMINAL JUSTICE AMONG MEXICANS IN ILLINOIS," PP. 279–281; PAUL S. TAYLOR, "CRIME AND THE FOREIGN BORN," PP. 204–207; AND ALIDA C. BOWLER, "RECENT STATISTICS ON CRIME AND THE FOREIGN BORN," PP. 100–102.

MEXICAN IMMIGRANT CRIME

But what was crime by Mexicans in the United States really like? Generally, all Mexicans stood vulnerable to the double standard with which justice was applied. Nonetheless, Table 1 shows that a significant regional difference existed in Mexican arrest rates. The immigrant *colonias* with the most developed forms of family cohesion, social networks, and time-tested immigrant institutions also experienced fewer incidents of police abuse, arrests, and Mexican-on-Mexican violence, and they had a greater ability to control combustible social situations. In the 1920s, this profile fits most border communities with more stable immigrant and Mexican American populations than industrial urban areas, such as Los Angeles and Chicago, where Mexicans had recently immigrated. Table 2 shows percentages of Mexicans who immigrated after 1920 for the most recent to the oldest *colonias.*

Clear-cut conclusions about Mexican criminality in the United States cannot be ascertained by viewing arrest rates by themselves. As

TABLE 2. PERCENTAGE OF MEXICANS WHO IMMIGRATED AFTER 1920, FOR MOST RECENT TO OLDEST *COLONIAS* (CHICAGO = MOST RECENT; EL PASO = OLDEST)

COLONIA	%	*COLONIA*	%
CHICAGO	78	SAN DIEGO	38
GARY	75	SAN ANTONIO	38
EAST CHICAGO	73	DENVER	34
DETROIT	66	PHOENIX	33
SAN FRANCISCO	51	DALLAS	32
LOS ANGELES	45	FORT WORTH	31
TUCSON	39	EL PASO	19
KANSAS CITY, MO.	40		

SOURCE: UNITED STATES BUREAU OF THE CENSUS, *FIFTEENTH CENSUS OF THE UNITED STATES TAKEN IN THE YEAR 1930, GENERAL REPORT OF STATISTICS BY SUBJECTS,* VOL. 2, P. 562.

the criminologist Richard Quinney professes, while arrests indicate the extent of certain forms of crime, they also reflect the policies and attitudes of law enforcement agencies. Thus, arrest statistics also reveal "a mixture of the *incidence of criminality and the administration of criminal law* [emphasis in text]."[10]

This assertion about the Mexicans' relationship with the police is more applicable when Mexicans were recently arrived. During 1913, thousands of destitute Mexicans fled Sonora into southern Arizona to escape the ravages of revolutionary violence. By November, Mexicans made up 80 percent of the Pima County jail criminal court cases according to a report in the *Los Angeles Times.* Similarly, police arrested 22 percent of the twelve hundred Mexicans living in Omaha, Nebraska, during 1923, mainly for disorderly conduct and petty theft. Because the arrest rate proved higher when compared with the general population, ostensibly Mexicans represented the most troublesome group in the city. Nonetheless, city officials freed most of those arrested, acknowledging that their greenhorn vulnerability, primarily the inability to speak English, resulted in unnecessary charges being levied against the newcomers.[11]

Mexican arrest rates in Chicago surpassed those of almost every other immigrant group. About 14 percent of the twenty thousand or so

Mexicans living in the city were arrested in 1929, compared with only 6 percent of the non-Mexican population. Mexicans comprised less than .006 percent of the total Chicago population, yet they made up .015 percent of the arrests. In comparison to other immigrant groups, the rate of Mexican arrests was still high (see Table 1). Although Chicago police arrested Mexicans disproportionately, their crimes were not serious. Jumping bail constituted 78 percent of Mexican felony charges in 1928–1929. Seventy-eight percent of Mexican misdemeanors involved drunkenness and disorderly conduct, while the remaining 22 percent consisted of carrying concealed weapons, assault, gambling, and traffic violations.[12]

In California between 1925 and 1930, over 12 percent of arrests involved Mexicans, while the Mexican proportion of the total California population in 1930 remained about 8 percent. As in Chicago, the California arrest rate for Mexicans was higher than for other immigrants. In San Francisco during 1929, Mexicans accounted for 1.5 percent of the arrest pool, even though less than 1 percent of the city's population was Mexican. Other immigrant groups, such as Irish and Italian immigrants, were arrested that year at rates lower than their proportion of the San Francisco population.[13] These disproportionate rates of Mexicans are partly attributable to non-Mexican immigrants being older and having lived longer in the United States. By the late 1920s, the aging "new immigrant" population had not been replaced by younger compatriots because of restrictions curbing southern and eastern Europeans. The result was an older European immigrant cohort that was less likely to clash with the law.

A relationship also existed between crime and regional locations. That is, the further away Mexicans lived from the border, the more numerous their arrests; *colonias* away from the border tended to be newer and located in industrial areas. In Los Angeles, from 1928 to 1929, 11.5 percent of all arrests were of Mexicans, who, according to the 1930 census, comprised only 8 percent of the city's population. On the other hand, in Imperial County, which borders Mexico, 34 percent of all arrests were of Mexicans, who composed 36 percent of the population in 1928.[14] Mexicans made up 50 percent of all 1929 arrests in Dimmit County, Texas (also on the Mexican border), although they were 73 percent of the population. However, if city life by itself contributed to Mexicans getting into trouble, the problem should have existed in San Antonio, the second largest city in Texas; in 1930, the San Antonio population was 232,000. Nonetheless, arrests of Mexicans were only 31 percent

of the total, while their proportion of the city's population was 35 percent—a sharp contrast to Los Angeles, Chicago, and Detroit.[15]

HUMAN INTERACTION AND DISPROPORTIONATE ARRESTS

The higher Mexican arrest rate outside border areas presents a paradox
because police treatment of Mexicans was more brutal in Texas and Arizona than in Los Angeles or Chicago (see Chapter 5). In fact, many
immigrants from West-Central Mexico forsook Texas for Detroit because of higher wages and technological opportunity, but they also believed they would not be as subject to discrimination and racism in the
Motor City.[16] Similarly, immigrants from Central Mexico bypassed Arizona for California because of better wages and attractive weather, and
significantly, because the state had a better reputation for treatment of
Mexicans.

Paul S. Taylor's observations in South Texas provide a clue to this
rural-urban dichotomy. He attributed the generally low arrest rate in
Dimmit County to a countryside milieu less conducive to crime than
urban areas. Anglos told him they could leave their homes for extended
periods without locking the doors.[17]

A second possible reason for fewer arrests along the border is that
Mexican behavior in Texas and Arizona conformed to Anglo expectations. Such a notion seen within the context of maintaining and control-
ling a labor reserve is not too far afield. In South Texas, Anglo farmers
in league with law officials imposed such a rigid "web of control" that
Mexican life revolved around the ruling group's economic and social
hegemony.[18] The extremely harsh police tactics and courtroom justice
in Texas perhaps served as a deterrent. In 1924, Mexico filed claims on
behalf of Mexicans in Texas who received five- or ten-year sentences
for stealing used clothing and for being involved in altercations with
Anglos.[19]

In Texas and the rest of the Southwest, the relationship between
law enforcement officers and Mexicans had been evolving for a longer
period of time than in urban industrial areas and Mexicans were segregated in their own part of town. Consequently, they did not "intrude"
into the lives of whites as much as in Chicago where Mexicans shared
residential areas in close quarters and in competition with whites.[20] In
border regions—Texas, Arizona, and New Mexico—the longtime presence of Mexican American court and law officials also allowed for a certain accommodation with the justice system.[21]

DEMOGRAPHY, REGIONAL ORIGINS, AND COMMUNITY STABILITY

Demographic factors go farther in explaining arrest disparities than the interracial and human interaction considerations raised above. A comparison of demographic characteristics within U.S. *colonias* demonstrates a correlation between arrests and these conditions: (1) the recency of the immigrant community, (2) regional origins in Mexico and regional destination in the United States, (3) the ratio of women to men and home ownership patterns, (4) the proportion of Mexican Americans to the Mexican-born, (5) unemployment patterns, and (6) age distribution, especially among males.

In the 1920s, about 80 percent of *colonia* inhabitants in the Midwest came from Central Mexico—Guanajuato, Michoacán, Jalisco, Zacatecas, San Luis Potosí, and Aguascalientes. Newly arrived and typically without family, these immigrants were attracted by higher paying jobs in the Midwest after they crossed the border. But immigrants from the Mexican interior were greenhorns by comparison. *Colonias* near the U.S. border were made up overwhelmingly of immigrants from northern Mexico. The majority of Mexicans working in the Imperial Valley, for example, migrated from Baja California, Sonora, and Sinaloa. The roots of Mexicans in Dimmit County were in nearby Coahuila and Nuevo León. Closer to home, they brought families or emigrated with a larger number of male relatives and friends from the same community. Even if not accompanied by families, proximity allowed *norteño* immigrants to return home to maintain intimate family contact more often than those from Central Mexico.[22]

In addition, during the 1920s border-area Mexicans had longer residency in the United States than immigrants who migrated farther north (see Table 1 above). The majority of San Antonio's Mexican population, for example, dated to the first Mexican influx in the 1890s. Thus, by the time *colonias* emerged in other cities, San Antonio's large Mexican community had firm roots. Similarly in Tucson, Sonoran immigrants developed reciprocity networks based on regional origins while the same process occurred in Lemon Grove, California (near San Diego), in relation to Baja California.[23]

Recency of immigration and incomplete families in the initial stages of *colonia* building resulted in disproportionate ratios of men to women, a factor contributing to disproportionate arrests because men commit more crimes than women. Additionally, lack of female companionship

FIGURE 6. DOUBLE WEDDING IN PHOENIX DURING 1933 OF ROSALES BROTHERS, RODRIGO AND ROBERTO, WITH GARCÍA SISTERS, ELODIA AND MERCEDES—ALL FROM ALTAR VALLEY OF SONORA. THE WEDDING PARTY WAS MADE UP OF FAMILY MEMBERS AND FRIENDS FROM THE SAME AREA. FROM AUTHOR'S PRIVATE FILES.

and family life fostered lifestyles that made young men vulnerable to arrest. The correlation here can be seen by comparing the ratio of single Mexican men to women in Table 3 to arrests by communities in Table 2. A higher incidence of home ownership in 1930 also points to community stability. In San Antonio, about 35 percent of the Mexican population owned property and homes. In Chicago, the figure was 8.5 percent, and in Detroit, 7 percent.[24]

A fourth consideration is that communities with larger numbers of U.S.-born ethnic Mexican Americans had less trouble with the law. A border judge in Maverick County, Texas, said the majority of cases tried before his court were not Texas Mexicans "but transients from across the border." In the late 1920s, 52 percent of Texas' convicts of Mexican ethnicity were born in Mexico even though only 42 percent of the Texas population was Mexico-born (see Table 4).[25] In addition, the Mexico-born were convicted of violent crimes more often and served longer sentences than Texas-born Mexicans for similar crimes, according to Wickersham Commission investigator Max Handman.

TABLE 3. RATIO OF MEXICAN MEN TO WOMEN FOR SELECTED CITIES, 1930

CITY	MEN:WOMEN	CITY	MEN:WOMEN
DETROIT	300:100	DENVER	115:100
GARY	274:100	LOS ANGELES	105:100
CHICAGO	210:100	PHOENIX	102:100
EAST CHICAGO	199:100	TUCSON	96:100
KANSAS CITY, MO.	148:100	SAN DIEGO	96:100
SAN FRANCISCO	122:100	SAN ANTONIO	91:100
DALLAS	122:100	EL PASO	80:100
FORT WORTH	116:100		

SOURCE: UNITED STATES BUREAU OF THE CENSUS, *FIFTEENTH CENSUS OF THE UNITED STATES TAKEN IN THE YEAR 1930,* VOL. 2, PP. 116–132.

But why were Mexican Americans not as vulnerable to arrest? In comparison to the immigrants, they probably understood the legal system better, had better political connections, were on the average older (see below), and the police, many of whom were Mexican American, more than likely showed greater hostility to those born in Mexico.

Unemployment and the extent to which social support systems existed emerges as a fifth factor in this analysis. Frequent economic downturns, felt more in urban areas, resulted in "last hired, first fired" patterns—the bane of Mexican immigrants. In 1930, even before the Great Depression ravaged the job market, 24 percent of Detroit's Mexicans were unemployed, although overall unemployment stood at only 5 percent. Significantly, Detroit police, in 1929, arrested Mexicans in higher proportions than anywhere else in the country. In Chicago, where Mexicans also had high arrest rates, 9 percent of job-eligible Mexicans were out of work. The overall unemployment rate hovered at 6 percent. In contrast, only 2 percent of Texas Mexicans were out of a job. The correlation between lower Texas Mexican joblessness to arrest rates is compelling, even when taking into account the difficulty of determining rural unemployment. Moreover, in an industrial city, jobless Mexicans faced harsher conditions than did jobless compatriots in towns like San Antonio or Tucson, which had higher levels of family and community reciprocity.[26]

TABLE 4. NATIVES OF MEXICO BY STATE, 1930

STATE	TOTAL ETHNIC MEXICAN POPULATION	BORN IN MEXICO (%)
INDIANA	7,612	78
ILLINOIS	21,570	75
MICHIGAN	9,778	73
MISSOURI	3,397	68
KANSAS	11,103	58
CALIFORNIA	199,359	54
ARIZONA	50,022	44
TEXAS	266,240	42

SOURCE: UNITED STATES BUREAU OF THE CENSUS, *FIFTEENTH CENSUS OF THE UNITED STATES TAKEN IN THE YEAR 1930,* VOL. 2, P. 446.

The sixth and most significant correlation to arrest rates is age distribution. Most arrests in the 1920s, regardless of region or race, were of males between the ages of eighteen and thirty-five. From 1929 through 1930 in Chicago, where 61 percent of the male Mexican population was between eighteen and thirty-five, the police arrested Mexicans at a rate three times higher than their overall proportion of the population (see Table 5). In San Antonio, where Mexicans had lower arrest rates, only 35 percent of the Mexican males were between the ages of eighteen and thirty-five.[27] Indeed, a decline in arrests required community maturity and stability. Until then, like extreme poverty and educational neglect, trouble with the law remained a cross for the newer *colonias* to bear.[28]

BARRIO BRUTALITY: INTERNECINE VIOLENCE

Negative reporting and racist stereotypes undoubtedly enhanced the reputation Mexicans had for violence, but because accounts of Mexican-on-Mexican brutality appear so often in historical records, the phenomenon begs for further examination. The old-timers I interviewed in the Chicago area, for example, were consistent in characterizing early *colonia* life as violent. In 1925, the Mexican consul in Chicago, immigrant leaders, and the East Chicago, Indiana, police chief met to ease *colonia*-police tension, exacerbated after a Mexican killed an officer. According

TABLE 5. PERCENTAGE OF MEXICANS BETWEEN THE AGES OF EIGHTEEN AND THIRTY-FIVE IN FIVE CITIES, 1930

CITY	%	CITY	%
DETROIT	61	LOS ANGELES	38
CHICAGO	60	SAN ANTONIO	35
SAN FRANCISCO	42		

SOURCE: UNITED STATES BUREAU OF THE CENSUS, *FIFTEENTH CENSUS OF THE UNITED STATES TAKEN IN THE YEAR 1930,* VOL. 2, PP. 749–750.

to José Anguiano, a leader in the Sociedad Cuauhtémoc during the 1920s:

The meeting was necessary because many Mexicans
blamed harsh police tactics for the tension, but Mexicans
were also violent—they drank and then fought. Sometimes a Mexican concluded his vendetta at the gate of the
Inland Steel plant where he followed his victim from
Mexico and shot him as he walked out of work.[29]

MEXICO AS A SOURCE OF VIOLENCE

Rising violence in Mexico during the advent of large-scale immigration was a corollary to rapidly shifting conditions in the Porfiriato and the Mexican Revolution. Intra- and inter-class strife and aggression, especially in West-Central Mexico, took place where land tenure systems underwent radical transformation and society remained in a state of flux.[30] According to statistics compiled by conservative Mexican jurist Ramón Prida in the late 1920s, murder arrests occurred more frequently in Central Mexico than in border states—the two main sources of immigration in this era. This can be attributed to the fact that in Central Mexican communities agrarian issues were hotly contested. Moreover, in this milieu peasants and workers who had been accustomed to absolute control by hacendados, along with mine owners, shoemakers, and *obraje* (cloth-making shop) owners, experienced liberation and a diminished respect for authority.[31] A United Nations study on the universal patterns of violence corroborates this. It states:

Statistical studies of the frequency of violent outbursts
in a number of nations over a period of years indicate

that violence is related to rapidity of social change. This may mean that such change brings with it new expectations and as a consequence, new frustrations leading to violence.[32]

Historian Luis González made the ironic observation that following the revolution in San José de Gracia, Michoacán, a quintessential immigrant-sending village, "Not everybody ate well, but it was a rare man who did not own a pistol. It was not easy to wipe out . . . machismo inherited from the past."[33] Paul Friedrich, who chronicled a pattern of homicides from the 1920s to the 1950s in Naranja, Michoacán, indicated that, "The great majority if not all were somehow political," meaning that community power struggles and land issues provoked the carnage.[34]

Ramón Prida was mystified when he discovered that rural people committed the greatest number of violent crimes in Mexico. In his words, "City dwellers engage in more crimes in other countries. Anyone who knew our peasants in the past realizes they were courteous and honest to a fault. So what has happened?" Prida concluded that agrarian reform created violent competition and rural dislocation.[35]

VIOLENCE, ALCOHOLISM, AND CULTURE

Ramón Prida explained violence by resorting to a popular stereotype of this period. "Mexicans," he asserted "have inherited the legacy of two warrior cultures—that of the Indians and the Spaniards. The Spaniards were addicted to violent conquest and the Indians to sacrifice."[36]

Even recent anthropological studies of rural Mexican communities infer that owing to specific Mexican cultural characteristics, drinking facilitates crossing the fine line from verbal to physical aggression. Or as Erich Fromm put it in a study of a Mexican village, "Most . . . violence, including murder, has resulted from sudden flare-ups in a cantina" because the aggressor "may be made to feel his impotence and frustration by a well-placed insult."[37] Octavio Paz, Samuel Ramos, and Eric Wolf explained *macho* aggressiveness through a theory of a mestizo male identity crisis in which insecurity is masked by belligerence and a desire, to use Paz' phraseology, to *chingarse* (screw over) a male rival.[38] Eric Wolf wrote that in the mestizo's individualistic desire for power, "all means are legitimate in this battle for personal control, even violence and death."[39] The ideas espoused by Frantz Fanon—that colonized people, unable to turn their anger and resentment on the colonizer, use their weaker, less threatening brethren as targets of aggression—offers another possible explanation.[40]

Nonetheless, alcohol consumption always seemed to be a factor when Mexicans committed crimes of passion. Luis González asserted that "cult violence, the habit of getting drunk, and an exaggerated sense of personal honor," all went together in San José de Gracia.[41] In Mexico, authorities often allowed tumultuous behavior to go unpunished, a permissiveness that could only encourage intragroup turbulence. William B. Taylor, in his brilliant study of violence in colonial Mexico, demonstrates that this attitude had early roots. Spanish officials rarely penalized Indians who murdered other Indians so long as such acts did not disrupt crown imperatives and remained geographically isolated.[42]

Paul Friedrich indicates that of the murders he recorded in Naranja in this century, "Only three of the seventy-six were actually punished by law and two of these lightly (that is, a night in the county jail)."[43] Undoubtedly, Mexican immigrants internalized this concept of punishment before crossing the border, but they did not encounter a similar impunity in the United States, especially in large industrial cities.

MEXICAN-ON-MEXICAN VIOLENCE IN THE UNITED STATES

José Anguiano, Eduardo Peralta, and other old-timers from Chicago who were interviewed for this study were consistent in affirming that Mexicans carried weapons in the United States because of the influence of the Mexican Revolution. Paul Taylor said Mexicans toted arms because "in Mexico the common folk wear knives so habitually as to regard them practically as part of dress."[44] Indeed, the arrest of Mexicans on weapons charges was a familiar occurrence in the U.S. *colonias,* as well as a constant source of grief. In 1916, the Kansas City consul secured the release of several compatriots arrested for carrying concealed weapons by convincing authorities that Mexicans were ignorant of such laws. He then threatened to cease intervening if immigrants continued to violate the prohibition.[45]

It is difficult to say to what degree the antisocial behavior described below is related to an anomic behavior that so many observers noted in Mexico because of industrialization during the Porfiriato and the social dislocation in the ensuing revolution. Certainly, if rapid social change provoked turbulence in Mexico, the immigrant environments of host communities in the United States contained similar catalysts.

Honor ignited male-on-male altercations. In the early hours of a Sunday during July 1932, David Duarte and his friends gathered around a car parked in front of his Glendale, Arizona, home. They drank, played the guitar, and sang. Duarte's daughter and her husband, Juan Díaz, also lived in the house. The latter objected to the singing because he wanted to sleep but Duarte refused to cease the merriment, telling Díaz, in front of friends, to shut up and go back inside the house. Insulted, the young Mexican shot and killed his father-in-law without warning.[46]

Rivalries related to competition over females all to often provoked male violence. In Tracy, California, railroad workers José Verduzco and Manuel Hernández were wooing the same Mexican girl and repeatedly threatened each other. Finally, José and his brother Zerefino fought a wild gun battle on July 8, 1923, against Manuel and his friend Esteban Alcaraz. At least seventy shots were fired in the melee in which Manuel, José, and Esteban died. Zerefino survived only to be shot and killed by policemen called in to quell the savage disturbance.[47]

Rejection by women also proved to be a constant catalyst to violence. "Rosita Alvírez," a very popular black-humor *corrido* (popular ballad), has the protagonist, Hipólito, taking out his revolver and killing the comely Rosita because she refused to dance with him. He pleads with her before the misdeed is committed, "Rosita please don't disdain me, everyone is looking." The song is supposedly based on a true incident from this period in Mexico, but at the very least it imitated life. For example, in June 1910, Basilio Martínez stabbed Bonita García to death at the altar of a Brownsville, Texas, church after her lover appeared and she refused to marry Martínez.

THE MIDWEST: AN ACCELERATION OF VIOLENCE

As *colonias* in the Midwest began to form, they experienced a greater volume of internecine turbulence than older, more stable southwestern Mexican communities (see comparative prison statistics in Chapter 9). In the Kansas City metropolitan area, six *colonias* emerged between 1910 and 1920. They contained about ten thousand immigrants, mainly from West-Central Mexico. According to historian Michael Smith, violent personal conflicts between weapon-carrying Mexicans became an integral part of *colonia* life.[48] Before the 1920s, the *colonia* had few stabilizing immigrant institutions. For example, in spite of a large number of Mexican Catholics, religious ministering from "Catholic authorities" proved inadequate. Smith concludes that the Church "responded belatedly and ambivalently to spiritual and physical needs."[49]

In northwestern Indiana *colonias,* about ten thousand recently arrived Mexicans lived in East Chicago and Gary during the 1920s. As in Kansas City, the *colonias* attracted businesses, Catholic and Protestant churches, and mutual aid societies—all institutions promoting cultural activity. They emerged, however, only after the large, young, *solo* (single men) group was diluted by the arrival of women, children, and middle-class entrepreneurs during the mid-1920s. In the meantime, housing remained scarce and expensive, forcing crowded living conditions. In East Chicago, for example, close to six thousand Mexican workers and their families lived in an area less than a square mile in size.

The majority of young single men worked in the steel industry at Inland, Youngstown, and U.S. Steel. When not working, they wandered through the streets, frequenting pool halls, speakeasies, and bordellos, or they traveled to Chicago where more recreational choices attracted them. They shared rooms with compatriots in arrangements called "hot beds"—one slept while the other worked or sought recreation in the streets. Unemployment threatened constantly. When they lost their jobs, young men were adrift, far from their family support systems in West-Central Mexico. These lifestyles promoted constant contact with the police, who did not hesitate to jail them for the slightest infractions.[50] Female scarcity in Midwest *colonias* intensified possessiveness in fathers, husbands, and boyfriends and brought out the worst in those deprived of female companionship. In South Chicago, for example, Gertrudis Londalús shot and killed Frank Zúnigo, who had married Londalús' former common-law wife. "He had gone to talk to the slain man and was called out into the hall. There in the semi-darkness he saw the flash of a knife," said South Chicago's *Daily Calumet.* The court released Londalús, based on a self-defense plea.[51]

Unlike Texas, violence in the Chicago area occurred mainly between males (see Table 6). Between 1928 and 1931, the *Calumet News* reported 32 violent Mexican-on-Mexican crimes in East Chicago and Gary, Indiana—none involved killing or injuring a woman. Most took place after 1929, a period that coincides with the rise of unemployment in these cities. The newspaper usually announced the incidents with a tone of moral indignation. On October 3, after reporting a number of violent events in the *colonia,* the newspaper led off a story with "Another Mexican arrested for murder."[52] The negative cast in *Calumet News* reporting was probably prompted by its support for repatriation. But crime news declined considerably as recently arrived *solos* were repatriated and Mexican families with longer residency remained in the area.[53] In neighboring Chicago, crime-related news in both Spanish-language newspapers and the *Daily Calumet* of South Chicago demonstrated internecine crime to have a similar intensity and character as in northwest Indiana. The newspaper sources for Chicago are reinforced by the

TABLE 6. MEXICAN-ON-MEXICAN VIOLENCE, 1900–1935 (N = 62)

LOCATION	MALE-ON-MALE	MALE-ON-FEMALE	FEMALE-ON-MALE
TEXAS	23	19	2
CHICAGO AREA	24	4	0

SOURCE: DERIVED FROM INCIDENTS DESCRIBED IN APPENDIX B.

"homicide log," a journal kept by the Chicago Police Department (see Table 7). Sixty Mexicans died violent deaths between 1922 and 1927, for instance. Of those, 60 percent represented crimes of internecine passion. Only blacks and Italians had a similar level of intragroup violence.[54]

SEX CRIMES

Rape represented the most common sex-related charge brought against Mexicans. In Los Angeles during 1928, 23 percent of the men charged with this breach were Mexican, which is much higher than their share of the city's population.[55] The female victims in these assaults almost always turned out to be Mexican. Statutory rape charges were the most common, a factor that stemmed partially from the male practice in Mexico of abducting young girls to serve as mates. There some aggrieved fathers avenged lost honor through violence; others simply accepted the liaison. But in the United States, Mexican parents complained to authorities. Police then charged kidnappers with statutory rape if sex had been performed. In Phoenix during December 1909, authorities arrested twenty-two-year-old Pedro Ricardo for statutory rape after he tried to elope with thirteen-year-old Antonia Medina. The couple married while Ricardo was in jail, but he was still convicted of the charges.[56] In more violent rape cases, Mexican victims most often knew the perpetrator, usually another Mexican.[57]

PREMEDITATED CRIME AND MEXICANS

Mexicans committed few premeditated crimes in comparison with other immigrant groups and the general white population. Their most serious offenses, as seen above, were impulsive assaults and homicides (see Chapter 9 for statistics on prisons). Unlike other groups, they did not figure prominently into organized crime except in smuggling along the border.[58] Other planned crimes consisted mainly of bootlegging,

TABLE 7. HOMICIDES IN CHICAGO BY ETHNIC-RACIAL GROUP, 1922–1927

	WH	BLK	ITAL	JEW	IR	EEU	CHI	MEX
TOTAL PROJECTED FROM ONE-OUT-OF-TEN SAMPLE								
	610	410	280	80	170	260	20	60
PROJECTED PERCENTAGES BY TYPE OF HOMICIDE								
TRAFFIC ACCIDENT	30	5	1	40	23	46	50	10
SAME-GROUP PASSION KILLING	23	54	18	—	23	15	—	60
ROBBERY VICTIM	18	10	4	40	17	23	50	10
ACCIDENTAL SHOOTING	7	2	1	—	1	7	—	—
POSSIBLE GANGLAND	5	—	21	11	1	4	—	—
KILLED BY POLICE	4	10	11	—	17	1	—	20
ABORTION	3	2	4	9	—	—	—	—
POISON	2	—	—	—	—	—	—	—
KILLED DURING CRIMINAL ACT	—	5	—	—	1	—	—	—
MOTIVE UNKNOWN	8	12	40*	—	17	5	—	—
TOTAL	100	100	100	100	100	101	100	100

WH = WHITE ANGLO OR UNKNOWN WHITE   ITAL = ITALIAN   EEU = EASTERN EUROPEAN
BLK = BLACK   JEW = JEWISH   CHI = CHINESE
IR = IRISH   MEX = MEXICAN

NOTE: ETHNIC DETERMINATION WAS MADE FROM SURNAMES AND CIRCUMSTANCES RECORDED IN THE HOMICIDE REPORTS. ONLY MEXICANS AND BLACKS WERE CONSISTENTLY IDENTIFIED AS SUCH IN REPORTS.

*KILLINGS OF ITALIANS, WHERE THE PERPETRATOR ESCAPED, HAD MANY OF THE EARMARKS OF ORGANIZED CRIME MURDERS, WHICH MAKES IT LIKELY THAT THE KILLER WAS ALSO ITALIAN. THUS, WHILE ETHNIC BREAKDOWN FOR GROUPS OTHER THAN MEXICANS AND BLACKS IS TENTATIVE, ITALIAN IDENTIFICATION WAS EASIER TO MAKE.

SOURCE: CHICAGO POLICE DEPARTMENT HOMICIDE LOGS, 1921–1927, ILLINOIS HISTORICAL SOCIETY ARCHIVES, SPRINGFIELD.

burglary, drug dealing, prostitution, armed robbery, and mugging. Customers or victims were usually other Mexicans. In Kansas City *colonias,* the record of Mexicans mugging or strong-arming other Mexicans for money or belongings is extensive. Sometimes robberies netted large amounts of cash, but usually the illicit proceeds proved negligible. In one incident, a Mexican holdup man fatally shot a compatriot, taking three dollars.[59]

Mexican consular officials and immigrant leaders often noted that unemployment during economic slowdowns forced usually law-abiding Mexicans into crime. At the height of the 1921 depression, Chicago Consul Francisco Pereda implored Mayor Hale to pay railroad fares to the border for destitute Mexicans who might turn to crime. Olivio Navarro, laid off from the steel mills in 1929 in Homestead, Pennsylvania, stole a carton of cigarettes and gave it to his Spanish landlord as a rent payment. But the landlord turned Navarro in to the police. After the Mexican consul explained the hardship situation to the judge, Navarro was released and deported.[60]

BOOTLEGGING AND DRUG PUSHING

In Arizona, where it was illegal to sell liquor to Indians, a lucrative trade involving Mexicans in illicit alcohol beverages had existed since the nineteenth century because of the state's large Native American population. For example, during 1907 near Yuma, law officials arrested Mario Hernández and Ignacio López as they carried a load of moonshine along the Colorado River into an Indian reservation. Both were turned over to federal authorities.[61]

During Prohibition, Mexicans made or bought corn whiskey, usually in small operations to sell among friends. In 1927, Los Angeles barber Felipe Montes explained that he borrowed fifteen hundred dollars to buy equipment to set up his shop. To make ends meet he turned to bootlegging. "I bought gallons of 'corn whiskey' or other kinds of whiskey in order to sell it to my friends. I sell it to them at $1 a pint and 25 cents a drink," he said. "When I'm not here my wife takes charge of waiting on them, and also when I am very busy," Montes added.[62] Bootlegging could be dangerous, however. Montes shared his constant fear of being arrested. In a dramatic family biography, *Rain of Gold,* Victor Villaseñor wrote of his father's exploits as a southern California bootlegger during this period, recounting close calls with the police and violent encounters with other bootleggers.

Marijuana use among Mexican immigrants can be traced to Mexico where smoking the drug had been extensive but not rampant.[63] Mexicans became associated with it in the same way Chinese were linked to opium. In 1926, East Chicago's *Calumet News,* for example, condemned marijuana use as a major *colonia* shortcoming. Los Angeles Mexicans purportedly used the drug extensively, and they accounted for almost half of all drug-use arrests there. Interestingly, they were not implicated as much in dealing or transporting marijuana into the city.[64] As in bootlegging, violence occurred among pushers. In Detroit during 1931, for example, a Mexican named Rodríguez shot and killed Ramón Santos after the latter, with the help of Gilberto Chapa, beat and cut him in the face during an argument over profits from marijuana sales.[65]

Mexican leaders and diplomats, however, consistently denied that compatriots used marijuana more than other ethnic groups. José M. Dávila, a Mexican border official invited to give a speech on immigration at the Claremont Colleges in 1927, absolved his countrymen of an undeserved reputation for criminality, saying that the "majority of them do not smoke 'marihuana' . . . contrary to the general belief." The Pittsburgh consul complained that the hardworking Mexicans in his district did not use the drug as much as other nationalities. But he admitted that unemployment forced many workers, including Mexicans, to sell the drug, which sold for between twenty-five cents and fifty cents per cigarette.[66]

Pandering for prostitutes does not appear as a major criminal activity for Mexicans in statistical data. For example, in Los Angeles, only 3 of 23 males arrested for violating the Mann Act (interstate transportation of prostitutes) in 1928 were Mexicans.[67] But anecdotal evidence shows that Mexican males plied the sex trade as panderers and bordello operators employing Mexican women or women from outside their ethnic group. When Lou Vidal tried to open up an El Paso dance hall in February of 1905, he and three dance-hall girls were arrested for prostitution. In February 1929, East Chicago police arrested Frank Ortega for pandering, and the following year they accused Adolfo Pérez of keeping an unsavory house that also sold illegal liquor and sex. For good measure, federal officers also charged him with illegal entry and deported him.[68]

MEXICAN WOMEN AND CRIME

In Los Angeles, authorities charged few Mexican women for being drunk and disorderly or for assault, a common cause of their male counterparts winding up behind bars. Julia Blackwelder's study of women in San

Antonio in the 1930s depression years corroborates this for San Antonio as well. Mexican females were arrested in proportion to their overall representation in the city, mainly for prostitution and "cottage industry" crime, such as bootlegging in their homes. This kind of activity, according to Blackwelder, would not compromise Mexicans' patriarchal notion of a woman's place within the *colonia*. The example provided above of how the Mexican bootlegger in Los Angeles depended on his family to dispense liquor suggests how Mexican women engaged in selling illegal liquor.[69]

Of the Mexican female lawbreakers, however, most engaged in prostitution. More Mexican professional prostitutes worked in the border regions than anywhere else. Mary Odom, in a study of female sexuality in the United States, identifies a fairly developed pattern of Mexican teenage prostitution in Los Angeles before 1920. During 1928, police put two hundred fifteen Mexican women in the Los Angeles County Jail for prostitution—13 percent of the total.[70] In San Antonio, observers estimated that Mexican females composed 40 percent of those practicing the profession in the 1930s. Border prostitution became more important when the U.S. military stationed large numbers of soldiers in the area during the Mexican Revolution. Although no reliable statistics exist for the El Paso–Ciudad Juárez region, most sources indicate that bordellos employed mainly Mexican women on both sides of the border. When city officials decided to shift the red-light district away from the center of town in 1903, many of the women threatened to move to Ciudad Juárez, but years later they were still plying their trade.

Other southwestern towns, especially mining communities, contained red-light districts employing Mexican women as well as numerous whites, although the specific ratio in this case is difficult to determine. Police ignored the vice until the mainstream community protested, then Mexican-born streetwalkers found themselves unceremoniously dumped south of the border.[71] During an antiprostitution campaign in Phoenix, police arrested and deported a number of Mexican women during August 1930. One thirty-two-year-old woman was charged with adultery because police caught her in a sex act but could not prove prostitution. She admitted being a street walker to the Phoenix consul, explaining that her husband had left her three years earlier and she had turned to the profession because he rejected reconciliation pleas. Besides, the woman added, "I paid my bribes to the police like everyone else. It is the Phoenix police who are as guilty as anyone else."[72]

Except in border areas, Americans did not consistently attribute prostitution to Mexicans, as they did other criminal stereotypes. This was especially true in the Midwest where Mexican males, themselves steady patrons of bordellos, frequently criticized working-class peers of other nationalities because they allowed "their women" to be prostitutes.[73] In the Midwest *colonias,* the relative lack of Mexicans in the profession probably stemmed from the paucity of Mexican women living in the region.

Unlike their male counterparts, Mexican females committed few violent crimes. Rather than being perpetrators, Mexican women more often wound up on the receiving end of brutality (see above). When Mexican females killed anyone, however, it was usually a male and under circumstances that pointed to self-defense. In June 1910, Manuel Navarro threatened to kill his lover with a gun. She lunged at him, and in the struggle the gun went off and blew away half his skull. In San Antonio, police arrested a sixteen-year-old girl in February 1919 for stabbing to death sixteen-year-old Alfredo Ochoa while the two were drinking "rot gut" whiskey and he began to beat her.[74]

SMUGGLING: HUMAN CONTRABAND

Smuggling from Mexico was a constant source of diplomatic friction throughout the Porfiriato and a continuous source of border disorder. This established way of life expanded during the Mexican Revolution when gunrunning attracted thousands of new adherents. Smuggling took an upswing in 1918 after President Wilson issued a sweeping trade embargo against Mexico because of diplomatic difficulties with Carranza's administration.[75] Human contraband became more common with the rise of immigration in the first decade of the twentieth century as the United States tightened its borders. After the 1917 Immigration Act, which required proof of literacy from immigrants and an eight-dollar head tax, ferrying them across the Rio Grande illegally became a lucrative trade.

The Mexico City newspaper *Gráfico* explained in 1920 that *coyotes,* as immigrant smugglers were known, worked so openly that the activity invited greater vigilance from the border patrol, and many immigrants trying to cross illegally had been shot.[76] In addition, smugglers often assaulted, robbed, or raped their clients. A 1923 government report told of how a *coyote* raped a teenage girl, while her family witnessed the ordeal from the opposite bank of the Rio Grande.[77] Moreover, the promises of *enganchistas* (labor recruiters), rarely bore out. In 1923, recruiters smuggled ten workers from Central Mexico across the border and enticed them to a lumbering operation in Bogalusa, Alabama, with promises of "magnificent daily wages." Once there, they crowded in with some fifty workers in an unhygienic stockade, "where company guards hindered their leaving." Some tried escape only to be returned and beaten by the guards.[78]

The 1924 Immigration Quota Act barred nonwhites from Asia and restricted southern and eastern Europeans, creating even more opportunities for alien smugglers because many of those barred by the Quota Act tried to enter the United States through Mexico.[79] Because Mexican labor still seemed indispensable in the United States, officials worried more about undocumented Europeans and Asians. Thousands of Asians and Europeans huddled at the Mexican border or in Cuba waiting to enter the United States. Most Europeans attempted to enter clandestinely through Cuba. According to one report, in January 1925, twenty thousand stood poised to make the journey to Miami. Asians, such as Chinese and Hindus, relied almost exclusively on Mexican entry. In September 1925, Mexico and the United States launched a joint effort to halt the clandestine entry of Chinese, who paid such high prices that a sophisticated ring of international agents sprang up at all major Mexican ports of entry to solicit their business. Asians arriving in Mexico were taught English, then smuggled into the United States. Even though the efforts to curb surreptitious entry targeted non-Mexicans, the increased vigilance hindered Mexicans from crossing as well. Eventually, labor markets became saturated, Mexicans became unwanted. By the end of 1925, Border Patrol agents turned more of their attention toward illegal Mexican immigrants.[80] Most activity focused on the Texas-Mexican border. H. H. Leonard, a Matamoros consulate official, submitted a detailed report in April 1925 listing the persons involved in smuggling and revealed rendezvous locations. Leonard felt that hundreds of criminals living on the Mexican side were "the main smugglers of aliens and liquors in commercial quantities. Most smuggling is carried as far as 155 miles up the Rio Grande River and downstream into the Gulf." He added that aliens wishing to enter went downstream to a farm or some small settlement and made arrangements for the trip across; there was always someone willing to risk serving as a guide.[81]

Most Mexicans caught entering without documents came from Central Mexico. Unlike many *norteños,* who knew how to cross many times in the course of one month without being bothered, immigrants from the interior had no knowledge of the territory and depended on *coyotes.* In some cases the *coyotes,* to remain immune from prosecution but still collect their fees, left unwitting aliens at a designated spot where agents had arranged to pick them up.[82] The price border crossers paid varied according to a number of factors. Basically, the least experienced paid more. José Anguiano's crossing sheds light on this disparity. By the time he arrived at the border from his native Guanajuato in 1918, he had been in the Mexican north for months. A Mexican border official, whom the teenaged Anguiano met through a prostitute for whom he ran errands, arranged for Anguiano to pay only about two dollars to cross on the ferry in the company of others in the same craft who were not as fortunate and less experienced. They were accompanied by *coyotes* who charged much more.[83]

SMUGGLING: LIQUOR AND DRUGS

The War Prohibited Act of 1918 created dry zones along the length of the border to force abstention on U.S. soldiers. It also made profitable the smuggling of a cheap but potent moonshine called *sotol* near El Paso. Extensive contraband rings emerged after the farther-reaching 1919 Volstead Act expanded opportunities.[84] As early as 1919, hundreds of El Paso's Mexicans organized into dope rings. A U.S. market for such illegal drugs as cocaine, morphine, and opium further propelled the illegal trade. Sold by druggists in Ciudad Juárez, cocaine, which just a few years prior went for thirteen dollars an ounce, commanded seventy-five dollars in 1925. Once conveyed across the Rio Grande most drugs made their way to the eastern United States.[85]

Leaders of contraband rings came from a variety of ethnic groups. Anglo American, Middle Eastern, Chinese, and Mexican merchants ran the large operations, but the rank and file were from the working-class *barrios* of border towns. Independent operators known as mules smuggled most of the liquor across in small quantities. Juárez official Andrés Morán estimated that 75 percent of the city's population, mostly natives of the border area, engaged in some kind of trafficking activity.[86] A U.S. Treasury agent branded them "ignorant Mexican desperados, paid from fifty cents to one dollar per sack, for handling liquor across the river on their backs or by pack mule."[87] The Mexican government lamented that, "Whenever there is any kind of economic crisis Mexicans find it the most difficult to find jobs and they turn to delinquency such as transporting liquor. They benefit very little from this endeavor and inevitably are caught and sentenced to penalties as long as five years imprisonment."[88] A popular *corrido* in the 1920s has a smuggler on a train taking him to serve a sentence at Fort Leavenworth wondering "if he will ever see his family again. . . . vowing never to smuggle again, he warns his countrymen to avoid landing in American jails, for once in, all your friends forget you." [89]

Authorities sometimes clashed violently with smugglers, a topic treated more extensively in Chapter 5. But the smuggling atmosphere also provoked violence not related to law enforcement efforts. In April 1928, the Los Angeles *La Opinión* reported the El Paso slaying of Guadalupe Morales at the Valverde Ranch, a well-known smuggler's watering hole near El Paso's Washington Park. The killing purportedly took place during a deal that went awry. Ringleaders duped hundreds of artless Mexicans into taking mule jobs because they were desperately poor, lamented the newspaper. Smuggler competition was so great in the 1920s that liquor and drug wars rivaled the border battles fought by political factions during the revolution. In January 1921, liquor smugglers fought a territorial battle near Laredo that left a large number of dead or wounded and forced one of the factions to retreat into Mexico. [90]

Large-scale trafficking bred corruption among officials on both sides of the border as well. Pedro Silva, previously an immigrant worker before settling in Ciudad Juárez to a life of contraband, told of a Texas Ranger captain stationed at Fort Bliss. Rendezvousing at the Valverde Ranch, the captain paid him two dollars for every case of liquor. Silva also negotiated an agreement with the ranger to make him immune from arrest. The arrangement was not always honored, he complained, judging by number of narrow escapes from arrest. [91]

BLAMING THE PURVEYORS

Eventually the public, blaming Mexico for border evils, demanded an end to smuggling and pressured politicians to act. During 1913, an article in the *Imperial Valley Press* condemning vice in Mexicali and Baja California, inspired Father F. Burelach, a prominent valley priest from Brawley, to write his congressman requesting that the federal government eradicate the evil. "Our country protects its citizens against the damage of foreign warfare, why should our country stand idly by when her citizens are exposed to this same danger at Mexicali under Mexican protection . . . ," he complained. [92] In February 1923, John W. Dye, U.S. consul in Ciudad Juárez, reported that a grand jury investigation in El Paso "revealed that drugs are being peddled to school children in El Paso." Dye had also learned of "the death of a prominent and popular society girl of El Paso, aged 17 years following a 'dope party' in Juarez." [93] The Ku Klux Klan entered into the picture as border moralists and vigilantes. Because of incessant threats by the Klan to stop smuggling, in 1921 an El Paso judge declared that Ku Klux Klan members who took the law into their own hands would be prosecuted. In 1926, the Calexico KKK, among many lobbyist groups, worked toward restriction of border smuggling and prohibition of access to border wickedness.[94]

Other Americans, however, had a divergent viewpoint on the cause of border corruption. Journalist Duncan Aikman, after visiting all of the border towns, wrote in a 1925 article that the vice centers mainly attracted Americans who simply recreated the evils that they were able to enjoy at home before Prohibition. At a 1926 conference in El Paso of the Home Mission Council, a Baptist settlement program, a resolution condemned "with shame the conditions of vice maintained largely by Americans along the Mexican border. Many of the larger gambling houses and saloons are operated and patronized by Americans, giving the Mexican an interpretation of American life which is a national disgrace."[95]

By January 1924, smuggling from Canada and Mexico was so widespread that a congressional bill was introduced to provide emergency prevention funding. In March 1924, assistant secretary of the treasury Andrew Moss ordered the closing of the international bridge at El Paso from 9 P.M. until 7 A.M. because whiskey and narcotics trafficking peaked during the late hours. Two weeks later, the practice was initiated in Laredo. At the same time, U.S. officials announced plans for building a 160-mile fence across the California boundary to have better control of the immigrants expected to cross the border in March to work in summer harvests.[96] Smuggling alarmed the Mexican government and law-abiding citizens on the Mexican side as well. In November 1924, Mexican secretary of foreign relations Ricardo Treviño consulted with U.S. treasury secretary Henning on bilateral agreements to control trafficking across the international line. In addition, during March 1925, El Comité Pro-Juárez in Ciudad Juárez petitioned the Chihuahua governor to crack down on drug smugglers. The Comité urged long jail terms for drug traffickers who brushed off fines, rehabilitation centers for addicts, and heavy penalties for those who in any way abetted traffickers.[97]

This universal concern over smuggling led to the convening of the binational conference in May 1925 to discuss mutual prevention efforts. The meeting resulted in a treaty, ratified in March 1926, in which both countries were held responsible for seizing contraband before it traversed the border.[98] Despite this well-meaning prescription, making even a small dent in illicit activity was an uphill battle. According to one report in Piedras Negras alone, four large wholesale liquor houses operated legally to satisfy the bootlegger market across the border. Much of the smuggling was done by American civilians and soldiers from Fort Clark, the report continued, in cooperation with Mexican dealers. The biggest deliveries were made in San Antonio, using little-traveled dirt roads. Profits made the risk seem worth it. For example, a case of Canadian Club Whiskey, which sold for $36 in Piedras Negras, brought $120 in San Antonio.[99]

As shall be seen in the remainder of this book, although Mexicans did not engage in professional crime to the same degree as the general population in the United States, they clashed inordinately with law enforcement officials and were well represented in criminal proceedings and within the incarcerated population. Crimes of passion or petty criminal activity, which was not too far removed from passion crimes in terms of premeditation, account for most of these unfortunate circumstances.

5| POLICE TREATMENT OF MEXICAN IMMIGRANTS

MEXICAN IMMIGRANTS FELT the negative presence of the police system from the moment they set foot on the U.S. side of the border. For example, in 1929, social worker Micaela Tafolla at San Antonio's International Institute, a YMCA immigrant assistance center, noticed an older woman who never left the building. She was waiting there with her daughters to travel on to Chicago to join a son. When Tafolla asked if she cared go out for some fresh air, the woman replied, "No, no, no, niñita, I would rather die than to see another Gringo with a pistol around his waist. He might stop and question me again."[1]

From the 1890s to the 1930s, perhaps as many as 20 to 25 percent of incoming Mexican immigrants were arrested or accosted by the police, often brutally. During the early twentieth century, many communities allowed ill-trained policemen to use such unconstitutional methods as the third degree (intense police questioning laced with torture), indiscriminate dragnets, and brutal arrest tactics on the powerless sectors of U.S. society. Mexican immigrants ranked among the most vulnerable of these victims (see Chapter 4 for statistics). Paul Warnshius noted that while two-thirds of Mexican arrests were for disorderly conduct, the charge "provides the police with what appears to be a convenient, colorless charge to which they can have recourse when the original accusation cannot be proved, and they are faced with possibility of their prisoner being discharged."[2]

Because American society valued Mexicans for their labor, law enforcement sought to assure employers that Mexicans would be maintained within a "web of control," as one scholar characterized methods used to keep immigrants malleable and accessible to work in Texas. Studies have shown that in Arizona mining communities, the function of the police in this century has been as much to keep the Mexican workers in check as to maintain public order.[3] The most direct manner of police intervention to benefit employers was squelching labor organizing. In turn of the century Los Angeles, according to Edward Escobar, "City officials, usually successful businessmen themselves, regularly assisted employers by passing anti-picketing and anti-radical ordinances. . . . No city agency, however, took a more active and direct role in protecting employers' interests than the Los Angeles Police Department."[4] Local police, the Arizona militia, and Arizona Rangers, also beat back Mexican miner strikes in Clifton-Morenci, Arizona, during 1903, and in Globe-Miami and Bisbee some years later. In the 1930s, the most intensive period of Mexican agricultural organizing in California up to that point failed largely because of police collusion with employers.

Although this study concludes that while the need to keep workers subordinated and under control is the overriding factor that explains police harshness toward Mexicans, other factors are woven into the interpretation. If the "web of control" mandate had been the only guideline for law officials, treatment of Mexicans would have proved less brutal. But because economic and political elites appreciated police loyalties, they did not interfere when local police used their power to fulfill more personal needs, unless labor sources were jeopardized. In addition, policemen had little to fear when charges of misconduct were brought against them. In Los Angeles, for example, between 1900 and 1917, Mexicans filed seventeen brutality charges against the city police; all but three were dismissed.[5]

THE BULLYING POLICEMAN

A permissive climate allowed policemen that were so inclined to vent sadistic tendencies by menacing Mexicans. These bullies thrived on the terror they instilled and acquired fearsome reputations in local barrios. In February 1910, Mexicans in the agricultural town of Colton, California, accused officer J. A. Magill of entering homes at all hours of the night, presumably looking for firearms, then pistol-whipping inhabitants. The City Board of Trustees, however, rejected the allegations and instead charged that the Mexicans had assaulted Magill. The *Colton Chronicle,* which did not as easily dismiss the charges, condemned the policeman's tactics, saying, "obviously he had great hatred for the Mexicans of 'Cholotown,'" as the barrio in South Colton was called.[6]

Police violence in Texas, perhaps more than in any other state, kept Mexicans within the web of control. Texas state representative Davidson told fellow lawmakers in 1919 that "the average Mexican citizen can only be controlled with an iron hand such as President Díaz exercised."[7] In spite of an obvious and blatant record of police mistreatment of Mexicans, Texas authorities rarely admitted the need for reform. During August 1927, Michoacán and Guanajuato newspapers published several letters written by Jesús González, a former immigrant living in Morelia, Michoacán, where he leveled a variety of accusations regarding the extremely harsh treatment of Mexicans by Texas law authorities. Even accounting for some hyperbole, his denouncements were mainly on target. But Governor Dan Moody's only reaction was to explore the possibility of using Mexican law to sue González for libel.[8]

The line between police actions to maintain the "web" constraint and a personal inclination to violence is often difficult to draw. For example, on the night of June 10, 1916, a deputy sheriff named Baily in Hitchcock, Texas, attacked three Mexicans caught riding a freight train. One had to be hospitalized in critical condition because of the injuries sustained from a severe pistol-whipping. Such tactics, according to the deputy, served to discourage the practice of jumping freight trains.[9] Here is the proverbial killing of two birds with one stone — one, the brutality discouraged a practice that railroad companies abhorred, and two, it allowed Baily to feel empowered and devoid of guilt.

As Mexicans followed job trails outside the Southwest, police harassment accompanied them. By 1916, perhaps as many as ten thousand Mexicans lived in Kansas and Missouri, primarily in six barrios within the Kansas City metropolitan area. According to one historical account, "Residents of the colonia . . . complained that overzealous law enforcement officers mistreated Mexicans, accosted and frisked them without due cause, and harassed women and children."[10]

POLICE CRIME AND MEXICANS

Officers who used their power to defraud or exploit Mexicans proved worse than bullying or vindictive policeman. The degree of corruption among large-city policemen is well known.[11] But many small towns also had criminal elements in the police. Transient Mexicans in these communities where they lacked family or friends posed easy targets for criminal policemen. In 1913, Mayor R. E. Johnson of Marble Falls, Texas, upset with his constable because he extorted from Mexicans, asked Secretary of State William J. Bryan to intervene. A Department of State underling informed Johnson that the agency had no authority over local government.[12]

The most incredible criminal act against Mexicans by police took place during December 1927 in Stanton, Texas, a town near Midland. According to the El Paso consul, deputies C. C. Baize and Lee Small promised work to Hilario Núñez, Norberto Díaz, and an unidentified third companion. The officers took them to Stanton, asking them to wait at a bank entrance while they went inside, supposedly to arrange employment. The deputies then came out with guns blazing, killing Núñez and Díaz and then claimed to have caught them in the act of trying to rob the bank. The third Mexican, although severely wounded, survived to tell the story. The killing, charged the consul, provided a ruse to claim a five thousand dollar reward offered by the Texas Bankers Association for apprehending bank robbers.[13]

Vagrancy, Police Raids, and Mass Roundups

Unless challenged by influential sectors of the community, police departments regularly employed timesaving but unconstitutional procedures. In the *colonias,* where protection rarely existed, police used sweeping dragnets in which scores of policemen rapidly appeared either to apprehend a fugitive, raid gambling houses, destroy neighborhood stills, arrest prostitutes and their clients, or control laborers. Vagrancy codes, for example, served to channel Mexican workers into situations that best suited employers. In South Texas, law officials arrested Mexican migrants as vagrants at the beginning of each cotton season and leased them to farmers. In Willacy County, this practice was called the "pass system." Once jailed, the "vagrant" worked off his fine in the cotton fields of farmers who had arrangements with county officials. Laborers leaving the region needed a signed pass indicating they were employed; otherwise they might be jailed in another county.[14] But when poor Anglos fell into the trap, the sheriff's enemies used it against him and the practice was eliminated.

The police arrested Mexicans en masse primarily to preempt the possibility that they would engage in criminal acts or become public charges. During the 1921 depression, thousands of destitute Mexican workers converged in cities in a hopeless quest for jobs. Public hysteria over the presence of unemployed beet workers in Denver prompted police to incarcerate hundreds of Mexicans on trumped-up charges of loitering. In March, San Antonio consul Enrique Puig charged that Dallas police arrested Mexican workers for vagrancy and meted out fifty-day sentences without providing a hearing. During the day they cleaned streets; at night the guards shackled them together at the ankles.[15]

During the mid-1920s mass arrests seemed to subside, but at the end of the decade, the U.S. economy slowed down again. During the winter of 1927–1928, Los Angeles unemployment reached one hundred thousand, creating an army of homeless men who converged on city parks to loiter. Every so often police raided these commons, picking up anyone not having a means of support. In January 1928, the Mexican community joined together in protest.[16] Organizer Agustín García claimed that once jailed, authorities forced many prisoners to work on public projects and paid them with a bus ticket to the nearest town. "These people are not vagrants," protested García, "they are just unemployed."[17]

The record of police raids in Texas is more violent, even if the orgy of law enforcement raids during the Plan de San Diego is not taken into account. In 1912, a sheriff and his deputies shot into the Ojo del Agua Ranch, a suspected bandit hideout, killing a sleeping Manuel Cantú who, relatives swore, was a law-abiding farm worker. The Mexican government's efforts to determine why the shooting took place came to naught.[18] As Chihuahita grew in South El Paso, so did police violations. In September 1918, for example, "Twenty plainclothes officers assisted by 18 uniformed officers swept the barrio in search of 'gunmen' and 'bootleggers.'" To confiscate guns, knives, and illicit liquor, the police stopped, searched, and arrested scores of innocent people. The police chief happily announced that all undesirable characters had been locked up or driven from the city.[19]

In midwestern states, Mexican transience and lack of support bases promoted vulnerability to police abuse. Because of the migration pattern this violence was evident first in the Great Plains and then in Chicago and Detroit. In February 1916, Kansas City policemen clubbed and took Mexicans to jail in paddy wagons because they roamed downtown streets on a Sunday morning. *El Cosmopolita* argued there was no provocation for these assaults. "Sunday is the only day that Mexican workers can get haircuts since they work six days out of the week and some shops remained open on Sunday morning to accommodate them."[20] By the 1920s, Chicago became the major midwestern destination for Mexicans. As Mexican numbers increased, so did raids and mass arrests. Police used such tactics, according to Spanish-language newspapers, to extort bribes or simply to harass Mexicans. *El Correo Mexicano* complained that in the fall of 1926 Chicago police arrested, without cause, twenty-eight Mexicans waiting to enter a Saturday night dance at the Hull House "simply because it suited their fancy."[21]

In Chicago, Detroit, and Kansas City, where "new immigrants" (eastern and southern Europeans) and their descendants resented and disliked Mexicans, the police, themselves of European background, allowed their prejudices to influence how they treated Mexicans. Chicago police-Mexican relations in particular became extremely tense. Paul Taylor explained the hostility by "the fact that the police in the districts inhabited by Mexicans were often first or second generation of the very nationalities which feel themselves in competition with the Mexicans."[22] Because Mexicans found it difficult to penetrate this structure, they quickly identified the police with their civilian ethnic rivals and tormentors. As late as the 1950s, for example, only one Mexican served as a policeman in the entire Chicago police force.

In the Southwest, the lack of large "new immigrant" enclaves blunted identification between policemen and particular ethnic sectors of the white community. Generally, southwestern law officers identified with other whites (Anglos) or with whites of their own class. But in Los Angeles, with an array of nationalities, Mexicans rarely accused policemen of siding with specific ethnic factions. Besides, the LAPD employed officers of Mexican descent, a factor that probably ameliorated tensions between Mexicans and the police.[23] This was certainly true in smaller communities in Arizona, New Mexico, and Texas. For example, many of the first law enforcement officers in Arizona's Maricopa County during the nineteenth century were Mexicans.

POLICE VIOLENCE DURING ARREST

The majority of police beatings and homicides occurred at the point of arrest when a policeman usually interfaced with a Mexican one-on-one. In an interview during 1927, Manuel Lomelí, a mineworker and a mutual aid society leader, summed up police-*colonia* relationships in Miami, Arizona. "The authorities deal very harshly with everyone," he related. "They beat one up while talking; they haven't any more than told one something than they hit one with a pistol barrel."[24]

This total lack of respect for a suspect was most common among the more vulnerable segments of society. Mexicans had been immigrating into Arizona since the nineteenth century, and by 1910, among all the states, only in New Mexico did the proportion of Mexicans to the total population exceed that in Arizona. Most Arizona police abuses took place in areas characterized by a rapid influx of immigrants rather than in regions where the Mexican population had long-standing roots; there was a geographic concentration of incidents linking police methods to the need to maintain the classic web used to control newly established labor forces.

In Tucson, an old Hispanic community, police problems reached their zenith in the late nineteenth century when the most immigration took place. One of the first Mexican organizations, El Centro Radical, for example, made protection from police a primary objective. Thomas

Sheridan, biographer of the Tucson Mexican community, asserts that by the 1930s Tucson Mexicans were more settled and that some of the city's police force included influential Mexicans.[25]

In contrast, between 1900 and 1920, thousands of Mexicans went to work in Salt River Valley agriculture and in southeastern Arizona mining towns, an influx that resulted in tension with the police. During 1913 when Francisco Rubio resisted Phoenix officer F. Murphy's efforts to jail him on drunk and disorderly charges, the enraged policeman repeatedly hit his captive in the stomach with such ferocity that Rubio later died in his cell. An investigation cleared Murphy of any wrongdoing.[26]

Police killings of Mexicans were even more acute in Arizona mining towns, which within a short period had drawn thousands of Mexicans to the state's most dynamic industrial sector. Extensive labor strife characterized early formation of these worker communities; consequently, relations between company-controlled police, Mexicans, and other workers was continually strained. John Welch, a half Mexican and longtime police chief in the archetypal mining town of Miami, had an especially fearsome reputation. In December 1931, Phoenix consul Luis Castro lamented that a Cochise County grand jury acquitted the officer after he shot to death Martín López y de la Torre. In the 1940s, labor leaders looking back at Welch's career designated him as the most villainous enemy of the Mexican working class.[27] But his self-image was quite different. When asked by a writer about the 1920s shooting death of Juan Lugo in a gun battle, the police chief said that in the main, Miami was peaceful, but "once in a while we have a criminal who gets out of line. But this class doesn't last long." [28]

One of the most flagrant examples of police overreaction occurred in Phoenix. During January 1929 officers learned that two Mexicans, Leo Bustamante and Mario García, and Puerto Rican Rudolph Vélez intended to burglarize the City Drug Store. Led by police captain M. F. Fraesier, five policemen waited to arrest them inside and outside the store. The officers watched the burglars break a window on the front door, enter, then go behind the display case to fill their bags. Then one of the patrolmen fired, and the others followed suit, "believing that their brother officers had been fired upon." Apparently the police chief, N. W. Matlock, had a standing order to always "shoot first before they get the drop on you." Twenty-year-old Vélez was wounded. A fatal bullet hit García, the oldest of the burglars, in the head as he slipped an ornamental clock into his bag. Bustamante, who had an amputated arm because of an automobile accident, was shotgunned through the heart. The police said the shootings were necessary because Vélez had a criminal record. None of the burglars were armed—not even with a knife.[29]

Texas was clearly in the forefront of police homicides at the point of arrest. A Mexican government study of Mexican immigrants in the United States killed by police between 1910 and 1920 concluded that the majority occurred in Texas. Texas officials themselves admitted this was the case. In 1918, El Paso consul Andrés García recommended that owing to mistreatment by law enforcement officers, Mexican workers should not be allowed into Texas under wartime waivers to the literacy requirements of the 1917 Immigration Act. T. C. Jennings, head of the Texas Labor Commission, anxious not to jeopardize Mexican labor during an expanding wartime market for Texas products, acknowledged the validity of the consul's concerns and pledged that measures would be taken to ameliorate the problem.[30]

But an inordinate number of slayings by police in Texas continued into the early 1920s. On August 25, 1921, at Driscoll, Deputy Hugh K. Kondall shot Adolfo Galván in the arm and then killed him with a second shot as the Mexican begged for his life. The officer gained his freedom after posting a twenty-five hundred dollar bond, pending a grand jury hearing, which was postponed and moved from one court to another until the issue was dropped. The Mexican ambassador in Washington, D.C., implored the State Department, "We ask your offices to take the necessary steps to not let this crime go unpunished."[31] Kondall then became a deputy sheriff in Karnes County and a year later shot and killed another Mexican, named José Flores. The issue was taken before the grand jury, but it also resulted in an acquittal.[32] In another case, Texas policeman Sam Bernard, who had a long history of brutality toward Mexicans, killed Alejo Quintanilla in 1922. In September, the Hidalgo County grand jury probed the homicide but referred the matter to its next session in February 1923. The probe then passed to the September session in which the grand jury adjourned without returning an indictment because "no witness could be found who could offer any evidence that would cast any reflection whatever on . . . this murder."[33]

Private guards, deputized civilians assisting in arrests, or inexperienced part-time police ("short call" officers) also inflicted gunshot wounds and injuries. At Washington-on-the-Brazos between Brenham and Navasota, army officer Sam H. Houston shot and killed a drunken Mexican who was "interfering with the police." He then claimed self-defense. Agustín Hernández was killed at a bar in Brady in McCulloch

FIGURE 7. NEWSPAPER CLIPPINGS OF POLICE KILLINGS IN HOUSTON. THESE KINDS OF HEADLINES WERE TYPICAL IN AREAS WHERE MEXICANS LIVED IN LARGE NUMBERS. FROM AUTHOR'S PRIVATE FILES, NEWSPAPERS UNKNOWN.

County, Texas, by Rube Burt, a night watchman who responded to a disturbance in the saloon on November 4, 1927. Hernández was so drunk he could hardly stand up, according to his friends, but the night watchman claimed Hernández came at him with a knife. Private guards also meted out violence in and around train stations and railroad camps where many transient Mexicans lived.

In 1927, a Los Angeles immigrant related an incident from years earlier that left him embittered toward the police:

Once a poor Mexican bought a bottle of whiskey to take
to his house and drink it . . . he noticed a policeman
drawing near. Then he slyly put his hand to his back
pocket in order to take the little bottle out and perhaps
throw it away when the policeman without much ado,
fired a shot at him and killed him. They didn't do any-

thing to that policeman; he is going about free. And there have been an infinite number of cases like that.[34]

Mexicans in California experienced fewer police homicides than those in Arizona and Texas during the 1910 to 1920 period, however. The high incidence in Texas reflected the large number of Mexicans living in that state. By 1910, Texas had absorbed almost 65 percent of all Mexican immigrants. Nonetheless, a continuing disproportionate incidence of police homicides in Arizona and Texas, even after California's Mexican population became the second largest in the country in the 1920s, points to a more blatant disregard for Mexican lives in these two states.

As the tide of immigration extended beyond the Southwest, so did episodes of police killing Mexicans. In Kansas, thousands of Mexicans lived in railroad camps on the edges of towns, areas which the police entered armed to the teeth, ready to do battle. On September 16, 1911, a policeman in Mackville, Kansas, ventured into a railroad camp to arrest a prostitute. Panicked workers tried to flee and the policeman fired and killed Pablo Ramos.[35] The Chicago police homicide ledgers for 1921 through 1927, handwritten records of persons who died at the hands of another human being (auto accidents and suicides included), show sixty Mexicans as victims. Of those, ten occurred at the hands of the police. No other ethnic group had a higher proportion of its members killed by law enforcement officers.[36] In Texas and Arizona, incidents of police violence against Mexicans declined considerably in the 1920s; at the same time they increased in Chicago.

Upper-class status did not protect Mexican expatriates from indiscriminate police tactics. The most publicized police violence toward Mexicans resulted in the 1931 death of the nephew of Mexican president Pascual Ortiz Rubio and another Mexican youth. In June, students Emilio and Salvador Cortés-Rubio and a friend, Manuel García Gómez, were motoring to Mexico after studying at Saint Benedicts College in Kansas. Near Ardmore, Oklahoma, two deputy sheriffs in plainclothes, Cecil Crosby and William E. Guess, thought the youths looked suspicious and followed their car from a highway hamburger stand. When Emilio, who was driving, stopped so Salvador could urinate, the policemen pulled up behind them. According to the only surviving student, Emilio Cortez Rubio, the youths had bought guns and ammunition to take back to Mexico and at first did not realize that the men in plainclothes were police. He put a gun on his lap to defend himself, he said, but when Crosby pulled him out of the car, he dropped it. The other officer, Guess, panicked and fired a number of volleys, killing Emilio's unarmed brother, who was still in front of the car, and García, who was in the passenger seat. The two officers were found innocent in spite of vigorous efforts by prosecutors who came under a lot of pressure from the Mexican government to show Guess had shot needlessly.[37]

THE THIRD DEGREE

A strenuous interrogation known as the third degree, usually accompanied by torture, elicited quick confessions and spared policemen the necessity of gathering evidence. A researcher who studied its extent in the 1920s observed that the third degree was most always employed with poor suspects because "the likelihood of abuse is less when the prisoner is in contact with an attorney. The poor and uninfluential are less apt to be represented."[38] Mexican suspects were prime candidates for the third degree. An Arizona lawyer who was half Mexican but had an Anglo surname wrote in the 1930s, "I have often been present when police interrogate these unfortunates. They will admit to anything even if they are not guilty."[39] In 1927, an El Paso Mexican woman was accused of setting fire to a kerosene-doused bed, killing her youngest child—allegedly an unwanted illegitimate baby. Arrested at midnight, she confessed after she was "relay-questioned without rest, and perhaps without food, for 35 hours." She later recanted however. When tried, she insisted that the fire was accidental and that officials threatened never to let her see the other children again unless she confessed.[40]

One of the most blatant applications of the third degree against Mexicans occurred in the mining town of Greaterville, Arizona, during April 1915. Pima County deputies Fenter and Moore visited the León family home to interrogate three brothers—José María, Francisco, and Hilario—whom they suspected had killed a Mrs. Loreta Yáñez and stolen her cattle. The brothers vehemently denied the accusations, so the deputies tried to coerce a confession—by hanging them until the brothers passed out. Hilario died immediately. José María was left out in the desert for twenty-one hours and when found was taken to his Greaterville home until a doctor could be summoned. Francisco, not as incapacitated, managed to find his way home.[41] Sheriff Thomas Forbes in Tucson assured incensed Mexican community leaders he would conduct a full investigation. José María died a week later from meningitis caused by oxygen starvation.

Widespread publicity given to the brutality resulted in a trial in which the deputies were found guilty of second-degree murder and sentenced to prison. The swift action, which at first pleased the Arizona Mexican community, ended in bitter disappointment. On February 13, 1917, the Arizona governor and the Board of Pardons and Paroles pardoned and released the former deputies.[42]

BORDER AUTHORITIES AND
VIOLENCE TOWARD MEXICANS

Because the core of Mexican criminality existed in towns along the border, Anglo border officials harbored some of the worst resentments toward Mexicans. On January 12, 1916, just a few days after the Santa Ysabel, Chihuahua, massacre of eighteen Americans (see Chapter 1), customs agent J. D. White shot Francisco Pérez to death in an Ysleta lockup after arresting him for riding a stolen horse across the border. But his sister in Ciudad Juárez told Mexican reporters that she had sent him on a simple errand to El Paso. Other Mexicans charged that the officials were avenging the massacre; after all, white civilians and soldiers had just gone on a rampage in El Paso Mexican neighborhoods. But customs officials insisted that the prisoner pulled a gun. The officer's acquittal by a grand jury enraged Mexicans further. El Paso chief of inspectors Zach Lamar Cobb, in a letter to Secretary of State Lansing, complained bitterly that Mexicans had no right to protest, considering the Villista atrocity.[43]

When the Immigration Border Patrol was formed in 1924 to augment the thinly staffed customs agency of the Treasury Department, undisciplined Texas toughs and former Texas Rangers served as the first recruits. According to Supervisor Clifford Perkins, patrol members dealt with Mexicans in a "rough shod fashion." Along the length of the border—from Tijuana to Matamoros—officers around Laredo had the worst reputation. Perkins was sent to the San Antonio office in the 1920s to clean up the mess but encountered resistance from the Laredo chief inspector who "proved to be a rough, tough, tobacco-chewing 'if they won't talk, work 'em over with a six-shooter' bully weighing well over 250 pounds."[44]

Because many Laredo patrol members were former Texas Rangers, Perkins said, they continued ranger habits and dealt with immigrants as criminals: "It took considerable indoctrinating to convince some of the inspectors they were not chasing outlaws, and we never did get it out of the heads of all of them, for we had to discharge several for being too rough." This "roughness would have been very injurious to the Patrol had there been any publicity," he admitted.[45]

Typically, mules who earned the smallest profit not only took the greatest risk of getting caught but were the most likely to be injured or killed by Border Patrol agents or hijackers who wanted their cargo. In 1929, the Department of the Treasury indicated that forty-five Mexican smugglers had been killed in trafficking battles since Prohibition was instituted. One list contained the names and circumstances under which twenty-one smugglers were killed by agents on both borders of the United States; sixteen were along the Mexican border, even though most illicit liquor came from Canada.[46]

The details of a widely publicized case near San Diego, California, demonstrate the danger Mexicans faced from authorities even when only peripherally involved in smuggling. In February 1931, immigration officials deported Rubén C. Pardo Zamora for illegal entry, but he returned to work at the Monserrat Ranch where Officers Joseph P. Byrne and Harry W. Cunningham arrested him again. When Pardo Zamora tried to escape, Cunningham fired at him at a distance of fifty feet, missed, but downed him with a second shot. Cunningham then handcuffed the mortally wounded Mexican as he lay on the ground.[47]

C. Kuykendall, district chief of the immigration office, justified the officer's actions because the young Mexican was an "incorrigible" whose deportation had stemmed from his having smuggled in fourteen pints of tequila. The San Diego district attorney agreed. On the other hand, E. F. Pearson, Pardo Zamora's boss for five years, said that he was among the most industrious workers. An article in the *San Diego Union* deplored the killing and said it was difficult to accept the accidental shooting explanation because the coroner's report revealed that Pardo Zamora was beaten, either before or after the shooting. District Attorney Tom Whelan of San Diego County reopened the case but the officers were again exonerated.[48]

THE RANGER CONCEPT: TEXAS AND ARIZONA

In both Texas and Arizona, state officers called Rangers dealt out extremely harsh justice to Mexicans. The Texas Rangers, much more famous than those in Arizona, had existed in various guises since the Texas Rebellion of 1836. The historian Walter Prescott Webb, who lavished praise on the officers, estimated that they killed anywhere from one thousand to five thousand Mexicans over the years.[49]

The print media painted these Texas lawmen with heroic strokes, fulfilling the public demand for romantic western lore. An article in the *New York Times* during March 1914 introduced the Rangers with the headline, "Texas Rangers, Who Ride Shoot and Dare." They made up "One of the World's Most Efficient Armed Organizations" whose motto was "Get Them When You Go for Them," said the piece, which swelled with admiration for the "derring-do of these men." It compared the Rangers with the Royal Canadian Mounted Police and asserted that their fame was "secure in English-speaking countries and most civilized lands where stories of grit and daring and coolness in the face of great danger are appreciated."[50]

The *Times* eulogy coincided with the anti-Mexican propaganda campaign being waged by the Wilson administration on the eve of the Veracruz invasion (see Chapter 1). Border tension was also at a fevered pitch. Governor Colquitt sent Rangers to Raymondville to counter live-stock rustling by border revolutionaries—an epidemic, according to local Anglos. Even Texas Mexican lawmen were slated for persecution if they sided with *rancheros* or were suspected of sympathizing with the bandits.[51] Some years later, Texas legislator José T. Canales from Brownsville accused the Rangers of unnecessary violence. "There was nothing but general stealing—they [Mexicans] stole saddles, arms and ammunition, and horses, but no life of an American in any way was threatened," he testified.[52]

But events surrounding the Plan de San Diego in 1915 provoked an orgy of killings by the Rangers, unmatched in the history of Texas Anglo-Mexican relations. According to Plan de San Diego leader León Caballo, alias Agustín Garza, the repression started in May of 1915. He showed a reporter a pocket of letters from Mexicans in Texas who wanted to return to Mexico because of repression in Texas. Said Caballo:

These . . . are from my people who cannot live any longer
in the state of Texas, as they are denied protection and
many have been killed by irresponsible armed posses
without reason. They are afraid to live there, and are
leaving small farms which they have purchased with the
savings of lifetime. Leaving everything behind they are
coming back.[53]

Dispatches of Rio Grande City consul Leoncio Reveles provide detailed information on the atrocities as they intensified in the fall of 1915. After rebels led by Luis de la Rosa attacked the village of Sebastian and killed a handful of whites, Texas officials accelerated their repression of Mexicans. A particularly intense firefight between rebels and Rangers at Las Norias Ranch that same month further intensified the struggle. Rangers arrested Juan Tovar in Banquete, a suspect in the battle, took him to the La Norias Ranch, and executed him without any explanation. But according to Reveles, Texas officers also killed nonparticipants. One of his reports indicates that Rangers executed workers on the Monte-cristo Ranch—Plutarco Garza, Ezequiel Tijerina, and Paulino Cerda—even though they had no affiliation with the insurrection. Reveles spoke to the appalled ranch foreman, Juan Vela, who said the victims' families were left in difficult straits. Garza had a wife and two children; Tijerina, a mother and father; and Cerda left eight children and a wife. Cerda in particular was an exemplary person who did much for his community, Reveles lamented.[54]

In August, a group of Rangers, led by Captain Tom McKee, accused Cenobio Rivas, a South Texas farmer, of harboring bandits. They told him to turn all the lights out at his ranch house while they waited outside to see if bandits would appear. When two Mexicans, who Rivas claimed were simple grubbers, knocked on the door and asked for a drink of water, the Rangers opened fire. Even after the Mexicans fell, the Rangers continued shooting into the house and killed fifteen-year-old Martina Rivas and wounded her brother George. The only assistance given by the State of Texas was to help bury the girl. José T. Canales undertook to collect damages, but eleven years later the state had not indemnified them, complained a family friend.[55]

By October 1915, calm had returned to South Texas and the Rangers were ordered to halt operations. At least five hundred persons had been killed in this period, according to Reveles.[56] But Villista aggressions early in 1916—the January Santa Ysabel massacre and the Columbus raid in March—further inflamed feelings toward Texas Mexicans, an antago-nism that was exacerbated when the troops of Pershing's expedition sus-tained numerous casualties at the El Carrizal clash with Carrancistas during June. During this period in El Paso, Rangers arrested Mexicans for openly harboring anti-American feelings. In one case they shot and wounded an eighteen-year-old Villista after trying to arrest him for recruiting.[57]

Even after border tensions cooled from the white-hot intensity reached during the Plan de San Diego and the Villista raids, Rangers continued to earn the hated *rinche* (ranger) epithet. After bandits, iden-tified in conflicting reports as either Carrancistas or Villistas, attacked the Brite Ranch on December 25, 1917, in the Big Bend area, brutally killing or wounding guests celebrating Christmas, Rangers and U.S.

troops pursued them into Mexico and allegedly killed several of their number. The Mexican government claimed that the persons slain in the foray had nothing to do with the raid.[58]

Then on January 25, 1918, Rangers went to a ranch near Porvenir, Texas, an isolated community of less than two hundred Mexicans, and arrested and then released three Mexicans whom they suspected of having participated in the Brite raid. They returned to Porvenir on the twenty-eighth, however, accompanied by Anglo ranchers and twelve U.S. Army soldiers who stayed on the outskirts while the remaining force took fifteen Mexicans, small farmers and stock owners, a mile out of town. There the Rangers and vigilantes executed their captives and mutilated their bodies with knives. Three were only teenagers. The rest of the village, mainly old men, women, and children, about 150 of them, fled to Mexico leaving behind their farms and stock. Juana Zorilla Flores, a grandmother of three of the victims, told army investigators that on "that awful night," her husband was taken away and killed. The local schoolteacher, the only white who lived in the village, did not allow her to see the mutilated body that lay in a row with twelve others.[59]

U.S. Army adjutant general James Harley ordered the disbanding of Company B of the Rangers, who were responsible for the massacre, and the resignation of its commander, Captain J. M. Fox. In a letter to Fox, the general wrote, "Your forced resignation came in the interest of humanity, decency, law and order and hereafter the laws and constitution of this state must be superior to the autocratic will of any peace officer . . . vandalism across the border can be best suppressed by suppressing it on the Texas side first."[60]

Less humane reasons propelled the curtailment on Ranger power, however. General Harley also referred to the trouble the incident would bring to international relations, including the conduct of the war in Europe. Moreover, as early as June of that year, Mexican officials warned that unless Texas prohibited Ranger attacks such as the Porvenir massacre, *braceros* (workers) would not be allowed into the state during the labor-scarce period of World War I. The threat greatly concerned both Texas and federal officials, who agreed to find a solution to the problem.[61] A report written by Howard C. Hopkins, a Department of Labor official, charged that Mexicans entering the country illegally and captured by Rangers were treated with "more brutality than [by] any other service." According to Hopkins, this played into the hands of pro-German Mexicans who wanted to prevent emigration to sabotage U.S. agriculture.[62]

In 1919, at special hearings motivated by the severity of Ranger brutality, numerous Texas officials, including legislator José T. Canales, called for curtailment of their authority. As Canales put it in a letter to C. H. Pease, a legislator who opposed his efforts, "I want to clear out a gang of lawless men and thugs from being placed . . . in the character of peace officers to enforce our laws." [63] This increasing public criticism tarnished the Rangers' romantic image. [64] In 1920, journalist George Marvin wrote an article in *World's Week* condemning Ranger atrocities. "There is no penalty for killing. . . . Reading over the Secret Service Records makes you feel as though there was an open season on Mexicans along the border," he lamented. [65]

Border tension declined somewhat in the first few years of the next decade but made a comeback in 1926 after President Calles repressed the Catholic Church and provoked the Cristero Rebellion. This rebellion unleashed a wave of violence throughout Mexico and along the Texas border at the same time that smuggling increased. Subsequently, Ranger and Border Patrol shootings also rose along the border. [66]

Nonetheless, the reports of Ranger atrocities decreased significantly in this decade. In fact, Rangers at times emerged as protectors of Mexicans. During the depression of 1921, at a time of Ku Klux Klan–inspired violence, Rangers secured the safety of Mexicans assaulted by masked men in towns like Ranger and Breckenridge. Then, as depression-related unemployment took a toll among American workers in 1931, Anglos blew up a Mexican mutual aid society building in Malankoff, Texas. The governor again sent Rangers to protect Mexican workers (see Chapter 6 for discussion on both eras).

The Arizona Territorial Legislature created a version of these Texas law officers in the spring of 1901 to curtail the cattle rustling and smuggling along the border, which was mainly done by Mexican outlaws. Many of the Arizona officers in fact were former Texas Rangers. [67] The Arizona Rangers achieved notoriety mainly for helping to suppress labor disputes involving Mexicans. In the Morenci strike of 1903, when thousands of Mexican strikers milled around the town, allegedly threatening white citizens, the Rangers were called in to keep the strikers from doing any damage. More conflict came when Arizona Rangers crossed the border into Cananea, Sonora, to rescue Anglo American personnel who had been besieged by Mexican strikers in June 1906. The Mexican government under Porfirio Díaz actually gave the Arizona officials military rank so they could put down the strike with the help of Mexican *rurales* (rural law enforcement officers).

FIGURE 8. A GROUP OF ARIZONA RANGERS IN WILLCOX, CIRCA 1908. REPRINTED, BY PERMISSION, FROM THE ARIZONA HISTORICAL FOUNDATION, HAYDEN LIBRARY, ARIZONA STATE UNIVERSITY.

The record of the Arizona officials is not as bloody as their counterparts in Texas. But as happened with the Texas Rangers, contemporaries and the media romanticized their image. After Arizona Ranger involvement in the Cananea strike caught attention in November 1906, an accolade appeared in *Harper's Weekly* stating that the officials "have been tremendous civilizing agents," who ridded the state of more than one "desperado" for whom the "proximity of Mexico, furnished a never-failing protection."[68]

The border-town killing of Ranger Jeff Kidder by Mexican police in an altercation at a Naco, Sonora, tavern in April 1908 generated resentment against Mexicans and enhanced the mystique of the force. Kidder, who had acquired a reputation as the bane of Mexican smugglers, apparently accosted a Mexican waitress after accusing her of stealing a dollar. Two Mexican police officers drinking in the bar then shot and killed the Ranger. A number of legends grew around this murder, which in reality occurred under rather seamy circumstances. One fantastic tale has Kidder killing five Mexicans before he died and then his captain riding out to rescue him, while standing off the Mexican army. But not all Rangers received such accolades. Billy Stiles, another Ranger, became a great embarrassment to the force when he was implicated in smuggling Chinese aliens, robbing a train, and other nefarious activities.[69]

RESISTANCE AGAINST LAW ENFORCEMENT OFFICERS

In a police slaying, regardless of the perpetrator's nationality, feelings of police fraternity bolstered by sympathetic public opinion impelled officials to retaliate vigorously once a suspect was identified. Mexicans believed, however, that a special vengeance was reserved for them in these incidents. The most famous case of this type is the Texas killing of Sheriff W. T. Morris of Karnes County by Gregorio Cortez on June 12, 1901. The ordeal began when the officer and a deputy went to the Mexican immigrant's ranch to inquire about a stolen horse. Because of a language misunderstanding, Cortez felt his life was threatened, and he shot Morris three times. Cortez then tried to flee to Mexico and the ensuing ten-day chase became one of the most publicized manhunts in Texas history. The fugitive did not make it to the border, but he gained enduring legendary status among Mexicans and Anglos alike. It took a number of trials over a period of four years before Cortez was finally hauled off to serve a life sentence at Huntsville. Significantly, Cortez was not jailed for the shooting of Morris, which the jury considered self-defense, but for the killing of Sheriff G. Glover who surprised him hiding out at the house of another Texas *ranchero* in Gonzales County two days after he fled the Karnes debacle.[70] Although many whites howled for his head— lynching threats abounded—Mexicans launched a massive effort to support a Mexican killing a U.S. law official. In the next few years, thousands of dollars were raised to pay B. R. Abernathy, who with a team of four lawyers, mounted a formidable defense. Even after Cortez was jailed, supporters continued to clamor for clemency, and in 1913 Governor Oscar Colquitt pardoned Cortez.[71]

Although many newspapers and influential whites demanded the death sentence even before Cortez was tried, Fred Opp, who represented another facet of Anglo opinion, directed an open letter to Governor Joseph D. Sayers in the *Mason County News* on July 5, 1901, asking that Cortez be shielded from being lynched. In addition, the piece condemned the unbridled vigilante justice by "reckless bands that have scoured the southern portion of this state recently . . . "[72]

But even when a Mexican killed an officer under less forgivable circumstances, police overreaction resulted in repression that alienated even middle-class Mexicans, who stood in a better position to provide financial and legal aid for fellow Mexicans who killed law officers. A professional criminal, "Little Phil" Alguin, alias Felipe Olguín, killed popular LAPD sergeant John J. Fitzgerald during July 1921 in a confrontation at a house used by burglars to store loot. The police offered a five hundred dollar reward for his capture and launched one of the most intensive manhunts in Los Angeles history. According to one account "groups of as many as two hundred officers . . . arbitrarily stopped citizens on the streets, arrested over a dozen known acquaintances of Alguin . . . and ransacked scores of private homes in their search for the suspected murderer." Alguin was eventually killed in Mexico by LAPD agents who illegally followed him across the border.[73]

Many Mexicans saw the police as a dangerous enemy and reacted accordingly. When Paul Taylor asked a Mexican immigrant in the Gary, Indiana, *colonia* why so many Mexicans carried guns, he responded, "One reason . . . is because of their relations with the police."[74] As a consequence, in the eyes of police, the marginalized "Little Mexicos" acquired a reputation for being extremely dangerous, and they, in return, gave no quarter. During November 1913, in Santa Paula, California, Juan Ortega killed city marshal H. M. Norman when he and several deputies attempted to quell a disturbance in which Mexicans were "shooting up the town."[75] As Martha Menchaca indicates, "In an attempt to defend Juan Ortega, they [the Mexicans] closed Mexican Town to all Anglo Americans including Anglo American policemen who tried to enter Mexican Town to arrest Ortega."[76] The altercation led to such hard feelings that nine years later the police were with a vengeance still confiscating weapons held by Mexicans (see Chapter 2).

Just a week after the alleged Phoenix plot by Mexican revolutionaries to raid city stores and banks was uncovered in 1914 (see Chapter 1), a posse of Americans fought a pitched battle with alleged Mexican horse thieves near Ray, Arizona, a mining town close to Phoenix. Four Americans and two Mexicans who hauled wood for mining operations were killed after the Mexicans took refuge in a canyon cabin and the Americans assaulted the building. Officials considered Pedro Smith, one of the Mexicans killed, and Ramón Villalobos, the only survivor of the shootout, union agitators. Two Anglo law officers and two employees at the Ray Consolidated Mining Company died in the shoot-out, which angered Anglo residents to such a degree that they drove all the Mexicans out of town.[77] Villalobos hanged for his part in this killing two years later but not before becoming a cause célèbre as compatriots tried to save him from the gallows.[78]

That economic downturns made for violence between police and Mexicans was more evident in the recession of the early 1920s. During September 1922, Mexican residents of Rosedale, a section of Johnstown, Pennsylvania, where Mexicans and blacks lived, killed three policemen during a battle. The mayor, a controversial figure who had already lost the primary bid for reelection, ordered all persons who had not lived longer than seven years in Johnstown, which was experiencing severe recession-related unemployment, to leave. This included the entire Mexican population of about four hundred.[79] During the 1926 industrial recession, when tensions between Mexicans and whites were at an all-time high in Chicago, a squad of policemen arrived at the Proviso railroad camp in December to quell a fight. One fell dead when Mexicans greeted them with a volley of gunfire, but the police killed two workers and wounded several others.[80]

Another case that became almost as famous as the Gregorio Cortez killing of Sheriff Morris involves the fatal shooting of LAPD detective Verne Brindley by Juan Reyna on May 11, 1930. Reyna, with brother-in-law Jesse Fountain as a passenger, accidentally backed his car into an unmarked police vehicle near downtown Los Angeles. According to Reyna, Brindley pulled him out by the neck, shoved him against the police car, and called him a "A dirty son of bitch of a Mexican." The policeman then threw him into the back seat of the police car, already crowded with two black prostitutes and a black police informer named Ansel Bartlett. Reyna was handcuffed to Bartlett and Officer Brindley then sat on Bartlett's knee for the trip to the police station. According to Reyna, Brindley kept hitting him with the barrel of his gun, but he wrested it away and shot both Brindley and the driver, Officer L. E. Williams. "I wouldn't have done any shooting if they had not done any hitting," protested Reyna. Brindley died later; Williams was only slightly wounded.[81]

In the trial which began August 18, Superior Court judge Marshall F. McComb impaneled six men and six women but excused the only one with a Spanish surname. Officer Williams denied Reyna's allegations that Brindley struck the Mexican but Bartlett, the black informer, supported Reyna's version. Reyna's lawyers contended their client was rendered temporarily insane by the blows but the prosecutor, Eugene W. Blalock, insisted the killing was premeditated and asked for the death penalty. Character witnesses described Reyna, a widower, as a hard worker, dedicated to supporting his mother and three children. On September 5, the case finally went to the jury after three weeks of testimony. Members of the Los Angeles *colonia,* which raised over four thousand dollars for lawyers' fees and to help support Reyna's family, anxiously awaited the verdict. But after sixty hours of deliberation, the jurors became deadlocked.[82]

A second jury was convened October 23, and the district attorney committed again to obtaining the death penalty. The trial only lasted a few days but this jury also had a difficult time in reaching a verdict and deliberated for seventy hours. Eventually the all-female panel found Reyna guilty of manslaughter and assault with a deadly weapon but recommended clemency. The reason for the long deliberation was that five of the jurors held out for acquittal. The judge sentenced Reyna to one to ten years at San Quentin on each count, allowing the sentences to expire simultaneously. This made him eligible for parole within one year. But on May 2 of the following year, an incredulous immigrant community learned that Reyna committed suicide, a topic that will be treated in greater detail in Chapter 9.[83]

The rapid influx of Mexicans into the Chicago area during the 1920s strained police-*colonia* relations to such an extent that the frequency of police killings was greater than anywhere else. A typically nationalistic 1920s response in the Mexican community to a "cop killer" incident occurred in the heart of South Chicago in 1930. When two plainclothes detectives, Louis Szewcyck and Daniel Collins, stopped Alfonso Reyes and Max and José García for "suspicious behavior" as they walked home on the night of January 15, Max García drew a gun and killed Szewcyck. The newspaper *México* and leaders of the *colonia* alleged the detectives approached the trio menacingly, without identifying themselves.[84] After the three were charged with first-degree murder, the Sociedad Mutualista de Obreros Mexicanos, led by O. B. Hernández, launched a campaign to save the men from execution. *México* implored the *colonia* to follow the lead of the society and contribute to a cause "which besides being just has been left in care of the Mexican Colony."[85] Delfina Villarreal, an organizer of the campaign, urged compatriots in an article in *México* "to contribute toward the defense of three, honest[,] hardworking accused men."[86] The trial started on May 15, 1930, and the *colonia's* effort resulted in a limited victory. The jury found Alfonso Reyes and José García not guilty, but Max García was sentenced to one to ten years for manslaughter.[87]

Few ethnic Mexican policemen existed in the United States, but attacks on Mexican American officers did occur in the border region. In 1913, as PLM member Jesús Rangel and his followers, known as "Red

Flaggers," prepared to cross the Rio Grande to join Zapatistas, they discovered Deputy Sheriff Candelario Ortiz and Sheriff Eugene Buck trailing them. Capturing them, they forced the officers to tag along. According to the *San Antonio Express,* "After enduring hardships of every description, heavy packs being loaded on their backs and their hands tied back of them, the band tried to force Ortiz and Buck to climb the bank of a creek. Buck climbed . . . after several attempts. Ortiz failed. . . . Then Ortiz was shot dead." [88] A posse caught up with the insurrectionists and attacked them. Rangel was captured alive but two of his men died in the gun battle. In a widely publicized trial, Rangel and one of his officers were sentenced to life at a federal prison, a penalty their supporters considered overly harsh. They became known in popular lore as *"los mártires de Texas."* [89]

KILLING OF BORDER AGENTS

Preventing liquor or drug contraband received greater priority than stopping illegal human cargo; therefore, violence became correspondingly higher in attempts to halt the former activities. In January 1908, liquor trafficker Juan Morales was tried in Laredo for the 1907 killing of Gregorio Duffy, a customs inspector at Rio Grande City. A mistrial was declared when the Mexican American jury, who some said sympathized with the accused man, could not reach a verdict. In 1918, a smuggler killed a passport agent in El Paso after he stopped a wagon that crossed the border laden with tequila. Passport agents, in this wartime atmosphere, became responsible for ensuring that immigrants entered at legal ports and for prevention of alien and liquor smuggling. The killing made headlines and eventually officers tracked down and killed one of the suspects in an ambush as he crossed the Rio Grande. [90]

Clifford Allen Perkins, the Border Patrol supervisor, wrote that by the end of the 1910s the violence provoked federal officials to carry more firearms and to employ less discrimination in identifying smugglers. According to Perkins, "alien smugglers had not been inclined to fight, liquor runners were. Most of them were criminals, wanted for a variety of major offenses in both the United States and Mexico, and they would fight at the drop of a hat, with pistols or rifles." [91] Perkins lamented that "Several [agents] were killed by shotgun blasts in the face when they answered their doorbell." [92] The danger made for trigger-sensitive agents who shot innocent Mexicans and even other officers mistaken for smugglers. But when smugglers killed border agents accounts are then bathed in sympathy. According to Perkins, "informing a woman that her husband, and the father of her children, has been killed in the line of duty is one of the hardest things that I have ever had to do." [93]

Nonetheless, while mainstream communities stood firm against any Mexican accused of slaying border officials, the Mexican community often sympathized with the suspect. In April 1926, U.S. customs officer W. W. McKee was killed by smugglers when he and three colleagues found a cache of illicit liquor out in the desert. Alfredo Grijalva, a Mexican rancher, was arrested for the killing but authorities freed him because the surviving officers failed to identify the rancher as part of the band. At the trial a Pima County deputy testified that Grijalva had been released so the other suspects still at large would feel safe. A Mexican witness, who had alleged that Grijalva and two others sought refuge at his ranch and divulged killing McKee, retracted his story and accused Pima County deputies of coercing him into making this admittance. Another witness who was at the same house had from the outset denied that Grijalva came to the ranch with the men who told of killing McKee. [94]

The Comité Pro Grijalva, organized by sympathetic members of Tucson's *colonia,* raised money for an appeal, and by December 1927, the group collected $1,223. But the Arizona Supreme Court affirmed the original judgment, and Grijalva had to begin serving his life sentence. Because Grijalva was a naturalized U.S. citizen, Nogales consul C. Palacios Roji initially only pledged support for Antonio Padilla, who was also accused of the murder. Influential relatives of the accused killer in Sonora intervened, however, and the Mexican government finally joined in the efforts for clemency. The state pardoned Grijalva in 1935 after extensive Mexican government and community efforts and deported him (see Chapter 9). [95]

This intense police-Mexican violence was a corollary to the friction that characterized general attitudes toward the immigrants from Mexico during this period. As shall be seen in the following chapter, Mexicans had as much to fear from American civilians as they did from the police.

6| Civilian Violence against Mexican Immigrants

FOR MEXICAN IMMIGRANTS, physical abuse from white civilians proved as vexing as the violence they received from the police. But like the other issues examined in this book, the mistreatment occurred within defined chronological and economic patterns. Table 8 suggests that violence against Mexicans loomed larger within the context of three historical situations: (1) the era of border violence fostered by the Mexican Revolution, (2) during and after World I—when employers recruited Mexicans into heretofore white work sectors, and (3) in times of economic slumps. The data also suggest that violence occurred within a regional timetable. For example, when attacks by whites tapered off in Texas, they rose in Chicago.

RACISM COMBINES WITH ECONOMIC ANXIETY

David Montejano and Susan Olzak best describe the economic competition among ethnic and racial groups that creates anxiety-provoked violence. For Texas Mexicans and Anglos, Montejano maintains that a political struggle between newcomer commercial farmers during this era and Anglo and Tejano cattle ranchers led to a breakdown in race relations. New labor and land-use exigencies resulted in the usurpation of Mexican property and a need to subordinate Mexican immigrants into labor reserves. These border uprisings, then, provided Anglo land speculators with an excuse to defraud Mexicans of land, paving the way for Anglo farmers.[1] Olzak, in speaking of influxes of blacks and new immigrants into areas where they had never worked, states, "Under such conditions it is not surprising that these newcomers are the victims of discrimination, violence, and exclusionary movements."[2]

But darker, more emotionally seated causes can explain violent incidents, often in tandem with economic factors. When Mexicans threatened Anglo cultural and racial hegemony, for example, whites justified taking the law into their own hands.[3] In studies on violence, Richard

TABLE 8. INCIDENTS OF CIVILIAN VIOLENCE TOWARD MEXICANS, 1900–1936

YEAR	TEXAS	ARIZ.	CALIF.	N. MEX.	SOUTH[A]	GREAT PLAINS & MID-WEST[B]	CHI-CAGO & ILLINOIS	TOTAL
1900–1910[C]	17	1				2		20
1911–1915	17	8	2			3		30
1916–1920	21	3	2	1	2	11	1	41
1921–1925	20	2	1		2	8	3	38
1926–1930	14	2	2	1		1	10	28
1931–1936	6		2		2	1	6	17
TOTAL	95	16	9	2	6	26	20	174

[A] SOUTH: ARKANSAS, LOUISIANA, AND MISSISSIPPI.
[B] GREAT PLAINS AND MIDWEST: COLORADO, INDIANA, KANSAS, MISSOURI, NEBRASKA, OHIO, AND OKLAHOMA.
[C] THE SAMPLE FOR THIS DECADE PROBABLY DOES NOT REFLECT THE ACTUAL DEGREE OF VIOLENCE FOR THIS PERIOD, SINCE THE SEARCH FOR DATA WAS NOT AS EXTENSIVE AS FOR THE YEARS AFTER 1910. THE NUMBERS DO NOT REFLECT INDIVIDUAL VICTIMS BUT RATHER REPORTS OF VIOLENCE IN WHICH ONE OR MORE MEXICANS WERE AFFECTED.

SOURCE: DERIVED FROM APPENDIX A.

Maxwell Brown demonstrates that the American emphasis on individualism propelled the Anglo common-law right of defending one's life, property, and family to a level of hair-trigger responses.[4]

Ultimately, this justification, combined with a lack of legal restraints, allowed white men to feel guiltless when they attacked individuals from minority groups because they were protecting their individual rights and an array of other possessions. Unfortunately, this form of empowerment, for some whites, fed an addiction to violence.

Racial abuse can flourish or decline in proportion to local elites' sanctions. David Garson and Gail O'Brien, who assert that when authorities clamped down on violence against blacks in the Reconstruction South when it began to affect whites, show that the abuse declined. In the 1920s, authorities at the behest of employers used Texas Rangers on more than one occasion to quell anti-Mexican riots because it interfered with economic stability.[5] The review of individual cases throughout the United States puts into clearer perspective the theoretical ruminations discussed above.

PERSONAL ATTACKS IN TEXAS

White civilians attacked Mexicans more often in Texas than in any other place. The state absorbed the initial and largest influx of Mexican immigrants before 1920, creating the classic negative feelings for new, incoming peoples that Olzak described. But more specific conditions have to be considered. An important one is that Mexican border violence, which escalated during the Mexican Revolution and provoked a hostile Anglo reaction during the "Brown Scare," was concentrated along the long border Texas shares with Mexico.[6] In addition, a deep-seated disdain existed in Texas for Mexico and its people that extended back to the Texas Rebellion of 1836.

Whichever underlying causes are most valid, the immediate trigger for violence against Mexicans in Texas can be found in historian C. L. Sonnichsen's notion that in Texas "the folk law of the frontier was reinforced by the unwritten law of the South and produced a habit of self-redress more deeply ingrained than perhaps anywhere else in the country."[7] Clifford A. Perkins, a Border Patrol official for forty years, similarly explained that "to hold onto what they had acquired with such difficulty, [Texas Anglos] and their descendants, with the assistance of equally tough hired hands, enlarged and consolidated their islands of rugged individualism into self-sufficient empires giving little more than lip service to outside authority."[8]

When attacking each other, though, whites could sometimes find themselves on the wrong side of the bars. But when whites assailed Mexicans or blacks they escaped punishment because arresting officers, judges, prosecuting attorneys, and juries accepted self-defense claims without question. A Texas rancher told Paul Schuster Taylor how his brother argued with two Mexicans over hunting dogs. When the Mexicans chased him, the Anglo shot them both, killing one and wounding the other. Because investigators allegedly found a half-opened long knife covered with sand and blood next to the dead Mexican, a grand jury acquitted him. His brother, said the rancher, insisted on a trial because he knew that no jury would convict him.[9]

This favored position for Anglos explains why many Mexicans did not retaliate when being attacked, a decision that transcends fear of Anglos or deference to caste. American labor radical William Z. Foster recalled a 1901 experience as a worker in East Texas where "[W]hites settled their own quarrels with gun and knife and dominated the Negroes and Mexicans by sheer terrorism."[10]

In the 1920s, more incidents of white individuals attacking Mexicans took place in the early part of the decade, a factor probably related to the recession that ravaged the Texas economy after World War I. Detailed assessment of these offenses, however, reveals the importance of the triggers discussed above as immediate factors. The killing of Pedro Saucedo, an act occurring a week after a young girl, Marie Schroeder, was found dead and raped near Rio Hondo, is a choice example of this process. On May 23, 1921, as Saucedo plowed a field, he called out in Spanish to a young, white girl walking on a nearby road. Panicking, she fled to a neighbor's house and watched the Mexican unhitch the plow horses, tie them to a tree, then walk toward the house. Thinking that he might harm her, the girl ran screaming to her own home, prompting her brother, Sam Gram, to run out to meet Saucedo and club him to death with a rifle butt.[11]

A local white official who considered Gram a troublemaker and Saucedo a hard-working, inoffensive man nonetheless felt that the thought of the Schroeder crime had driven Gram into a murderous rage when he saw his sister presumably being pursued. A number of postponements delayed the grand jury hearing. A year later Gram received an acquittal after he entered a self-defense plea, even though a Mexican witness, Carlos Adams, testified to the contrary and Saucedo's employer, H. C. West, corroborated the general feeling that Saucedo was a responsible man with good character. The defense lawyer, on the other hand, insisted that Gram avenged the honor of his sister.[12] Adding to the tragedy of this incident is that after deputies arrested four young Mexicans in the Schroeder killing, townspeople lynched one of the suspects, Pedro Saucedo's nephew.

When a Mexican national's killer was an influential Mexican American, the Mexican government protested as vehemently as if a white had been the perpetuator. In Hidalgo County, for example, on January 15, 1923, Texas Mexican Máximo Díaz, a former deputy sheriff and justice of the peace, accused his Mexican-born neighbor, Inés Rivas, of trespassing as the latter mended a fence separating their farms. An argument ensued and Díaz shot Rivas twice, the second time as the man lay on the ground wounded.[13] Manuel Téllez, concerned about Díaz' influence, unsuccessfully pressed for a change of venue. Díaz' trial in October 1923 lasted two days. After seven hours of deliberation the jury, which contained at least four Texas Mexicans, became deadlocked and the judge discharged the panel. The next year in April, Díaz faced trial again, but this time the jury considered the case for only one hour and exonerated the defendant even though ten witnesses testified he did not act in self-defense.[14]

Téllez wrote to Secretary of State Charles E. Hughes that the "whole of the Mexican community in South Texas now feels that no offense committed by an American citizen against a Mexican citizen will ever be punished, regardless of evidence or severity of the crime." [15]

Because killings of Mexicans reached epidemic proportions during this era, on August 23, 1924, the San Antonio consul and Mexican immigrant leaders went to Austin and implored Texas officials to intervene in local cases where whites murdered Mexicans. The consul protested that in the past two years grand juries in Hidalgo County had failed to indict the killers of eight Mexican citizens. Governor Pat Neff told the group that his hands were tied and though he agreed with their protestations, he could not force a grand jury to bring about indictments.[16]

PERSONAL ATTACKS OUTSIDE OF TEXAS

In a Mexican government study of American civilians' attacks on Mexicans during the 1910s, Arizona came in a close second to Texas. As in Texas, authorities often ignored these violations, which effectively encouraged them. For example, W. H. Heltrip slew Jesús Arias during January 1913 in Yuma, claiming self-defense, and authorities did not charge him. A bartender of "Austrian descent" on November 12, 1912, beat a drunken Tomás Soto when he created a disturbance at a bar in the mining town of Miami. The next morning Soto's body was found a few yards from the saloon, but the bartender fled and could not be found, according to local authorities. The Cochise County coroner diagnosed his death as coming from "wet brain"; consequently the sheriff did not file charges.[17]

As in Texas, if Mexicans succeeded in inflicting injures on whites in Arizona, the response was predictable. When, during a drunken melee in Phoenix, amid the Día de San Juan festival on June 24, 1900, Mexicans killed two Anglos, Anton Olsen and T. W. Stewart, Governor Murphy condemned the Mexican celebration and the *Arizona Republican* announced that Sheriff D. L. Murray offered an eight-hundred-dollar reward for the "Mexican greaser" killers. Publishers of *El Demócrata* became indignant and called for a meeting of all Mexicans to protest the plainly racist reaction of white Arizona officials. Later that year, the state legislature banned future celebrations of this Mexican holiday.[18]

The sources on attacks of Mexicans yield fewer incidents for California than for Texas or Arizona, even though the state sustained intensive immigration in the first two decades of the century. Likewise, a review of Los Angeles' *La Opinión* in the 1920s reveals far fewer reports of Anglo mistreatment of Mexicans than San Antonio's *La Prensa* during the 1910s.

Similarly, no incidents of white violence against Mexicans are recorded for northern New Mexico in the Mexican government violations list and very few appear in such newspapers as *La Voz del Pueblo* of Las Vegas, New Mexico.[19] Immigration to those areas was slight, however, and Mexican Americans, most of whom were U.S. natives, protected themselves more effectively than could recently arrived immigrants elsewhere. Still, in the Midwest, the heart of the destination for many new arrivals, assailants or killers of Mexicans did not receive immunity as routinely as in Texas or Arizona. On August 15, 1924, Tom Reece murdered Luis Amézquita Gomar in Jackson County, Illinois, after an argument. Arrested and convicted, Reece received a twenty-five-year sentence and the judge denied his motion for a new trial.[20]

U.S. soldiers stationed on the border who came from states with no Mexican population, many of them black, soon internalized the prejudices common among border-dwelling whites. Military personnel also disliked Mexicans because of atrocities attributed to them during the revolution. They killed hundreds of Mexicans, ostensibly in the line of duty, but on other occasions innocent civilians died or suffered injuries in incidents not even remotely linked to legitimate operations. According to the jurist Ramón Prida, who as a Mexican refugee worked as translator for the *El Paso Morning Times* during the Mexican Revolution, Mexicans had much to fear from U.S. military personnel along the border, whom Prida considered the dregs of society.[21] During January 1916, for example, soldiers joined in the riots against Mexicans after the Santa Ysabel massacre, beating Mexicans on the streets. Ricardo Silva, in June 1917, complained to the Kansas City consul that U.S. soldiers arrived at a railroad work site near Manhattan, Kansas, searched the Mexican workers for arms, then cudgeled the track workers with their rifles for no reason.[22]

ATTACKS ON WOMEN

It is hard to determine the number of sexual assaults on Mexican women by men of other ethnic groups because it is likely that most of the crimes were not reported. The scant record that does exist, however, suggests that authorities, at least in Texas and Arizona, did not charge attackers if they were whites. Mexican women who worked in taverns or cafes were particularly vulnerable. A diplomatic protest charged that in May 1926, H. M. Craig, a mine foreman at Douglas, Arizona, drank too much at a cafe and made unwanted advances toward the waitress, a woman named Asunción Aguilar. Failing to seduce her, Craig then beat her, according to the report. Aguilar later refused twenty-five dollars that the judge offered to discourage her from pressing charges. In Redford, Texas, during 1917, Carmen Salazar charged that after a drinking bout, two white teachers attempted to enter her home to rape her and her daughter Paula, but the unexpected return of her son thwarted the plan. Efforts by the San Antonio consul to have the teachers prosecuted were to no avail. In 1926, Edward Beeman, a soldier from Fort Sam Houston, and some other soldiers walked down a dark road near Luling, Texas, when they came across a Mexican man fixing a flat tire while his wife stood by. The soldiers attacked the couple, and Beeman raped the woman, María Treviño de García. The Mexican government and the Mexican community were outraged when military officials had the soldier transferred.[23]

HOMICIDES AND VIOLENCE IN THE WORKPLACE

Next to police violence, Mexicans experienced the worst physical abuse in the workplace, usually at the hands of employers who controlled Mexican workers through intimidation by the brandishing and frequent use of firearms. But finding work represented the ultimate fulfillment for immigrants, even though arduous conditions and danger awaited them in most Mexican-designated jobs. Discriminatory firings and recessions brought long-term unemployment and destitution. So when Mexicans worked, they stayed on the job as long as they could stand it, but their vulnerability increased the power that employers had over them. Or as a California fruit grower asserted, "We want the Mexican because we can treat them as we cannot treat any other living man . . . we can control them by keeping them at night behind bolted gates, within a stockade eight feet high surrounded by barbed wire . . . We can make them work under armed guards in the fields." [24]

As with other kinds of attacks, Texas had the worst record of employer violence. A Mexican immigrant from Forester, hearing that Alvaro Obregón's administration was redistributing land in 1924, wrote him that he and a number of other *paisanos* wanted to return home because "I have been here but a short time and am appalled at the treatment which we receive at the hands of the bosses who treat Mexicans with the greatest amount of cruelty." [25] This brutality stemmed from many causes. When Mexicans attempted to ameliorate problems collectively, through individual negotiation, or by resistance (that is, quitting in an insolent manner), violence often resulted. In January 1919, lumber company owner Almond Robinson came to Thorndale, Texas, to personally crush a wildcat strike by Mexican workers. In speaking to spokesman Jesús Navarrete, Robinson lost his temper and hit him with a stick. During the beating, the stick slipped out of Robinson's hands; Navarrete picked it up to defend himself, and Robinson shot him. The wounded Navarrete fled, only to die a few days later. After a grand jury exonerated Robinson, the San Antonio consul protested that the panel ignored testimony of Mexican witnesses who testified that Robinson hit the unarmed Navarrete first.[26]

Texas railroad workers suffered the greatest abuse from violent bosses. When labor radical William Z. Foster cooked for a Southern Pacific repair crew in the East Texas town of Echo, he remembered that "the most hard-boiled boss was 'Lige' Gardner, timekeeper and gunman" and that with "gun in hand, he terrorized the Mexican laborers." [27] Repair-crew foremen were pressured to finish a job quickly to accommodate train schedules, but railroad work attracted mainly newly arrived Mexicans unacquainted with routine tasks. Consequently, a foreman's perception of malingering or insubordination often sparked violent temper tantrums.[28]

Anglo farmers used strong-arm tactics to avoid complying with sharecropper contracts or to avoid paying wages that were due, especially during times of slim profit margins. But Anglo farmers also expected unquestioned compliance from Mexican workers. Defiance sparked fits of frenzy that went beyond the calculated decision to simply evict a sharecropper and forfeit his wages. For some farmers, these dynamics provided an opportunity to vent an uncontrolled anger that impunity from the law fostered. Jesse Adams, "a rich and influential man of the place," on May 24, 1920, at the Keystone Ranch near Pearsall shot Bernardino Campos. Adams and Campos had disagreed over work quality, and the Mexican quit, shouting angrily that "he would leave as soon as he received his pay." Adams followed Campos to his home, where the argument escalated, and shot him twice with a pistol in front of the employee's wife.[29]

The ability of Texas farmers to demand extreme deference from their Mexican help required cooperation of local officials who ignored employer abuse of Mexicans. Gonzales County Attorney Horace Dun can wrote to Governor W. P. Hobby explaining why he chose not to prosecute A. P. Thames in the killing of farmworker Ramón Ramírez in 1920. After hearing testimony from the wife and mother of the dead man and from the defendant, the grand jury found that Thames acted in self-defense, he said. He then added, "From my personal knowledge of Thames's crop this year I can say that he is the greater loser by the Mexican's death and the departure of the other Mexicans from the premise. Instead of there being a good crop there is almost a failure due to its not being worked."[30]

Boss abuse outside Texas, while not as common, was just as violent. On May 9, 1912, Phoenix farmworker José Castro's boss beat him senseless and knocked out most of his teeth. A justice of the peace ruled that no criminal charges could be filed. In October 1920, near Chandler, Arizona, farmer C. H. Kunce beat employee Crispín Ruvalcaba with a tree branch for stealing, after a local constable handcuffed him.[31]

In California, influence did not always immunize white bosses from prosecution. In the Imperial Valley during April 1932, rancher Joseph Robert Hatfield and two friends, Robert Robertson Kloss and Jack Williams, drank homemade beer in the ranch brewery and shot off pistols against its adobe wall. Two ranch hands, Tom Robinson and Victor Gómez, joined the drinking party while another worker, Alejandro Villa, stayed away. When Gómez stepped outside to urinate after "getting sassy," Hatfield, shot and killed him through the window. Perhaps he was not aiming at him, but the bullet struck Gómez in the back of the head. Panicking, Hatfield, Kloss, and Williams tied up the Mexican's body and threw him into the Alamo River. After they finished covering their tracks, Hatfield and his friends held Gómez' workmate Robinson against his will, but he managed to escape and expose the murder.[32]

On May 18, Elmer W. Heald, Imperial County district attorney, submitted the case to the grand jury. Judge Vaughn N. Thompson put the panel members under guard to prevent tampering. In the meantime, Caléxico consul Edmundo L. Aragón, with the help of El Centro's Comisión Honorífica Mexicana, gathered information that might aid in the prosecution. Two days later the three accused men pleaded innocent, at which point Imperial County sheriff John Thetford announced that newly found evidence indicated Gómez carried a knife when he was shot. Deputy Sheriff Rodney Clark found the "new evidence" five days after the killing in the trunk of his car when he changed a flat tire. District Attorney Heald, responding to Mexican community charges that this was a ruse, assured that the prosecution would be vigorous. In addition, the Mexican community had Anglo American support, the most important being from the *San Diego Sun,* which throughout the ordeal exhibited marked sympathy for the victim.[33]

The grand jury indicted all three men and their trial began on June 20. Heald requested sequestration of the jury to keep the Imperial Valley Immigration Committee, a nativist group to whom Hatfield's attorney, Ernest R. Utily, served as an advisor, from influencing the group. Utily, a former county district attorney, built his case on the knife being found near Gómez' body, but weakening the case against the defendants was the mysterious disappearance of Alejandro Villa, the other witness to the crime. The jury found Hatfield guilty of manslaughter after a three-day trial and his lawyers appealed immediately. Kloss and Williams were found not guilty, but Heald prosecuted them for concealing a crime. On October 18, 1932, another jury found them guilty and each of them received sentences of one to five years in prison.[34]

Such incidents were not as common outside of the Southwest but they occurred nonetheless. For example, on January 22, 1913, Margarito López and Samuel Espinoza complained to their boss at a Grandfield, Oklahoma, railroad work site about time computation and were promptly fired. They continued arguing, and the foreman shot at them, wounding López. Police arrested the foreman but soon released him.[35]

BEATING THE BOSS TO THE PUNCH
Unionization played an important role in defending against abusive supervisors, but Mexican workers also protected their interests with-

out organizing. Mexican farmworkers in Texas, for example, commonly traveled in groups and insisted on being hired as such. These independent work crews, usually made up of families, close friends, or *compadres* (extended family members through godparenting), were less vulnerable to exploitation and boss violence. This was also the case in Arizona and, undoubtedly, in other areas as well.[36] Jesús Valle, a printer by trade and native of Sinaloa, remembered in a 1927 interview that years earlier he had had a heated argument in the cotton fields near Phoenix, Arizona, with a foreman who tried to cheat him. They called each other names, and when the foreman threatened him with a gun, "all the '*chicanada*' (the Mexican folk) came to my help, and we came mighty near to lynching him."[37]

At times, Mexicans beat their bosses to the punch in inflicting real physical damage. Aurelio Pompa, who killed his boss at a Los Angeles work site, achieved legendary status for standing up to him even though San Quentin officials executed him for the crime (see Chapter 8). Basil Pacheco, who organized one of the first informal work stoppages by Mexicans in the 1920s when he worked at East Chicago's Youngstown Steel Company, remembered proudly during a 1975 interview that while working on a railroad repair crew in Washington, he hit his foreman broadside with a shovel, then fled for his life.[38]

INTERETHNIC PEER VIOLENCE IN THE WORKPLACE

Even though Mexicans frequently fought during their off-hours, at work they mustered up more solidarity and mainly fought with workers of other nationalities. Altercations with non-Mexican workers, however, occurred more often in the less-segregated work sectors outside southwestern agricultural job sites where Mexicans toiled alongside other ethnic or racial groups as peers. In these cases, the justice system was less one-sided. For example, a black named Wallace Hall went on trial for the stabbing death of Juan Ramírez at the Swift Packing Plant in Kansas City. Four Mexicans and two Poles asserted Hall killed Ramírez, but Hall's lawyer stated that the Mexican belonged to a race of cutthroats with fiery eyes. Prosecutor James Enright successfully discounted this justification. The jury found Hall guilty, and he was sent to prison.[39] In many of the Ford plants in Michigan, racism, which was fueled by intense speedups and workforce reductions, took a psychological toll, provoking many job-site altercations. During March 1929, Fernando Albañiz, a Ford worker in Rouge, Michigan, was fired for pulling a knife on a fellow white worker. At the same plant, another Mexican lost his job for knifing a white worker.[40]

MOB VIOLENCE AGAINST MEXICANS

Mexicans, sometimes with the blessing of lower officials, were collectively attacked by other ethnic groups, especially when they entered a new labor sector or competed for jobs during economic slumps.[41] The potential for such incidents increased during the revolution when Mexican border banditry and revolutionary violence was endemic. Generally, worker resentment was also greatest in the raw-material-producing West where the vagaries of world markets provoked more general economic insecurity.

But as has been the case in the other forms of violence discussed thus far, the trigger for mob action was not always clearly economic. Such innocuous rituals as the *fiestas patrias* (Mexican Independence Day celebrations), for example, provoked Anglo backlashes. A September 1910 newspaper report that Madero supporters had infiltrated festival committees in San Antonio and Del Rio angered white Texans, who now saw the *fiestas* as subversive and wanted them canceled. In May 1912, Anglo miners invaded a Cinco de Mayo festival in Twin Buttes, about forty miles from Tucson, attacked the Mexican workers, then took down and tore up Mexican flags on display for the holiday.[42]

Mexican violence against whites was a radical departure from expected behavior and often resulted in mass retaliation. At a baseball game in Falfurrias during March 1910, a fight broke out among the spectators watching a Mexican and Anglo boy fighting in which the Mexican got the better of his opponent. When the Mexicans cheered, a free-for-all fight broke out. Local officers, under Sheriff José Guerra, broke up the skirmish, but an Anglo suffered a slight stab wound. Guerra arrested B. García, one of the ballplayers from nearby Alice, and later released him on a five-thousand-dollar bond. Aware that local Anglos wanted to punish García, the sheriff sent Deputy Doroteo González to accompany the accused Mexican on the train back to Alice. A mob of Anglos, however, converged at the station before the train departed, two boarded the train and while one threatened Deputy González with a pistol, the other, Dave Dolan, shot García in the back as he tried to flee. Guerra arrested Dolan then released him on a ten-thousand-dollar bond—eventually the Starr County Grand Jury dismissed the charges.[43]

Widespread anti-Mexican feelings were provoked by the anti-American student riots in Mexico City and Guadalajara, which were sparked by the November 1910 lynching of Antonio Rodríguez in Rock Springs, Texas. Anglos, reacting to sensationalism, feared a connection between border insurrectionists led by Francisco Madero and the anti-

American episodes in Mexico. The Department of State advised Governor Campbell to take precautions to protect American citizens along the border.[44]

Angry over the reported atrocities committed against Americans in the riots, F. W. Meyer, a hatter from Bonney, Texas, penned a letter to President Taft. "Because . . . an admitted low lifed mexican Criminal, who murdered a Texas Woman and destroyed an American HOME, the Mexicans murder good Americans because said greaser got his just dues" [*sic*], he wrote bitterly.[45] Other angry Texans retaliated by attacking Mexican immigrants. The backlash was so severe that on November 15 the Carrizo Springs consul took in immigrants to protect them from being clubbed by Anglos who heard rumors of Del Rio Mexicans marching to Rock Springs to avenge the lynching.[46]

In the Midwest, collective violence against Mexicans stemmed more clearly from economic resentments. In Chicago, during the spring of 1919, thousands of veterans demobilized at the end of the Great War jammed employment agencies or were forced to panhandle in the street. As pressures mounted, railroad companies even dismissed black and Mexican workers and gave the jobs to white veterans.[47] This was also a time of vigorous labor organizing by militant but chauvinistic labor unions that did not bridge racial gaps. Strikes in the steel mills and stockyards during 1919 were defeated by importing strikebreakers, many of them blacks or Mexicans. Such initial contacts with these minority groups inevitably created extreme racial tension. On July 30, 1919, at the height of the white-black riots rocking Chicago's stockyard neighborhoods, Fred Schott and five other whites attacked Federico González and José Blanco, two young stockyard workers. Both Mexicans were severely injured, but Blanco managed to fatally stab Schott, and Chicago police promptly charged him with first-degree murder. The Chicago consul provided legal assistance, and Blanco was acquitted.[48]

The 1921 recession unleashed a record wave of anti-Mexican feelings in which the most violent reaction was evident in North Texas and Oklahoma, labor sectors Mexicans entered for the first time during the war. As bad times approached, former Texas governor James E. Ferguson, who lived in Temple, the heart of Texas nativism and populism, published in December 1920 a bitter invective against Mexicans in his *Ferguson Forum*. It read in part:

America for America, when brought home means Texas
for Texans. It should mean that we are going to have less

Mexicans swarming across the border into Texas. . . .
The Mexican people have not improved one bit with
civilization. . . . They are not disposed to and have no
desire to become real Americans and never will be. . . .
The farming interests don't need Mexicans. . . . Absentee
landlords ought not want and should not be permitted
to import a Mexican population to occupy Texas to the
exclusion of or even in competition with red blooded
Americans. The Railroads should not be permitted to
continue to bring thousands of these Mexicans and take
the place of native Americans who need the money and
have no other intention but to be a good citizen, loyal
and true to the stars and stripes.[49]

As unemployment rocked the oil industry during February 1921,
pressure from white workers in Eastland resulted in the dismissal of
Mexicans hired during the war. The Mexicans were too destitute to
leave, however. "People in Eastland want something to be done about
the huge number of Mexicans coming and seeking jobs," a newspaper
reported.[50] In nearby Ranger, posted admonitions also appeared. When
Mexicans who already had been idle for six weeks did not heed them,
mounted masked men, allegedly members of the Ku Klux Klan, broke
into their homes, destroyed furniture, mistreated women and children,
and warned them not to compete with American labor. A beleaguered
group under the leadership of Primitivo R. Castillo sought help from
authorities but was told that leaving town seemed the most prudent
action. About one hundred refugees fled to Fort Worth and signed a
petition through the Mexican consul asking the Mexican government to
help end their mistreatment and provide repatriation funds.[51]

When the immigrants did not leave immediately after the ultima-
tum, "one of the most severe breaches of individual liberty took place,"
La Prensa of San Antonio protested. "Nothing is better evidence that
Mexicans in this country are willing to obey the law and be good citizens
than the restraint they show when they are attacked." At the office of
San Antonio consul Francisco Pérez, a *La Prensa* reporter interviewed
the male heads of four banished families who came from West-Central
Mexico and concluded that "they just are humble men." The refugees
disclosed that at least five hundred of their countrymen were still in
Ranger, unable to leave. Consul Pérez sought funds to transport the besieged Mexicans to the border so they could return to Mexico.[52]

White workers also attacked Mexicans in Cisco, Texas. According to a telegram to Consul Pérez from Aristeo Solorio, a Cisco oil worker, attackers threw rocks at Mexicans and threatened their lives if they refused to vacate the town. Governor Pat Neff finally sent Captain Hickman and a group of Texas Rangers to protect Mexicans in the afflicted areas, a maneuver that apparently quelled the violence.[53]

When competition provoked white-worker vengeance, white elites—influential employers and officials—protected Mexicans for financial as well as humanitarian reasons. District court judges E. A. Hill and E. L. Davenport appealed "to all sensible and law abiding people to join in an energetic condemnation" of the violence. The Eastland *Daily Oil Belt News* published letters written by Robert D. Gordon and Kenneth B. Turner, who "vigorously protest the actions of the past few days." The letters encouraged authorities to protect Mexican workers, crucial as they were to the economy, and pointed out that the mistreatment could affect the way Americans working in Mexico were treated. By the end of February, a semblance of peace returned to Ranger and the surrounding areas. *La Prensa,* consistently critical of the Mexican consular service in the past, credited Consul Pérez with pressuring Neff to act quickly.[54]

Black workers also resented Mexicans during the recession. Throughout the 1920s, black leaders often railed against the threat from Mexicans who "were taking bread from the mouths of colored people."[55] Early in 1921, 90 percent of the Mexican workers in Fort Worth were jobless after black and white workers coerced employers into firing Mexicans. Both whites and blacks marched on city hall after city officials received an anonymous letter threatening to blow up the building unless they discharged Mexicans from city construction projects. Attempts to force Mexicans out of jobs continued throughout the rest of the year.[56]

Next to Texas, Oklahoma experienced the greatest number of anti-Mexican incidents during the crisis. In March 1921, Merced Lara and Pedro Villarreal complained to the Tulsa, Oklahoma, consul that after a recruiter named Greenman took forty-five Mexican workers to a refinery in Nowata, armed Anglos arrived in an automobile caravan demanding that the contractor fire his charges. The intimidated contractor complied, and after he released the Mexicans without pay, the white workers accompanied them to the Tulsa train station. Lara and Villarreal protested that pressure throughout the state prompted mining companies, refineries, and oil fields to fire Mexicans, forcing them to live in destitution.[57] In the meantime, several Oklahoma farmworkers wrote Tulsa consul Enrique R. Rodríguez asking for repatriation, complaining that white workers had assaulted them and that local authorities ignored their appeals for help.[58]

By May, when severe deprivation racked *colonias* throughout the United States, President Alvaro Obregón decided to fund repatriation. That month, Galveston consul G. Meade Fierro announced a repatriation plan for East Texas. To be eligible, immigrants had to register with the consulate either directly or by mail if they lived too far from Galveston. Fort Worth authorities decided to fund deportation for twelve hundred Mexicans, the majority of them men. At this point the Comisiones Honoríficas Mexicanas were founded to assist in this effort (see Chapter 3).[59]

In 1921, the worst year of the recession, manifestations of anti-Mexican feelings lingered on, especially in the Texas oil belt. Following a November 1922 lynching of a Mexican in Breckenridge, about three hundred members of the Owls Fraternal Club marched through the Mexican section threatening to burn down houses unless the Mexicans left town. After protestations by the Mexican Embassy, Secretary of State Charles E. Hughes directed the governor of Texas to protect the town's Mexicans. The turmoil subsided only when a "multitude of Mexicans and Negroes left town after being threatened."[60] The turbulence caused by the economic downturn did not seem to affect Mexicans in California and Arizona as much. In 1923, a number of cross burnings around the mining communities of Globe and Miami alarmed many Arizona Mexicans, but they were spared the ferocity of the Texas and Oklahoma incidents. Similarly, that same year reports of Ku Klux Klan cross burnings aimed at intimidating Mexicans came out of Santa Barbara, Ventura, and Richmond. In Richmond, the burnings coincided with a concerted effort to segregate Mexicans in black neighborhoods.[61]

American workers also continued to resent Mexicans for strike-breaking. In June 1922, four unemployed Mexican men, two of them brothers named Resíndez, left recession-ridden Chicago at the same time the nation's soft-coal miners were in the midst of one of the longest coal strikes in U.S. history—it lasted 161 days. The passenger train carrying the Resíndez brothers and their companions made an unscheduled stop at West Frankfort, a small coal-mining town in southern Illinois permeated by labor tension. Ten miles away in Herrin, strikers had recently executed nineteen captives, including a hated supervisor, after winning a battle against company guards, supervisors, and strikebreakers. The four Mexicans had not intended to disembark in West Frankfort, but when the train stopped, they entered the station cafeteria where strikers attacked them. The Resíndez brothers, although seriously injured, managed to escape, but two unidentified companions died in the turmoil. One leaped to his death from a slag heap as he fled from his pursuers.[62]

Anti-Mexican violence subsided with the end of the recession, but the agricultural economy again faltered in 1926, and outbreaks recurred, especially in Texas. That year, Americans clamored for intervention in Mexico because of President Calles' decision to repress the Catholic Church and enforce a section of the Mexican Constitution that threatened American oil interests. The Houston consul complained that in December, hooded Ku Klux Klan members attacked about fifty Sugar Land Mexicans and thirty blacks, forcing them to leave town. Most of the Mexicans were humble peons, the consul said, and whites targeted them because they accepted low wages. Indeed, San Antonio consul Humberto Valenzuela warned earlier in the year that trouble was brewing because Mexicans worked for $1.25 a day, wages so low that even blacks would not take them.[63]

In midwestern industrial cities that year, the crisis provoked hostilities from other ethnic groups—that is, Poles and Italians—an enmity stemming from competition for jobs, housing, and the use of public parks. In 1926 thousands of unemployed Mexican beet workers converged in Chicago hoping to find work. Because Poles resented Mexicans more than any other ethnic group, Paul S. Taylor labeled this year as the "era of Mexican-Polish troubles," so extensive were clashes between the two groups.[64]

COMPETITION OVER PUBLIC FACILITIES

The use of public facilities by Mexicans provoked intense hostility from whites. The barring of blacks was clearly defined by years of tradition and in Southern states by Jim Crow laws. Mexicans were similarly excluded, especially in Texas and Arizona, but authorities did not uniformly enforce their segregation. Migrant Mexicans did not know where they would encounter such barriers or when whites would decide to exclude them. On August 24, 1925, a group of about one hundred Anglos assaulted fourteen Mexicans attending a Kansas City fair at Shawnee Park. The Mexicans escaped, thanks to the police, who then told them to stay at home if they did not want trouble with Americans.[65]

On the July 4 holiday in 1931, Chicagoans escaped to the beaches of Lake Michigan. For some years now, South Chicago Mexicans had shared the beach at Calumet Park with Poles and Italians in an uneasy truce. Deteriorating economic conditions and subsequent ethnic squabbling severely tested the tacit agreement, however. The first arrivals staked out a space at the overcrowded beach, according to ethnic and family arrangements, and then protected their territory for the rest of the day. About mid-afternoon, Mexican teenagers had a watermelon fight and one of the rinds landed on a Pole on the next beach space. The incident escalated into a minor riot in which rock-throwing Poles and Italians ejected the Mexicans from the park. Both sides drew knives, and two Mexican girls were seriously injured. Police arrested rioters from all the ethnic groups on a variety of infractions, but they did not charge the men responsible for the attack on the girls.[66]

VIOLENCE DURING THE GREAT DEPRESSION

Unemployment during the Great Depression, as had been the case in 1921, encouraged threats and violence toward Mexicans. The number of these incidents, however, appear to be fewer. Certainly, working-class animosity existed, but it was expressed more at the rhetorical level. The *San Angelo Evening Standard* received a letter in June 1930 from the "Darts and Others" that said, "We are forming a club known as the darts and our aim is to clean up this city making working conditions better for Americans. You will hear from us from time to time. [A]s our good work progresses each member will work separately not knowing any other member. All Mexicans must leave."[67]

But violence existed nonetheless. In May, disgruntled workers in Malakoff, an oil company town near Dallas, took more concrete action. On May 19, 1931, unknown persons dynamited the "Mexican Hall," a gathering place for Mexicans who worked for the Malakoff Fuel Company—an act of retaliation that the *Dallas Dispatch* attributed to the hiring of Mexicans during the economic crisis.[68] After the blast, placards attached to the wrecked hall read "LEAVE TOWN, DAMN PRONTO." When county sheriff C. G. Pharris ignored a request from Dallas consul Juan E. Achondo that he protect Mexican workers, the consul appealed to the Malakoff Fuel Company. The company's director, who came personally to Malakoff from Dallas, assured the consul the company would protect Mexicans, then called Governor Ross Sterling, who dispatched Texas Rangers to the troubled town.[69] Soon after that Governor Sterling announced that Rangers had already arrested an individual for the bombing. This satisfied President Pascual Ortiz Rubio's government, which was under a lot of pressure to act decisively in this latest outrage.[70] Officers of the Unión General de Trabajadores Mexicanos en Los Estados Unidos de America in Dallas, to whom the bombed hall belonged, were not as optimistic. They telegraphed President Ortiz Rubio to thank him for his efforts, but warned that danger still loomed in Malakoff. Once the Texas Rangers left, whites again became aggressive and local officials refused to act. This message prompted Ortiz Rubio to personally press consular officials to pursue the matter further. The Rangers returned and local officials purportedly arraigned an accused bomber in Tubbleville, a neighboring town.[71]

White-worker attacks on Mexicans continued in the depression era. In Newport, Arkansas, during June 1931, Tránsito Velásquez, a foreman for a vegetable packing company, complained that twenty-five to thirty Anglo Americans went on a rampage looking for Mexicans to shoot, but the police dispersed the mob. Velásquez said he was then arrested and jailed for no reason. His wife bailed him out and Velásquez' boss, Allen Mayer, came to his house and told him and the other Mexicans to leave town immediately. He paid him $38.50 as part of his salary but did not allow him to pack. Velásquez fled with his family, leaving their belongings behind—furniture, clothing, a stove, and other items.[72]

In response to an inquiry from Oklahoma City consul Joaquín Amador, the Newport police chief blamed the Mexicans for the riot. Two of his officers quelled a disturbance on June 30 in "Mexican town" and arrested eight persons of both races. Velásquez, whom the chief described as the Mexican ringleader, made death threats against the Newport populace. According to the chief, "Those Mexicans had not worked but thirty days and they were causing considerable trouble among the inhabitants of that part of town and were mainly responsible for the affray that took place."[73]

In Chicago, continuous attacks on Mexicans by other ethnic groups seemed endemic in 1931, perhaps because of depression-related hopelessness. In its May 20 issue, *El Nacional* warned about the danger of walking the streets because Italian youth gangs robbed Mexicans with impunity. A few days prior, according to the newspaper, a gang attacked two Mexicans, beating one up severely and chasing the other back to his neighborhood. "There is an assumption that some Italian politicians protect them [gang members]; when one is caught by the police he is freed . . . with this procedure the neighborhood is terrorized."[74]

THE LYNCHING OF MEXICANS
IN THE TWENTIETH CENTURY

Lynching, that is, taking a prisoner out of a jail cell or simply arresting suspects to execute them without due process, dramatically affected Mexicans in California, Arizona, New Mexico, and Texas during the nineteenth century. But only two apparent lynchings of Mexicans could be found for southwestern states other than Texas during the early part of the century—one in Arizona and the other in New Mexico. Outside the Southwest, seven Mexicans are known to have been lynched, two in Colorado, two in Oklahoma, two in Nebraska, and one in Kansas. In Texas, however, perhaps as many as thirty lynchings of Mexicans, depending on how the practice is defined, took place after 1900. This tally does not include all illegal executions, however.

In 1904, the body of a Mexican was found dangling from a tree in the desert near Globe, Arizona, riddled with bullets. The *Arizona Republican* presumed the killing to be a lynching. The last illegal execution in Arizona was of a white. In 1918, a mob hanged Starr Daly after he killed James Gibson and sexually assaulted his victim's wife. Daly triggered the mob action when he boasted that he would not hang because the voters had abolished capital punishment the previous year.[75]

No lynchings of Mexicans were found for California in this century. Unlike Texas, reaction to a Mexican attacking a white did not seem to send California Anglos into a lynching frenzy. In March 1914, Epitacio Valenzuela shot and killed an unarmed but drunken Delbert Wardlow, after the Anglo assaulted Valenzuela at a speakeasy that the Mexican operated in Orange County. Valenzuela received a light sentence for manslaughter, but as far as can be ascertained, this crime did not create a lynching atmosphere.[76]

The decline of illegal executions of Mexicans in Arizona and California simply reflects the ending of the lynching phenomenon in those states after the turn of the century. But that lynchings continued outside the Southwest is probably due to the newness of immigration to these areas.

During September 1919, in the midst of a steel strike in Pueblo, railroad section hands José González and Salvador Ortiz were jailed on suspicion of killing a patrolman named Jeff Evans. Incensed whites, many of them workers who resented Mexican strikebreakers working in the mills, distracted the police by calling in a riot at the steel works. Night captain John Sinclair responded with all of his men, leaving only the desk man to mind the police station. An armed mob marched to the jailhouse, held the official at gunpoint, and forcibly took the Mexicans in a caravan of automobiles to the edge of town and hanged them twenty-four feet apart from girders of the Fourth Street bridge.

In California, the only known lynchings in this century do not appear to have been racially motivated. In December 1920, a mob took three whites, accused of raping two young women and killing a policeman trying to capture them, from their Santa Rosa jail and hanged them. The last known lynching in California took place in San Jose during 1933 when two whites who kidnapped and murdered Leopold Hart, the rich scion of a department store family, were dragged from their cells and hanged.[77]

LYNCHINGS OF MEXICANS IN TEXAS

According to a study by David Chapman, twenty-four lynchings of Mexicans took place in Texas between 1889 and the 1920s—one of the victims was a woman. Ninety-four blacks and fourteen whites encountered the same fate during the period. Of those, nine were women—one white and eight black. The disproportionate execution of blacks by lynch mobs follows a pattern typical of Southern states. Motivations ranged from murder and rape to simply "acting uppity." Chapman's study concludes that even though more Mexicans experienced lynchings than whites, racism did not figure as often as a motive as it did with black lynchings. He points out that most of the incidents took place during 1915, when whites retaliated for the Plan de San Diego uprising.[78]

Nonetheless, one reason Texas is the only state with extensive illegal executions of Mexicans in this century is because it is there that racial attitudes toward them most closely paralleled those held toward blacks. Next to the Antonio Rodríguez lynching discussed above, the most notorious illegal execution was that of Antonio Gómez. In June 1911, in an attempt to eject fourteen-year-old Gómez from a store, a fight ensued and the boy stabbed a German American to death. While awaiting trial, a mob took him from jail, beat him, hanged him, and then dragged his body around town tied to the back of a buggy. In February 1913, Juvencio López and two other unidentified Mexicans were lynched after town officials accused them of murdering a policeman near Raymondville.[79]

To avoid these blatant violations of justice, Mexicans took the law into their own hands. In December 1914 Ysidro González and Francisco Sánchez killed jailer Henry Hinton in an escape from the Oakville jail.

A posse immediately captured González who was tried and found guilty. San Antonio judge W. W. Walling sentenced him to death. Sánchez, captured later, had to be transported back to Oakville under heavy guard because of lynching threats. As a consequence, Mexicans from Oakville and neighboring communities unsuccessfully attacked the courthouse to obtain González' freedom. Sánchez was saved from the lynch mob, but authorities executed him legally in the spring of 1915. González, in spite of extraordinary efforts to keep him out of the mob's hands, was lynched. A mob took him from jail and fired three shots into his body. A third Mexican in the Oakville jail charged with complicity in the Hinton killing avoided lynching because the jail guard was increased.[80]

The 1921–1922 recession deepened hostility toward Mexicans. In March 1921, Mexicans allegedly murdered a young girl named Marie Schroeder near Hondo, exacerbating the tension already present because of a poor economy. Officers took suspect Salvador Saucedo to the scene of the crime and released him to a lynch mob. In November 1922, an angry mob of white workers took Elías Villarreal from his cell, where he awaited trial for fistfighting with an Anglo in the Rio Grande Valley town of Weslaco, and hanged him. Labor rivalry had been rampant in the town, and Villarreal, afraid of what might happen to him, managed to ask for help from the Corpus Christi consul, who attempted to ensure Villarreal's protection but failed.[81] During the same month in Breckenridge a Mexican named Zarate, also involved in a fight with an Anglo, was jailed and lynched even though the Mexican consul requested safekeeping from local authorities. The *New York Times* editorialized that the lynching "reflected racial animosity that would stop at nothing. Not the most inoffensive Mexican would be safe in such a community."[82]

But as Chapman points out, the motivation for lynching Mexicans differed in some important ways. For example, his study did not find one instance of a Mexican's illegal execution because he acted uppity or because he paid attention to a white woman. The sight of a mixed couple—Mexican and white—did not send whites into a frenzy of violence as often happened if blacks breached such taboos. Many Mexicans, in fact, married white women in Texas. Representative José T. Canales, for example, a prominent Texas Mexican who identified ethnically with Tejanos, married Annie Wheeler in Houston during 1910.

This chapter examined two aspects of white civilians' attacks on Mexicans: violence caused by the employer's need to control Mexican workers or by white workers anxious about competition, and violence suffered at the hands of individuals who used Mexicans to fulfill needs that transcended economic anxiety, that is, racist hatred. Regardless of what provoked these assaults, they occurred with such frequency that immigrants from Mexico had to live in perpetual fear of such reprisals, a phenomenon that made survival in the United States difficult at best.

7 | MEXICANS AND JUSTICE IN THE COURTROOM

DURING THE REVOLUTION, when law and order in Mexico broke down, the justice system became extremely arbitrary and limited the Mexican's experience with the courts. Mexicans could either be summarily shot by military officials for forgery or be ignored when they murdered or raped. Involvement in a property dispute, an accusation of theft, an assault, or a murder might have brought the common Mexican before *jefes de acordada* (local magistrates), but rural dwellers, and even urbanites, rarely faced a judge, mainly because of a lack of law enforcement personnel.[1] Mexicans from all classes facing a trial knew they could potentially influence the outcome, if not with money, through network connections. For poorer Mexicans, the *patrón,* who wanted them back at work, or the village priest served as the most effective advocates.[2]

Thus, Mexican immigrants must have met with bewilderment the discovery that U.S. courts granted them little latitude, though looser arrangements were available for others, particularly Anglos. Even within respectable middle-class society, which boasted an anticorruption ideology, judicial influence peddling existed. Nonetheless, in the United States, excepting large cities like Chicago, the orbit of those able to manipulate the judicial system was much smaller than in Mexico. For the newly arrived Mexicans, however, access to influence in the courts remained virtually unavailable.

THE COURTS, LANGUAGE, AND MEXICANS

Mexican immigrants frequently found themselves before a judge facing charges that would not have been brought to court in Mexico—drunkenness, carrying a concealed weapon, traffic violations, poaching in orchards, statutory rape, and so forth. Communication difficulties made the judicial process even harder to navigate. Mexican defendants often did not understand court proceedings and their testimonies, even when translated, lost the resonance given to truth by effective communication. In Los Angeles, Sevariano González was sentenced to life imprisonment in January 1903 for the killing of Charles Underwood, a murder González swore he did not commit. No direct evidence linked González to the crime. Nonetheless, prosecutors persuaded a judge to waive a jury trial. According to the Mexican government, the monolingual González could not object because the court did not provide him an interpreter. In 1913, a Texas Mexican consular official declared that even honest judges convicted innocent Mexicans who, scared, confused, and unable to speak English, appeared vacillating and showed a guilty demeanor. During 1916, so many Kansas City judges sentenced Mexicans without the benefit of an interpreter that Mexican consul Jack Dancinger advertised through *El Cosmopolita* that his office would provide interpreters.[3]

As the volume of immigration proliferated in the 1920s, the language issue became even more crucial, especially in communities where the recently arrived did not have a broker group of Mexican Americans or long-term resident immigrants. In the 1920s, Paul Warnshius, who studied crime and Mexicans in Chicago, identified a Mexican's inability to speak English as the main reason for inadequate defenses in Illinois courts. Municipal court magistrates, he indicated, made few attempts to furnish interpreters for Mexican suspects. Poles and Italians had this service, on the other hand, because persons of those nationalities worked in the courts. Of ninety-eight Mexicans he interviewed in Illinois prisons, only twenty-seven understood their trial proceedings.[4]

Paul Warnshius described what he considered the typical arrest process in Chicago for the Mexican who did not understand English:

A Mexican is picked up on "suspicion," and charged
with disorderly conduct. The officer saw him do nothing.
At the trial, the officer comes forward, the Mexican is
brought in and the prosecutor will say something[,] and
before he knows it[,] the Mexican is back in his cell convicted. He was then obliged to pay a fine, and if he
doesn't have it[,] he serves out the days at the Bridewell
lockup. The Mexican might have been asked to provide a
statement[,] but he doesn't know it.

He also related the case of a Mexican for whom court officials denied an interpreter because, "evidently, the judge was satisfied with the man's guilt and felt no need of listening to his testimony."[5]

In California in 1920, a Mexican American attorney advised Simón Ruíz, a seventeen-year-old Mexican accused of killing his Anglo boss while burglarizing his home, to throw himself on the mercy of the court. The jury convicted Ruíz, and a judge sentenced him to hang at San Quentin. According to the *San Francisco Call,* because he did not understand the proceedings, Ruíz "learned of his fate through a Spanish-speaking prisoner, who sat next to him at a prison theatrical performance. With the sudden realization that he was on death row, he was overcome and his shrieks of horror almost broke up the performance."[6]

Warnshius maintained that even if a Mexican's case went to the jury, the court procedure was usually stacked against the defendant. In 1924, Chicago Mexican consul Lorenzo Lupián filed a claim before the Mexican Claims Commission in a case involving Bernardo Roa, Roberto Torres, and Gregorio Rizo. Lupián said the three Mexicans, accused of robbing and killing an elevated-train ticket agent named Johnson during November 1923, were railroaded by the judge and the prosecutor.[7] He claimed that no witnesses were brought on the defendants' behalf during the two-day trial that resulted in an arbitrary verdict "because all the evidence was purely circumstantial and in no way does it prove their guilt."[8]

THE JUDGES

Because Mexican defendants often pleaded guilty, they rarely were tried by a jury. Consequently, American judges who regularly and openly expressed disdain for Mexicans and for Mexico became the sole legal arbiters of their destiny. Undoubtedly, Mexicans encountered acts of beneficence from judges as when the justice of the peace in Douglas, Arizona, Ben Rice, opened up the doors of the jail and let out the prisoners on September 16, 1910, to celebrate Mexican Independence Day.[9] But the historical record reveals a generally more malevolent relationship between the American judiciary and Mexican immigrants. Lower echelon judges with little or no legal training could be the most arbitrary. A 1913 Mexican consular report from Galveston complained that judges were one of the major sources of discrimination against Mexicans in Texas:

There is so much prejudice that court cases involving
Mexicans are always decided automatically against the
Mexican. . . . County judges in Texas pay for their salary
from fines. Americans and even other foreigners, because

they are well organized, make good cases and get off. The
poor[,] ignorant Mexican is left to take up the slack and
winds up paying the judges salary.[10]

In an angry exchange of letters, the Mexican consul in Globe, Arizona, Gustavo G. Hernández, in the spring of 1918, accused Justice of the Peace E. A. McEahern of violating the rights of Tomás González and Simón Espinoza.[11] The former, Hernández charged, died after his release from jail for wife beating, because he did not receive medical attention for pneumonia while in his cell. Moreover, Hernández reported, González was never charged with any crime during fifty-one days of his imprisonment. McEahern replied that he gave permission to the local sheriff to jail the Mexican without any formal arraignment but only after González' wife repeatedly complained of being abused. As far as González being ill, the judge responded, "I talked to him the day before we released him, and he seemed perfectly healthy to me. Besides, anyone who has the strength to beat his wife cannot be very sick."[12] In the case of Espinoza, McEahern jailed him because he quit making payments on a car that cost him sixty dollars of which he still owed twenty. Hernández consulted a lawyer who told him that a justice of the peace did not have the authority to jail any person for not making payments.[13]

In Chicago, the prejudice manifested by Chicago judges and jurors toward Mexicans astonished Paul Warnshius. One judge even told him "the Mexican is a born bandit not to be trusted." Such an attitude, undoubtedly, affected the conviction rates of Mexicans, twice that of "other nationalities" during the 1920s. Furthermore, Warnshius discovered that judges and prosecutors repeatedly pressured Mexicans charged with felonies to waive their right to a jury trial by pleading guilty, usually without the presence of defense counsel or interpreters.[14]

Judges, at times, allowed prejudices stemming from political conditions or perceptions of immorality in Mexico to weigh on decisions regarding Mexicans. In Los Angeles, a 1914 labor rally, sponsored by a Mexican-dominated Industrial Workers of the World local, led to a riot in which a policeman sustained serious injuries when he and fellow officers plowed into the crowd. They then arbitrarily arrested over seventy demonstrators, but only twenty were arraigned. Of those, the court dropped charges against the only two whites arrested and ten Mexicans. The jury found the remaining eight Mexicans guilty of rioting and assault, and they received sentences of one to two years in prison. The presiding judge explained:

I have given careful consideration to the case, and I have
taken into account the nationality of the accused. If the
men came from a country where they were accustomed
to liberty and into a land where the iron heel of oppression was ever present, it would put a different aspect to
their actions. But they came from Mexico to the United
States and were allowed the full privileges that are
accorded our citizens. I am going to impose sentences
that will warn all such agitators that they cannot dispute
men who have been vested by the people of the land with
authority to enforce the laws.[15]

Years later in another California case, a judge revealed a similar
prejudice at a sentencing. The events leading to the judge's injudicious
remarks began on the morning of May 21, 1929, when two Mexican
money couriers from the Aguacaliente Casino in Tijuana were taking
the previous night's receipts to a San Diego bank. As their car turned a
corner on the winding highway between Tijuana and San Diego, a band
of white "eastern types" cut them down with machine-gun fire. The two
casino employees, José Borrego and Nemesio Monroy, died instantly.
After San Diego police apprehended two of the six gang members soon
after the robbery, they were tried and convicted of premeditated murder. Because of the brutality of the crime, the Mexican government
pressed for a death sentence and general public opinion seemed to con-
cur.[16] Judge J. N. Andrews, however, sentenced M. B. Colson and Robert
Lee Cochran to life imprisonment and justified the lighter penalty by
holding Mexico partially responsible for the misdeeds of the two holdup
men. After discussing the rise of crime in southern California and laud-
ing the slain Mexican couriers for their commitment to duty, the judge
launched a verbal assault on San Diego's neighboring Mexican city:

Tijuana perhaps should be charged as an aid in this
crime. Much woe and misery have been brought into
San Diego and to this court because of the border resort.
That awful spot across time, figuratively speaking, should
be wiped out. And this I believe will be done through the
moral awaking of the people of the Mexican Republic
and by the Mexican President.[17]

The judge's action was influenced by allegations three years earlier that
the rape of two San Diego white girls by Tijuana police officials provoked

the mass suicide of the girls' entire immediate family. Nonetheless, San Diego consul Enrique Ferreira indicated that he could not understand why the judge attacked Tijuana because the gangland hijacking took place in typical American fashion.[18]

During the Great Depression, Maurice E. Crites, superior court judge of Lake County, Indiana, where Gary and East Chicago are located, was appointed chairman of the Indiana Harbor Welfare Committee, which provided relief for thousands of unemployed workers and their families in this highly industrialized county. To alleviate the demand on welfare coffers, the committee, in conjunction with the American Legion, initiated a massive repatriation program for "the removal of the nationalists [*sic*], especially the Mexicans." [19] In East Chicago, Mexicans wanting to remain in the United States were legalizing their status, with the help of the Immigrant Protective League and local Spanish-language newspapers, an activity of which Crites disapproved. The judge told East Chicago high school students in 1930 that he doubted the ability of foreigners, including Mexicans, to be good citizens since they were only "one half American," even after they naturalized.[20]

As a state judge, Crites did not administer the oath of allegiance to Mexicans becoming citizens, a process he obviously opposed. But this was not true in the case of federal judges who might also harbor anti-Mexican feelings. On December 12, 1935, Timoteo Andrade stood before Judge John Knight of the First Federal Circuit Court in Buffalo awaiting a citizenship swearing-in ceremony. Andrade was shocked when Knight rejected his application because of his Indian heritage. Until the 1950s, naturalization law denied citizenship to many non-whites, but the exclusion did not apply to Mexicans, primarily because of the 1897 *Rodriguez v. Texas* decision, allowing Mexicans to naturalize because of the 1848 Treaty of Guadalupe Hidalgo. Judge Knight, using a legal interpretation provided by the California-based Joint Immigration Committee, ruled the Rodríguez decision to be unconstitutional. He based much of his judgment on a more recent case denying citizenship to a Canadian Native American. Alonso McLatchey, chairman of the Joint Immigration Committee and a member of the family publishing the nativist *Sacramento Bee*, persuaded John Murf, the naturalization officer in charge of Andrade's proceedings, to collude with Judge Knight and reject Andrade's application.[21]

The Mexican government, alarmed over the possibility that such a decision would prevent future immigration, considered appealing the case. After a legal analysis, Mexican officials concluded that the Knight decision was constitutionally defensible. They opted for behind-the-scenes diplomacy. Meanwhile Sumner Welles, the State Department Latin American affairs specialist, concerned with damage to President Franklin Roosevelt's Good Neighbor Policy, assured the Mexican ambassador in Washington that immigration officials would permit Mexicans to enter the United States in spite of the decision. The consul general in New York City then paid four thousand dollars to a prominent attorney and close friend of the judge to influence Knight to expunge the decision. In this manner, a history-changing event did not take place.[22] Andrade, a native of Jalisco, was sworn in as a citizen, according to his widow, "with a lot of pride, and with no ill-feelings against the United States."[23]

One of the most unhappy examples of a judge's prejudice toward Mexicans can be seen in the 1931 jailing of Chicago vice consul Adolfo Domínguez. At this time, Great Depression unemployment exacerbated ethnic hostility toward Mexicans, an enmity manifested by local neighborhood policemen. Domínguez managed the consulate's *atropello* (violation) division and as seemingly arbitrary arrests of Mexicans increased in the 1930s, the aggressive official scurried in and out of courtrooms attempting to assure justice for his compatriots. On the morning of July 7, the vice consul, accompanied by attorney John Baker and a small group of Mexican citizens, entered Judge Thomas Green's courtroom to determine why white assailants of two Mexican girls hurt at a Fourth of July race riot were not charged.[24]

Judge Green, apparently fed up with Domínguez' remonstrations, launched into a tirade upon learning of the vice consul's presence. According to Baker, he shouted at the top of his lungs that "the consul was no good, the Mexican Government was no good, that the consul was not taking care of his job properly . . . ," ending his invective with, "Shut up or I'll throw you in the can." Domínguez did not shut up quickly enough, and Green sent him off to the county jail to serve a six-month sentence for contempt of court.[25] Mexican ambassador Manuel Téllez learned about the incident the next day and protested the jailing of a presumably immune Mexican diplomat. The Department of State, sensitive to the international implications of Judge Green's action, had already acted. The judge's action could not have come at a worse time. Less than a week before Domínguez' jailing, deputy sheriffs, on a dark Oklahoma highway, killed two Mexican youths who had been studying in the United States and were motoring back to Mexico. One was a nephew of Mexican president Pascual Ortiz Rubio (see Chapter 5). The State Department, consequently, sought to quickly suppress the Chicago incident, cabling Governor Louis Emmerson in Springfield to request his help in averting any further complications.[26]

In Chicago, cooler heads had already prevailed. Over Green's objections, another judge freed Domínguez on his own recognizance. Green remained defiant throughout the whole affair. When reminded by a prosecutor in his courtroom that the vice consul enjoyed diplomatic immunity, Green exploded, saying "it would take nothing short of an act of President Hoover" to change his mind. Then he added, "I'm an ex-Marine myself and that's the way we Marines handle things. I don't see why people . . . scrape to these consuls and ambassadors. They've got to be put in their place."[27] Meanwhile the judge retained the services of an American Legion attorney to represent him in all future deliberations. He soon changed his mind, however, after Chief Justice Sonseteby of the Illinois Supreme Court, at the behest of Governor Emmerson, persuaded Green to expunge the original sentence and issue a statement admitting his error. The Department of State sent an official apology to Mexico through Ambassador Téllez and the international imbroglio ended.[28]

THE PROSECUTORS

The unwillingness of prosecutors to pursue convictions in cases where whites had perpetuated crimes against Mexicans served as a continuous source of exasperation for the Mexican community. During February 1920, law officers Frank Taylor and Luther Moore killed Ernesto Flores and Carnación Cornejo in Colorado, Texas, a few miles from El Paso, because they suspected them of cattle rustling. Examination of their wounds revealed that the officers had summarily executed Flores and Cornejo. So much hostility existed toward Mexicans locally, however, that the families of the murdered men could not persuade county attorneys to prosecute the case. In response to Mexican Embassy entreaties, the secretary of state asked for information from the governor of Texas, but the case was dropped.[29]

INCOMPETENT DEFENSE

As important as the attitudes of judges were in determining how Mexicans fared in the judicial system, the quality of their defense figured more crucially. In nineteenth-century California courts, for example, Mexican Americans found it difficult to obtain justice because of the lack of competent Spanish-speaking lawyers. It was not until 1872 that the first Mexican American lawyer started practicing in Los Angeles.

This privation prevailed in other areas where Mexicans lived during this era, but southwestern Mexicans eventually acquired political influence that helped offset the lack of lawyers of their own ethnic background.[30] In this century the new immigrants were not as fortunate. As more Mexicans came before the bench, many threw themselves, without counsel, on the mercy of the court. Even when Mexicans had a legal advocate, incompetence, indifference, and laziness characterized the attitudes of many lawyers who took responsibility for their defense. In 1910, Chihuahua native Francisco Márquez was sentenced to hang on October 28 for the 1909 murder of P. B. Hodges in Yuma, Arizona. Márquez, who survived two lynching attempts, was convicted, although he maintained he killed Hodges in self-defense. The victim's family, prominent in Yuma society, demanded and got the death penalty. Because Márquez lacked funds to hire a lawyer, the trial judge appointed two friends of the deceased Hodges to defend him. Moreover, members of the mob that tried to lynch him, family friends, and members of the victim's lodge were put on the jury. Márquez' attorneys pleaded temporary insanity and made no other efforts to introduce evidence.[31]

At times, Anglo defense lawyers sympathized with public antipathy toward Mexicans on trial and, as a result, neglected to provide an adequate defense for their clients. A judge in Deming, New Mexico, appointed a reluctant Buel R. Wood to represent seven defendants accused of killing U.S. Army engineer Charles Dewitt Miller during Pancho Villa's 1916 raid on Columbus. Wood made a lukewarm effort against a prosecution that did not even place most of the accused men at the raid. Assistant District Attorney J. S. Vaught told the jury in his opening statement "that the state would prove that the defendants were in the vicinity . . . and were assisting in the perpetuation of a felony. He would not expect to show," he admitted, "that any of them had actually shot Miller or had even been close by when he was killed." After the hangings, Wood, in a letter to the *Deming Graphic,* called the many critics of the whole process "chicken-hearted" and agreed with general public opinion that the hanged men "had come to the end they deserved."[32]

Understandably, such ineptitude ignited legal defense efforts in the immigrant communities. The plight of Pedro Cano, convicted of the 1924 killing of a white Salt Lake City prostitute, caught the attention of Mexican immigrants throughout the country because of acute irregularities in the proceedings. None of the interrogating policemen spoke Spanish, a point the lawyer appointed to defend the monolingual Mexican immigrant failed to demonstrate at the trial. Cano's mother hired another lawyer who immediately asked for a change of venue on the basis that court officials and police investigators had shown exceptional partiality, but the motion was denied by the presiding judge. An openly hostile jury found Cano guilty and sentenced him to death. Similarly, in California, a dramatic fund-raising effort to save Mauricio Trinidad from the gallows after he was convicted of killing a farmer in 1926 was prompted by dismay over an inadequate defense. His lawyer made a ten-minute defense plea without introducing evidence or producing witnesses.[33]

Warnshius made it a point to demonstrate that Chicago lawyers who defended Mexicans were incompetent. Of the ninety-eight Mexican prisoners Warnshius interviewed at different Illinois prisons, only nineteen believed they had adequate defense at their trials.[34] Paul S. Taylor, also referring to Chicago, noted that witnesses for the defense often failed to show up because of job requirements. Moreover, once incarcerated, Mexicans found it difficult to contact someone on the outside who could help their case. Normally, said Taylor, the lawyer's duty required securing such support but they rarely made the effort.[35]

A Chicago Mexican leader complained to Paul Taylor in 1925 that lawyers and policemen, at times, colluded to defraud Mexicans. When police arrested a Mexican, he said, a lawyer took his money, made bribes at City Hall, and then officials released the now impecunious detainee. Anthropologist Robert Redfield cited an example of two Mexicans in Chicago whom police arrested for larceny in 1925. They did not speak English, but a Spanish-speaking runner for an attorney approached them, promising his boss would get them off. Without waiting to be officially hired, the attorney represented them, pleaded them guilty without their consent, and charged them fifty dollars.[36]

A SQUARE DEAL IN THE COURTROOM

Although courtroom horror stories regarding Mexicans can be told about almost any location in the country, cases of more nearly equal treatment stand out mainly outside Texas and Arizona. Paul Warnshius observed that even though lawyers and judges in the Illinois Superior Courts treated Mexican defendants disdainfully, proceedings were held in a more dignified setting—not as hurried or mechanical as in city and county courts.[37] To the joy of the *colonia,* in January 1926, Judge James Martin Smith of the Lake County, Indiana, Superior Court dismissed a case against Agustín González for assaulting Barney Jenassanki for lack of evidence, even though an East Chicago policeman testified that he saw the assault.[38] Similarly, on December 15, 1931, in Chicago, a jury acquitted Santiago Rivera of murder charges after he killed a man accused of sexually molesting his mother. Judge B. David, who freed Rivera, stated, "I would have done the same as this young man had done in those circumstances; therefore, in the Law's name I declare you innocent." *El Nacional* approved of the judge's decision and Rivera's action "because the bandit who had trampled his honor had bragged of his deed." [39]

Sympathetic court officials were more evident in California, which had a larger number of progressives than in any other state in the Southwest. Simón Ruíz, an underage Mexican sentenced to hang at San Quentin in 1921 for killing his white foreman in a robbery, received support from prominent Anglo businessmen and women, such as attorney Mabel Dorn Hirst, the daughter of a judge from Monterey County who was a member of the Progressive Party. A leader in the Pathfinders prison reform group, Hirst circulated petitions throughout California protesting Ruíz' execution. Also, San Bernardino Judge J. W. Curtis, who sentenced Ruíz to death, recanted and recommended a commutation to Governor Stephens. The prosecutor and most of the jury members who convicted him also signed a clemency petition on Ruíz' behalf.[40]

In the 1930s, New Dealers appointed a number of federal judges more sympathetic to the plight of defendants. Alberto Velasco, imprisoned in Illinois during 1930 for first-degree murder, benefited from these changing attitudes. In 1945, Federal District Court Judge Elwyn Shaw, a Roosevelt appointee, released Velasco from prison after deciding that when Velasco killed Juvenciano Horta in a fight after Horta refused his drunken solicitations to have paid sex with a "gay Polish woman," the circumstances appeared more like self-defense than premeditated murder.[41]

COMPETENT LAWYERS

Lawyers chosen by defendants or the Mexican consuls performed much better than court-appointed attorneys. Some accused Mexicans had money to pay lawyers' fees in minor brushes with the law, but it was impossible for most to sustain expenses in long-drawn-out cases. Mexican consuls had special budgets to hire lawyers for these purposes, and, as a result, the names of some attorneys—for example, Raymond Hall of Hutchison, Kansas—appear repeatedly in consular records. Hired by the Kansas City consul in January 1916, Hall managed to reduce charges against Joaquín Valdez from first-degree murder to manslaughter in the killing of Arcadio González in a 1915 fight. In Chicago, Mary Lee Spencer was frequently retained by the consul. It is hard to measure her effectiveness because on occasion immigrants criticized her for poor performance, while at other times the Mexican community lauded her. In one case she persuaded a judge to dismiss charges against a Mexican who ran over an elderly Anglo farmer outside of Chicago during 1931 as he and his family were driving back to Mexico. Spencer achieved the most publicity when she defended Robert Tórrez, one of three Mexicans convicted of killing Assistant Warden Herbert Klein in 1926 during an escape from the state prison at Joliet, a story told in greater detail in Chapter 8.[42]

Consulate lawyers sometimes developed close relationships with individual consuls. Enrique Ferreira, while serving as consul in Nogales, Arizona, hired attorney Fred Noon to defend Mexicans. In 1923, Noon took over from the incompetent lawyers who had failed to appeal in the case of Plácido Silvas, who, along with Manuel Martínez, was convicted of killing an Anglo couple during a 1921 robbery. Martínez received the death sentence and Silvas, life (see Chapter 8). Noon persuaded Martínez to admit before he was hanged that he falsely implicated Silvas so Noon could get Silvas a pardon; he was finally released in 1933. When the Foreign Ministry assigned Ferreira to San Diego in the late 1920s, Noon followed his friend and appeared frequently as a defense attorney for accused Mexicans in San Diego consular reports.[43] A 1988 television movie portrays him as representing the plaintiff in the now famous Lemon Grove desegregation case. In the film, his brilliant interrogation of local school board members and teachers resulted in a judgment against the Lemon Grove School Board.

In incidents that garnered a lot of publicity, the Mexican government did not spare expense in providing support for expatriates. As indicated in Chapter 3, in the case of the four young Mexicans accused of bombing the federal courthouse in New York City during 1927, the Mexican government reportedly hired one of the best firms in the city. In 1921, New York consul general Ramón P. de Negri hired Grace Hamilton, a successful New York City criminal lawyer, to help him in the unsuccessful effort to influence Governor Alfred Smith to commute the death sentences of Enrique García and Agustín Sánchez. The two were executed at Sing Sing Prison anyway in January 1921 (see Chapter 8).[44]

Consular money often had ceilings, however, so community organizations had to take up the slack. Los Angeles' La Liga Protectora Mexicana and La Confederación de Sociedades Mexicanas kept lawyers on retainer specifically for defending Mexicans. The most extensive effort by these organizations was in helping Mauricio Trinidad after an incompetent lawyer made minimal efforts in his trial for murder (see above).[45] The Los Angeles law firm of Charles J. Orbisson, which represented Juan Reyna, who had killed a Los Angeles policeman, asked for a minimum advance of five hundred dollars, a sum Reyna's family could not raise. Consular officials and private Mexican organizations then coordinated fund-raising to help cover the cost, but the lawyers were not satisfied and withdrew. Los Angeles consul Rafael de la Colina then asked his legal consultant, Robert P. Carey, to take on the defense and began a press and radio collection campaign to raise the twenty-five-hundred-dollar legal fee, which could be paid in installments. Within a few weeks, the Unión de Obreros Mexicanos and other organizations came up with $2,736.[46]

MEXICAN AMERICAN AND SPANISH-SPEAKING LAWYERS

Because few Mexican-immigrant lawyers qualified to practice in the United States, Anglo Americans who did not speak Spanish usually defended Mexicans. A notable exception was Robert G. Estill in East Chicago. A former missionary who had lived in Mexico and in the Mexican community of Kansas City, Estill moved to Indiana, studied law, and set up his own business. "He knows Spanish and is opposed to drug trafficking in the Mexican community," editorialized *El Amigo del Hogar* in a frank endorsement.[47] On another occasion he helped organize a meeting between the consul, the East Chicago police chief, and members of the *colonia* to ameliorate an extremely estranged relationship. Estill became Lake County district attorney and achieved fame for pursuing the arrest and prosecution of John Dillinger. His promising career fizzled, however, when he posed for photographers embracing the notorious bandit-killer.[48]

Most Mexican American attorneys spoke both Spanish and English. They frequently proffered services to the immigrant community either to help *la raza* or because Mexicans were their only clients. Generally, they seemed to be competent even though many lost cases which were very difficult to defend.

Prominent among Mexican American lawyers was Manuel González. Early in his career, the World War I veteran became secretary to the U.S. military attaché in Madrid. In the 1920s, he actively participated in fledgling Mexican American organizations such as the Order of the Sons of America and in 1929 became a founding member of the League of

United Latin American Citizens. Because he lived in San Antonio, the seat of the consul general, Mexican officials often asked him to serve as a friend of the court in trials of policemen who killed Mexicans.

In 1931, when the young attorney represented the Mexican government at the Oklahoma trial of the two deputies who killed two middle-class students from Mexico, he flamboyantly made his war record known while addressing the court.[49] In 1937, González again served as a friend of the court in the trial of two policemen who beat thirty-seven-year-old Mexican immigrant Elpidio Cortez to death in the Houston city jail. Although González was not pleased with the verdict, he had high praise for prosecutor Dan Jackson and his assistant for mounting a vigorous effort.[50]

More successful were San Antonio lawyers Jesús Rodríguez and Santos Valdez who, in 1928, managed to obtain a manslaughter conviction for client Joaquín Cadena, although the prosecutor had vigorously sought a first-degree murder verdict. Cadena had stabbed his Mexican wife to death as she exited a San Antonio movie theater with another man. The lawyers then, unsuccessfully, attempted to overturn the manslaughter conviction when they discovered that the state legislature had removed the specific charge for which Cadena was convicted from the criminal code.[51]

Phoenix attorney, Gregorio "Greg" García was among the most active Arizona criminal lawyers in defending Mexicans. García and Consul Alejandro Martínez led the successful 1926 campaign to obtain a commutation for a deranged Ramón Escobar, sentenced to hang for killing his wife in a jealous rage.[52] García also served as the main lawyer in the case of Alfredo Grijalva, the southern Arizona rancher accused of killing a customs official in 1926. Grijalva was found guilty, but García presented a defense vigorous enough to cast some doubt and the judge sentenced Grijalva to life imprisonment rather than giving him the death penalty. García belonged to the Alianza Hispano Americana and in the 1930s went on to become a founding member of the Latin American Club, a "Mexican-American Generation" organization (of persons born in the United States of Mexican ancestry who predominated in leadership positions after the 1930s in Mexican communities in the United States) that supported the Democratic Party and the New Deal. In the 1940s and 1950s, he worked with attorney Ralph Estrada in desegregation cases in the Phoenix area.[53]

8| CAPITAL PUNISHMENT AND MEXICANS IN THE UNITED STATES

BECAUSE MÉXICO LINDO—ERA leaders were convinced that judges discriminated when meting out capital punishment to their people, they and their government expended prodigious amounts of political energy attempting to obtain commutations. From their vantage point, they saw the death sentences as a corollary to courtroom abuses, police brutality, and disproportionate arrests. Statistics on how many Mexicans died legally at the hands of executioners, when they died, and at what ratios they died in comparison to whites follow the same significant patterns of the other issues discussed in this book. Executions were more intensive during the period of heavy immigration and declined as the *colonias* and their institutions aged. In addition, more executions took place during the time of border turbulence, a phenomenon that is probably interrelated (see Table 9).

ARIZONA

In Arizona between 1873 and 1910, out of forty-five persons executed, there were twenty whites, ten Mexicans, eight Indians, four blacks, and three Chinese. In 1910, the Arizona white population constituted about 70 percent of the population. After 1910, with increased immigration of both Mexicans and whites, the execution disparity widened even more. Between 1910 and 1934, of thirty-two executions in the state prison at Florence sixteen were Hispanics, including one Spaniard. Eight whites, four Chinese, two blacks, and a Cherokee Indian, which most accounts portray as a white, met the same fate. The only female to hang was white.[1]

The Porfirian administration, in reality, had more success in protecting Arizona Mexicans than subsequent regimes—at least until diplomatic stability returned in the 1920s. Francisco Márquez, in 1910, was the last condemned Mexican to receive clemency in the United States before Díaz' ouster. Early in the same year, a Yuma, Arizona, judge sen-

TABLE 9. EXECUTIONS IN ARIZONA, CALIFORNIA, NEW MEXICO, AND TEXAS, 1901–1935

YEAR	WHITE	MEXICAN	BLACK	INDIAN	ASIAN	TOTAL
1901–1905	27	18	18	3	1	67
1906–1910	15	11	32	1	1	60
1911–1915	19	11	27	1	1	59
1916–1920	17	15	13	1	5	51
1921–1925	28	23	33	0	0	84
1926–1930	34	7	33	0	0	74
1931–1935	43	8	33	0	0	84
TOTAL	183	93	189	6	8	479
%	38.2	19.4	39.5	1.3	1.7	100

SOURCE: M. WATT ESPY AND JOHN ORTIZ SMYKLA, "EXECUTIONS IN THE UNITED STATES, 1608–1987: THE ESPY FILE" (ANN ARBOR: INTER-UNIVERSITY CONSORTIUM FOR POLITICAL AND SOCIAL RESEARCH, 1990), MACHINE-READABLE DATA FILE 8541.

tenced him to hang for the murder of P. B. Hodges, an influential Anglo. In October, his appeal to the Arizona Supreme Court failed despite numerous errors pointed out by the defense. Since May 1910, when Márquez should have hanged, Mexican Ambassador Francisco León de la Barra had been applying diplomatic pressure through the Department of State to gain him a stay of execution. Arizona Mexicans and the chaplain at the prison in Florence clamored for clemency at the same time that they somewhat unjustifiably criticized the Mexican government for inaction. In fact, territorial governor Richard P. Sloan caved in to diplomatic pressure and on October 22 commuted Márquez' death sentence.[2]

In the 1910s, every person executed at the new state prison at Florence was Hispanic, even though several whites had received death sentences (Mexicans counted the Spaniard as one of their own). In this era, newly forming immigrant institutions could not mount effective defense efforts, and during the Mexican Revolution, Mexico's ability to intervene had diminished considerably. Additionally, Anglo hostility increased during this period of border strife, a factor that might have served as a catalyst to Mexicans receiving death sentences. But more crucially, large-scale immigration provoked a volatile relationship with the Anglos,

FIGURE 9. FIVE MEXICANS CONDEMNED TO DIE AT THE STATE PRISON IN FLORENCE, ARIZONA, ON THE SAME DAY IN MAY 1915. THEIR SENTENCE CREATED A STIR AMONG MEXICAN IMMIGRANT ACTIVISTS. REPRINTED WITH PERMISSION FROM FOTOTECA DE LA SECRETARÍA DE RELACIONES EXTERIORES, MÉXICO.

especially law officials. Four out of eleven Mexicans executed between 1910 and 1920 received the death sentence for killing policemen.

Between 1910 and 1913, the Mexican community hardly protested the hangings at Florence of five Hispanics, probably because few defense-minded organizations existed at this point. The Mexican government remained silent as well because after Porfirio Díaz fell, the various factions claiming to rule Mexico were too distracted by internal power struggles to respond to immigrant mistreatment. However, the temper of the community changed in 1915. Of the twelve men awaiting execution on death row that year, seven Americans (one was a black) and five Mexicans—Francisco Rodríguez, Eduardo Pérez, N. B. Chávez, Miguel Peralta, and Ramón Villalobos—were scheduled to hang for unrelated crimes on the same day in May. Juries had convicted Villalobos and Chávez of killing law officers; Rodríguez and Peralta had killed their wives. Preventing this mass execution became one of first issues of the newly organized Liga Protectora Latina.[3]

Governor George W. P. Hunt, a progressive Republican and a foe of capital punishment, managed to postpone the executions through legal maneuvering even though in the previous year's election, when voters reelected him, a referendum stripped him of clemency powers. These passed to the Board of Pardons and Paroles, headed by capital punishment advocate Attorney General Wiley Jones. Hunt pressured the board and even convinced Secretary of State Robert Lansing to request clemency for the Mexicans. The State Department rapidly obliged, concerned that the executions would exacerbate serious border problems provoked by the Plan de San Diego revolt in South Texas.[4] La Liga Protectora Latina and Douglas consul Ives Levelier circulated petitions and personally met with Hunt and the parole board in Phoenix. The group pointed out that a referendum to decide the death penalty's future was pending, arguing that the condemned Mexicans' fate should await the outcome. Nonetheless, four of the condemned men hanged. Ramón Villalobos was first, in December 1915. The other three died the following year— Francisco Rodríguez in May, Chávez in June, and Peralta in July. Only Pérez, who had killed another Mexican, received a commutation from the board.[5] In contrast, the board commuted the sentences for the seven Americans on death row. After the four Mexicans hanged, a white man named Robert Dayton Talley still faced the gallows. But to the dismay of the Mexican community, the parole board granted Talley a ninety-day reprieve until it was known whether or not the voters would abolish the death sentence. They did, and Dayton Talley did not hang.[6]

Arizona voters, however, motivated by a dramatic rise in murders, reinstated capital punishment in November 1918. During the two-year capital-punishment respite, seventy-nine killings took place in contrast to forty-seven in 1915–1916.[7] Of nineteen killers convicted during the grace period, only four were Mexicans. Nonetheless, on April 16, 1920, Simplicio Torres, who killed a Williams policeman, became the first person executed once the death penalty became legal again. The Arizona Mexican community then launched an intense but unsuccessful campaign to save Torres.[8]

After Torres, the Mexican community did not contest executions as persistently, even though four Mexicans hanged in the next two years. Perhaps these latest executions did not stir deep feelings among Mexicans because during this period prison officials also hanged two whites and an Armenian, Martin Nichan, whom the *Arizona Republican* identified as a nonwhite.[9] After 1922, however, vigorous protests against executions resumed. They were brought on by the highly publicized plight of Manuel Martínez, who was convicted of killing an Anglo grocer couple during a robbery in Ruby, a mining town near Nogales. His case received more attention than other hangings because in 1921 the Obregón government traded Martínez illegally for Francisco Reina, an exiled rebel living near Nogales, Arizona. In addition, Martínez and Plácido Silvas, also indicted in the slaying, made an unsuccessful but dramatic escape, which captured the imagination of the Arizona Mexican community (see Chapter 7). The Mexican community also believed that the all-white jury at the trial held in Nogales had a priori made up their minds to a guilty verdict. Then in what appeared as incompetence, Martínez' lawyers failed to meet a sixty-day deadline to appeal the sentence.[10]

Criticism of Martínez' illegal extradition threatened to derail the formation of Comisiones Honorífica Mexicanas in Arizona (see Chapter 3) so the Foreign Ministry ordered Phoenix consul Roberto Quiroz to lead the campaign to save Martínez. With Jesús Franco, then an El Paso journalist and Comisión organizer, Quiroz traveled to various Arizona *colonias* announcing these intentions. The consulate then hired the Douglas firm of Robinson and Anaya, who obtained a stay and a writ of habeas corpus, putting the case on the appeal circuit. The firm even sent a lawyer to Washington to prepare a possible Supreme Court appeal.[11] The newly minted Comisiones organized by Franco in practically every *colonia* in the state then deluged the governor's office with clemency requests. The Arizona governor also received requests from numerous organizations in Sonora and the Sonoran state legislature.[12]

When the stay expired, Martínez was resentenced to hang on August 11, 1924. Quiroz, with the consulate lawyers, began preparation for an appeal to the U.S. Supreme Court, but he fell ill and did not file in time. A commutation from the Board of Paroles remained Martínez' only hope, but now it refused a request from Mexico, and the unlucky Mexican hanged as scheduled.[13] Although the Martínez mobilization was unsuccessful, it revealed to Arizona officials a Mexican community with enough unity to launch formidable campaigns to protect Mexicans. The Mexican community also felt their efforts were worthwhile because after the execution nine men and one woman died at the gallows in Florence before another Mexican hanged.

The failure to prevent the 1934 execution of Fred and Manuel Hernández for the killing of Charles P. Washburn, a prospector from Needles, California, brought back some of the old frustrations, however. The gas chamber was used for the first time and Manuel, seventeen when he committed the crime, became the youngest person to be executed in Arizona. The Mexican government could not help because the brothers were born in the United States, but a major community campaign to save the two followed. The Superior Court affirmed the original sentence in an appeal bid, but the mother of the two boys traveled tirelessly throughout the state urging people to sign petitions for clemency. To no avail, for the boys died on July 6, 1934.[14]

NEW MEXICO

In the early years after New Mexico's annexation by the United States, more Anglos died by execution than Mexicans even though Anglos constituted a minority. Paradoxically, as the number of Anglos grew, more Mexicans hanged in proportion to the overall population. A reason for this is that tension and violence wrought by economic warfare and social change in the 1890s involved many Hispano natives who committed crimes punishable by execution.[15]

After 1910, the geography of where capital punishment applied to Mexicans shifted from the northern to the southern part of the state and executions began to take on more racial overtones. The change coincided with an influx of Mexican immigration to that area and the rise of border violence during the Mexican Revolution. The most publicized multiple execution followed the hysteria resulting from the Villista raid on Columbus in 1916. Army officials arrested twenty-four Mexicans for participating in the raid and for the killing of a U.S. Army mining engineer, Dewitt Miller. Eleven were captured in the raid itself, but soldiers in Pershing's punitive expedition seized the others in Chihuahua when paid informers identified them as participants. Three separate trials decided their fate in Deming, but controversy surrounded the proceedings because extradition procedures had been ignored during the arrests in Mexico.[16] The first trial during April 1916 lasted less than a week. Six of the captured Mexicans—Eusebio Rentería, Taurino García, José Rodríguez, Francisco Alvarez, José Rangel, and Juan Castillo—were found guilty of killing the officer. None of the men played pivotal roles in the raids, and one of them, José Rodríguez, claimed he was forced to ride with the Villistas as a horse tender. No witnesses actually saw the defendants shoot the American officer and prosecutors could not place five of the men in the raid with any kind of certainty. In a separate trial, the jury found Juan Sánchez, whom soldiers captured at Columbus, guilty as well. He was one of only two defendants who witnesses conclusively identified as being at the Columbus attack. Carranza's government demurred in providing support until the trial drew so much international attention that the issue could not be ignored. After the judge meted out death sentences, Mexico paid an attorney to appeal the case.[17]

State officials then transferred the seven condemned men to the New Mexico State Penitentiary in Santa Fe, fearing that the Luna County jail could not withstand a rumored lynching attempt. Mexican groups throughout the nation and Anglo sympathizers saw the trial as a sham and petitioned Governor William C. McDonald for clemency. The governor provided a three-week reprieve and rescheduled the execution for June 9. Only Juan Sánchez and Francisco Alvarez died on the appointed day because McDonald issued yet another stay for the remaining five. He also commuted the death sentence of José Rodríguez to life in prison because he had been impressed into Villa's army only two weeks before the raid and did not even know the raid occurred north of the border. After the stay expired, the remaining four—Rentería, Rangel, García, and Castillo—hanged to accolades from many New Mexicans, including the lawyer who defended them.[18]

In 1920, four New Mexico natives captured by the celebrated lawman, Elfego Baca, for the killing of wealthy Socorro cattleman Abrahám Contreras were found guilty but not sentenced to die. Pedro Saíz received a life sentence, but his confederates served thirty-year sentences, each with a chance at parole. This stood in stark contrast to the fate of the alleged participants in the Columbus raid who hanged even though their guilt was seriously in doubt. Only one Mexican hanging for a crime of passion in this century can be ascertained from the record. After receiving two reprieves from New Mexico's governor, Julian Romero went to the gallows on April 11, 1918, for the murder of his young wife.[19] That more did not hang is attributable to the banning of capital punishment in New Mexico after the 1920s, an act intimately connected with the state's grisly history of executions.

MEXICANS AND CAPITAL PUNISHMENT IN TEXAS

In the last twenty-five years of the nineteenth century, Texas officials executed more Mexicans than in the same time span in the beginning of the twentieth, even though their number had by then increased dramatically. The late nineteenth century is a period of large-scale immigration to Texas—approximately 150,000 Mexican immigrants lived in the state during 1910. Moreover, more Mexicans hanged in the first seventeen years after 1900 than in the period from 1917 to 1935 (66 percent in first span). This first era corresponds to border turmoil during the Mexican Revolution. Basically, Mexicans died from legal capital punishment roughly in proportion to their overall share of the Texas population between 1901 and 1935. For every Mexican executed, two whites and seven blacks met the same fate. In 1930, Mexicans made up 7 percent of the population.

In addition, in the 1920s, the number of legal Mexican executions in Texas was lower than in Arizona and California, whose combined Mexican population stood equal to that of Texas. This hardly comforted Texas Mexican civil rights activists, however, because mobs there lynched more compatriots in this century than in the rest of the country combined. In addition, Texas posses and law officers performed more summary executions of Mexicans than officials in other states. In other words, law officers and civilians dispatched by other means Mexicans who might legally have wound up on the gallows. Moreover, before 1923 it is more difficult to ascertain the exact number of legal executions for Texas because scholars of capital punishment have not uncovered records to the same degree as in other areas. Nonetheless, efforts to save Mexicans from the gallows in Texas abounded and although the results were mixed, activists in the state had more success than in Arizona and California.

One of the most prolonged efforts to save a Mexican ended on May 11, 1914, when León Cárdenas Martínez, Jr., was executed for the 1911 murder of Emma Brown in Pecos. Cárdenas claimed to be sixteen years old at the time of the murder, a factor which should have spared his life—Texas law forbade the execution of minors. According to Cárdenas Martínez' father, officers took the boy to the murder site, held a gun to his head, and told him that if he confessed they would him protect from a menacing lynch mob.[20] During the July 1911 trial, incensed townspeople forced León Cárdenas Martínez Sr. to abandon his butcher shop and take his family out of town—the mob included the Reeves County sheriff. The Mexican Protective Association of San Antonio, headed by D. R. Dávila, raised money to appeal the sentence. In Reeves County, local whites broke up support meetings. At the trial, a jury of Anglos ignored efforts by lawyers to demonstrate that León Cárdenas was under the legal age for execution. In addition, the sheriff prevented his lawyers from interviewing the defendant properly, and community pressure intimidated them into not appealing the case.[21]

In October 1913, the Mexican government, aided by a community fund, hired lawyers J. F. Cunningham and Robert P. Coon to file a writ of habeas corpus with the Texas Court of Appeals to get the sentence reviewed. The request postponed the hanging, but the original judgment was eventually affirmed. Cárdenas' lawyers then appealed to the U.S. Supreme Court, a move that prolonged the young Mexican's life for almost two years. When the case came before the high court in October 1913, Cárdenas Martínez' lawyers failed to follow through on some technical requirements, and the justices dismissed the case.[22]

From the outset, Mexicans on both sides of the border responded enthusiastically to the crusade. The boy's father belonged to the PLM, and members of the group offered aid. In April 1914, just a month and a half before the scheduled execution on May 11, Waco's Mexicans formed the Comité de Defensa. Meetings were held at the houses of middle-class Mexican women, and the main activities were fund-raising and publicity efforts. San Antonio's *La Prensa* also joined the drive, providing organizers with more widespread coverage. Support from other Texas newspapers, including Laredo's *El Guardia del Bravo,* added to the effort. Hundreds of clemency petitions circulated in various Texas towns and were sent to Governor Colquitt. That month in Los Angeles, the Industrial Workers of the World held a mass rally at the *placita* to protest the execution.[23] Diplomatically, Mexico could do nothing because of the invasion of Veracruz on April 21. Huerta's government, however, asked Spanish ambassador Juan Raino to call on Secretary of State William Jennings Bryan on behalf of the condemned Mexican on May 9. Bryan dutifully communicated this request to Governor Colquitt, who still refused to commute the sentence, and on May 11, 1914, León Cárdenas Martínez hanged for the murder of Emma Brown.[24]

Even the obvious insanity of a Mexican murderer did not deter the vigorous pursuit of a death sentence. In San Antonio during the summer of 1921, fourteen-year-old Theodore Bernhart and a group of boys teased and threw rocks at a demented Clemente Apolinar Partida as he drank from a small spring. Infuriated, Apolinar retaliated by catching Bernhart and crushing his head with a rock and gouging out his eyes. As a boy, Apolinar's family had committed him to an insane asylum after his skull was cracked by a blow to the head. The San Antonio Mexican community wanted to have Apolinar declared mentally incompetent, but an all-white jury found him guilty of first-degree murder, and Partida became the last person to hang legally in Texas at Huntsville in February 1923 (the electric chair was used after this). The Mexican government did not become involved because Apolinar was born in Texas.[25]

Seemingly unmeritorious cases became causes célèbres, not simply because the death penalty threatened the life of a *paisano* but because the ordeal also romantically captured the imagination of the community. In 1923, Frank Cadena, in a drunken state, killed his sister-in-law after she spurned his advances. Sentenced to hang, his case was unsuccessfully appealed after a momentous campaign. Romantic notions tinged the murder, however, a factor that fueled the clemency campaign. Supporters felt that Cadena deserved, at most, a life sentence because they considered death too harsh for one "who was a criminal for love" as one stanza of a corrido written in his honor asserts. Huntsville officials executed him on June 23, 1924.[26]

Rape in Texas could be punishable by death but only one incident exists on record in which this ultimate punishment was assessed against Mexicans. In 1928, Clemente Rodríguez and Ezequiel Servín, both twenty, were sentenced to death for raping and robbing a white girl who attended Breckenridge High School. They hijacked the car driven by the girl's boyfriend, robbed the couple, then raped the girl.[27] San Antonio consul Santibáñez and a community campaign tried to have their sentence commuted but to no avail. Just as for blacks who raped a white victim, Anglos felt compelled to punish such a transgression by a Mexican with death. The state electrocuted Servín and Rodríguez at the Huntsville prison on September 7, 1928.[28]

Police killings brought quick retribution. Victor Rodríguez and Nicandro Muñoz were sentenced on June 19, 1931, to die in the electric chair for killing customs agent Burt Ellison at a Harlingen dance. Officers also implicated José María López, but he received a sentence of ninety-nine years. At the last minute, Governor Ross Sterling provided a reprieve for Rodríguez and Muñoz so that lawyers could appeal on the basis that their original trial lawyer had not been admitted to the bar. Moreover, Rodríguez' father swore that Ellison's real killer had fled to Mexico and that his son did not even attend the dance. The appellate court denied Rodríguez' appeal motion; they heard Muñoz' bid, but then affirmed his death sentence. On October 30, 1931, officials executed both at Huntsville.[29]

Nonetheless, in Texas, community efforts to save the lives of condemned Mexicans resulted in greater success than anywhere else, primarily because of the political links that the Mexican leaders forged with white politicians. As early as 1917 the pharmacist, Francisco Chapa, persuaded Governor James Ferguson to commute the death sentence of Juan Mata and Rosendo Barrera to life imprisonment. The two had been convicted of killing Eugene Smith during a robbery, although the Mexican community believed that the evidence was insufficient. In 1917, La Liga Protectora Mexicana, Chapa, and the Mexican government enthusiastically supported the campaign. Mata's father, however, not satisfied with a commutation, pressed throughout the 1920s for his son's release.[30]

FIGURE 10. PEDRO SÁNCHEZ WITH PRIEST. CONDEMNED TO HANG IN
TEXAS, HE RECEIVED A LAST-MINUTE COMMUTATION, THANKS TO COMMU-
NITY AND MEXICAN GOVERNMENT PRESSURE. REPRINTED, BY PERMISSION
OF MARY JO FRENCH, DAUGHTER OF JESÚS FRANCO, FROM JESÚS FRANCO,
EL ALMA DE LA RAZA, PRIVATE PRINTING IN FRENCH'S FILES.

A double execution of Pedro Sánchez and José Flores for killing a
jailer in Marlin, Texas, was scheduled for January 1921. Defense attorneys, however, maintained that Sánchez never touched the weapon used
to beat the jailer and that his only crime was befriending Flores. This
argument persuaded Governor Jack Campbell to commute Sánchez'
sentence to life after the Mexican government initiated a campaign to
save him. Alvaro Obregón's rise to the Mexican presidency is partially
responsible for this victory because he cultivated a better relationship
with Governor Campbell than Carranza did. This success coincided with
two other major efforts in California and New York (see below).[31]

A Mexican killer could more easily avoid the noose or the chair if
the murder victim was another Mexican. Prison records at Huntsville
show many Mexican convicts imprisoned for various degrees of homicide but most had killed one of their own. Five Mexicans and one white

awaited transfer from the Bexar County Jail to Huntsville in February 1928 to be electrocuted. The governor commuted the death sentence for the white, Pete McKenzie, to life. The Mexicans were Anastasio Vargas, Juan Flores, Ezequiel Servín, Clemente Rodríguez, and Adán Bazán. Only Servín and Rodríguez, convicted of raping a white girl, died.[32] Flores' sentence stemmed from his having killed a Mexican American boy during a store holdup in San Antonio. The mother of the victim, who ran the business, identified him as the killer, but Flores insisted it was a case of mistaken identity. Governor Moody, at the behest of Flores' lawyer, Bartolo Corrigan, gave the convict two reprieves and finally granted commutation because of weaknesses in the original prosecution.[33] Moody provided Vargas, whom the police accused of killing a Mexican woman and beating up her husband, with a commutation after he had received three reprieves. In October of that year, after an intensive community campaign, Vargas was given a full pardon along with four white prisoners.[34]

The successful campaign to obtain commutation of Raúl Ramiro Galván's death sentence in 1936 suggests that at this late date, Mexicans received more consideration when killing a white man than earlier in the century. This was especially significant because Galván, a resident of Ciudad Juárez, was convicted of killing customs agent Ivan Scott during a 1935 shoot-out in El Paso. The Mexican government assumed an active role in seeking clemency but only after prominent Ciudad Juárez and El Paso citizens organized El Comité Pro-Galván and pressed for mercy. A factor in this case is that by the time of Lázaro Cárdenas' presidency, Mexico's diplomatic relations with the United States had improved considerably. When the State Department pressured Texas governor James Allred, Anglo Texans bitterly opposed the commutation. However, when the State Department promised Allred that Mexico would illegally extradite a Mexican American wanted for murder who was holed up in Chihuahua, Allred acceded.[35]

CALIFORNIA

More Mexicans were executed in California in the 1920s than in Arizona and Texas combined; eleven in comparison with four in Arizona and five in Texas. In October 1926 alone, three Mexicans died at the gallows. Various factors could explain this disparity. The most apparent is that as immigration tapered down in the other states discussed above, it increased in California. Of the nineteen Spanish-surnamed individuals hanged between 1893 and 1934 in California, fifteen (79 percent) succumbed during the 1919 to 1934 period. Mexicans composed 16 percent of the total executed during this specific period, exceeding the percentage of Mexican males in the California population in 1930, which was never more than 7 percent of total.[36] Between 1916 and 1918 four Hispanics hanged, but only one of the executions seems to have been contested by the Mexican government. In 1918, Governor William D. Stephens commuted Ladislao Guerra's death sentence to life imprisonment as a result of immigrant and Mexican government pressure.

By 1920, so many Mexicans were on death row throughout the country that this period is characterized by interlinked crusades that gave the saving of Mexicans from the gallows national prominence. One of the most dramatic efforts was waged in California. Jalisco native Simón Ruíz was only seventeen when he killed railroad foreman Tom Miller as he and two other Mexican companions burglarized Miller's house. Ruíz' lawyer maintained that an older man named Eduardo Miranda pressured the impressionable Ruíz and Antonio Varela, his equally youthful *paisano* from Jalisco, to kill the foreman of a railroad work site in Sperry, California. Miller allegedly treated Mexicans like slaves and constantly insulted them.[37] On October 26, 1920, Ruíz and Varela were tried in San Bernardino and found guilty of first-degree murder. Miranda, who was granted immunity, was the star witness. The judge sentenced Ruíz to hang at San Quentin on January 14, 1921, and condemned Varela to life imprisonment.[38]

San Francisco general consul Enrique Liekens, upon learning of Ruíz' ordeal, presented Governor Stephens with a hastily circulated petition, signed by eight hundred Mexicans, asking for a commutation. A life sentence with time off for good behavior would make Ruíz eligible for parole after seven years.[39] Before the scheduled execution on January 14, Alberto Mascarena, who replaced Liekens as San Francisco consul general, continued to press for the commutation. Attorney Antonio Orfila, hired by the consulate, obtained appeals for clemency from the judge who sentenced Ruíz, from the prosecutor, and from all jury members who had found him guilty.[40]

Now the campaign, with the support of Anglos who opposed capital punishment, began to snowball. During January 1921, Julio Arce, editor of *Hispano América,* began a Spanish-language press campaign on Ruíz' behalf. More crucial support, which attracted supporters from outside the Mexican community, came from Fremont Older, publisher of the *San Francisco Call.* He assigned Alma S. Reed, editor of the public welfare section, to the story. Her first installment, replete with color and emotion, appeared the day before the scheduled execution. At the last minute, Governor Stephens ordered that the execution be postponed for fifteen days.[41] Reed, supported by a number of California women's clubs, then lobbied for a state constitutional amendment to abolish capital punishment of minors and continued writing on Ruíz' behalf in the *Call,* which drew more supporters. When the first stay expired, Governor Stephens postponed Ruíz' execution until March 11, 1921. Solicitations poured into Sacramento from the Women's Christian Temperance Union, the California Civic League, Masonic lodges, and the San Francisco Forum. Supporters responded from outside of California as well.[42]

The value of non-Mexican backing was not lost on Consul Mascarena. On March 3, the day a group of prominent San Francisco women met with the governor to ask for clemency, Mascarena noted, "It is hoped that with the help of these women who are so well-known with the authorities of the state that they will obtain a favorable outcome."[43] Pressured by the crusade, Governor Stephens postponed the execution from March 11, 1921, to August 26. Within days, Berkeley legislator and well-known progressive Anna Saylor, supported by a number of California women's groups, introduced a bill in the state assembly to eliminate the death sentence for minors. It passed shortly thereafter. Governor Stephens now had no choice. He could not in good conscience allow an execution of a minor with the new law on the books, even though it did not apply retroactively. On July 1, 1921, the governor commuted Ruíz' sentence to life, and the young Mexican eventually obtained a parole.[44]

Alma Reed, immediately after this campaign, traveled to the Yucatán on an archeological expedition. There she met Yucatán's socialist governor, Felipe Carillo Puerto, who divorced his wife to marry the onetime journalist. Counterrevolutionaries executed Carrillo just two weeks before the wedding, but Reed continued living as a celebrity in Mexico from time to time. Many years later, Reed recounts, a man in his mid-forties approached her and said, "Don't you remember me? I am Simón Ruíz. You saved me from the gallows such a long time ago."[45]

With the Ruíz effort, Mexicans acquired a wealth of experience that was useful in later campaigns to save Mexicans from the gallows. But, as elsewhere, the degree to which the Mexican community and the Mexican government supported clemency efforts depended on a number of factors. In particularly abhorrent crimes, efforts to save a condemned compatriot were not as intense. Gregorio Chávez, a fifty-year-old farm worker from the Imperial Valley, died on March 2, 1923, for the 1922 killing of thirteen-year-old of Jovita Hurtado. Chávez, incensed that his wife left him for Luis Hurtado after years of physical abuse, stalked her with the intention of killing her. In one attempt, the wife narrowly escaped with their two-year-old child. Chávez then went after Hurtado, but when he shot at him, the bullet ricocheted, killing Hurtado's daughter instead. When Chávez hanged, *Hispano América* simply indicated that he "went to the gallows completely serene and asked if the noose would be destroyed." [46]

The well-known effort to save Aurelio Pompa from execution contrasts drastically to the Chávez incident. On the morning of October 19, 1922, at the site of the new Los Angeles post office, Pompa, then twenty-one, killed William McCue, the carpenter Pompa served as a laborer. The prosecution contended that Pompa used tools without McCue's permission and in an ensuing argument, he struck the ambitious young Mexican with his fist and the side of a saw blade. Pompa, according to this version, went home, returned with a revolver, and without warning shot McCue twice, once in the heart. Mexican witnesses, however, swore that a second argument ensued before Pompa took out a gun and shot McCue. Police arrived just in time to prevent white workmen from lynching Pompa. In April 1923, Pompa was convicted of first-degree murder and he received the death sentence.[47] In November, attorney Frank E. Domínguez appealed the sentence, citing errors and a contention that the verdict was contrary to law, but Superior court judge Russ Avery affirmed the original judgment.[48] The Mexican community perceived the slaying as self-defense. An editorial appearing in *Hispano América* captured the highly charged pro-Pompa sentiment:

The threat of the gallows is being brandished in the case
of another Mexican whose name is Aurelio Pompa.
Never mind that he had to kill to protect his own life and
on top of that, half of the jury was in favor of finding
him innocent. For the sake of humanity and love of justice, we must mobilize in order to save that unfortunate.[49]

This sentiment prompted a campaign that netted three thousand dollars, even before the Mexican consul decided to help coordinate fund-raising. Jesús Heras, editor of *El Heraldo de México,* served among the most ardent of supporters. The California Mexican community, Pompa's mother, and even President Obregón's mother pressured the Mexican president to intercede. Obregón then sent an appeal to Governor F. W. Richardson, and supporters gathered 12,915 signatures petitioning for clemency, but Richardson did not commute the sentence. Pompa's execution on March 3, 1924, shocked and grieved the Mexican community, and he became an instant folk martyr.[50]

The Cruz Azul Mexicana of San Francisco arranged for the remains to be taken on a Friday night to an Italian American mortuary, where hundreds of Mexican people who filed past the body also saw Pompa's mother grieving at her son's side the whole night. In Los Angeles, hundreds more viewed the corpse for two nights at the Mexican Undertaking Company. On Monday, Pompa's remains were sent on to Sonora where he was buried in an elaborate funeral at his hometown of Caborca.[51]

Four Mexicans were scheduled to be executed at San Quentin at the end of 1926. Alfonso Rincón and Willy Adams, also known as Guillermo Franco, would hang October 8 for the killing and robbing of T. K. Ullman at his ranch house near Los Angeles. Mauricio Trinidad was scheduled to die October 14 and José Sandoval on November 15. On October 3, La Confederación de Sociedades Mexicanas held a rally at the Los Angeles *placita* to drum up support for the convicts. In a fiery speech, organizer Adolfo Moncada exhorted the crowd of supporters to go to the Confederación office and sign petitions urging clemency. Los Angeles consul Francisco A. Pesquiera sent Vice Consul José Quijano to appeal directly to Governor Richardson.[52]

Of the four, Trinidad's circumstances generated the most sympathy. He had killed Luis Hernández in Colton during 1925, but a witness who disappeared supposedly could have corroborated Trinidad's claim of self-defense. Then his lawyer addressed the jury for only ten minutes, did not call a single witness to testify, nor did he question any of the prosecution's witnesses. Immediately, fund-raising began to hire a competent lawyer. In northern California, El Comité de Defensa de Mauricio Trinidad of Richmond, the Sociedad Cruz Azul Mexicana, the Club Chapultepec and the Comisión Honorífica Mexicana of San Francisco joined the effort. In Los Angeles, such organizations as La Liga Protectora Mexicana and La Confederación de Sociedades Mexicanas raised funds as well. The newspapers *Hispano América* of San Francisco, *El Heraldo de México,* and *La Opinión* of Los Angeles enthusiastically provided publicity. Trinidad's new lawyer was hired too late for an appeal, so countless petitions descended on Governor Richardson, who remained oblivious to the supplications. Trinidad hanged as scheduled on October 14, 1926. Nonetheless, the efforts to save Trinidad demonstrated that by the mid-1920s a significant network of ethnic solidarity now spanned the state.[53]

With maturity within *colonia* institutions, the ability to obtain clemency for California Mexicans improved. In September 1928 Tomás Alvarez was scheduled to die alongside Earl J. Clark, a San Pedro, California, bootlegger and pimp who killed a sailor and robbed him. Governor C. C. Young gave Alvarez, who had killed his common-law wife while drunk, a last-minute commutation, primarily because of efforts made by the Mexican consulate. Clark hanged.[54] Another successful effort came in the 1934 case of Apolonio Campos, whom the police arrested for the shooting death of Ignacio Núñez in Blythe. Apparently Riverside County attorney Karl Redwine offered him a life sentence in return for a guilty plea. Nonetheless, Judge O. K. Morton sentenced Campos to death, despite an affidavit sworn by Campos' attorney, John Waite, that he had agreed to the plea bargain.[55] Governor Frank Merriman commuted his sentence after Secretary of State Cordell Hull, at the behest of Ambassador Fernando González Roa, made the request.[56]

OUTSIDE THE SOUTHWEST

At least twenty-three executions of Hispanics took place in states outside the Southwest between 1910 and 1930; most were probably Mexican. In Illinois, which had the majority of the Mexicans in the Midwest, only two hanged between 1920 and 1935. As shall be seen below, there would have been two more if it had not been for escape attempts. New York, with a much smaller Mexican population, sent three Mexicans to the electric chair in the 1920–1935 period.[57]

One of the most intensive efforts to save condemned Mexicans came in the cases of Agustín L. Sánchez and Enrique García, who were scheduled to die at New York's Sing Sing Prison in January 1921. The Mexican government and the expatriate community throughout the United States mustered extraordinary but unsuccessful efforts to persuade two New York governors to commute the sentences. García claimed he acted in self-defense when he killed a man named Andrew during a New York City fight. An Olean, New York, jury found Sánchez guilty of killing a Spaniard, José Lizarraga, on September 19, 1919. According to Sánchez, a man and a woman killed Lizarraga in a mugging attempt as he and his Spanish friend walked through an Olean park. Police found a comb belonging to Sánchez at the scene, and the jury did not believe his story.[58]

Mexican government efforts to save the two started in April 1920, before Venustiano Carranza's ouster from the Mexican presidency. The governor of Tamaulipas, Sánchez' native state, requested clemency directly from Secretary of State Bainbridge Colby because Carranza had severed relations with Washington. Colby transmitted the request to

Governor Alfred Smith, who promised to review the case, but only after it had undergone the appeal process.[59] After Carranza's demise, the Mexican government's ability to affect the treatment of expatriates improved. In December 1920, after García's appeal was denied, Manuel Téllez, Obregón's representative in Washington, continued to request a commutation from Governor Smith. New York consul general Ramón P. de Negri also appealed directly to Smith, who took no action and devolved the petitions to Governor-elect Nathan A. Miller.[60] De Negri, with the help of New York City criminal lawyer Grace Hamilton, continued the clemency efforts after Miller took office. The governor rejected the first petition, saying the original judgment was affirmed by the appeal court. De Negri sent a telegram to Miller begging him to reconsider, but the governor insisted he could not put clemency above the law nor could he interfere with court procedure.[61]

In the meantime, Manuel Téllez sent an emotional protest to Colby complaining that Governor Miller disregarded "thousands of petitions sent to him . . . by humane and educational societies, labor organizations, and some Governors of this Great Union, His Excellency the Governor of Panama, and even the very employers for whom Sánchez worked."[62] De Negri, suspecting García to be deranged, persuaded Governor Smith, before his term expired, to have García tested; he was deemed competent to be executed. A few days before the execution, however, Grace Hamilton told the press that newly discovered evidence demonstrated Sánchez' innocence and continued to insist that García was mentally deranged. De Negri then asked for a reprieve but Governor Miller refused to familiarize himself with the case because delays would bring the justice system into disrepute.[63]

Meanwhile, Consul de Negri conveyed to various consulates the urgency of mobilizing local constituencies to participate in the campaign. In response, Mexican women in New York's Círculo de Santa Teresa organized fund-raisers and appealed for clemency from Smith. *La Prensa* of San Antonio, whose circulation extended widely outside of Texas, began a publicity drive. The effort soon centered on Sánchez because his plea seemed more convincing. Multiple petitions were sent from throughout the country to the state house in New York. *La Prensa* publicized a letter from Sánchez' mother to Governor Smith imploring him to grant mercy to her son.[64] Francisco A. Chapa, editor of *El Imparcial de Texas,* sent telegrams to governors of New Mexico, Arizona, Mississippi, California, and Colorado to persuade them to ask for clemency. San Antonio's Pan American Round Table, a group of Anglo and Mexican American businessmen and the Anglo American Chamber of

Commerce in Mexico City also joined in raising funds and in petitioning Governor Miller.[65] In San Francisco, Consul Enrique Liekens and *Hispano América* mobilized the Bay Area Mexican community, which was in the in the midst of trying to save seventeen-year-old Simón Ruíz (see above). Countless letters, petitions, and telegrams were sent to President Woodrow Wilson from hundreds of Mexican organizations, in itself a remarkable demonstration of consular networking and México Lindo solidarity. Even Cuban cigar workers sent a petition from Tampa, Florida.[66]

Lack of diplomatic recognition, however, weakened the hand of President Obregón, who replied to one of de Negri's cables by saying that he regretted "that at the moment it is difficult to intervene because we do not have an ambassador in Washington."[67] Nonetheless, pressure from Sánchez' mother, brother, and labor unions forced Obregón to stay on track.[68] E. Martínez, secretary general of the Comité Regional de Obreros Mexicanos (CROM), wrote the president asking for intervention, emphasizing that Sánchez had been a union mechanic in Linares, Nuevo León.[69] Obregón, in his rise to power, had become greatly indebted to Mexican organized labor, and he could not easily ignore such requests.

In December, Obregón turned to American border governors he had befriended as he rose to prominence—W. P. Hobby of Texas, Octaviano A. Larrazola of New Mexico, and Thomas E. Campbell of Arizona. Directing telegrams at the three, he indicated that lack of recognition had tied his hands and that he needed their intervention. The governors immediately solicited clemency from Governor Smith, who replied that the case now devolved to Governor-elect Nathan Miller. Further requests to Miller simply elicited the stock response that he had the case under careful consideration.[70]

Manuel Téllez then tried unsuccessfully to persuade the Supreme Court to issue a writ of habeas corpus in the Sánchez case, but to the dismay of the thousands of clemency supporters the execution took place on January 28, the first during Miller's term. President Obregón called for a day of mourning and declared that no work would be done in government offices as a symbol of protest.[71] García insisted until the very end that he killed Andrew in self-defense. In a handwritten will, Sánchez professed his love for his mother and left her his belongings: a watch, a gold chain, and clothes.[72]

In Illinois during 1927, Mexican organizations marshaled another well-publicized attempt to save a Mexican from execution. Roberto

Tórrez was convicted and given the death sentence, along with six other convicts, including two Mexicans, for the slaying of Deputy Warden Peter M. Klein during an escape on May 5, 1926, from Joliet State Prison. After a number of other escapes and killings during escape attempts, only three of the original seven, Roberto Tórrez, Charles Duschowoski, and Walter Staleski faced the gallows (see Chapter 9). On July 16, 1927, the three became the last persons to hang in Illinois. Until the final moment, South Chicago Mexican residents fruitlessly continued their efforts to save Tórrez. Chicago consul A. L. Mondragón and Tórrez' lawyer, Mary Lee Spencer, for example, made last-minute appeals to Governor Len Small.[73]

Six hundred observers crowded eagerly into the jail yard, pushing, shoving, and showing passes that had required influence to obtain. Outside the jail, an estimated thousand persons awaited official word that the execution had taken place. In the crowd were Consul Mondragón and Mary Lee Spencer. Both had just returned from a futile all-night effort to find a judge who would issue a writ for a stay for Tórrez, whom they claimed had gone mad. Indeed, the convict, who had been a singer, seemed demented. Reportedly, he asked the Will County sheriff, as he lowered the noose around his head, if he wanted to hear "La Paloma." At a signal that the men were dead, Chicago paperboys with preprinted editions hit the streets hawking the news to hundreds of customers who clamored to get copies. At least fifteen thousand persons filed past their bodies at the Joliet Funeral Home, and the police had to be called in to keep order. Among the mourners stood members of the Joliet Mexican *colonia* and other Mexicans who made the trip from Chicago. They came to see Tórrez' remains because he, along with the two other Mexicans, had become a hero in three escape attempts—one escaped prisoner, Bernardo Roa, was never recaptured (see Chapter 9).[74]

9| DOING TIME FOR MEXICANS IN THE UNITED STATES

LAW AUTHORITIES in the United States arrested between 15 percent and 20 percent of the Mexican immigrant population, mainly male, during the period from 1900 to 1930. Although it is difficult to determine how many of those arrested actually spent time in a cell, it can be assumed that most did. A smaller number were convicted and confined to state or federal prisons, an experience that altered their lives more dramatically. Incarceration for Mexicans in the United States reflected their overall experience in the country. Non-Mexican prisoners and personnel treated them with disdain, officials segregated them from whites, and job assignments reflected the labor segmentation common outside the confines of jails. In addition, the complaints of the Mexican government, the experiences of the immigrants themselves, and the observations of researchers of the period are unanimous in declaring that Mexicans tended to serve more jail time than the general population.[1]

With stability and longer-term residence, the likelihood of Mexicans being imprisoned lessened. This occurred within a differential timetable where the possibility of jailings tapered off first in the older *colonias* of the Southwest and declined last in areas of new immigration.

LOCAL JAILS

More Mexicans spent time in local jails than in state or federal penitentiaries. In municipal and county lockups, turnkeys lacked training, conditions were filthy, and food was abysmally inadequate. Moreover, officials put Mexicans in these "hoosegows" more often than members of other groups, mainly because of their precarious economic condition. Paul Warnshius pointed out that in Chicago during the 1920s the inability to pay fines for minor offenses landed most Mexicans in jail: "$10 . . . would be [a] huge fine especially if it meant . . . going to the Bridewell [lockup] for lack of cash . . . leaving his wife and children to keep the wolf from the door the best they could."[2] Consular official

Enrique Santibáñez wrote in a 1930 book that "the Mexican is held in jail indefinitely because he is so poor that he cannot pay his fine, unlike the sheriff who shoots down a Mexican."[3]

Vagrancy arrests rid the streets of unemployed Mexicans during economic downturns, but law officials used it for more pernicious purposes as well. In Texas, a common practice was to attach arrested Mexicans to private employers who paid off fines in return for chattel labor. A Grayson County deputy sheriff on January 25, 1923, arrested eight Mexicans on vagrancy charges as they waited to be picked up at the Denison train station after they had been sent there by a Houston employment agency. Not understanding the proceedings, they signed a form waiving their rights to a hearing before a judge and were delivered to a private contractor on a road project. The gang foreman beat one of the Mexicans, Octavio Escutia, because he worked too slowly, charged the report. At night, they tried to sleep in a locked "narrow and malodorous pen" with five black prisoners, where they remained "squatting as there [was] very little space."

"ILLEGAL ALIENS" IN LOCAL JAILS

During economic slumps, border-area jails were filled beyond their capacity. During the 1908 recession, the consul in Naco, Arizona, protested that immigration agents crammed detained Mexicans into a hermetically sealed, twenty-by-fifteen-foot wooden structure. At the consul's behest, María González, a woman nursing a one-year-old baby, was taken out and put in more comfortable quarters.

In 1929, labor markets were again saturated and no relief appeared in sight. Congress now passed an act making illegal entry punishable by up to two years in prison, a one-thousand-dollar fine, or both. The law gave amnesty to Mexicans living illegally in the United States since 1921 and allowed them to apply for citizenship, but the majority of Mexican immigrants without resident status had entered after that date. Secretary of Labor William Doak launched a nationwide campaign in which both local police and federal agents rounded up and locked up undocumented aliens, mainly first-time immigrants from Central Mexico, with common criminals for two or three months before deporting them.[4]

BRUTALITY IN LOCAL JAILS

Mexican immigrants complained more about mistreatment in local jails than they did about state prisons, especially in Texas. In March 1914, a

Mexican in Giddings wrote the general consul in San Antonio about the woes of his friend Calistro Castro:

They took him prisoner and threw him in jail for nothing, where the jailer insulted then shot him point blank
while still in his cell, inflicting serious wounds. Castro
still has two years to serve out his sentence. Consul, we
crave justice! We want to be heard, we want to prove our
honor and patriotism! We want these indignities to end![5]

Unfortunately for Mexicans in Giddings, Mexico's diplomatic influence was at a low ebb and the San Antonio consul did not respond to their plaintive request. The United States invaded Veracruz the following month, and the Foreign Ministry became distracted with propaganda and diplomatic issues. Moreover, it refused to provide travel money to the consul to travel to Giddings.[6]

One of the greatest jailhouse tragedies involving Mexicans occurred in the El Paso County jail during March 1916, two months after the Santa Ysabel massacre. According to officials, someone lit a cigarette as convicts bathed with gasoline to get rid of lice. The subsequent explosion engulfed the jail in flames. Freshly doused convicts lit up like dry tinder, a report said—nine died. The El Paso mayor blamed the prisoners for negligence, but the Mexican community suspected that someone intentionally set the fire to avenge Villista atrocities.[7]

DOING HARD TIME—MEXICANS IN U.S. PRISONS

Mexicans dominated penitentiaries in the Southwest after the Anglo takeover, but incarceration of Chinese, Anglos, blacks, and criminals from other ethnic groups reduced their proportion within a few years. Because of immigration, by 1900, the Mexican share had increased dramatically.

In 1882, seventeen of the sixty-six prisoners at the Arizona Territorial Prison were Mexicans. When the new Arizona Territorial Prison in Florence opened in 1910, the 279 Mexican convicts detained there made up 60 percent of the population. Arizona's Mexicans then stood at no more than 30 percent of the total population for the state.[8] Throughout the 1910s, the majority of Hispanic convicts in Arizona were Mexican-born. By 1920, about 76 percent of the ethnic Mexican proportion, which remained 60 percent of the total, came from Mexico. The steady increase from the 1880s to the 1920s reflected the continuous arrival of

FIGURE 11. GUARDS AND MEXICAN PRISONERS IN FRONT OF A CELL BLOCK AT ARIZONA STATE PRISON AT FLORENCE. REPRINTED, BY PERMISSION, FROM THE JOSEPH AND GRACE ALEXANDER COLLECTION, ARIZONA COLLECTION, ARIZONA STATE UNIVERSITY LIBRARIES.

new immigrants from Mexico to Arizona's modernizing sectors. Paul Warnshius indicated "recent immigrants have the odds against them in their attempt to be law-abiding, hence the proportion of crime is likely to be larger than those who have been in this country a longer period of time."[9]

As the proportion of the Mexican-born population decreased from previous years or became older, the number of imprisoned Mexicans declined notably. The Phoenix Mexican consul in 1929 reported only 97 Mexican-born men out of about 150 ethnic Mexicans at the Florence penitentiary. The other 225 prisoners were non-Mexican; it was the first time since the 1880s that Mexicans were a minority in the system. The Phoenix consulate took some of the credit for the decline, claiming its intervention had led to many releases (see below). More important is that the aging of both Mexican-born males and the coming of age of Mexican Americans combined with the slowing of immigration, meant

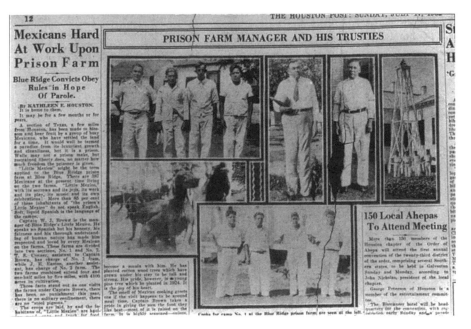

FIGURE 12. CLIPPING OF ARTICLE ABOUT BLUE RIDGE FARM FROM THE *HOUSTON POST,* JULY 17, 1932. THE ARTICLE PAINTS A SANITIZED PICTURE OF LIFE ON THE FARM. COPYRIGHT 1932 HOUSTON POST. ALL RIGHTS RESERVED. REPRINTED WITH PERMISSION.

that the ratio of incarcerated U.S.-born Mexicans to those born across the border started to shift.[10]

Statistics on imprisoned Mexicans in Texas before 1920 are difficult to come by, but it is likely, judging by the Arizona example, that as immigration abated in the 1920s, the number of those incarcerated declined. In 1926, for instance, only about 10 percent of the 3,063 convicts in the system were Mexican, about the same as their share of the state's population. Authorities imprisoned blacks disproportionately, however, while the incarcerated white population stood much smaller than their overall level in the state. In 1926, various facilities housed Mexicans, but the Blue Ridge Farm near Houston, with 253 convicts, was exclusively for first-time Mexican offenders. As in other prisons during this time, only a small number of the Mexicans at Blue Ridge understood English—the majority came from Mexico.[11]

In California during 1854, Mexicans, South Americans, and native *californios* composed about 12 percent of the two hundred convicts at San Quentin. By the end of the nineteenth century, the proportion of imprisoned Mexicans rose, and it continued to grow during the first two decades of this century. In 1919, Ramón P. de Negri, Mexican consul general at San Francisco, visited San Quentin and claimed that Mexicans composed almost one-fourth of the convict population, which stood at about fifteen hundred, but according to Governor C. C. Young's Fact-Finding Committee, only 13 percent of the convicts at San Quentin were Mexican that year. This source also indicates that by 1929 the proportion remained about the same, although the Mexican population almost quadrupled in California during the decade; as in other states, the Mexican prison population declined. In the Folsom Penitentiary, which housed a recidivist population, Mexicans accounted for only 6.6 percent of the convict population in 1929 (2,083 total), much lower than their proportion of the general prison population in California.[12] Unlike the ratio in Texas, however, Mexicans imprisoned in all California prisons represented a larger proportion than their overall population in the state.

In the Midwest, imprisonment of Mexicans in the 1920s was even more disproportionate than in the Southwest. Jackson State Prison in Michigan as of March 1927 held thirty-six men born in Mexico, 1 percent of the total prison population; the overall Mexican population in the state was .01 percent of the total in 1930. And this figure did take into account that other Michigan facilities housed other Mexican felons. Paul Warnshius' study showed that during the 1920s Mexicans in Illinois state prisons declined slightly, from fifty-five in 1924 to forty-six in 1930; about 90 percent of both counts came from Mexico. Significantly, the number of Mexican prisoners fell even as the Illinois Mexican population increased. Regardless of the decrease, in 1930 Mexican convicts composed about 1 percent of the total prison population although composing only 0.004 of the Illinois population. There is no way of determining the Illinois Mexican population for 1924, but it was probably smaller than in 1930, making their imprisoned proportion higher. A more dramatic decline occurred at the Kansas State Prison in Lansing. In 1916, forty-six Mexicans, 5 percent of the institution's inmates, served sentences. Ten years later, however, the facility housed only twenty-eight Mexicans.[13]

WHY MEXICANS WENT TO PRISON

The courts imprisoned few Mexicans for professional or organized crime convictions. Petty larceny, burglary, or crimes of violence predominated in the felony charges lodged against them. Of the ninety-seven Mexican-born convicts in the Arizona State Prison in 1927, fifteen

were convicted of assault—four had used fists or feet, and eleven inflicted wounds with deadly weapons. Fourteen were imprisoned for
homicide—two for first-degree murder. Sex violations and a not-for-
gain crime accounted for eight incarcerations. Petty larceny convictions
put twenty-seven Mexicans in the penitentiary, making it the second
biggest reason for serving long-term sentences. Only three served sentences for armed robbery, usually the crime of professionals. Of the
remaining, thirty-two served sentences for such crimes as arson, kidnapping, property damage, and so forth.[14] Phoenix consul Manuel Payno,
who considered the penalties overly harsh, stated, "Many of these unfortunates have been sentenced, according to what I have been told, to
five, seven and even ten years in prison for minor assaults, nonviolent
robberies, consuming bootleg liquor, etc. etc."[15] Prison records show
that about 140 whites served life sentences or were executed in comparison to 114 Mexicans between 1875 and 1935.[16]

In Texas, violence-related convictions and petty crimes also resulted in long-term imprisonment. The state housed most Mexicans in
the segregated medium-security farm at Blue Ridge, but unfortunately
a breakdown of their crimes is not available. However, the crimes of
ninety-seven Mexicans in the maximum security prison for repeat offenders at Huntsville during 1930 provides an idea of felonies committed
by Texas Mexicans. For example, none were incarcerated for armed robbery, which accounted for 40 percent of the crimes committed by
whites, and less than 1 percent for blacks. Another white man's crime
was forgery, which usually meant passing bad checks or the more skilled
crime of counterfeiting. Forgery accounted for only 1 percent of the total
crimes for Mexicans, 9 percent for blacks, and 17 percent for whites.
More Mexicans served time for homicide (25 percent of their group)
than whites (14 percent) or blacks (15 percent).[17]

The 1919 Mexican consul's report on San Quentin Mexicans did not
state precisely what crimes put the men in the penitentiary. "Many were
arrested for minor violations," the official said, "but because of their
poverty and ignorance they are given long sentences." Three waited on
death row and the rest "are purging long sentences which range from
just a few months to life terms," he said.[18] Paul S. Taylor attributed this
imbalance to Mexicans pleading guilty more often than others and because of their inability to finance a proper defense.[19] More precise data
for Folsom Prison demonstrate that Mexicans went to prison mainly for
impulse crimes or for minor theft and drugs (see Table 10).

In Illinois, violent crimes sent more Mexicans to prison than in
other states. They composed only 1.5 percent of the total number of con-

TABLE 10. MEXICANS IN FOLSOM PRISON BY CRIME, SEPTEMBER 1929

CRIME	TOTAL CRIMES FOR ALL	TOTAL CRIMES FOR MEXICANS	MEXICANS AS % OF TOTAL	% WITHIN MEXICAN GROUP
MURDER, MANSLAUGHTER, ETC.	169	14	8.3	10.1
SEX	117	8	6.8	5.8
ROBBERY	390	10	2.6	7.2
BURGLARY	568	54	9.5	39.1
DEADLY WEAPONS	64	8	12.5	5.8
LARCENY, ETC.	187	15	8.0	10.9
FORGERY, BAD CHECKS	333	3	.9	2.2
POISON ACT (DRUGS, ETC.)	71	11	15.5	8.0
ESCAPES	42	5	11.9	3.6
MOTOR VEHICLE ACTS	59	1	1.7	.7
ALL OTHER	82	9	17.3	6.5
TOTAL	2,082	138	6.6	100

SOURCE: MEXICANS IN CALIFORNIA: REPORT OF GOVERNOR C. C. YOUNG'S MEXICAN FACT-FINDING COMMITTEE, P. 199.

victs in 1924, yet 3 percent of all incarcerated for homicide were Mexicans. Within their own group, 30 percent of all Mexican prisoners served sentences for murder in comparison with 15 percent for Arizona and 22 percent for Texas.[20] Warnshius' study provides insights into the world of Mexicans in Illinois prisons. He interviewed ninety-eight Mexican convicts in various state prisons and in the Chicago Bridewell lockup. Of those, only twenty could afford a lawyer. His research also hints as to what might have made this world so violent. Most of the prisoners were young—64 percent under thirty. Seventy percent were single and had lived in crowded boarding houses, which Warnshius asserted "would many times be productive of crime."[21]

PRISON CONDITIONS

In 1925, the National Society of Penal Information, Inc., conducted a prison study that concluded conditions in U.S. prisons had barely improved from the wretchedness of the previous century. Without exception, medical attention, recreation, living quarters, and quality of prison staff was substandard, even by the modest expectations of the day.[22] In 1917, Texas legislators Frank Holladay, J. G. Nealus, and F. O. Fuller inspected the prisons and announced convicts could expect daily whippings and all kinds of other indignities.[23] Four years later another investigative committee issued a similarly critical report.[24] The outcry notwithstanding, the prison climate changed slowly, if at all. In November 1927, journalist Ernest Booth published an exposé in the *American Mercury* on Texas prison conditions that reverberated throughout the United States. In response, a number of people pressed Governor Dan Moody to reform the system. Chicago attorney Stephen Love wrote Moody and asked him to remedy conditions, "for the sake of humanity." Moody called the story fiction and denied that such conditions existed.[25]

Similar conditions prevailed in California prisons. San Quentin and Folsom officials continued, into the 1920s, such practices as chaining prisoners to the walls, putting them in a wet cell doused with lime that caused fumes to burn nose membranes raw, or keeping the insane in an unwholesome cell block called "Crazy Alley."[26] In the documentary film *Ballad of an Unsung Hero,* the subject, Pedro González, a Los Angeles radio personality imprisoned at San Quentin in the 1930s, remembers a hated punishment in which convicts stood in a sewage-filled cistern on tiptoe to avoid swallowing filth.[27] A reform movement in the 1930s ended many of these abysmal conditions. Arizona seems have initiated reform earlier. By all accounts, circumstances improved in Arizona after the infamous Yuma Territorial Prison shut down in 1909 and was replaced with a more modern facility in Florence.[28]

NON-MEXICANS IN PRISON

These wretched conditions existed for all convicts regardless of background, albeit those with influence fared much better. For example, outside intervention affected white inmates more than racial minorities. The Texas State Archives contain numerous letters from outsiders asking the governor to give special consideration to white convicts, while only two asked for the same consideration for Mexicans.[29] In the influence-ridden atmosphere of Illinois, prisoners with connections lived in relative luxury while guards and other convicts endured abysmal conditions. Some of the prisoners set up shacks in the middle of the exercise yard and openly "sold young offenders as homosexual prostitutes."[30] Warden Joseph E. Ragen complained when he took over the

Joliet complex in 1935 that privileged convicts had special food delivered to their cells, wore expensive civilian clothes, and surrounded themselves with a retinue.[31]

Similarly, at Fort Leavenworth, white prisoners who had acquired considerable influence on the outside before being incarcerated on federal convictions continued to enjoy privileges once in. Charles S. Wharton, an ex-congressman from the Chicago area, wrote a book about his experience at the federal penitentiary where he served three years for a corruption conviction during the 1920s. Throughout the work, Wharton alludes to the influence wielded by white mobsters and about his own relatively privileged position.[32]

Hardly any prison employees were of Mexican background, and the practically all-white guards and officials treated Mexicans with disdain. In 1899, Martín Aguirre became warden and Joseph Aguirre chief of guards at San Quentin, but how these two Los Angeles brothers of *californio* background affected the life of Mexican convicts is unclear. Political detractors mainly singled out their tenure as one riddled with corruption and mismanagement, and they were quickly ousted. In 1930, all the paid personnel at Blue Ridge and Huntsville prisons in Texas were Anglos or blacks. In 1939, of the thirty guards at the Arizona State Prison, three had Spanish surnames.[33]

PRISON LIFE FOR MEXICANS

In 1925, *Hispano América* publisher Julio Arce made an impassioned plea to *colonia* members, the consulate, the ambassador, and California officials to investigate the situation of Mexicans at San Quentin, "an institution where they suffer numerous indignities and prejudices from the personnel and other prisoners alike."[34] Similarly, Charles S. Wharton in his book on Fort Leavenworth admits that blacks, Mexicans, and Indians did not enter the orbit of advantage that he and his white cronies enjoyed. One Mexican who killed another man in a fight spent years in solitary confinement in a "gloomy cell with only one window at the top to give air and a cold half-light. No view of sky or star, no picture to stimulate his imagination, not a word from another human being broke that horrible existence."[35]

Mónico Dúran, a convict serving a life sentence at Huntsville State Prison in Texas, protested to San Antonio consul Enrique Ruíz in April 1921 that guards subjected Mexicans on a daily basis to "cruel indignities." The consul implored Governor Pat Neff to intervene and stop the abuses. The majority of Mexicans in Texas, however, served their sentences at the Blue Ridge Farm, where conditions were worse.[36] In December 1929, the Mexican Embassy protested that the 260 prisoners at the farm served questionably long sentences, performed extremely hard labor, were subjected to floggings, and were attacked by guard dogs. In one incident, Anastasio Reyna fell ill on a farm detail and asked for assistance, but the guards forced him to go back to work. Reyna collapsed with blood gushing out of his mouth and was left to recline on the ground without medical attention. Within an hour, Reyna died from sunstroke, and at sundown his body was carried out of the fields on a horse cart used to transport fodder.[37]

In Arizona, the infamous territorial prison in Yuma had one of the worst reputations in the country. But reforms in the 1910s at the Arizona State Penitentiary in Florence resulted in improvements under George W. K. Hunt, a Progressive governor who also opposed capital punishment.[38] In 1934, Arizona governor B. B. Moeur invited civil rights activist and lawyer Rafael Estrada to visit the prison at Florence and interview the Mexican prisoners. Estrada, a Moeur supporter, probably had a vested interest in concluding that the prisoners "had nothing but warm praise for Warden A. J. Walker, who treated them very well" and that they "received the best of attention, were better fed and clothed and received the best of education." But whatever his motives, fewer complaints about the Arizona prison appear in the sources than for institutions such as those in Texas.[39]

In the Midwest, prison officials treated Mexicans no worse than other prisoners. Paul Warnshius found that Illinois prison guards were not as prejudiced against Mexicans as Chicago policemen.[40] After inspecting local jails in Detroit and the state penitentiary at Jackson, Michigan, in 1927, Detroit consul Joaquín Terrazas concluded that "our compatriots are treated correctly, their cells are clean and the convicts appear well-kempt."[41]

WORK IN PRISON

In May 1916, the editor of *El Cosmopolita* found Mexican convicts worked alongside white prisoners in prison coal mines at the state prison in Lansing.[42] At San Quentin, Mexicans were also not segregated in job assignments, as shall be seen in the discussion on violence below. That the segmentation existing outside the walls followed Mexicans into prison is much more evident in Texas and Arizona. At Huntsville, for example, only whites had such skilled jobs such as electricians, sheet-metal workers, brick masons, or clerks. Most blacks and the small groups of Mexicans worked as cleaners and stewards, or worse, had no work assignments at all.

At the old Yuma facility in Arizona, Mexicans made horsehair relics while Anglos served as carpenters and in trusty positions, which required English skills. During the 1890s, politicians and other public figures hotly debated leasing prisoners, the majority of them Mexicans, to private companies so that they could build canals, highways, and railroads. In 1896, the *Arizona Sentinel* argued for the use of convict labor because "Mexicans commit crimes on purpose to be incarcerated in prison where they get plenty to eat and no work." When the new penitentiary in Florence was built between 1908 and 1911, officials brought groups of convict labor from the old facility in Yuma and housed them in temporary tents. Thirty-five convicts arrived in the searing Arizona summer heat during July and August of 1908 and dug the ditch where the wall foundation was poured. Of those, thirty-one were Mexican. By the time the workers completed the prison in 1909, all the Mexicans from the old Yuma prison had worked at building the prison. The convicts that remained to move all equipment and furniture from the old facility to Florence were white. Only seventy-five non-Mexicans out of two hundred fifty actually saw labor in the building project. In contrast, as early as 1909, and well into the 1920s, work gangs from Florence assigned to contract labor in building roads comprised mainly white convicts.[43]

At the segregated Blue Ridge farm, work assignments for obvious reason were more diverse. Convicts at the four-hundred-acre farm tended rice and sorghum, kept livestock, and were assigned to all tasks necessary to keep the prison working.[44] In 1927, a former convict remembered that a judge and jury made up of prisoners meted out assignments such as cleaning and washing floors for infractions.[45]

EVERYDAY LIFE
Like other convicts, some Mexicans had hobbies to make institutional life bearable. At San Quentin, convict Ramón García painted a life-size painting of Jesus Christ on the laminated wall of his cell, creating a sensation among prisoners of different backgrounds, many of whom prayed before the image. Judge H. T. Dewhurst, who learned about García's talent, helped free him and took a collection from among San Francisco Bay–area friends to send the young convict to art school.[46] Horacio de la Peña wrote poetry in his San Quentin cell. *Hispano América*, in 1919, published one of his poems, "Mi Delito" ("My Crime"), which captured the

experience of many Mexican convicts. The saga reflects de la Peña's road to prison. Unemployed after arriving from Mexico, de la Peña forged a check to pay for three days' lodging in a hotel and to buy food. Although he tried to return part of the ill-gotten money to the check victim after finding work, he was arrested anyway. He received a fourteen-year sentence, but in 1919, the warden recommended de la Peña for parole.[47]

In 1928, Amador M. González, a reader of *La Opinión* while a prisoner in McAlister, Oklahoma, wrote to columnist Rudolfo Arango proclaiming proudly that "until now . . . my record is clean because I want to show American authorities that a Mexican can behave well." He had spent his two years in jail working in the shoe factory and playing in the prison band. Arango wholeheartedly approved and called him a credit to Mexicans in the United States.[48]

Prison officials rarely showed sensitivity to ethnic diversity among the inmates. Lack of cultural sensitivity kept Mexicans from the few activities designed for rehabilitation or recreation. The Joliet Prison library, for example, had thirty thousand volumes in 1930, but only six were in Spanish. In 1917, after *El Cosmopolita* lamented lack of reading materials for the forty Mexican convicts confined at the state prison in Lansing, Kansas, the Mexican consul in Kansas City launched a community campaign to collect books in Spanish for the prisoners.[49]

Still, not knowing English impeded participation in the prison mainstream. An *El Cosmopolita* reporter noted in 1916 that four Mexicans who spoke no English remained in the state prison in Lansing, Kansas, after completing their sentences because they could not fill out release papers.[50] At the Folsom Penitentiary in California, the fact that Mexicans violated prison rules more often was attributed "to a more imperfect knowledge of English than to any general tendency to insubordination."[51] When Paul Warnshius asked a Joliet Prison psychologist if using English tests on Mexicans really measured intelligence, the official replied that not knowing English demonstrated mental deficiency.

Cultural starvation and the necessity to learn English, then, served as an impetus for Mexicans to integrate into American life, even within the prison system. Warnshius believed that Mexicans learned to read and write English at Joliet faster than compatriots who remained in their Chicago enclaves.[52] The most spectacular example is that of Alberto Velasco, in prison for the 1931 killing of a compatriot during a fight in Chicago. Because Velasco did not understand the English proceedings, he did not learn of his life sentence until he arrived at the Joliet State Prison in Illinois. Ironically, while in prison Velasco learned the language and enough law to file a writ of habeas corpus and plead his case before a federal circuit court judge in Chicago, which released him.[53]

PRISON VIOLENCE

Although internecine violence was a major cause for Mexicans going to prison, once in, they mustered more solidarity upon discovering infighting had to be avoided when confronting other inmates and prison personnel.[54] Interethnic rivalry and violence at Joliet occurred mainly between Irish and Italian prison gangs, but prisoners kept it in check themselves through negotiation and truces. Because convicts exerted control, the killer of another inmate feared more from the victim's associates than from officials. Although only a small group, the intensity of Mexican cohesion allowed them to defend themselves adequately at Joliet.[55]

A San Quentin biography indicates that in the 1920s "Mexicans were looked down as 'Mexes,' 'greasers,' and 'chili chokers,' but they were tolerated as long as they kept their own company."[56] But Mexicans did not always comply with this expectation. A fight broke out in February 1925 as twenty Mexicans and thirteen whites walked along a corridor leading to a jute mill where they worked. The guards entered the fray on the side of the white prisoners, beating Mexicans with their clubs. When the tumult ended, both groups had sustained serious injuries but thirty-six-year-old Antonio Hernández lay dead, clubbed to death by a guard. In another fight on the same day, a white was stabbed, and a Mexican suffered severe head injuries. In reporting the battle, *Hispano América* inveighed, "Mexicans have been subjected to ill-treatment by the majority of American inmates to the point that a breaking point had to be reached."[57]

Two months later violence broke out again. Andrés Gómez stabbed Lawrence Mahach, an American Indian, while they cleaned the lavatory. Convicts Harry Allen and Harold T. Smith retaliated by killing Miguel Gómez the following day (no relation to Andrés). Later, two unidentified Mexican convicts stabbed Frank Williams to death. The riots distressed Mexicans on both sides of the border. In Mazatlán, Sinaloa, for example, hundreds of Mexicans demonstrated in front of the U.S. Consulate to demand an investigation into the killings.[58]

But in Huntsville in Texas and in the Arizona prison, Mexicans were kept more separated through labor segmentation and even in segregated cells, thus less friction occurred with other groups. At Blue Ridge, however, they had no choice but to be together and tension among the

Mexicans was intense. There, however, prisoner cliques maintained tight internal discipline and kept violence down to a minimum.[59]

LEAVING PRISON: THE LEGAL WAY

Incarceration for Mexicans could end by one of four methods: being found not guilty or having a conviction overturned, completing a sentence or obtaining parole, escaping, or dying. When freed, authorities always deported them if they had entered the United States illegally. In 1930, Texas officials had retainers for eighty-nine Mexican prisoners awaiting their release to arrest them for other crimes—fifty-six were for illegal entry. At San Quentin, 175 Mexicans scheduled to be released in 1926 were to be deported because they entered the country illegally. Authorities could also expel Mexicans convicted for felonies even if they had legal permanent residency. Significantly, parole boards always seemed more amenable to freeing Mexicans on the condition that they be evicted from the country.[60] Mexican convicts welcomed any kind of release from prison, even if it meant banishment.

Even so, such discharges were difficult to obtain. In Arizona, white prisoners who received a parole or whose life sentence was reversed, spent about a year and a half less in prison, on the average, than the Mexicans who gained similar releases.[61] In 1921 when "law and order" candidate Pat Neff was elected governor of Texas, he eliminated the parole board; only executive clemency could now provide early releases. *El Imparcial de Texas* protested that clemency would require political influence, which, for Mexicans, was hard to come by. Eight years later, Dallas lawyer T. Gorre and Professor Ira P. Hildebrand, a Southern Methodist University prison reformer, complained that only outside influence brought hopeful prisoners to the governor's attention.[62]

Although 10 percent of Huntsville's population was Mexican, Mexicans received only about 3 percent of the early discharges and furloughs given convicts between 1927 and 1930.[63] In 1928, Huntsville prisoner Manuel González Abalardo, after serving fifteen months of a two-year sentence for smuggling aliens, complained to the San Antonio consul that officials released white inmates after serving only a year of a comparable sentence. With the consul's help, three months after writing his letter González gained his freedom, but immigration officials immediately deported him.[64]

Because of this discrimination, the Mexican Foreign Ministry announced periodically that its consulates would serve as advocates for early releases. In 1914, *La Prensa* indicated that the Mexican government would attempt to obtain freedom for Mexicans in Texas prisons and have them returned to Mexico. When Alvaro Obregón assumed the presidency in 1921, he gave clemency to thousands of convicts in Mexico and suggested that Mexican prisoners in the United States be given the same consideration.

More successful intervention efforts came later in the decade when the Mexican Foreign Ministry implemented a more systematic approach to helping Mexican convicts. In 1929, San Diego consul Enrique Ferreira arranged for car thief Guadalupe Rivas to be expelled to Ciudad Juárez instead of Manzanillo, Colima, after Rivas' mother pleaded that her son needed to be with relatives in Ciudad Juárez because of an epileptic condition.[65] Kansas City consul Alfredo C. Vásquez convinced the Kansas Parole Board to free Ramón Navarro in 1930 after he served eight years of a twenty-two-year armed robbery sentence in the state penitentiary. In May of the same year, a South Dakota court dropped charges for lack of evidence after Consul Vásquez provided an attorney for murder suspects Nicolás Unzueta, Manuel Cardones, and Humberto Contreras. They had been arrested in the killing of an Anglo in Fort Robinson the previous year.[66]

The greatest advocacy efforts were made in Arizona, where the disproportionate jailing of Mexicans propelled a community campaign that pressured consular officials to obtain releases. When Governor George W. P. Hunt, known for a "magnanimous" concern for prisoners, lost a reelection bid in 1928, Phoenix consul Manuel Payno persuaded the lame-duck governor to pardon a number of Mexicans imprisoned for minor crimes.[67] Also, the popular crusade to save Alfredo Grijalva, convicted with Antonio Padilla of the 1926 killing of a customs agent, prompted other efforts to get early releases in Arizona. Payno presented a petition signed by over one thousand people to the Board of Pardons and Paroles on May 15, 1929, pointing to the suffering of Grijalva and his family and to the numerous errors in his case. Grijalva's wife died of consumption while he was in prison and his children had to be supported by public charity. Even so, the board did not discharge Grijalva.[68] In July 1930, persistent consular officials renewed their efforts but to no avail. In March 1933, the board again considered Grijalva's release. José E. Torres, now the Tucson consul, and prominent Arizona Mexicans attended the meeting to influence the proceedings. Again, the board declined clemency to the model prisoner.[69] Finally, the board paroled Grijalva on June 14, 1935, and he was immediately deported. Eight other Mexicans received paroles that year.[70]

LEAVING PRISON: ESCAPE

If Mexicans found it difficult to obtain paroles and furloughs, escape became an alternative. Often underpaid guards took bribes to look the other way while convicts prepared their departure. Guards were also distracted by the large amounts of gambling, drinking, and other vices available inside prisons. Convicts found Texas jails among the easiest to bolt. A white bank robber serving a ninety-nine-year sentence escaped in 1928, prompting A. Spears, a bank cashier from Cisco, to write to Governor Moody deploring the frequency of breakouts.

The more alienated Mexicans harbored an even greater desire to escape. The underfunded and porous Blue Ridge Prison was a particularly abhorrent facility. No more than an open farm, Blue Ridge had far too few guards and barricades to keep Mexicans from abandoning what was their worst experience in the United States.[71] Once out, Mexicans in Texas had a good support network—that is, family or friends and large barrios where they could more easily disappear. Moreover, escapees could easily return to Mexico if they reached the border. Of fifty-three convicts that fled Texas prisons between March 3 and March 29, 1927, nine had been housed at Blue Ridge. By April 6, ten fugitives still eluded officials; two were Mexicans. Fifty-six convicts escaped between October 30 and November 20 of 1929—eight of them Mexicans from Blue Ridge. Of twenty still at large at the end of November, six came from the Blue Ridge group.[72] On April 10, 1926, while a Blue Ridge guard read a magazine, J. E. Marino and five other convicts slipped out through an opening made by removing a windowpane. They fled to Houston and hid out at a relative's house before hopping a freight train to San Antonio where they spent fourteen days with another relative before being captured. Their freedom lasted a month.[73]

Brutal conditions at the Arizona Territorial Prison in Yuma provoked many escape attempts in the nineteenth century, mostly by Mexicans. Many Arizona Mexicans escaped from the state prison at Florence as well. Of ninety-six Mexican-born prisoners incarcerated in 1927, seven had made escape attempts. Two—Juan Esparza, sentenced to ten years for a Greenlee County robbery, and Francisco Bojórquez, serving two years for larceny in Santa Cruz—were not captured for more than four years. Esparza escaped on March 31, 1920, but officials caught him on February 13, five years later. Bojórquez' stretch of freedom was shorter—from May 1922 to December 1926. Mexicans, it seems, escaped more often than non-Mexicans, probably because for a long time they constituted the majority of those behind the walls. A list of convicts serving life sentences or waiting to be executed at both the territorial and state prisons between 1900 and 1935 shows that seven Mexicans and six non-Mexicans tried to flee.[74]

A dramatic series of Illinois escapes in 1926 and 1927 demonstrates that Midwest Mexicans also supported *paisano* fugitives. In 1924, a Cook County judge sent Bernardo Roa, Gregorio Rizo, and Roberto Tórrez to Joliet after they were convicted of robbing and killing an El train ticket agent. The Mexican community, the Spanish-language newspapers, and the Mexican consul believed that the South Chicago police framed them.[75] On May 5, 1926, the three Mexicans and four white prisoners killed Assistant Warden Peter M. Klein, a former South Chicago policeman, and made their first escape by fleeing into the Will County countryside. Local farmers and townspeople captured all but one of the escapees—twenty-nine-year-old James Price. The posse severely shotgunned Roa, who almost died.[76]

The events angered much of the general public, but among Chicago Mexicans, the fugitives became heroes. Will County officials investigated allegations that Klein belonged to a parole-selling ring headed by Will Colvin, chairman of the Board of Pardons and Paroles. The newspapers also reported that Chicago police had arrested Klein for selling bootleg liquor while still warden and for allowing prisoners to leave the prison and commit robberies so they could raise money for paroles.[77] After a dramatic trial during late November 1926, all six convicts were sentenced to hang on March 11, 1927, in the Will County jail. The judge sentenced James Price to death in absentia. In South Chicago and Joliet, Mexican organizations like the Sociedad Mutualista Guadalupana raised funds so that Roa, Tórrez, and Rizo could appeal, but the three Mexicans quietly prepared for a second escape.[78]

Juanita Gallardo, Roa's South Chicago girlfriend and Greorgio Rizo's brother, Salvador, smuggled files and saws embedded in bananas, apples, and roasted chickens. Roa concealed the tools in the crutches that he used because of his injuries, and while he and Rizo slowly filed the cell bars, Tórrez played the guitar and sang "La Paloma," muffling the sounds of scraping tools. The trio broke out March 11; they had received a stay of execution after forcing a county guard to drive them to East Chicago, Indiana, where the vehicle collided into a telephone pole. They took a taxi for the last leg of the journey to South Chicago, but the police had prepared a trap. In an ensuing gun battle, Rizo, the taxi driver, and two policemen fell. Rizo, who was not expected to live, miraculously pulled through. One of the wounded policemen, Leo Grant, died March 14. Roa, who hobbled away on a crippled leg amidst the gun battle, was hidden and fed by *paisanos* in the sprawling Carnegie Steel Works until "the heat" subsided. He escaped first to Canada, and then to Mexico, where he was never caught.[79] On June 13, 1927, Rizo and Tórrez and the remaining three death-row convicts attempted a third escape from the Will County jail that cost Rizo his life. Charles Schrader, one of the remaining condemned five, was never seen again. Joliet police arrested nine local Mexicans for conspiracy in this final bid. Of the seven indicted in the killing of Klein, only three—Roberto Tórrez, Charles Duschowoski, and Walter Staleski—remained to hang on July 15, 1927.[80]

During the period of the Mexican Revolution, U.S. prisons held many Mexican notables, the most famous being Ricardo Flores Magón, who spent much time in local jails at the Arizona Territorial Prison in Yuma, in the new state prison in Florence, and at the Federal Penitentiary in Leavenworth, Kansas. Victoriano Huerta, once president of Mexico, also purged time in a Texas prison. But Pascual Orozco, the lapsed revolutionary, was the most famous Mexican to escape from an American prison. Federal agents arrested Orozco with Huerta in June 1915 for conspiring, on U.S. soil, to overthrow President Carranza and was imprisoned at Fort Bliss, Texas. He escaped two months later, and a posse killed him and a number of his followers for livestock rustling.[81]

Another Mexican jailed for political reasons who made a dramatic escape attempt was the anarchist William "Wenceslao" Laustauneau. Not as celebrated or as well known as Orozco or the members of the PLM, Laustauneau, A. F. Salcido, and the Italian, Frank Colombo, led the Morenci Copper strike of 1903. Convicted of inciting a riot in the three-day work stoppage where armed workers milled through Morenci making demands, the judge sentenced Laustauneau to two years at the Arizona Territorial Prison. After serving four months, he and four Mexican convicts tried to escape on April 28, 1904, by taking hostages. Guards fired into the group, foiling the escape. Laustauneau received an additional ten years and became an Arizona folk hero among Mexicans and unionists alike.[82]

LEAVING PRISON: DEATH

The ultimate way of leaving prison or jail was death, and execution was the most public of prison deaths. But more often, convicts succumbed from confinement-related illnesses and poor medical attention. Local lockups had woefully inadequate medical facilities, but the larger in-

FIGURE 13. WILLIAM H. "WENCESLAO" LAUSTAUNEAU'S MUG SHOT TAKEN
AFTER HE WAS IMPRISONED AT THE ARIZONA TERRITORIAL PRISON IN
YUMA, ARIZONA, IN 1903. REPRINTED, BY PERMISSION, FROM MARTHA M.
MCELROY, "WILLIAM H. LAUSTAUNEAU: MENACE OR MARTYR," CHICANO
RESEARCH COLLECTION, ARIZONA STATE UNIVERSITY LIBRARIES.

stitutions also did not provide satisfactory care. At the tuberculosis farm
at Huntsville, where ten of the fifty patients were Mexicans, guards
forced extremely sick prisoners to work, then gave rations of "sour corn
bread, fried mushy biscuit dough, and beans which were not very well
cooked."[83] The deplorable conditions prompted officials, in 1927, to release Pablo Martínez so he could die more comfortably at home.[84]

Convicts also could escape their circumstances by killing themselves. The most notorious jail suicide was that of Juan Reyna at San
Quentin, who had been given a relatively light sentence for the 1931 killing of a Los Angeles policeman. On May 4, 1931, prison officials announced that Reyna stabbed himself to death only five months before he
could apply for a parole.[85] San Francisco consul A. Lubbert, although he
had some doubts about the suicide, at first concurred that Reyna died of
a self-inflicted wound and had "swallowed something corrosive."[86] Im-

migrant leaders speculated that guards murdered Reyna so he would not get a parole. The press in Mexico City and elsewhere in the Mexican Republic gave credence to the speculations and on May 28, R. Cervantes Torres, secretary of the Confederación Regional de Obreros Mexicanos, joined in the chorus of demands for a thorough inquiry.[87] Reyna's family was also convinced of foul play because in his letters to a female friend, to his children, and to his mother, he appeared optimistic about his eventual parole.[88]

Because of the troublesome relationship with the law, Mexicans wound up imprisoned in large numbers in every state where they worked, and their treatment while jailed reflected the general prejudices that Anglo Americans had for Mexicans. Consequently, the community, especially the Mexican government, sometimes with success, pressured state governments to affect reform. The number of imprisoned Mexicans decreased as the immigrant communities acquired greater longevity and better defense mechanisms. The final chapter of this book treats extradition. Once a wanted Mexican, sometimes an innocent one, crossed the border, he was relatively secure from extradition. The reasons for this had much to do with reluctance of Mexican authorities to return fugitives to face American justice. Still, the desire to nab Mexicans who had committed crimes in the United States led to arbitrary, sovereignty-violating procedures.

10| EXTRADITION BETWEEN MEXICO AND THE UNITED STATES

SINCE THE NINETEENTH CENTURY, Mexican criminals in the United States have sought refuge by crossing the border into Mexico. Once there, they became relatively secure from extradition, mainly because of the reluctance of Mexican authorities to return fugitives to face American justice and because of an inadequate and unclear extradition policy. But, as shall be seen below, American authorities also resisted returning U.S. citizens who committed crimes in Mexico. An extradition arrangement with Mexico had been signed in 1861, but the process broke down during the French Intervention. Besides, in this agreement the responding country was not obliged to turn over its nationals to the requesting country.[1] In 1869, the U.S. emissary in Mexico, Nelson Perkins, requested permission to allow American authorities to pursue Comanches and Kickapoos who raided ranches on the Texas side of the border. The Department of State claimed that Benito Juárez had agreed to this in 1866 when he found himself in El Paso del Norte (Ciudad Juárez) beleaguered by Maximilian's forces and in need of American help. Juárez, now ensconced in Mexico City with Maximilian long executed, replied that he, as president, could not make such a decision. Only the Mexican Congress could do so.[2]

The most sustained impetus for an extradition arrangement came from Texas authorities during the 1870s when border livestock rustling was rampant. In 1877, Texas governor Richard Coke pleaded before the U.S. Senate to have two regiments of cavalry stationed in his state because of incessant raids. "American stock raisers who could do so abandoned their ranches and sought safety in the towns," he lamented. Wealthy Mexicans south of the border encouraged cattle rustling forays, alleged Coke, a practice common since the Juan Nepucemo Cortina raids in the late 1850s. A wealthy landowner, Cortina ran afoul of the law in Brownsville and retreated into northern Tamaulipas; from there he conducted bandit raids into South Texas. The hands of law officials in

Texas were tied, asserted Coke, because bandits simply slipped back into Mexico.[3]

In reality, U.S. Army troops and Texas Rangers regularly chased Indians and Mexicans who drove Texas cattle across the Rio Grande, extradition treaty or no. Mexico consistently protested these extralegal pursuits, but eventually the Díaz government gave permission for American soldiers and Texas Rangers to make arrests in Mexico only if apprehension was done in "hot pursuit."[4] Even so, the arrangement did not allow for extradition of criminals who escaped into Mexico undetected or were not caught when being pursued. Moreover, Mexican officials only returned U.S.-born suspects attempting to find refuge in Mexico. Governor Richard Coke, finding the agreement unsatisfactory, recounted an incident in which a Tamaulipas judge refused to return four Mexican bandits who killed Americans in two different Texas counties. After a number of delays, Mexico and the United States signed a more binding treaty on February 22, 1899. It identified extraditable crimes and stipulated the bilateral steps necessary to request return of wanted criminals. Significantly, the agreement did not allow either nation to deny a request if the fugitive was a citizen of the responding nation. The treaty's provisions were only infrequently applied, however. Americans found the flexible, hot-pursuit policy the most useful instrument for returning suspects from Mexico.[5]

After the fall of Díaz, all agreements collapsed and retrieving suspects without the Mexican government complaining or resisting became more difficult than ever. During May 1911 in the Arizona mining town of Silver Bell, a Mexican circus performer known as *el payaso* (the clown) Quintero killed a compatriot in a fight and escaped to Mexico. To catch Quintero, Deputy Sheriff Edward S. McCuen followed Quintero's wife, whom he had left behind in Silver Bell, to his hiding place in Imuris, Sonora. McCuen arranged for Quintero to be jailed in Nogales, Sonora, until Arizona officials filed extradition papers. Díaz' government, collapsing under Francisco Madero's challenge, ignored the requests. When rebels took over Nogales and opened the doors to the local *calabozo,* Quintero escaped—*el payaso* was never seen again.[6]

A cursory look at diplomatic records for this period shows that extradition requests from both governments abounded, but they do not seem to have been honored by either nation.[7] After Pascual Orozco's failed attempt to oust Madero in 1912, his supporters resorted to raiding into Texas for supplies and cattle. At first U.S. troops along the border showed restraint in pursuing rustlers because, unlike conditions in the

Porfiriato, U.S. soldiers now risked clashing with revolutionary armies if they crossed the border. An aggravated Secretary of State Philander Knox wrote to Ambassador Henry Lane Wilson in Mexico City late in 1912, asking him to persuade the now more nationalistic Mexicans to allow more latitude.[8] But as border banditry increased in the 1910s, respect for Mexican sovereignty declined proportionately. This prompted a steady string of accusations, which U.S. officials routinely denied, often with transparent alibis.

Military reactions to bandit incursions reached a high point in 1919. Relations strained even more as both countries issued a stream of charges and countercharges. According to the Mexican government, on April 1, 1919, American soldiers pursued bandits, who had attacked the Brite Ranch and killed the owner, to San Antonio, Chihuahua. There they captured and shot Hermenegildo Domínguez and also wounded a Señorita Meléndez with a stray bullet. Neither Domínguez nor the woman were given medical attention according to Mexican officials. Troops arrested eight other Mexicans and interned them at Fort Bliss, but after several days, officials released them for lack of evidence. The U.S. Army did detain Domínguez, however, and released him to Texas authorities, not for taking part in the Brite raid but because the previous year he had fled to Mexico after being accused of murder. Ambassador Ignacio Bonillas charged that in pursuing the raiders, soldiers took advantage of the incursion to arrest the Mexican who was convicted of murder.[9] In 1921, Domínguez' lawyers appealed his conviction by arguing that extradition procedures were not followed by either government. The court of appeals affirmed the conviction, however, and Domínguez stayed in a Texas prison.[10]

In a similar incident, troops crossed into Chihuahua in August 1919 to secure the release of two American aviators being held for ransom by an outlaw named Jesús Rentería. Americans ransomed only one of the pilots and then decided to enter Barrancos de Guadalupe to capture Rentería. Unable to find him, they arrested six Mexicans and took them across the border to Marfa, charging them with draft evasion and with belonging to Rentería's band. Within a month, the army released them after an investigation showed they were not guilty of either charge.[11] A week later a party of fifty U.S. soldiers crossed the border heading to the same area "on hot trail in pursuit of Mexicans who had crossed the border . . . and driven livestock belonging to American Citizens." They arrested night watchmen Francisco Jáquez, Esteban Maldonado, and Alberto Venegas. Federal authorities also released them, however, after the

El Paso consul general demonstrated that the "evidence against them was insufficient to warrant their detention." [12] Raids netted eighteen captives within five months. Only one, Hermenegildo Domínguez, was still imprisoned by the end of the period.

The most celebrated and expensive border crossing became Pershing's "Punitive Expedition" designed to arrest Pancho Villa and his officers for the 1916 raid on Columbus, New Mexico. Pershing's troops, using paid informants, captured only twenty Villistas, whose role in the Columbus raid was insignificant. The arrests came under heavy criticism, both in the United States and Mexico, because the U.S. military extradited the men, then delivered them to Luna County authorities illegally [13] (see Chapter 1 for more examples).

During and after the Revolution of 1910, extradition procedure bogged down more than ever, but a succession of Mexican governments, wanting the return of dangerous political foes who found refuge in the United States, gave Anglo American authorities leeway in abducting wanted criminals on Mexican soil. During the revolution itself, practically every faction in power made numerous extradition requests if they believed their enemies to be on American soil. These included such revolutionary figures as Pascual Orozco, Venustiano Carranza, and José Vasconcelos. In the summer of 1913, believing Carranza had crossed into the United States, Victoriano Huerta's government attempted to have him extradited, accusing him of malfeasance while in office as governor of Coahuila. [14]

Mexico continued unsuccessful attempts at retrieving political enemies into the 1920s. Ignacio Morán y Mariscal is an example; he defected to de la Huerta's rebellion in 1923 while consul in Germany, fled to New York when it failed, and became director of the Spanish Publishing Company. During March 1924, Ambassador Manuel Téllez "requested the provisional arrest . . . of Moran with a view to his extradition on the ground that he had unlawfully appropriated $20,000 while acting as consul general of Mexico in Germany." According to a Department of State official, "Moran's extradition was not complied with as the Department took the position that the offense was not committed within the jurisdiction of Mexico." [15] In April 1924, José Ibarra and José Robles, also members of de la Huerta's rebellion, fled to El Paso where police picked them up on vagrancy charges. When the Mexican Embassy learned of the jailing, it demanded their return, but U.S. immigration officials used a technicality to deny the request. The "Mexican government does not demonstrate any reason for this deportation," indicated Carl White, an immigration officer at the Department of Labor.[16] These denials were probably guilt concessions to de la Huerta, who also became an exile. At one time influential Americans supported his uprising when it was unclear if President Alvaro Obregón would tamper with oil properties held by Americans.

Because resorting to legal channels did not work for the Mexican government, they used other methods. In March 1921, Mexican officials traded Manuel Martínez, wanted for murder in Arizona, for Francisco Reina, a Villista general who wreaked havoc in Sonora during a series of 1917 raids. With permission from Arizona officials, Mexican agents crossed to Nogales, Arizona, on November 26, 1921, and seized Reyna, who had taken his pregnant wife to Nogales to get medical attention. Mexican officials quickly tried the former guerrilla leader and executed him.[17]

The most notorious "extradition" was of the land reform advocate from Coahuila, Lucio Blanco. Like Emiliano Zapata, Blanco emerged from the chaos of the Mexican Revolution with an untarnished reputation as being true to his ideals. After Carranza's assassination, Blanco fell from favor among the new ruling clique led by Alvaro Obregón and from his South Texas exile, he plotted to overthrow the government. Mexican agents learned in the spring of 1922 that Blanco's plan to take over Nuevo Laredo military installations and use the border town as a launching pad for further insurrection was gaining many adherents. A worried President Obregón instructed Secretary of the Interior Plutarco Elías Calles to extradite Blanco and arrest him. Early in the morning of June 7, 1922, Calles' agents, posing as weapons purveyors, lured Blanco to the Laredo, Texas, town square and kidnapped him, purportedly to take him across the river to the Mexican side on a raft. The next day, however, Blanco's body was found on the Texas bank of the Rio Grande. John Valls, the district attorney of Webb County, where Laredo is located, and a friend of Blanco, swore revenge. In 1929, when Calles, who had just finished his term as president, planned a visit to Washington, D.C., he had to ask for Department of State intervention to safely enter the United States at Laredo. Valls had issued an arrest warrant for Calles for the murder of Blanco![18]

American officials in the extradition game behaved similarly, albeit not similarly motivated by political considerations. In 1904, a professional smuggler, Antonio Félix, brought a shackled Juan Puebla across

FIGURE 14. THE YOUNG AND CHARISMATIC LUCIO BLANCO CAME FROM THE
ELITE FAMILIES OF COAHUILA, YET HE CHAMPIONED THE COMMON MAN.
HIS EXTRADITION AND MURDER ELICITED MUCH ANGUISH. REPRINTED, BY
PERMISSION OF MARY JO FRENCH, DAUGHTER OF JESÚS FRANCO, FROM
JESÚS FRANCO, *EL ALMA DE LA RAZA,* PRIVATE PRINTING IN FRENCH'S
FILES.

the Mexican border to El Campo, California, at the point of a gun. San
Diego sheriff Charles Hammel, who arrested Puebla on charges of killing a man in a bar fight in Santa Monica during 1898, only to have him
escape, paid Félix to carry out the abduction. Arrested later by Americans for smuggling Chinese, Félix, in musical-chairs fashion, was extradited, probably illegally, and the Mexicans charged him with the kidnapping of Puebla. The Mexican government nonetheless pressed California
officials for the return of Puebla. But Acting Secretary of State Robert
Bacon apprised the Mexican ambassador of a Supreme Court decision
in the 1890s that upheld the arrest of a man named Ker, even though an
Illinois official kidnapped him in Peru and brought him back where
other Illinois officials arrested him.[19] The extradition process went more
smoothly when officials returned fugitives not native to the country doing the expelling.

In 1918, three Anglos escaped the Tombstone, Arizona, jail, robbed the Vásquez Circus Company of eight hundred dollars, and then crossed the border into Sonora. The Mexican government acted quickly to find them and helped Arizona officials comply with the extradition request after the circus owners, who were Mexican citizens, appealed directly to Mexico. In March 1928, California extradited Abraham Kirsh from Mexico for a Los Angeles bank robbery, in a procedure marked by extraordinary cooperation between the Los Angeles Police Department and Mexican officials.

No case appeared in the records examined for this study, however, of an Anglo American who committed a crime in Mexico and who was then delivered to the Mexicans, legally or illegally. During 1932, for example, Baja California authorities pressed for the return of accused murderer Millard K. Davis. His lawyers argued successfully before a federal court in Los Angeles that Davis could not be extradited because the Mexican request used the vague word "homicide," a crime category that in the United States included manslaughter, a nonextraditable charge. To the dismay of Mexican diplomats, the U.S. Circuit Court of Appeals in Los Angeles upheld the lower court's ruling.[20]

Mexican officials resisted returning Mexico's nationals as well. Cochise County sheriff Edward Hood traveled to Hermosillo, Sonora, from Arizona in 1922 to negotiate the extradition of Arcadio Chávez, wanted as an accomplice in the Bisbee murder of Jesse Fisher. Manuel García and José Pérez, already sentenced to life for the killing, had implicated the fugitive. After the killing took place, Chávez crossed the border but at the behest of Cochise County officials was put in an Agua Prieta, Sonora, jail, and "feeling safe," he confessed the murder to the Mexican police. Francis J. Dyer, the U.S. Consul in Nogales, Sonora, protested that Mexican federal officials in Hermosillo were uncooperative, apparently claiming that because the United States did not recognize Obregón's administration, extradition agreements were invalid. The Sonora governor agreed that extradition provisions were suspended, but he still offered to cooperate. Negotiations ensued, albeit without much Mexican enthusiasm. Federal official Jesús P. Ruíz informed the Nogales U.S. consul that a coroner's report was needed and that Cochise officials had sixty days to comply; otherwise Chávez would go free. In the meantime, Chávez' lawyer filed an *amparo* (writ) stating Chávez was being held illegally, and by the time Cochise County officials complied with the Mexican request, a federal judge had freed Chávez.[21]

Still, Mexican authorities, at least before the 1940s, seemed more willing to return their nationals than vice versa. During 1933, Juan Díaz killed his father-in-law, David Duarte, in Phoenix during a drunken altercation and fled to Villa Hidalgo, Jalisco. Duarte's widow went to Consul E. E. Cola and pleaded for his extradition. The consul then made extraordinary arrangements to obtain the capture and jailing of Díaz in Jalisco.[22] In 1935, a judge in Zacatecas turned down an *amparo* request from Rubén Bravo Leal, who had been jailed pending a hearing on an extradition request from the state of Michigan. To the dismay of Hector Delgado Ayala, a Mexico City columnist, Mexican officials allowed Bravo Leal to be taken back to Michigan even though a "writ filed in his behalf stated clearly that compatriots accused of crimes on the other side of the 'border' are unlikely to be given a fair trial."[23]

The amount of red tape involved in extradition and the likelihood that the host country would reject a properly channeled bid prompted authorities on both sides to continue employing illegal means to apprehend wanted fugitives. In 1936, the governor of Chihuahua, mistakenly thinking he had the power under the 1889 treaty to do so, turned Efrén Hinojos over to Texas officials without due hearing.[24] A few years later, Mexican newspapers reported accusations against agents from the Mexican Department of the Interior operating in Nuevo Leon who allegedly turned over Mexican fugitives to Texas authorities for a bribe. Even Ignacio García Téllez, who was secretary of the interior under Lázaro Cárdenas, was implicated in this scandal. He defended himself successfully by saying the accusations were politically motivated by right-wing malcontents in the Mexican Congress.[25] Mexico resorted to this illegal process mainly to return dangerous exiles, whereas the United States continues to this day to use this extralegal method to return fugitives suspected of common crimes.[26]

BERNARDO ROA BERBER: A SLIPPERY EXTRADITION ROAD

The example of a twenty-five-year effort to extradite Bernardo Roa Berber, after his escape from Illinois, provides significant insights into both the legal process and the psychological stimulus that drove the extradition process. Impetus first came from Hjalmar Rehn, the Illinois state attorney who prosecuted the murder case of Assistant Warden Klein during the 1926 jailbreak from Joliet (see Chapter 9). Joseph E. Ragen, who became warden in 1935, continued the quest until 1952.[27]

Roa was born in Santiago Marviato, Michoacán, in 1900. As a boy he lived in La Hacienda de la Toba in the *municipio* of San Francisco de

FIGURE 15. BERNARDO ROA'S MUG SHOT TAKEN WHEN HE WAS FIRST IMPRISONED IN 1924 IN CHICAGO. FROM RECORD GROUP 84, RECORDS OF U.S. FOREIGN SERVICE POSTS, GUAYMAS, MEXICO, OFFICIAL CORRESPONDENCE 1928, VOLUME 3, FILE 200, COURTESY NATIONAL ARCHIVES AND RECORDS ADMINISTRATION, COLLEGE PARK, MARYLAND.

la Rivera, Guanajuato. When he was a teenager, revolutionaries tried to impress him, but he and his brother escaped from the countryside to the relative safety of Mexico City. Like many other boys growing up during this violent era, Roa lived outside the law. After Mexico City police jailed him twice in 1923, he crossed illegally into the United States and within a year Chicago police arrested him on charges of killing an elevated-train ticket agent. Roa escaped twice from Joliet—once, only to be returned, in 1926 and then successfully in 1927. To avoid detection, he fled to Canada, rather than returning to Mexico, after leaving Chicago. When the ardor to find him cooled, he crossed the width of the United States and the length of Mexico, worked in the chicle industry of Yucatán, then settled in Mexico City as a taxi driver along with his brother Jesús.[28]

Will County offered a five-hundred-dollar reward for any information leading to Roa's arrest.[29] Rehn sought the extradition with what his son characterized as "Norwegian stubbornness."[30] On one occasion, having received a tip that Roa was in Florida, he suspended his schedule and took a train south. Most of the time, however, the official worked through the Department of State, which instructed its consuls to look out for Roa. In October 1928 in Guaymas, Sonora, Consul Hubert S. Bursley wrote Rehn that both Roa and Price might be in La Paz, Baja California, and urged him to make extradition arrangements. Fortunately the Department of State cautioned against haste. The man believed to be Roa turned out to be a Japanese doctor who had lived in La Paz for a number of years.[31]

In Mexico, word of the reward spread, making Roa's refuge tenuous at best. In June 1932, a Mexico City detective, Alfredo S. Gómez, informed Dudley G. Dwyre, U.S. consul general in Mexico City, that the taxi driver fugitive had been in an accident and jailed at Mexico City's Belém Prison on a weapons charge. Rehn, who often stated he would not rest until Roa hanged, persuaded Will County officials to reinstate the expired reward offer.[32] Such enthusiasm prompted the State Department to instruct its embassy to pressure Mexican officials to arrest Roa. Foreign Minister Manuel Téllez, who, as the 1920s ambassador to the United States, had protested numerous injustices against Mexicans, assured Mexican cooperation. However, by the time Detective G. Domenzain of the Mexico City police was assigned to retrieve Roa from Belém, the fugitive had been released.[33]

In November 1932, Gastón Leherper, a former Mexican Secret Service agent, supposedly located Roa, but his source of information turned out to be in error. The U.S. Embassy made another request to the Mexican Foreign Ministry in February 1933. The Mexico City police chief replied that an agent "D" (Domenzain) had discovered that Roa had fled to Canada. United States officials were skeptical, however, and State Department pressure continued. At the end of the year, Mexican authorities again assured the United States that Roa would be sought but with little result. Efforts were renewed in January 1934 after Ambassador Josephus Daniels reminded the Foreign Ministry that the United States still desired the extradition. The Mexicans responded as usual, promising full cooperation.[34]

After this period of activity, a hiatus developed in the Roa extradition efforts even though the State Department sporadically reminded Mexicans about the case. Then, Mexico City police, in November 1935, announced that a man believed to be Roa had been jailed. They could only hold him, however, if the U.S. Embassy made a request in writing. An inexperienced Embassy official named Thomas D. Bowman treated this latest disclosure lightly, however. He neglected to inform the ambassador and waited days for Department of State authorization. In the meantime, the police released the man suspected of being Roa "for lack of cause."[35]

Nonetheless, officials in Illinois kept the extradition issue alive. While the State Department exerted pressure on Mexico, Secretary of State Cordell Hull, without much enthusiasm, asked Governor Henry Horner of Illinois if Roa's return was still desired. The governor emphatically assured Hull that Illinois still wanted Roa and that the reward offer was valid despite the years that had passed. By now, Joseph Ragen had assumed the warden post at Joliet and "vowed . . . that he would do everything in his power to bring Bernard Roa back." He wanted his "inmates to realize that Illinois will track down fugitives, no matter how long it takes or how far they have gone." [36] In the meantime, Federal Police colonel Ignacio Sánchez announced that authorities had lost track of the fugitive. The U.S. Embassy continued to emphasize the need to find Roa. One embassy official who considered the policy of offering a reward unwise because it could encourage Mexican officials to act in a mercenary fashion said that "in this case the exception is justified." [37]

By now Ragen provided the only impetus for extradition. "At every opportunity he talked with everyone who might be of help, from State Department officials to policemen, in the hope that something might be done," his biographer wrote.[38] In January 1936, J. Edgar Hoover sent Roa's complete dossier to the Mexico City police, prompting a sensational article on the front page of *Excelsior* with the bold headline "TERRIBLE BANDIT IN MEXICO, FUGITIVE IS AUDACIOUS AND DECISIVE." The exaggerated article indicated that, at the behest of U.S. officials, the metropolitan police sought a fascinating Mexican who had turned into a terrible gangster and

makes frequent trips to the United States to commit his misdeeds, but as soon as he is aware that the authorities are on to him, he slips back into Mexico until the zeal to capture him cools off and then he returns to Mexico City, where he resides in the federal district.[39]

Once the issue became public, the Department of State decided, in March 1936, to advertise the reward. The department also warned Ambassador Daniels that the reward money should not be perceived as coming from the U.S. government. Under the renewed pressure, Mexican officials asked for more information on Roa, a request that Warden Ragen gladly provided. On October 1, federal agent Luis G. García claimed a friend of Roa had written to the fugitive in Chicago at 606 Federal Street, but it took three months for the news to reach Illinois. When Chicago police checked out the address, it turned out to be a parking lot that at one time contained an apartment building where unidentified Mexicans had lived.[40]

The desire to have Roa returned continued to wane on all fronts— except for Warden Ragen. In 1938, he heard from someone in his network of Mexican contacts that Roa was in Puebla (a false lead). At his prodding, Illinois attorney general Otto Kerner, in September, asked for a State Department progress report. Green H. Hackworth, a legal advisor, despaired at yet another request. He reminded Kerner just how much time the State Department had spent on the matter and that Illinois officials had been informed of Roa's supposed Chicago residency. He asked pointedly if they had followed up on the lead and finished by saying that Illinois officials should be more specific about Roa's hiding place if they wanted the department to act.[41]

In October of that year, Colonel Alfredo González, a police commander in Mexico City, informed the U.S. Embassy that agent J. Ignacio Delgadillo knew the fugitive's whereabouts. The U.S. Embassy informed officials at the Foreign Ministry, who did nothing for over a month. Delgadillo, however, who mistakenly thought Roa had escaped from San Quentin and that a five-thousand-dollar reward existed for his return, decided to negotiate directly with American diplomats in Mexico City.[42] The cagey agent, however, who insisted he knew exactly where Roa lived, withdrew cooperation when a U.S. Embassy officer told him the reward was only five hundred dollars. He later changed his mind and revealed that Roa served as a police inspector in Pénjamo, Guanajuato, and that influential people, including the state governor, shielded him. Delgadillo then offered his own "influence" to kidnap Roa and deliver him to American authorities; apparently he found no takers.[43]

Still enthusiastic, Illinois officials announced that the reward had been upped to one thousand dollars. Ramón Beteta, now secretary of the Foreign Ministry, acknowledged on November 11 that federal authorities wanted to arrest Roa but that Delgadillo had disappeared during the time it took to exchange the dispatches and that the escapee had fled to Canada. Mexican enthusiasm was frankly dampened by Delgadillo's mercenary attitude.[44] The U.S. Embassy, which pledged to continue pressing Mexican officials to find Roa in Mexico, saw the story as a red herring. Roa might have left Guanajuato but not for Canada. According to the police chief of Pachuca, Hidalgo, who sent a telegram to Warden Ragen, Roa hid out in that city.[45] In January 1939, another volley of information sparked yet more hope about apprehending the escapee. A Spaniard named J. C. Alba told Mexican officials that Roa, going under the aliases of Francisco González and Pedro Díaz, lived in an *ejido* near Pénjamo, Guanajuato. On January 6, the U.S. Embassy again went to Beteta, who assured the Americans that Roa would be arrested at this hideaway. Romeo León Orantes, a high-ranking administrator at the attorney general's office, was not as enthusiastic. He demurred taking any action for a month and told colleagues that he found the whole affair distasteful because the informant, Alba, a foreigner, seemed motivated solely by the reward; the effort again bogged down.[46]

In December 1940, Jesús Morales, another *guanajuatense* who wanted to rid his state of Roa, wrote by means of the U.S. Embassy to President Franklin D. Roosevelt, bypassing Mexican officials because he distrusted the government. He assured Roosevelt that Roa lived near Palo Verde at a ranch only minutes by car from the village railroad station but cautioned that Roa, guarded by eleven armed agrarians, was extremely dangerous. Morales advised the Americans that only the Mexican federal police could capture the fugitive because state and local authorities would protect him. Department of State bureaucrats ignored Morales' request, however, so in February 1941 Morales wrote again to President Roosevelt, essentially repeating the same information.[47] After this second letter, the State Department conveyed the information to Illinois officials, but Secretary of State Hull now wondered openly if Roa was worth all this trouble. He wrote to Governor Dwight H. Green, pointedly asking if, considering the age of the case, Illinois still wanted extradition. Besides, Hull explained, the extradition now appeared more difficult because Mexico felt the process had gone on too long. Hull did not count on Ragen's obsession with Roa, however. He was probably disappointed when Green informed him that the warden insisted on continuing the effort. An intense exchange of diplomatic dispatches took place that spring but neither side took any visible action.[48]

In April 1944, yet another *guanajuatense,* Juan Ramírez of León, offered to assist in Roa's apprehension. Claiming Roa had killed his brother, Ramírez seemed more motivated by vengeance than the reward. But now Illinois officials seemed indifferent. No one in the state house knew much about the Roa case. They were not even sure if the United States had an extradition treaty with Mexico. The State Department assured Illinois attorney general George Barret of Roa's extraditable status, but the official, overwhelmed by the procedure, did not follow through.[49] By the end of the 1940s, Warden Ragen seemed to be the only party interested in Roa's return. In 1948, the FBI informed him that Mexican authorities had imprisoned Roa at Guanajuato's Granaditas Prison for growing *amapola* (opium poppies) on a wealthy farmer's land near León, Guanajuato. Ragen immediately contacted Governor Green, who again initiated the extradition process. The U.S. Embassy made the usual remonstrations and the Foreign Ministry routinely promised complete cooperation. The Mexican attorney general then offered to delay Guanajuato's legal proceedings against Roa so that the United States could process the extradition. The State Department then asked Governor Green to make the decision.[50]

Ragen himself then wrote directly to Secretary of State George C. Marshall, assuring him that Will County and his office truly wanted Roa back to execute him. Illinois had only forty days to prepare the extradition papers, but within two weeks the attorney general's office amassed eleven photo copies of every item necessary for the package, and on April 22, the U.S. Ambassador delivered the formal request to the Foreign Ministry. Ragen and Green became even more optimistic when President Harry S. Truman assigned Secret Service agent Roy Doerfler to retrieve Roa in Mexico City.[51]

In the meantime, Roa, from prison, protested the extradition to President Miguel Alemán. In an eloquent, typewritten letter, Roa explained he was awaiting trial for a narcotics charge, but if returned, Illinois officials would execute him for a crime he did not commit. Indeed, at the trial for the killing of Assistant Warden Klein, the defendants claimed that only one escapee, Charles Duschowoski, stabbed the prison official to death.[52] The Mexican attorney general, however, at the behest of Alemán, told Foreign Ministry officials that he did not favor extradition because Mexican law only allowed for a maximum penalty of fifteen years for the crimes for which Roa would be executed in the United States.

Mexican Foreign Ministry officials attempted to mollify the Americans by reminding them that Roa would serve twelve years on a narcotics conviction and that his criminal record in the United States made it doubtful he would get an early release. The State Department was clearly disappointed by the decision because they had not doubted the sincerity of the promise by Mexican officials to yield the elusive escapee. More than anything, the Department of State dreaded informing Illinois officials. But Roa's being in a jail seems to have calmed Ragen, especially since the State Department assured him they would pursue the case upon his release.[53]

Roa did not serve twelve years as the Mexican attorney general had promised. Prison officials freed him in August 1949 after he spent less than one and a half years in Granaditas. Again, Ragen urged for extradition, a request that was dutifully conveyed to Mexico. Although U.S. officials had publicly bemoaned the Mexican recalcitrance that prevented the extradition in 1948, they decided not to press too hard so as not to jeopardize contemporary extradition requests that were considered more important. Rather than being frank with hopeful Illinois officials who spent so much time and money preparing the documents, the department told them that Roa's extradition efforts were continuing.[54] "We will bring up the case with Mexican authorities from time to time for hope that a decision be reached in the near future," Embassy official Taylor G. Belcher wrote to the State Department in August 1949.[55]

In Illinois, Ragen refused to give up, and he continued to pressure Washington. Mexican officials, at this point, decided to put an end to the wearisome issue. In July 1952, Luis F. Canudas Orezza from the Foreign Ministry wrote, "It is my opinion that extradition is not possible because we do not have capital punishment in Mexico for murder and he is Mexican. Besides the statutes of limitation of fifteen years has passed."[56] Finally, in November 1952, the Foreign Ministry told the U.S. Embassy point-blank that Roa's extradition would not be allowed.[57]

In 1957, Gladys Erickson, Ragen's biographer, wrote:

Thirty-two years have passed since Roa's crime, and he is
now fifty-seven years old. A good many people have forgotten that the man existed. But Ragen is still on his trail,
and continues to pester federal officials concerning the
case. He admits that he does not have much hope of
achieving his end, but he has no intention of giving up.

Ragen wanted to hang Roa even though that punishment had been deemed inhumane and changed to electrocution in 1927. "As far as Warden Ragen knows, Roa is the only man alive who can be legally hung in Illinois," Erickson said. Ragen felt justified in pursuing his goal because "the man's crimes were too atrocious and their meaning to the men behind the walls at Statesville too important."[58] Roa's hanging, nonetheless, would have contrasted with the consideration given James Price, the white escapee also convicted in the Klein killing, whose death sentence had been rescinded. In 1935, New York authorities had imprisoned Price under the alias James Meadow for robbery and extradited him to Illinois in 1936. The board of pardons commuted his death sentence to 150 years' imprisonment and he died at Joliet Prison in 1963.[59] As to why he did not insist on hanging Price, Ragen said, "We were at a loss to obtain evidence to convict him. . . . We finally persuaded Price to plead guilty. In that way we felt we were seeing [that] justice was well served. . . . Price was as much involved as anyone else in the murder and escape."[60]

Roa remained the quintessential survivor, but years of turmoil wore

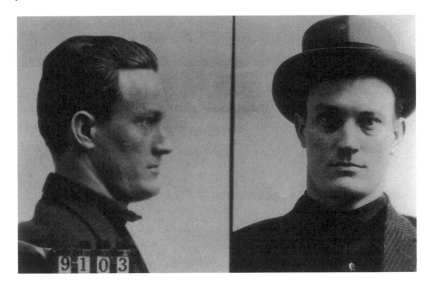

FIGURE 16. JAMES PRICE, WHO WAS CONVICTED OF THE KLEIN MURDER ALONG WITH BERNARDO ROA AND THE OTHER ESCAPEES. FROM RECORD GROUP 84, RECORDS OF U.S. FOREIGN SERVICE POSTS, GUAYMAS, MEXICO, OFFICIAL CORRESPONDENCE 1928, VOLUME 3, FILE 200, COURTESY NATIONAL ARCHIVES AND RECORDS ADMINISTRATION, COLLEGE PARK, MARYLAND.

down his body. He died in August 1965 at a hospital in León, Guanajuato, while Elodia, the wife of his nephew Jesús Roa, rocked his head. Perceptions of Roa held by many Mexicans contrasted to those of his Illinois pursuers. Even those who remember him from his *ejido* chieftain days when he did not hesitate to have a dissident punished, perhaps with death, saw a certain fairness in the way he ran the collective farm.[61] José Anguiano, a law-abiding East Chicago steelworker since the 1920s who served as an immigrant leader and businessman, returned to visit his native San Francisco del Rincón, Guanajuato, in the 1940s. At a local *ejido* fiesta, a companion pointed to a man sitting at the head table and said, "Do you know who that is? That is Bernardo Roa." Anguiano was awed, "I could not believe my eyes that I was finally looking at this man of whom I had heard so much about back in Chicago."[62] During a 1988 interview in León, Elodia, the wife of Roa's nephew Jesús, fully aware of her uncle-in-law's tumultuous past, exclaimed, "He was a wonderful, generous man." His nephew, who kept some news clippings about his notorious uncle, said, "I knew someone would write his story—it is too exciting to be ignored."[63]

| Conclusion

DURING THE TWENTIETH CENTURY, conditions improved for Mexicans in the United States and civil rights activism partially explained these gains. This book shows that the México Lindo generation in protecting itself can take some of the credit for this accomplishment. In addition, this activism also provided a foundation for future civil rights movements. The examination also provides important insights into the nature of racism and ethnic prejudice that the dominant, mainstream society has held toward Mexicans. Below are some of the major conclusions that can be drawn from the evidence provided in this study.

THE "TROUBLESOME BORDER" AND
PROXIMITY TO MEXICO

The images coming out of Mexico during the period of revolution perpetuated an image of Mexicans as violent, dangerous, and treacherous. Texas congressman John C. Box summed up this feeling in 1920 as he urged that immigration laws not be waived to allow entry of Mexican workers in 1920.

> Americans found they could not live with them on genial
> terms in Texas 80 years ago. In a contest which arose
> then the Mexican showed both his inferiority and savage
> nature. The same traits which prevailed with them in the
> days of the Alamo and Goliad show themselves the deal-
> ings with each other and with the Americans now. . . .
> Villa, Huerta, Orozco, Carranza and their bands and
> the conditions of Mexico now are exhibits of Mexican
> character.[1]

Few Anglos discerned that special circumstances in the Revolution created an atmosphere promoting violence and atrocities in Mexico.

193

Instead, Americans believed this violence to be intrinsic to Mexican character, a conviction that allowed them to rationalize and justify mistreatment. As one historian has put it, "The additional hysteria of wartime America only amplified and aggravated the already existing prejudice and discrimination. It was a pretty sorry time when there was no justice for innocent, apolitical Mexican Americans."[2] In Mexico, resentment toward the United States also increased during the turmoil. It stemmed mostly from immigrant treatment, but Mexicans were also sensitive to constant Mexico-bashing by U.S. politicians and the press. The pounding resumed in 1926 when President Plutarco Elías Calles repressed the Catholic Church and threatened to enforce Mexican subsoil rights. The U.S. government criticism, although welcomed by militant Catholics, generally rankled Mexican nationalists. Then a violent Catholic reaction known as the Cristero Rebellion unleashed a lawlessness not seen since the 1910s. Some Americans were again abused, generating demands for intervention.

In November 1926, *Excelsior* accused Americans of besmirching Mexico's reputation in order to continue exploiting Mexican resources with impunity. In addition, the newspaper charged that bashing also created a favorable atmosphere for U.S. citizens with cases before the Joint Claims Commission for property damage and deaths during the revolution. The campaign made it appear that Mexicans were peculiarly prone to atrocities, said *El Universal*, but it ignored the heinous behavior of Europeans and Americans during World War I.[3]

THE LEGACY OF MÉXICO LINDO ACTIVISM AND DEFENSE

Such a hostile atmosphere provoked Mexican immigrants to defend themselves by adopting an immigrant nationalism which I term México Lindo. This orientation emerged everywhere there were Mexicans but was especially strong in *colonias* with large numbers of recent immigrants. Nonetheless, *norteño* and native southwestern Hispanic traits were crucial in contributing to identity in older communities, which had already established an orientation not as closely linked to Mexico. The older Hispanics with weaker ties to the old country were in a significantly better position to help immigrants if they chose to do so. In the newer *colonias*, immigrants depended more on the Mexican government for cultural orientation and help as a broker for problems they encountered in U.S. society. Still, more similarity existed than differences in the degree to which they adhered to the México Lindo ideology.

Indeed, even Mexicans born in the United States claimed Mexican citizenship upon encountering legal problems. South Texas' *El Defensor,* a newspaper with a Mexican American orientation, lamented in 1930 that Mexican immigrants had the lowest record of naturalization and that descendants of Mexicans who lived in Texas before it became part of the United States registered with Mexican consuls. In 1923, even Mauro Parisi, an Italian doomed to hang at San Quentin, claimed to be Mexican to sustain his clemency request through the San Francisco Mexican consulate.[4] Mexican government emissaries also discouraged naturalization and encouraged children born in the United States of Mexican parents to remain Mexican citizens and maintain Mexican-ness. Indeed, Mexicans when compared with other immigrants have one of the lowest naturalization rates—undoubtedly, the attitude of their government had something to do with this.

Reinforcing this protectionist attitude were the Mexican consuls. In this first era of large-scale immigration the consuls served as an important source of protection for Mexican expatriates. Penniless immigrants caught in legal predicaments sometimes had no other recourse than the consular service. The sociologist Emory Bogardus indicated that

by remaining a citizen of Mexico and by calling on the Mexican consul for assistance, the Mexican can secure justice, whereas if he becomes an American citizen he feels helpless. He does not understand our courts and is not able to secure as adequate a hearing as if he remains a Mexican citizen.[5]

MEXICAN CRIMINALS

But unfortunately for Mexican immigrants, their criminal behavior, mainly internecine violence, attracted inordinate attention from law enforcement agencies. Between 1910 and 1930 Mexicans, especially the most recently arrived, clashed with the law more than other immigrant groups. But by the end 1920s, the arrest rate of Mexicans began to decline as *colonias* aged, especially along the border. This contrasted with the police-Mexican strife created by a rapid Mexican influx into Chicago and Los Angeles during the same period.

The tendency for internecine violence can be partially attributed to characteristics brought by the immigrants from Mexico. At the time of immigration, Mexico confronted drastic social and economic changes that weakened values, mores, and class subservience. Although it is unclear whether the pathologies defined by Paz, Ramos, Wolf, Fanon, and

Fromm in Chapter 4 stimulated disorder, it is certain that alcohol use facilitated violence. Finally, abuse in the United States from whites exacerbated and added new tensions that enhanced the inclination to violence. Such a climate existed in many early-forming new immigrant communities, regardless of ethnicity, a condition that invited the attention of law enforcers and the risk of police and judicial abuse.

For-gain crime was not as common among the Mexican immigrants as it was for other immigrants. Even when committing such misdeeds, the acts were mainly spontaneous and not that far removed from being as impulsive as crimes of passion. Most often, poverty forced relatively honest immigrants into desperate acts of criminality. There were some professional criminals in drug dealing, bootlegging, and larceny outside the border area, but for-gain crime consisted mainly of smuggling along the border. Even there, poverty and lack of opportunity induced most of those Mexicans who participated. Why Mexicans were not involved on a larger scale in gangland crime has something to do with the lateness of their emigration to large cities like Los Angeles, Chicago, and Kansas City. Just a few years after Mexicans arrived, the end of Prohibition cut short an avenue to organized crime that had accrued to the children and grandchildren of such older groups as Italians, Jews, and the Irish. Tragically, what got Mexicans into trouble with the law was crime that very rarely paid off.

POLICE VIOLENCE

As has been stated in Chapter 5, police-Mexican violence declined by the end of the 1920s in the Southwest. An economic explanation for this is that because competition over labor declined during the Great Depression, the web of control applied to Mexican labor eased—thus, the extremes of police mistreatment would have been tempered. But enveloped in this paradigm are a whole array of emotions that cannot be portrayed within the context of structural change. One involves the manner in which Anglos and their institutions reacted to the massive inflow of sometimes rowdy immigrants during the revolution and the negative emotions spurred by border lawlessness during this same era. But apart from the emotional reaction to perceived atrocities by Mexicans, simple prejudice and opportunity to engage in sanctioned violence motivated police brutality. When border conflict came to an end and Anglos began to accept Mexicans as they spent more time in the United States, the antipathy diminished. Such a turn of events became as powerful a catalyst in easing racism and repression as improved or evolved economic conditions.

Moreover, homicide and beatings by police created a lasting residue of resentment and bitterness among Mexicans in the United States. Besides seeing policemen as their tormentors, the brutality they experienced or witnessed left in Mexicans a disdain for and resentment of police for years thereafter. In Arizona, five out of eleven Mexicans executed between 1910 and 1925 had killed law officers. In California also, two executions of Mexicans during the 1920s stemmed from convictions in police killings. The same trend is seen in areas outside the Southwest as delineated in the section on capital punishment. The phenomenon of Mexicans supporting compatriots accused of this crime was further assessed in these discussions as well.

Finally, non-Mexican support for ending police abuse was more apparent in urban areas outside of the Southwest, especially where the influence of the Progressives held sway. In California, English-language newspapers often condemned anti-Mexican atrocities and white middle-class women supported clemency campaigns for Mexicans condemned to the death sentence, for example. The Immigrant Protective League often interceded to help Mexicans in areas where the organization was active. Intervention attempts by the immigrant community and its government did not go unheeded by American officials, but they lacked the impact of protests that included mainstream white Americans.[6]

CIVILIAN VIOLENCE

Many times Anglo employers found Mexicans unwilling or unable to conform to onerous expectations of industrial work—on-the-job danger, new technological demands, and rigid timetables of production. But whenever they had a power relationship over Mexicans, they settled these disputes with violent impunity. Moreover, when Mexicans trespassed caste prerogatives, employers, especially in agricultural work, reacted with a fury borne out of race anger. Mistreatment also made for troublesome Mexicans at the work site, which, in a vicious circle, required bosses to use terror tactics.[7] But bosses, at times, tormented Mexican workers to the breaking point simply because they enjoyed power. On other occasions, employers motivated by gain created conflict by cheating Mexicans out of their wages.

The abuse was most prevalent in Texas. Legislator José T. Canales testified in 1919 at the state hearings on violence in South Texas that "some Mexicans were not paid by men who employed them. Some of those Mexicans were beaten and mistreated . . . and in that manner agitated the friction between the two races."[8] An explanation for this wider margin of violence in Texas is that more Mexicans worked as sharecroppers or owned property in Texas; therefore, disputes over profits and land occurred more than in California and other states. Also smaller family-owned farms predominated and agriculturalists tended to have a personal relationship with Mexican workers and felt they had the right to control recalcitrant workers by any means they chose. Ultimately, what lubricated the structure of abuse is that in Texas justice officials were less likely to punish aggressors.

It should also be pointed out that in the Midwest, especially in the Chicago area, violence by individual civilians came later, coinciding with interethnic tension created by a delayed influx of Mexicans into cities in the 1920s. By then, civilian violence against Mexicans had subsided in smaller communities of the Southwest.

Collective action by working-class whites against Mexicans was often carried out with the blessing of the local authorities. This reveals the existence of a deeply embedded inequality sanctioned by American social and value structures. Ultimately, however, the state and influential employers attempted to prevent anti-Mexican violence perpetuated by class groups below them, such as white workers and local police. This was especially true if turbulence interfered with labor needs. Local police, on the other hand, acted less decisively in protecting Mexicans or in investigating the crimes committed against them. This can only be attributed to their identification with whites aggrieved by the Mexican presence. The clear affinity existing between Polish policemen and Polish workers in Chicago is a case in point.

The motives for lynching Mexicans, even in Texas, did not follow precisely the same pattern as for blacks. Less violent outbreaks occurred against Mexicans for breaching racial etiquette—paying attention to white women or not deferring to whites. Unlike the segregation of blacks, informal understandings varying from region to region rather than civil codes enforced Mexican segregation. For individual Mexicans, darker racial appearance and lower-class affiliation determined exclusion, whereas whites demanded racial apartheid from all blacks, regardless of class. For example, miscegenation laws did not prohibit Mexican-Anglo marriages.

Somewhat paradoxical is the apparent decline of abuse during the

1930s, a time of economic disaster. If this is the case, what are the reasons? It is likely that the sight of Mexicans leaving rather than arriving eased tensions. And it could also be that by the 1930s, authorities were more responsive to the demands for protection made by the Mexican expatriate community.

THE COURTS AND DEFENSE LAWYERS

Technically, Mexicans had access to all of the guarantees the judicial system had to offer all Americans. But they lacked cash to purchase adequate defense, a handicap made worse by the added obstacle of prejudicial judges and juries. Ultimately, immigrants kept faith and at times perseverance paid off in wresting their rights from an American justice system which at the very least had an ideological commitment to fairness.

Nothing suggests a correlation between either competency or incompetence and the Mexican ethnicity of lawyers. However, if good communication between lawyer and client result in a stronger defense, Mexican American lawyers had an edge. The record contains abundant examples of defense efforts by incompetent or uncaring white lawyers, which resulted in unfavorable outcomes for Mexican defendants. But another unfortunate factor was that white judges and juries were prejudiced against Mexican American lawyers. Eagle Pass consul Samuel Pereyra reported that he would not hire Mexican Americans because of the bias against them.[9] Significantly, working with the consulates to defend Mexican nationals probably politicized Mexican American lawyers into becoming civil rights warriors.

CAPITAL PUNISHMENT AND MEXICAN IMMIGRANTS

Executions of Mexicans rose during the 1900-to-1920 period, an era of heavy immigration, revolution-linked violence, and labor duress—and declined when immigration waned in the late 1920s. In Arizona, thirteen of the seventeen Mexicans who hanged between 1910 and 1934 were executed before 1925, even though four times as many Mexicans lived in the state during 1930 than in 1910. In these two decades, the immigrants and their children achieved stability as immigration tapered off in the 1920s. Organized community protest, as well as more effective diplomatic intervention in the 1920s, also had a sobering effect on arresting officers, juries, and judges, making it more difficult to send Mexicans to the gallows. After the Hernández brothers execution in 1934, only three

U.S.-born, Spanish-surnamed individuals out of thirty-four died in the gas chamber before the Supreme Court abolished capital punishment in 1970; the list contains no Mexican nationals.

A similar decline is evident in New Mexico and Texas. In New Mexico, of course, this stems from the abolishment of the death sentence in the 1920s. Executions in the state before 1900, however, were not accompanied by the same degree of ethnic or racial tension as in other southwestern states. It is not surprising that a large proportion of those hanged were Spanish surnamed since New Mexico's population ranged between 60 to 80 percent Hispanic during the nineteenth century. Moreover, Hispanic authorities and juries served in the process of sending their *paisanos* to the gallows.[10] This changed after 1910 when the roll of those who hanged consisted mainly of Mexican nationals who crossed the border and committed crimes. In Texas, the decrease stemmed from the same reasons as in Arizona, albeit a more developed structure of protection and political connection among Mexicans resulted in more acts of clemency.

In California, and in states outside the Southwest, the decline in executions came later than in border states where large-scale immigration was evident much earlier. As in Arizona and Texas, executions tapered off with immigration and as the defense institutions acquired more maturity.

The Mexican community did not always rally behind a compatriot condemned to death. In Canon City, Colorado, two Mexican American brothers, one of them a minor, were executed during July 1934 for brutally murdering and mutilating an entire Anglo family, then trying to burn down their farmhouse with the bodies inside. *El Tucsonense,* which the same year had joined the energetic effort to save the Hernández brothers, merely noted "Luis and Juan Pacheco, 30 and 18 years old respectively will die together in the gas chamber. . . . The brothers pleaded guilty and will not appeal because they do not have money, *nor friends.*"[11]

When the community and the Mexican government did intervene, they could provide Mexicans with important legal assistance sometimes not available to other Americans. For example, the efforts to gain clemency for Roberto Tórrez in Will County, Illinois, exceeded anything that was done for the two white men that hanged with him. In general, by the end of the 1920s, there is no doubt that Mexican government efforts, the clemency movement, and more effective legal defense were much more successful than in previous years in offsetting the bias in applying capital punishment to Mexicans.

IMPRISONMENT OF MEXICAN IMMIGRANTS

In all the prisons surveyed for this era, the Mexican population declined, suggesting that Mexicans went to prison less as they aged and spent more time in the United States. That Mexicans returned to prisons in the era of this study less often than other groups is suggested by the smaller proportion of Mexicans at such recidivist institutions as Folsom State Prison in California or Huntsville in Texas, in comparison with institutions for first-time offenders. Three reasons account for this: few Mexicans were professional criminals, their youthful demographic profile had not yet allowed for enough releases to create a critical core of potential recidivists, and officials deported most Mexican nationals after their release.[12]

By present-day standards, prison conditions were abysmal. But while all prisoners suffered regardless of race, observations that Mexicans, like blacks, were more vulnerable to institutional maladies abound. This was especially true in Texas where Mexicans had their own prison. Ultimately, insensitivity to the cultural needs of Mexicans and the difficulty in obtaining releases proved to be just as debilitating as the wretched conditions in the prisons.

EXTRADITION

Americans who attempted to extradite fugitives from Mexico often found themselves bogged down in bureaucratic red tape, and Mexican officials, at times, proved uncooperative. This certainly occurred in cases where Americans followed procedure as outlined in extradition agreements. Personal reasons often fueled a reluctance to cooperate, that is, individual resentment against Americans, lack of motivation, and so forth. A collective attitude also probably accounts for this lack of cooperation as well. Just as Mexican immigrants perceived their compatriots, whom mainstream society saw as pure criminals, as victims of the justice system, Mexican authorities sympathized with compatriots who they felt escaped unjust conditions by coming home. Moreover, memories of American officials and military personnel violating Mexican sovereignty by seizing fugitives in Mexico did not put Mexicans in a mood to cooperate. Therefore, Americans often turned to extralegal means to bring back Mexicans. In many cases, they had the collaboration of counterparts in Mexico whose desire for reciprocity or bribes assured such cooperation. Even Warden Ragen, remote as he was in Joliet, established a cooperative network with Mexican police. Such efforts eventually led to the emergence of official international law enforcement cooperation between both countries in efforts to deal with crime and to bring back criminals wanted in the United States.

APPENDIX A

WHITE AND BLACK CIVILIAN VIOLENCE AGAINST MEXICANS

NOTE: In some cases assailants may have been law officers. Determination was made as precisely as the information in the source allowed.

June 1900. Phoenix. A Mexican was killed in Ray, Arizona, allegedly in retaliation for the killings of the whites at Día de San Juan celebrations in Phoenix. AHSRE, 12/7/238.

August 1901. Félix Martínez was lynched in Karnes County, Texas. The reason he was executed is unknown. Chapman, pp. 103–104.

1908. Kenedy County, Texas. A rape charge motivated a mob to hang Carlos Muñoz—it is not known if the rape victim was white. Chapman, pp. 103–104.

February 1908. Groesbeck, Texas. Walter Thetford killed Manuel Acosta with a butcher knife after having had trouble with him. *Houston Chronicle*, February 10, 1908.

February 1908. Fort Worth, Texas. The Mexican consul in San Antonio, Texas, inquired into the murder of Dan Gallegos by Palmer Maddox. *Houston Chronicle*, February 23, 1908.

March 1908. Alpine, Texas. Antonio Casas was shot and killed by county surveyor John Harmon. *Houston Chronicle*, March 15, 1908.

June 1908. Houston, Texas. John Nobles is going on trial for killing a Mexican. *Houston Chronicle*, March 15, 1908.

July 1908. Harrisburg, Texas. Bernaldo Luna was shot and killed after he confronted W. E. Eason, who fired him from a railroad job. *Houston Chronicle*, July 31, 1908.

October 1908. El Paso, Texas. S. A. Wright killed a Mexican miner when he was attacked. *Houston Chronicle*, October 29, 1908.

November 1908. Houston, Texas. A Negro attacked a Mexican girl in the fifth ward area. *Houston Chronicle*, November 10, 1908.

March 1910. San Antonio, Texas. Nelson Watters is pleading self-defense on the murder charge of Juan de la Rosa. *Houston Chronicle*, March 12, 1910.

August 1910. El Paso, Texas. Tom Hall shot Pedro Benavides for stealing cattle. Hall surrendered. *Houston Chronicle,* August 9, 1910.

November 1910. A man named Opei, a descendent of Kickapoo immigrants from Mexico living in Oklahoma, was lynched after killing a police chief in the town of Anadarko. *La Gaceta de Jalisco,* November 14, 15, 1910.

November 1910. A mob hanged Liborio Estrada near Austin—the reason for the slaying is unknown. *El País,* November 17, 1910.

November 1910. Galveston, Texas. Anglos clashed with Mexicans who "displayed an impudent attitude" after riots in Mexico City. Rice, pp. 47–48.

November 1910. In Kenedy County, Texas, Anglos beat Mexicans, chasing them across the border when they cursed at Americans. Rice, pp. 47–48.

November 1910. A riot in Carrizo Springs, Texas, resulted in two stabbings of Anglos and the beating of eleven Mexicans and wounding of two in shootings. Rice, pp. 47–48.

November 1910. Drunken Americans at Rio Grande City picked fights with Mexicans who had never heard of the Rodríguez lynching or the Mexico City riots. Rice, pp. 47–48.

November 1910. In construction camps and ranches in Webb, Duval, La Salle, Dimmit, and Starr Counties in Texas, Anglos attacked "sullen and threatening" Mexicans. Rice, pp. 47–48.

November 1910. In Starr and Zapata Counties, Mexicans fled across the border "fearing they will be killed by cowboys." Rice, pp. 47–48.

February 1911. Scribner, Nebraska. An armed mob of townspeople stormed the jailhouse, dragged out Juan González, and hanged him. *El Cosmopolita,* February 27, 1911.

June 1911. Raúl Mendoza was killed in Miami, Arizona, by an individual named Sutter White. The motive for this killing is uncertain. AHSRE, 11/19/24.

June 1911. George Adams, a foreman for the Santa Fe Railroad in San Bernardino, California, beat Isabel Ramírez to death after they argued over the tallying of hours. AHSRE, 11/19/24.

December 1911. El Centro, California. The foreman of a farm, Henry Shirley, shot Felícitos González. AHSRE, 11/19/24.

March 1912. Sinton, Texas. An Anglo, in retaliation for a feud with other Mexicans, shot and wounded transient José E. Franco as he slept in a train station. AHSRE, 12-7-18.

August 1912. San Antonio, Texas. Francisco Garza and Manuel Gutiérrez were killed at La Volanta Ranch by an American named Alonso Alee after an argument over property. AHSRE, 11/19/24.

December 1912. Dallas, Texas. José Puente was shot and killed by an American bartender because Puente did not heed sign indicating Mexicans were not allowed in the bar. AHSRE, 11/19/24.

January 1913. Grandfield, Oklahoma. Boss fired railroad workers Margarito López and Samuel Espinoza after argument over wages, but then shot López. *La Prensa,* January 27, 1913.

June 1913. At restaurant in Tiague, Texas, Mauricio Guzmán got into a fight with Jim Alison who gave him such a hard blow on the head that the Mexican died. AHSRE, 11/19/24.

July 1913. At July 4 celebrations Anglo revelers tore down Mexican flags at the consulates in Tucson and Douglas, Arizona, and in Pharr, Texas. *La Prensa,* July 10, 1913.

August 1913. Victoriano Godina was killed near Little River, Texas, by Americans named Manuel López and John Gregory, both U.S. citizens. AHSRE, 11/19/24.

September 1913. Texas. William Garner admitted to police that he shot and killed Lucio Abargo because he did not like Mexicans. AHSRE, 11/19/24.

November 1913. Miami, Arizona. José Pérez and M. Ortiz were killed by American soldiers during a race riot. AHSRE, 11/19/24.

September 1914. Luis Guevara was assaulted by four white men on a Houston, Texas, street. *Houston Chronicle,* September 18, 1914.

April 1915. Charco, Texas. Leocadio Díaz was killed at the Powell Ranch near Charco, Texas, after a dispute over wages. AHSRE, 11/19/24.

June 1915. South Texas. Roberto Tobías and José Vargas refused to go work and were beaten by the Moore brothers, their employers, and thrown in jail. AHSRE, 11/19/24.

February 1916. W. Ligget shot and killed 62-year-old Gregorio Rivera during a property dispute. AHSRE, 11/19/24.

April 1916. Brawley, California. An Anglo American who killed Francisco Maga was tried in court, which showed partiality, and freed. AHSRE, 11/19/24.

April 1916. Texas Mexicans Francisco Prieto and Felipe Luján killed Mexican citizens Jesús Chávez and Fabian Trujillo in Ruidoso, Texas, and were not arrested. AHSRE, 11/19/24.

May 1916. Union City, Oklahoma. Americans threatened to blast Mexicans out with guns if they did not leave the community. *El Cosmopolita,* May 20, 1916.

November 1916. Delfino González was killed by William McInnis in Com Ingalls, Louisiana, with a shotgun. They had argued over a debt of $1.50. AHSRE, 11/19/24.

January 1917. Runge, Texas. Two armed and drunken Anglos and a Mexican Texan forced Cosme Galván to feed them at his cafe. They insulted him and left without paying. AHSRE, 11/19/24.

February 1917. Kansas City, Missouri. Local farmers lynched a Mexican railroad worker accused of killing an Anglo farmer near a railroad camp. *El Cosmopolita*, February 24, 1917.

February 1917. José Martínez was shot and killed by an unnamed American citizen in Nebraska. AHSRE, 11/19/24.

February 1917. Kansas City, Missouri. José Castillo was shot and killed by T. Charles. AHSRE, 11/19/24.

June 1917. Rio Hondo, Texas. Charles Soathoff shot and killed Vicente Pérez, who was traveling with his family, after accusing the Mexican of stealing from his ranch. AHSRE, 11/19/24.

Fall 1917. Texas Ranger identified as David killed Antonio Pérez at El Baroso Ranch near Rio Grande City, after the Mexican attacked him for making sexual advances toward his wife. NA, RG59, 311.121, P411.

October 1917. An army truck carelessly driven by an American soldier ran over David Herrera in Miami, Arizona. The Mexican died from his injuries. AHSRE, 11/19/24.

April 1918. W. L. Flucker, a ranch foreman near Roswell, New Mexico, shot at employees Carlos Conal and Lucas López. Conal died. AHSRE, 11/19/24.

June 1918. Anacleto Vargas was killed in downtown El Paso, Texas, by American soldiers. AHSRE, 11/19/24.

August 1918. Texas farmworker Roberto Romero cursed at his boss, H. H. Burch, who then broke his nose and ribs. AHSRE, 11/19/24.

February 1919. Eugenio Calvillo was killed by some American soldiers because he would not sell them liquor. It turned out that Calvillo did not have any to sell. AHSRE, 11/19/24.

March 1919. Fabens, Texas. Andrés Nájera, foreman of the Ivalde Ranch, fought a duel with an Anglo and both died in a hospital near El Paso, Texas. *El Imparcial de Texas*, March 20, 1919.

April 1919. Near San Antonio, Texas. Luis Esparza was shot by M. W. Ward at Esparza's farm job. AHSRE, 11/19/24.

April 1919. José Martínez was killed by his foreman at a farm near Weslaco, Texas. AHSRE, 11/19/24.

April 1919. Longino Ortiz was killed by the foreman on a farm near Kansas City, Missouri. AHSRE, 11/19/24.

April 1919. Bartlesville, Oklahoma. A Mexican who worked in a cafe was shot in the head by a dentist who became angry at the worker for an undetermined cause.

Another Mexican, David Cantú, was beaten by five or six Anglo Americans because he had a white girlfriend. Later, a law official led an unsuccessful attempt to lynch Cantú. United States, Department of State, *Papers Relating to the Foreign Relations of the United States,* 1919, vol. 2, pp. 534–535; AHSRE, 12-8-58.

May 1919. Rockport, Texas. Jesús Aguirre, a shipyard worker, was beaten up by Americans and they were not arrested. AHSRE, 11/19/24.

July 1919. S. H. York spent only a few hours in jail for killing a Mexican named Hernández in Mobile, Alabama. AHSRE, 11/19/24.

July 1919. Perfecta Solís was shot dead by Sergeant Major H. Hastings at a park in El Paso, Texas. He was hunting rabbits. AHSRE, 11/19/24.

July 1919. Washington, D.C. Francisco Rosales was assaulted and robbed during riots between whites and blacks. AHSRE, 11/19/24.

July 1919. José Blanco and Elizondo González were attacked by mob in Chicago, Illinois, during race riot. Blanco stabbed one aggressor and González was seriously wounded. NA, RG59, 311.121, R71.

August 1919. Texas. Strong words over political conditions in Mexico escalated to fisticuffs; then a white named Bowen took out a gun and shot Julio Martínez. AHSRE, 11/19/24.

October 1919. At a Dinero, Texas, railroad work site, a foreman named Sharp shot and killed Antonio Torres when he disobeyed an order. AHSRE, 11/19/24.

November 1919. Kansas City, Missouri. George Madupe killed Tito Quintana because the Mexican was having illicit relations with his wife. AHSRE, 11/19/24.

December 1919. Kale, Texas. After Thomas Campbell fired Luis Rodríguez from his railroad job, the foreman shot Rodríguez as he and his wife prepared to leave their railroad-car home. AHSRE, 11/19/24.

February 1920. Colorado, Texas. Frank Taylor and Luther Moore, suspecting Ernesto Flores and Encarnación Cornejo of cattle rustling, summarily executed them. NA, RG59, 311.1213 F661.

April 1920. San Pedro, California. Miguel Gallegos was killed by a taxi driver, Clarence D., who claimed the boy tried to rob him. NA, RG59, 311.1213 G13.

November 1920. Youngstown, Ohio, Salvador Díaz was shot and wounded by Ross Flory in an argument over a rent debt—charges were never filed against the landlord. NA, RG59, 311.1213 D54.

March 1921. Granite City, Illinois. Striking steel workers beat Emerterio Melyosa, Guadalupe Rodríguez, and Jesús Becerra at pool hall frequented by strikers. NA, RG59, 311.1213 M48.

March 1921. Nevada. Federico Díaz was shot and killed by Charles de Beck, alias "Coyote Bill." The Mexican government complained that local police did nothing. NA, RG59, 311.1213 C15.

April 1921. White men attacked nude Mexican mine workers bathing in a water-filled quarry in Pittsburgh, Oklahoma. *La Prensa,* May 15, April 7, 1921.

August 1921. Bartlesville, Oklahoma. Anonymous warnings appeared on Mexican homes demanding they leave within twenty-four hours or face the consequences. *Hispano América,* August 6, 1921.

December 1921. Kansas City, Missouri. In the midst of a meatpacking workers' strike, Owen Devens, a black picketer, killed strikebreaker Antonio Hernández. NA, RG59, 311.1213 M48.

February 1922. Cameron County, Texas. Manuel Duarte was lynched. Chapman, p. 111.

March 1922. Texas. N. H. Free, a railroad site foreman, fired Juan Hernández, then shot and killed him after argument. Hernández allegedly drew a knife. NA, RG59, 311.1213, Hernández.

October 1922. San Diego, California. J. M. Heath, a construction foreman, killed Ricardo Chaboya with a shovel after he fired him and the Mexican refused to leave. RG 59 311.1213 Chaboya, Ricardo.

December 1922. Pearsall, Texas. Frank Rhodes killed Manuel Zapata. Rhodes claimed self-defense. NA, RG59, 311.1213 Zapata.

October 1923. Texas. A demented Mexican attacked passengers with a knife on train. He was subdued by other passengers, beaten, and shot to death. *Hispano América,* October 27, 1923.

March 1924. Houston, Texas. Primitivo Saldaña, an elderly pecan-candy vendor, was hospitalized for a concussion after a black assailant hit him in the head and robbed him. *Houston Chronicle,* March 12, 1924.

April 1924. Elgin, Texas. When farmer Charles Rolff and Santos Campos fought over wages, a gun Rolff pulled discharged harmlessly but Campos was given a ten-year sentence. TSA, RG 301, Box 56.

May 1926. The newspaper *México* complained that Mexicans were being accosted and robbed almost daily by Poles in South Chicago, Illinois. May 15, 1926.

October 1926. Policemen of Polish descent were accused of exhibiting partiality when investigating the vandalizing of a Mexican-owned business by Polish gang. *México,* October 12, 1926.

November 1926. Chicago, Illinois. A Mexican was killed in assault by Poles. *México,* November 27, 1926.

1927. A Mexican reporter remembers watching an Anglo in West Texas severely beating a Mexican while the victim's friends watched. Gamio Papers, File No. 4, Box 1.

1927. Kerrville, Texas. Loreto Hernández, a cafe owner, recalled that a bus driver ejected him from a crowded bus after he refused to relinquish his seat to an Anglo. Gamio Papers, Box 1, File No. 7.

1927. Manuel Pérez remembers being beaten by his foreman because he dropped bucket of molten copper at a smelter in Wiles, California. Gamio Papers, Box 2, File No. 13.

January 1927. Chicago, Illinois. *El Correo* reported an attempted mugging of a Mexican by ten Italians, implying the act was racially motivated. January 3, 1927.

January 1927. Chicago, Illinois. Mexican assaulted surprised Poles without means of defense, corner of 14th place and South Halstead. *El Correo,* January 8, 1927.

January 1927. Chicago, Illinois. A Mexican walking home at night was mugged by ten Italians. *México,* January 23, 1927.

April 1927. Assaults on Mexicans are frequent on Taylor between Halstead and Canal in Chicago, Illinois. *México,* April 30, 1927.

July 1927. Chicago, Illinois. Italians attack and shoot Mexicans at Taylor and Halstead. *México,* July 20, 1927.

August 1927. Three Mexicans were involved in a scuffle with Poles in Chicago, Illinois, which resulted in the stabbing death of a young Polish man. *La Noticia Mundial,* August 21, 1927.

August 1927. Zavala County, Texas. An unidentified Anglo killed Benjamin Izquierdo and Antonio Durán in self-defense. TSA, RG 301, Box 80.

November 1927. Chicago, Illinois. A Polish American killed Juan García because the Mexican was having a relationship with the wife of the assassin. *La Noticia Mundial,* November 20, 1927.

March 1928. San Patricio, Texas. Ripley L. Terrel, a rich landowner, shot Abelardo González dead moments after their cars collided on a county highway. *La Prensa,* March 4, 1928.

November 1928. Sutter Creek, California. An Anglo American shot and killed Leonardo García after the Mexican followed him home from a restaurant where they had argued. *La Opinión,* November 22, 1928.

December 1928. Bonanza, Colorado. A. O. Burgess gunned down Cecilio Galindo over a gambling argument. Burgess was freed by grand jury. NA, RG59, 311.1213, Galindo.

1929. A Mexican in Corpus Christi, Texas, said, "An American killed a Mexican for not getting out of his way. It was no use trying to fight the case." Taylor, *An American-Mexican Frontier,* p. 171.

1929. An American in Nueces County offered that Mexicans never went to court against Anglo aggressors because the law would not support them. Taylor, *An American-Mexican Frontier,* p. 171.

Late 1920s. Hamilton, Texas. After Mexicans refused to pick cotton because Johnson grass overran the fields, the infuriated farmer and his friends threatened to lynch them. Vargas, p. 17.

Late 1920s. Texas. After a walkout, an employer locked remaining workers in a garage, threatening to kill anyone else who left. Taylor, *A Spanish Mexican Peasant Community*, p. 49.

June 1930. Alamo, Texas. Rufino Barriero quit his farm job and demanded his wages from Bret Julian, who shot him instead in front of his wife. *El Defensor*, June 27, 1930.

January 1931. Tom Green County, Texas. Anglo workers signed a petition demanding the firing of Mexican workers from county highway construction. *El Defensor*, January 16, 1931.

January 1931. Terre Haute, Indiana. A mob of white workers converged on Mexican railroad workers and forced them to give up their jobs. Balderrama and Rodríguez, *Decade of Betrayal*, p. 99.

May 1931. Chicago, Illinois. Domingo González was shotgunned to death in a drive-by shooting for being stool pigeon by mobster Joseph Montana. *El Nacional*, May 6, 1931.

May 1931. Chicago, Illinois. A gang of Italians attacked two Mexicans, beating one up severely and chasing the other back to his neighborhood. *El Nacional*, May 20, 1931.

May 1931. Luis Méndez charged that Polish gangs living in his South Chicago, Illinois, ward beat him and took $100. *El Nacional*, May 27, 1931.

May 1931. Malakoff, Texas. The "Mexican Hall" in the middle of the *barrio* was bombed by white workers who wanted Mexicans to leave town. AHSRE, IV-325-68.

May 1931. A white man attacked Julio Domínguez in Malakoff, Texas, after Mexican mutual aid society building was bombed. Domínguez was forced to leave town. AHSRE, IV-325-68.

June 1931. Sheriff Haynes of San Angelo, Texas, received a letter threatening Mexicans, signed "The Unemployed, South With Mexicans." *San Angelo Evening Standard*, June 13, 1931.

June 1931. *San Angelo Evening Standard* in Texas received a letter from the club "Darts and Others" which said "our aim is to . . . make working conditions better for Americans." (The group wanted all Mexicans to leave town.) *San Angelo Evening Standard*, June 13, 1931.

June 1931. A white man who violated a six-year-old Mexican girl in San Antonio, Texas, was freed by a judge because the man became severely ill. *El Nacional*, June 27, 1931.

June 1931. Chicago, Illinois. Nineteen-year-old María Rosales was abducted by three men assumed to be Italian, but the assault was frustrated by the arrival of the police. *El Nacional*, June 29, 1931.

July 1931. Chicago, Illinois. Rock-throwing Poles and Italians ejected Mexicans from Calumet Beach at Fourth of July celebration. Interview, Eduardo Peralta.

July 1931. Newport, Arkansas. Twenty-five to thirty Anglo Americans went on a rampage looking for Mexicans to shoot. AHSRE, IV/186/51.

August 1931. White workers forced Mexican tenant farmers in Mississippi to abandon their plots area and seek repatriation. Balderrama and Rodríguez, *Decade of Betrayal,* p. 99.

May 1932. Imperial Valley, California. Ranch hand Victor Gómez was shot by his drunken boss, Joseph Robert Hatfield, for an undetermined reason. AHSRE, IV-187-21.

March 1934. On the corner of 108th Street and Torrence in South Chicago, a Polish gang assaulted Luis Vargas, taking his passport and two dollars. *La Lucha,* March 28, 1934.

Winter 1933–1934. Visalia, California. Farmers attacked striking Mexican farm-workers, killing two. Balderrama and Rodríguez, *Decade of Betrayal,* pp. 65–66.

December 1935. El Paso, Texas. U.S. Army private E. F. Lassiler broke into Juan Artalejo's house and struck Artalejo, who died from a cerebral blood clot. The soldier was freed. NA, RG59, 311.1213, Artalejo.

Appendix B

**MEXICAN-ON-MEXICAN VIOLENCE IN TEXAS
AND THE CHICAGO AREA**

January 1908. In San Antonio, Texas, Leandro Martínez slashed his wife with a razor after a fight over money. *Houston Chronicle,* January 17, 1908.

January 1908. A Mexican in El Paso, Texas, prevented an Anglo miner from eloping with his sister by killing them both. *Houston Chronicle,* January 24, 1908.

February 1908. Seguín, Texas. José Fernández was jailed for fighting with and killing Silvestro Cabello at a dance. *Houston Chronicle,* February 2, 1908.

March 1908. Mexican was jailed in Bastrop, Texas, for beating his son to death. *Houston Chronicle,* March 9, 1908.

April 29, 1908. Houston, Texas. R. Rafael was assaulted by two Mexicans when they attempted to rob him. *Houston Chronicle,* April 29, 1908.

May 1908. San Angelo, Texas. Daniel Flores shot Jesus Muñoz at a dance. *Houston Chronicle,* May 1, 1908.

May 1908. El Paso, Texas. Máximo Arando went on trial for the murder of Doroteo Vigil in a bar fight. *Houston Chronicle,* May 28, 1908.

June 1908. Accusing her of infidelity, Mexican in Gonzales, Texas, killed his wife and son, then wounded his mother-in-law and a girl. *Houston Chronicle,* June 2, 1908.

June 1908. New Braunfels, Texas. Rómulo Vidiales was shot and wounded in a dispute over a woman. *Houston Chronicle,* September 20, 1908.

August 1908. San Angelo, Texas. Pólito Ponce surrendered after killing Juan Caraleo in a dispute. *Houston Chronicle,* August 26, 1908.

September 1908. Marlin, Texas. Santos González, suspect in the killing of Juan Flores, was sought. *Houston Chronicle,* September 3, 1908.

December 1908. Texas. Santiago Garza seriously wounded a Mexican who took him for another man and shot him. *Houston Chronicle,* December 3, 1908.

June 1910. Ignacio López was arrested in San Antonio, Texas, for the murder of his father. *Houston Chronicle,* June 11, 1910.

June 1910. San Antonio, Texas. When Manuel Navarro threatened his lover with a gun, she lunged at him and the gun went off, blowing off half his skull. *Houston Chronicle,* August 11, 1910.

August 1910. El Campo, Texas. Mexican shot Charlie González in a "quarrel over a woman." *Houston Chronicle,* August 11, 1910.

August 1910. Inhabitants of Lockhart, Texas, search for Geraldo López for the killing of another Mexican in a fight. *Houston Chronicle,* August 15, 1910.

August 1910. Goliad, Texas. Antonio Castillo was jailed for cutting Caseus Vela with a dagger. *Houston Chronicle,* August 18, 1910.

November 1910. San Angelo, Texas. Fernando Martínez was shot to death by a Mexican who fled town. *Houston Chronicle,* November 22, 1910.

December 1910. Three Mexicans in Galveston, Texas, allegedly killed José García during a fight. *Houston Chronicle,* December 28, 1910.

April 1913. An intoxicated Loralis Rosales attacked passersby with a knife in the Mexican section of San Antonio, Texas. *La Prensa,* April 24, 1913.

April 1913. San Antonio, Texas. Emilio Vidal, who had a long-standing dispute with Alfredo Arocha, shot and killed him after the latter knifed him. *La Prensa,* April 24, 1913.

May 1913. In Houston, Texas, Candelario Treviño killed his wife with an ice pick and gun during a drinking bout—he was sentenced to prison for 25 years. *La Prensa,* May 29, 1913.

October 1913. *La Prensa* announced the "cowardly" killing of rancher, José Rincón near Seguín, Texas. Two Mexicans were suspected. October 30, 1913.

February 1914. Texas. Pablo García was jailed for brutally beating his twelve-year-old daughter. *Houston Chronicle,* February 23, 1914.

April 1914. Galveston, Texas. Alfredo Zúniga "lost his temper" and killed his wife, his mother-in-law, and himself. *Houston Chronicle,* April 4, 1914.

June 1914. Houston, Texas. Abel Flores shot Hortencia Luna and then himself. *Houston Chronicle,* June 11, 1914.

July 1914. Houston, Texas. Jesse Valdez killed his wife and then himself in a fit of jealousy. *Houston Chronicle,* July 24, 1914.

September 1914. Houston, Texas. Mariano Guerrero was arrested for abduction and rape after eloping with his thirteen-year-old sweetheart. *Houston Chronicle,* September 17, 1914.

October 1914. Luling, Texas. Manuel Martínez shot and killed Luis Serna because he suspected him of an having an affair with his wife. *Houston Chronicle,* October 28, 1914.

February 1917. Brownsville, Texas. Pedro Pérez killed his wife and then himself after failing to find a job. *Houston Chronicle,* February 9, 1917.

February 1919. San Antonio, Texas. A sixteen-year-old girl stabbed to death sixteen-year-old Alfredo Ochoa while the two were drinking rotgut whiskey. *El Imparcial de Texas,* February 27, 1919.

December 1919. Georgetown, Texas. With an ax, Juan Chabolla killed Anastasio Bravo, his wife, and daughter. Chabolla claimed all of them attacked him. NA, RG59, 211.1213 B72.

August 1921. Galveston, Texas. Sixteen-year-old Virginia Aguirre shot and killed her nineteen-year-old boyfriend, George Stevens. *Houston Chronicle,* August 16, 1921.

December 1921. El Paso, Texas. Prudencio Ramírez claims he accidentally stabbed his wife trying to defend her from an intruder who entered their bedroom. *La Patria,* December 17, 1921.

August 1922. Chicago, Illinois. Benito Castro was stabbed in rear of 550 Taylor Street during fight with two other Mexicans—Rico de Oro is suspect. Chicago Police Homicide Log, ISA.

December 1923. South Chicago, Illinois. Juan Saldona stabbed José Botello to death in argument over pool game. Chicago Police Homicide Log, ISA.

April 1923. Chicago, Illinois. Jesus Alcantar, twenty-four, was fatally shot by Luis Alcaraz in quarrel. Chicago Police Homicide Log, ISA.

February 1926. Chicago, Illinois. Edward Rodríguez stabbed twenty-two-year-old waitress, Etta McDowell, when she rejected him. *Daily Calumet,* February 13, 1926.

March 1926. Jesús González and Luis Contreras shot and killed Reyes Silva in San Pedro, Texas, because he was courting a girl Contreras wanted as his girlfriend. *El Cronista del Valle,* March 29, 1926.

May 1926. Chicago, Illinois. John Juárez and Tony Almido were arrested out of six Mexicans who "were staging a near riot." One had to be taken to the hospital. *Daily Calumet,* May 6, 1926.

August 1926. Chicago, Illinois. Manuel Rejes was shot to death by Juan Visianaiz who escaped; during quarrel. Chicago Police Homicide Log, ISA.

1927. La Salle County, Texas. An intoxicated Carlos Corona beat his wife to death with iron bolt. *People v Corona,* 300 SW 80 (Court of Criminal Appeals of Texas, 1927).

February 1927. Chicago, Illinois. Gertrudis Londalús shot and killed Frank Zúnigo in an argument caused by Zúnigo marrying Londalús' common-law wife. *Daily Calumet,* February 22, 1927.

May 1927. Chicago, Illinois. In a group fight, Joe Rangel, 24, cut Ignacio Cazárez' throat and then another Mexican almost cut his ear off. *Daily Calumet,* May 7, 1927.

September 1927. East Chicago, Indiana. A seventeen-year-old Mexican American was stabbed and killed by boyfriend after she broke off the relationship. Our Lady of Guadalupe Church Death Records, East Chicago, Indiana.

September 1927. Chicago, Illinois. Bartolomé Guerra, in a drunken state, beat Angel Sandoval to death with stove iron at Illinois Central railroad camp. *México,* February 13, 1929.

January 1928. Houston, Texas. At a Mexican restaurant shooting, owner Max Martínez, detective Pete Corrales, and twenty-five-year-old Juanita Guzmán died. *Houston Chronicle,* January 4, 1928.

February 1928. Chicago, Illinois. In poolroom brawl, Candide Ojeda, twenty-nine, struck Hilario Flores, twenty-five, with stick but was taken to hospital with stab wounds. *Daily Calumet,* February 21, 1928.

February 1928. Chicago, Illinois. Jesús Dolf was assaulted by Antonio Záñez with knife. *Daily Calumet,* February 23, 1928.

March 1928. Mission, Texas. Friends took twenty-one-year-old F. Frausto to the hospital where he died from stab wounds sustained at an all-night drinking party. *La Prensa,* March 5, 1928.

April 1928. A man named José was stabbed to death in East Chicago, Indiana. *Calumet News,* April 8, 1928.

August 1928. Jesús, a steel worker from Jalisco who lived in a boarding house next to Inland Steel, died from stab wounds in East Chicago, Indiana. Our Lady of Guadalupe Church Death Records.

February 1929. At a Gary, Indiana, hospital Miguel Fernández was in critical condition but his foe was only slightly wounded after a gun battle. *Calumet News,* February 4, 1929.

March 1929. East Chicago, Indiana. A Mexican died after he was stabbed by a compatriot who escaped. *Calumet News,* March 30, 1929.

March 1929. Angel Guarda was shot by Anselmo Jiménez as latter crossed a Chicago, Illinois, street; over love affair. *México,* March 23, 1929.

April 1929. Juan Godínez and Pascual Velasco fought over a telephone booth in front of a South Chicago, Illinois, restaurant. Velasco died from knife wounds. *México,* April 16, 1929.

March 1930. A Mexican was killed in the East Chicago, Indiana, *colonia.* Juan Rodríguez was charged later but acquitted for lack of evidence. *Calumet News,* March 18, 1930.

May 1930. East Chicago, Indiana. A Mexican shot and killed his son-in-law after the younger man threatened to kill the assailant's daughter. *Calumet News,* May 16, 1930.

June 1930. Gary, Indiana. A Mexican was near death from gunshot wounds— another Mexican shot him after a violent argument over a girl and a gambling debt. *Calumet News,* July 16, 1930.

February 1931. Gary, Indiana. A Mexican customer stabbed a compatriot pool-room operator in a fight over a soda bottle refund. *Calumet News,* February 7, 1931.

March 1931. Chicago. Carlos Franco, drunk and in a fit of passion, beat Gregoria G. de Márquez and shot her twice because she rejected his advances. *El Nacional,* March 14, 1931.

April 1931. *El Nacional* condemned Jesús Barragán, alias "the Monkey," for the "cowardly" stabbing death of Francisco Bravo, a pool-hall proprietor in South Chicago, Illinois. April 1, 1931.

May 1931. Twenty-nine-year-old Francisco Juárez was hospitalized in South Chicago after his roommate, Salvador R. Gutiérrez, stabbed him. *El Nacional,* May 13, 1931.

June 1931. A Mexican was wounded in East Chicago gunfight between two Mexicans over a watch. *Calumet News,* June 6, 1931.

August 1931. East Chicago, Indiana. Miguel Barragán stabbed his son-in-law to death because he had been beating his daughter. *Calumet News,* August 9, 1931.

October 1931. The *Calumet News* complained of "Another Mexican knife fight in Gary, Indiana." October 3, 1931.

October 1931. *Calumet News* told of a Mexican in East Chicago, Indiana, who was arrested "for injuries due to his reckless knife." October 31, 1931.

October 1931. *El Nacional* announced the discovery of the beheaded corpse of "El Veneno" in an alley in South Chicago, Illinois. October 26, 1931.

October 1931. A *Calumet News* story reported three knife fights involving Mexicans in East Chicago, Indiana. October 14, 1931.

November 1931. An East Chicago, Indiana, stabbing prompted the headline in the *Calumet News,* "Another Mexican murdered." November 23, 1931.

January 1932. Chicago, Illinois. A man named Paniagua made repeated advances to Ildefonso de la Cruz' wife. The husband stabbed Paniagua to death. *El Nacional,* April 23, 1932.

February 1933. Gary, Indiana. Juan García stabbed grocer Rafael Muro to death when he chastised García for reading a newspaper without purchasing it. *El Nacional,* February 4, 1933.

June 1933. Houston, Texas. A Mexican named Fidencio eloped with his underage girlfriend María, and her parents filed charges. *Houston Chronicle,* June 23, 1933.

Notes

Introduction

1. See John Higham, *Strangers in the Land,* for penetrating insights into the often negative reaction to European immigrants.

2. Karen J. Winkler, "Scholars Say Chicano-Studies Field 'Revolutionized' by Issues of Diversity," *Academe Today* (reprint from *Chronicle of Higher Education,* September 26, 1990).

3. Peter Skerry, *Mexican Americans,* passim.

4. Richard Griswold del Castillo, *The Los Angeles Barrios, 1850–1890,* pp. 108, 116. See also Gilbert G. González and Raúl Fernández, "Chicano History," *Pacific Historical Review* 58 (November 1994): 469–498, for discussion of economic structural differences between nineteenth- and twentieth-century experiences of Mexicans in the United States. For a discussion of the process in Texas, see Guadalupe San Miguel, *"Let All of Them Take Heed,"* pp. 6, 38.

5. See Arnoldo De León and Kenneth L. Stewart, *Not Room Enough,* passim, for a slightly revisionist work on the degree to which Mexicans were integrated into local government in Texas.

6. See Rodolfo Acuña, *Occupied America,* passim, and Alfredo Mirandé, *Gringo Justice,* passim. Both authors see the justice system as simply oppressive for all Mexicans, regardless of era.

7. See Reginald Horsman, *Race and Manifest Destiny,* and Philip Wayne Powell, *Tree of Hate.*

8. Ricardo Romo, *East Los Angeles,* pp. 89–111.

9. *New York Times,* November 10, 1926.

10. "Prison Reforms in Arizona," *Charities and the Commons* 1907: 333.

11. William J. Bowers, *Legal Homicide,* pp. 73–79, 272–273.

12. *Differential application of the law* also means discriminatory treatment at every level of the legal system.

13. See Matthew Donald Esposito, "From Cuauhtémoc to Juárez" (Master's thesis, Arizona State University, 1993), for discussion of the rise of nationalistic symbols in the Porfiriato.

14. Kerby Miller, *Emigrants and Exiles,* passim.

15. *El Imparcial de Texas,* March 6, 1919; *Houston Chronicle,* May 4, 1919; Roberto Treviño, "Prensa y Patria," *Western Historical Quarterly* 22 (November 1991): 451–472; Carole Christian, "Joining the American Mainstream," *Southwestern Historical Quarterly* 92 (April 1989): 559–595; Thomas E. Sheridan, *Los Tucsonenses,* pp. 76, 100–106.

16. Reprinted in *La Opinión,* October 5, 1926 (my translation). Henceforth, translations from Spanish are mine unless otherwise indicated.

1. THE MEXICAN REVOLUTION, BORDER MEXICANS, AND ANGLOS

1. John M. Hart, *Revolutionary Mexico,* passim, discusses the United States' economic domination of Mexico.

2. *Houston Chronicle,* January 12, February 3, June 21, 28, and 29, July 2, September 13 and 30, and December 11, 1908; W. Dirk Raat, *Revoltosos,* pp. 47–53. James A. Sandos, *Rebellion in the Borderlands,* passim, discusses how antiradical sentiment is extended to exiled *revoltosos.*

3. Alan Knight, *The Mexican Revolution,* vol. 1, pp. 22–23, and David Pletcher, *Rails, Mines, and Progress,* passim, discuss failed entrepreneurship in Mexico during the Porfiriato.

4. "Memory of a Man," The John Peck Family Manuscript, Arizona Historical Society Archives (henceforth cited as AHSA), p. 385.

5. J. T. Dickerson, State Board of Public Affairs, Guthrie, Oklahoma, to Philander Knox, secretary of state, November 25, 1910, National Archives (henceforth cited as NA), RG 59, 812.00/498.

6. Romo, *East Los Angeles,* pp. 91–108.

7. Luther Ellsworth, consul in Piedras Negras, to Department of State, August 30, 1910, and Ellsworth to Department of State, October 13, 1910, NA, RG 59, 812.00/400.

8. Alance A. Miller, U.S. consul in Tampico, to Department of State, September 6, 1910, and Miller to Department of State, September 15, 1910, NA, RG 59, 812.00.

9. Undated communiqué from U.S. consul in San Luis Potosí, fall 1910, NA, RG 59, 812.00.

10. F. Arturo Rosales, "The Lynching of Antonio Rodríguez: An Historical Reassessment" (manuscript), p. 12.

11. Berta Ulloa, *Revolución intervenida,* pp. 29–35.

12. B. Johnny Rube, "Raid Mexican Insurgents Once Attacked Border Town," *Yuma Sun,* October 24, 1986, p. 11.

13. Raat, *Revoltosos,* p. 246; Hart, *Revolutionary Mexico,* p. 255; Rudolfo Rocha, "The Influence of the Mexican Revolution on the Mexico-Texas Border, 1910–1916" (Ph.D. dissertation, Texas Tech University, 1981), p. 123; Memorandum, Department of State, Division of Latin American Affairs, September 5, 1912, NA, RG 59, 812.00.

14. Rocha, "The Influence of the Mexican Revolution on the Mexico-Texas Border," pp. 124–127.

15. Hart, *Revolutionary Mexico,* pp. 283, 290; Ulloa, *Revolución intervenida,* p. 77.

16. Knight, *The Mexican Revolution,* vol. 1, pp. 72–73.

17. *La Prensa,* July 5, 22, 1913.

18. *La Prensa,* September 11, 1913; Rocha, "The Influence of the Mexican Revolution on the Mexico-Texas Border," p. 182.

19. Hart, *Revolutionary Mexico,* p. 268; Rocha, "The Influence of the Mexican Revolution on the Mexico-Texas Border," p. 115.

20. Rocha, "The Influence of the Mexican Revolution on the Mexico-Texas Border," pp. 162, 166; *New York Times,* August 7, 1913.

21. J. A. Fernández, San Antonio consul general, to Secretaría de Relaciones Exteriores (henceforth cited as SRE), November 10, 1913, Archivo Histórico de la Secretaría de Relaciones Exteriores (henceforth cited as AHSRE), 16-9-182.

22. *Los Angeles Times*, November 15, 1913.

23. *New York Times*, March 16, 17, 1914.

24. Mario T. García, *Desert Immigrants*, p. 186; Don M. A. Coerver and Linda B. Hall, *Texas and the Mexican Revolution*, pp. 77–78; *Houston Chronicle*, April 24, 25, 27, 1914; Rocha, "The Influence of the Mexican Revolution on the Mexico-Texas Border," pp. 162, 168.

25. *Arizona Republican*, August 8, 9, 10, and 11, 1914.

26. Ibid.

27. Rocha, "The Influence of the Mexican Revolution on the Mexico-Texas Border," pp. 248–249; *El Cosmopolita*, February 27, 1915.

28. Glenn Justice, *Revolution on the Rio Grande*, pp. 9–12; Anita Harlan, "The Battles of 'Ambos Nogales,'" AHSA, MS 332, p. 10; García, *Desert Immigrants*, pp. 188, 192.

29. García, *Desert Immigrants*, pp. 192–193; Romo, *East Los Angeles*, p. 101.

30. *El Paso Times*, May 8 and 16, 1916. Justice, *Revolution on the Rio Grande*, p. 11, indicates the boy was four years old.

31. *Houston Chronicle*, May 14, 1916.

32. Charles H. Harris III and Louis Sadler, "The Plan de San Diego and the Mexican–United States War Crisis of 1916," in *Border Revolution*, ed. Harris and Sadler, pp. 89–90; Sandos, *Rebellion in the Borderlands*, p. 161; *Houston Chronicle*, May 14, 1916.

33. *El Paso Times*, May 16, 1916. *El Cosmopolita*, May 20, June 24, 1916.

34. Harris and Sadler, "The Plan de San Diego and the Mexican–United States War Crisis of 1916," pp. 86–89.

35. James Rodgers, Department of State, to Cándido Aguilar, June 16, 1916, AHSRE, 12-7-229.

36. G. H. French to Adjutant General of U.S. Army, Washington, D.C., February 27, 1917, NA, RG 59, 812.0144.

37. *Houston Chronicle*, April 8, 1917; Justice, *Revolution on the Rio Grande*, pp. 11–12; John A. Pope to Melquiades García, Mexican consul in Laredo, August 18, 1917, AHSRE, 16/2/192; Harris and Sadler, "The Plan de San Diego," p. 97.

38. *El Cosmopolita*, December 12, 1917.

39. *Houston Chronicle*, December 26, 1917; Coerver and Hall, *Texas and the Mexican Revolution*, pp. 118–119.

40. *El Cosmopolita*, December 8, 1917; *New York Times*, December 25, 1917; Alvin A. Adee to Henry Wilson, March 9, 1918, NA, RG 59, 711.12; ibid., 311.12.

41. *El Cosmopolita*, January 26 and February 9, 1918; *El Imparcial de Texas*, March 7, 1918.

42. Justice, *Revolution on the Rio Grande*, pp. 49–55.

43. Hart, *Revolutionary Mexico*, pp. 342–343.

44. Raat, *Revoltosos*, p. 261.

45. *New York Times*, January 6, 1917; Harris and Sadler, "The Plan de San Diego," pp. 91–92; see Richmond, *Venustiano Carranza's Nationalist Struggle, 1893–1920*, pp. 203–211, for a thorough discussion of the German connection.

46. *El Imparcial de Texas,* September 5, 1918; Harlan, "The Battles of 'Ambos Nogales,'" p. 3; Oscar J. Martínez, *Fragments of the Mexican Revolution,* pp. 194–196.

47. *El Imparcial de Texas,* July 24, 1919.

2. MÉXICO LINDO MOBILIZATION

1. Sarah Deutsch, *No Separate Refuge,* pp. 203–204; David Montejano, *Anglos and Mexicans in the Making of Texas, 1836–1986,* pp. 167–174.

2. Edward J. Escobar, "Race and Law Enforcement" (manuscript), p. 92.

3. Andrés Avila, interview, April 23, 1927, Manuel Gamio Papers, Box 1, File 3.

4. *La Prensa,* April 20, 1914.

5. *Arizona Republican,* January 8, 1919; *El Imparcial de Texas,* March 18 and April 4, 1919.

6. David Villaseñor, interview, May 3, 1927, Manuel Gamio Papers, Box 2, File 11. John Chávez, *The Lost Land,* pp. 63–84, discusses Mexican immigrant resentment of U.S. imperialism in Mexico.

7. *El Imparcial de Texas,* June 13 and 29, 1918; *Houston Chronicle,* February 19, 1924; Charles H. Harris III and Louis Sadler, "The 1911 Reyes Conspiracy," in *Border Revolution,* ed. Harris and Sadler, pp. 31–33.

8. *El Mosquito,* April 6, 1919; Richmond, "Mexican Immigration and Border Strategy during the Revolution, 1910–1920," p. 279.

9. *La Opinión,* March 17 and October 14, 1928.

10. *El Imparcial de Texas,* November 23, 1920.

11. *El Imparcial de Texas,* January 13, 1921.

12. *México,* October 20, 1928, microfilm reel 62, Chicago Historical Society, Chicago Foreign Language Press Survey (henceforth cited as CFLPS).

13. *La Opinión,* September 24, 1926; *New York Times,* January 5, 1926.

14. *La Opinión,* September 23, 1928.

15. Juan Gómez Quiñones, "Piedras contra la luna," in *Contemporary Mexico,* ed. James Wilkie, p. 523; *El Amigo del Hogar,* February 21 and March 14, 1926; *La Opinión,* March 25, 1928.

16. See Guadalupe San Miguel, *"Let All of Them Take Heed,"* and Mario T. García, *Mexican Americans,* for discussions on the extensive efforts of the Mexican American generation to desegregate in Texas. For a California emphasis, see Gilbert G. González, *Chicano Education in the Era of Segregation,* passim.

17. Secretaría de Relaciones Exteriores, "Suspuesta exclusión de niños mexicanos en las escuelas de Tejas," *Diario Official* (c. November 1910), AHSRE, pp. 415–516; Scott W. Solliday, "The Journey to Rio Salado: Hispanic Migrations to Tempe, Arizona" (Master's thesis, Arizona State University, 1993), pp. 100–102; David Ray García, "The Romo Decision and Desegregation in Tempe" (Senior thesis, Arizona State University, 1993), passim.

18. Judith Fincher Laird, "Argentine Kansas," pp. 104–105; Transcript of School Segregation Testimony by Superintendent of Schools for Argentine, Kansas, NA, RG 59, 311.215, Kansas City; *New York Times,* May 14, 1929; Roberto R. Alvarez, Jr., *La Familia,* pp. 148–161.

19. *Hispano América,* August 9, 1919; September 8, 1923; *La Opinión,* September 11, 1928; Enrique Santibáñez, consul in San Antonio, to Amador Candelaria,

president of the Comisión Honorífica Mexicana, Austin, Texas, July 30, 1930, AHSRE, IV-78-26; Ehlalie Appelt to Secretaría de Relaciones Exteriores, November 4, 1929, AHSRE, IV-75-28.

20. Ibid., pp. 17–18; *Houston Chronicle,* December 30, 1914; *Hispano América,* March 7, 1925.

21. *La Prensa,* June 26, 1913; *El Cosmopolita,* December 16, 1916.

22. Acuña, *Occupied America,* p. 161.

23. Arnoldo De León, *Mexican Americans in Texas,* p. 38; Neil Foley, "Mexican Migrant and Tenant Labor in Central Texas Cotton Counties, 1880–1930: Transformation in a Multicultural Society," *Wooster Review* 9 (Spring 1989): 95–99; Dennis Nodín Valdés, *Al Norte,* pp. 1–29; Carey McWilliams, *Factories in the Fields,* passim.

24. Arnoldo De León, *Ethnicity in the Sunbelt,* p. 13; Montejano, *Anglos and Mexicans in the Making of Texas,* p. 104.

25. Montejano, *Anglos and Mexicans in the Making of Texas,* p. 116; Acuña, *Occupied America,* p. 161.

26. Sheridan, *Los Tucsonenses,* pp. 89–90; José Amaro Hernández, *Mutual Aid for Survival,* pp. 75–83; James D. McBride, "The Liga Protectora Latina: A Mexican American Benevolent Society in Arizona," *Journal of the West* 14 (October 1975): 82–90; *Arizona Republican,* November 12, 1914; *The Oasis,* April 15, 1899.

27. *La Gaceta Mexicana,* May 1, 1928; Frank Gibler, interview, Houston, Texas, May 12, 1977; Frank Gibler to Governor Dan Moody, December 4, 1928, Texas State Archives (henceforth cited as TSA), RG 301, Box 42.

28. Hernández, *Mutual Aid for Survival,* p. 79.

29. *La Opinión,* September 23, 1926; Romo, *East Los Angeles,* p. 145.

30. Michael M. Smith, "Mexicans in Kansas City: The First Generation, 1900–1920," *Perspectives in Mexican American Studies* 2 (1989): 29–58.

31. Hernández, *Mutual Aid for Survival,* p. 75; Paul S. Taylor, *Mexican Labor in the United States: Chicago and the Calumet Region,* p. 152.

32. *Houston Chronicle,* January 14, 1908; *La Prensa,* November 20, 1913; Thomas Martin, lawyer to Dallas Mexican Consulate, to Antonio Villarreal, secretary of Secretaría de Agricultura y Promoción, March 12, 1915, AHSRE, 1/5/11; Emilio Zamora, *The World of the Mexican Worker in Texas,* pp. 142–143.

33. Cardoso de Oliveira, Brazilian Embassy, to William S. Bryan, secretary of state, January 25, 1915, NA, RG 59, 311.1221, R16.

34. Francisco Olivares, Phoenix consul, to SRE, October 11, 1912, AHSRE, L-E-828; *El Imparcial de Texas,* December 12, 1918; Comité Pro-Defensa Estrada to Plutarco Elías Calles, president of Mexico, June 1, 1927, Archivo General de la Nación (henceforth cited as AGN), Presidentes, Calles-Obregón, 104-M-49; *Hispano América,* June 11, 1927; Romo, *East Los Angeles,* p. 54; *La Opinión,* March 31, 1928.

35. See *El Imparcial de Texas,* 1917–1921, for this regular feature.

36. Romo, *East Los Angeles,* p. 158; *La Opinión,* March 23, 1928.

37. Jesús Franco interview, c. April, 1927, Manuel Gamio Papers, Box 2, File 6.

38. Pedro de la Lama interview, 1927, Manuel Gamio Papers, Box 1, File 1.

39. Juan Rodríguez, *Crónicas diabólicas de "Jorge Ulica"/Julio G. Arce,* pp. 9–20.

40. *El Tucsonense,* April 3, 1923.

41. Hernández, *Mutual Aid for Survival,* p. 79; Sheridan, *Los Tucsonenses,* p. 174; *La Opinión,* September 9, 10, 14, 23, and 29, 1928.

42. Paul S. Taylor, *Mexican Labor in the United States: Chicago and the Calumet Region,* pp. 143–144.

43. Smith, "Mexicans in Kansas City," pp. 48–49.

44. Ibid., p. 48.

45. *La Gaceta Mexicana,* February 15, 1927; *México,* March 16, 1926, CFLPS.

46. *El Cosmopolita,* June 21, 1919; *El Amigo del Hogar,* September 15, 1927.

47. *El Nacional,* September 19, 1931, November 30, 1931, and April 23, 1932, CFLPS.

48. Manuel Gamio, *The Life Story of the Mexican Immigrant,* p. 199.

49. Ibid., p. 202.

3. THE CONSULS AND MÉXICO LINDO

1. Studies that discuss aspects of the consular service are Albert Camarillo, *Chicanos in a Changing Society,* pp. 92, 119, 149, 151; Griswold del Castillo, *The Los Angeles Barrios, 1850–1890,* pp. 119–120; and García, *Desert Immigrants,* pp. 99–504. Studies that contain extensive discussions of consular performance are Gómez Quiñones, "Piedras contra la luna," pp. 497–498; John Martínez, *Mexican Emigration to the United States, 1910–1930;* Mario T. García, "Porfirian Diplomacy and the Administration of Justice in Texas, 1877–1900," *Aztlán* 16 (1985): 1–26; Lawrence Cardoso, *Mexican Emigration to the United States, 1897–1931;* Raat, *Revoltosos;* Francisco E. Balderrama, *In Defense of La Raza;* Francisco E. Balderrama and Raymond Rodríguez, *Decade of Betrayal;* Romo, *East Los Angeles;* Smith, "Mexicans in Kansas City," pp. 29–58; Manuel Gamio, *The Life Story of the Mexican Immigrant;* Manuel Gamio, *Mexican Immigration to the United States;* Douglas W. Richmond, "Mexican Immigration and Border Strategy during the Revolution," *New Mexico Historical Review* 57 (July 1982): 279; and George J. Sánchez, *Becoming Mexican American,* pp. 108–125.

2. *El Observador Mexicano,* July 23, 1898; *El Ocasional,* November 21, 1898.

3. Luis G. Zorrilla, *Relaciones políticas, económicas, y sociales de Mexico en el extranjero,* vol. 3, p. 12.

4. Raat, *Revoltosos,* pp. 182–183.

5. *Revolt,* March 16, 1912.

6. García, *Desert Immigrants,* p. 184.

7. *El Cosmopolita,* October 2 and December 10, 1915.

8. Gómez Quiñones, "Piedras contra la luna," pp. 511–513; *El Cosmopolita,* April 14 and October 15, 1914; February 24 and March 17, 1915; October 2, 1915.

9. Julio Arce to Cándido Aguilar, secretary of SRE, October 21, 1916, AHSRE, 23-21-156.

10. Ibid.

11. Ramón P. de Negri, consul, to Aguilar, December 2, 1916; Sub-Secretario del Estado del Interior to Rafael Nieto, sub-secretario, SRE, June 19, 1917; both in AHSRE, 23-21-156.

12. De Negri to Aguilar, February 11, 1918, AHSRE, 23-21-156. In 1916, *El Eco de México* received a subsidy of $650 a month to promote *carrancista* sentiment. The government of Mexico also funded New York City's Columbus Publishing Com-

pany, which published *El Gráfico*. Sánchez, *Becoming Mexican American*, p. 111; Douglas W. Richmond, *Venustiano Carranza's Nationalist Struggle*, p. 190.

13. *El Cosmopolita*, June 22, 1918.

14. Raúl R. Domínguez to Aguilar, June 13, 1918, AHSRE, 12-6-81. See Deborah J. Baldwin, *Protestants and the Mexican Revolution*, passim, for *carrancista* ties to Protestants.

15. Richmond, *Venustiano Carranza's Nationalist Struggle*, pp. 192–193; Diego Fernández, Mexican Embassy, to Bainbridge Colby, secretary of state, March 25, 1920, NA, RG 59, 311.1221 C39.

16. J. J. Uriburu, for the "American Latin League," to Emilio Salinas, consul in Los Angeles, January 17, 1910, Ramo Trabajo, AGN, 137-22-11; Romo, *East Los Angeles*, p. 154.

17. *El Cosmopolita*, October 11, 1919, reprinted in *El Mosquito*, October 11, 1919.

18. Zorrilla, *Relaciones políticas, económicas, y sociales de Mexico en el extranjero*, vol. 3, p. 219.

19. García, "Porfirian Diplomacy and the Administration of Justice in Texas," p. 2.

20. Ignacio Mariscal, SRE, to Ramón Corral, "Summary of Reports from Los Angeles, San Francisco, and El Paso," March 12, 1908, Ramo Gobernación, AGN, 1A-907-8-1-1.

21. Quoted in Escobar, "Race and Law Enforcement," p. 19.

22. Acuña, *Occupied America*, p. 161; Gómez Quiñones, "Piedras contra la luna," pp. 504–509; undated clipping of *El Imparcial de Texas*, NA, RG 59, File 811.12.

23. Gómez Quiñones, "Piedras contra la luna," p. 496.

24. *La Prensa*, January 11, 1913.

25. Gómez Quiñones, "Piedras contra la luna," pp. 504–509.

26. J. A. Fernández, San Antonio consul general for Mexico, to SRE, November 10, 1913, AHSRE, 16-9-182.

27. Both quotations from Sub-Secretario de Gobierno to Secretario de Fomento, Colonización e Industria, October 3, 1913, Trabajo, AGN, 8–31.

28. *La Prensa*, September 18, 1913.

29. *New York Times*, July 5, 1913.

30. *New York Times*, May 9, 1914.

31. Sub-Secretario de Gobierno to Secretario de Fomento, Colonización e Industria, October 17, 1913, Trabajo, AGN, 58-3.

32. Smith, "Mexicans in Kansas City," p. 41.

33. *El Cosmopolita*, June 24, 1916; *La Prensa*, October 18, 1916.

34. Cardoso, *Mexican Emigration to the United States, 1897–1931*, p. 65.

35. Gómez Quiñones implies that consular intervention in helping Mexicans to register went against the interests of immigrants. See his "Piedras contra la luna," p. 521. Lawrence Cardoso gives an opposing explanation in "Labor Emigration to the Southwest, 1911–1920, Mexican Attitudes and Policy," *Southwestern Historical Quarterly* 84 (April 1973): 400–416; he sees the intervention as an effort to assure that immigrants would not be jailed.

36. Cardoso, *Mexican Emigration to the United States, 1897–1931*, p. 67; Martínez, *Mexican Emigration to the United States, 1910–1930*, p. 44.

37. Gustavo G. Hernández, consul in Globe, Arizona, to Thomas J. Croaff, presi-

dent, Arizona State Federation of Labor, May 10, 1918; Hernández to George W. P. Hunt, governor of Arizona, May 21, 1918; Hernández to Alberto J. Pani, Secretaría de Industria, Comercio y Trabajo (henceforth cited as SICT), May 29, 1918; all in AGN, Trabajo, 137-20.

38. Richmond, *Venustiano Carranza's Nationalist Struggle*, p. 231; see *El Cosmopolita*, January 1, 6, and 20, February 3, 17, 19, and 24, March 3, and November 17, 1917, for accounts of these changes.

39. *El Imparcial de Texas*, November 28, 1918.

40. Romo, *East Los Angeles*, p. 156.

41. Gómez Quiñones, "Piedras contra la luna," pp. 519–521; Raat, *Los Revoltosos*, pp. 273–274.

42. Andrés G. García, consul general, El Paso, to SICT, February 28, 1918, Ramo Trabajo, AGN, 137-22-11; *El Excelsior*, December 24, 1918.

43. Cardoso, *Mexican Emigration to the United States, 1897–1931*, pp. 66–67. Gómez Quiñones, "Piedras contra la luna," pp. 518–520, presents a critical assessment. See Richmond, *Venustiano Carranza's Nationalist Struggle*, pp. 189–194, and Richmond, "Mexican Immigration and Border Strategy during the Revolution," pp. 279–280, for positive appraisal.

44. See Chapter 8 on Mexicans on death row. Cardoso, "Labor Emigration to the Southwest, 1911–1920," p. 407; Martínez, *Mexican Emigration to the United States, 1910–1930*, p. 73.

45. Jesús Franco, *El alma de la raza*, p. 23.

46. Balderrama, *In Defense of La Raza*, pp. 9–10; Cardoso, *Mexican Emigration to the United States, 1897–1931*, pp. 105–106; Martínez, *Mexican Emigration to the United States, 1910–1930*, p. 74; Zaragoza Vargas, *Proletarians of the North*, p. 231, fn. 34. See Chapter 5 for discussion on recession-related riots against Mexicans.

47. Atilaño Saldaña to Alvaro Obregón, May 1, 1924, Ramo Presidentes, Obregón-Calles, AGN, 241-E-K-1; M. G. Prieto, Phoenix consul, to SRE, September 29, 1923, AHSRE, 38-11-111.

48. "Mexicanos emigrantes, medidas sugeridas para controlar sus energías," Report to President Alvaro Obregón, June 10, 1922, AGN, Ramo Presidentes, Obregón-Calles, 711-M-30; *New York Times*, September 12, 1922; Balderrama, *In Defense of La Raza*, pp. 7–11; Cardoso, *Mexican Emigration to the United States, 1897–1931*, pp. 113–114.

49. Cardoso, *Mexican Emigration to the United States, 1897–1931*, pp. 113–114.

50. See Stanley R. Ross, "Dwight Morrow and the Mexican Revolution," *Hispanic American Historical Review* 38 (November 1958): 506–527, for examples of Sheffield's and Kellogg's Mexico bashing.

51. *La Prensa*, January 3, 1927.

52. Alan Knight, "Popular Culture and the Revolutionary State in Mexico, 1910–1940," *Hispanic American Historical Review* 74 (Fall 1994): 393–444. See also Baldwin, *Protestants and the Mexican Revolution*, passim, for a discussion of Sáenz' Protestantism.

53. *La Opinión*, January 6, January 24, February 22, and May 5, 1928; *La Prensa*, February 22, 1928.

54. John J. Morton to Frank Kellogg, secretary of state, January 10, 1927, NA, RG 59, 711.12/863.

55. Secretaría de Educación Pública, Comisión Técnica Consultiva, typescript, Eduardo Hernández Chazarro to SRE, August 21, 1931, AHSRE, IV-212-14.

56. Balderrama, *In Defense of La Raza,* pp. 77–78.

57. Eduardo Hay to consuls, circular, 1936; Manuel Esparza to Lázaro Cárdenas, 1936; both in Ramo Presidentes, Cárdenas, AGN, 17-1/50.

58. *Chicago Tribune,* November 9, 10, 11, 1924; Paul S. Taylor, "Crime and the Foreign Born: The Problem of the Mexican," in *Report on Crime and Criminal Justice in Relation to the Foreign Born, for the National Commission on Law Observance and Enforcement,* no. 10, ed. Edith Abbott, p. 231.

59. Department of State, "Internal Memorandum," June 12, 1926, NA, RG 59, 812.918.

60. *La Opinión,* September 10, 29, 1928.

61. Gamio, *The Life Story of the Mexican Immigrant,* p. 152.

62. *El Amigo del Hogar,* December 6, 1925.

63. John Parker, governor of Louisiana, to Secretary of State, May 17, 1921, NA, RG 59, 311.122 L88; David I. Garrett, district attorney of Monroe, to Thomas O. Harris, secretary to the governor of Louisiana, May 20, 1921, NA, RG 59, 311.122 L88. On Arturo Elías having an unsavory reputation, see Gómez Quiñones, "Piedras contra la luna," pp. 507–508; Raat, *Revoltosos,* passim.

64. Escobar, "Race and Law Enforcement," p. 168.

65. Translation of *El Universal* article, September 1927, in NA, RG 59, 311.1221, del Hoyo. See James Stuart Olson, *The Ethnic Dimension in American History,* p. 122, for the Sacco-Vanzetti execution.

66. *El Universal* article, September 1927, in NA, RG 59, 311.1221, del Hoyo.

67. J. Willis Cook, American minister in Mexico, to Secretary of State, September 29, 1927, and Francis White to "Certain American Consular Officers in Mexico," September 28, 1927, NA, RG 59, 311.1221, del Hoyo.

68. J. Edgar Hoover to Robert F. Kelley, Department of State, December 20, 1927, NA, RG 59, 311.1221, del Hoyo.

69. Manuel Téllez, Mexican ambassador, to Charles E. Hughes, October 11, 1923, Hughes to F. W. Richardson, governor of California, October 22, 1923, F. W. Richardson to Hughes, October 22, 1923, and Téllez to Hughes, October 11, 1923, NA, RG 59, 311.122, Santa Paula. See Martha Menchaca, *The Mexican Outsiders,* pp. 46–50, for police relations with Mexicans in Santa Paula.

70. *El Nacional,* April 29, 1930, CFLPS; *United States ex rel Velasco v Ragen,* 158 F2d 87 (7th Cir, 1946); Rafael Aveleyra, consul in Chicago, to SRE, April 31, 1931, AHSRE, IV/344/44; M. Jesús Gallo, secretary to Manuel Avila Camacho, president of Mexico, to President Camacho, Presidentes, Camacho, AGN, 575.1/87.

71. Frank Kellogg, secretary of state, to Miriam Ferguson, governor of Texas, April 19, 1926, and Calles to Manuel Hernández, editor of *El Horizonte,* March 11, 1926, NA, RG 59, 311.1212, José Puig Casuranc; *El Cronista del Valle,* March 11, 1926.

72. Raúl Aguirre Manjarrez, general de la Brijada, D.F., to Lázaro Cárdenas, president of Mexico, 1936, AGN, Presidentes, Cárdenas, 573.12/6.

4. MEXICAN CRIMINALS IN THE UNITED STATES

1. Edith Abbott, ed., *Report on Crime and Criminal Justice in Relation to the Foreign Born,* p. 72.

2. Taylor, "Crime and the Foreign Born," p. 239; Don D. Lescochier, "The Vital Problem, Mexican Immigration," in *Proceedings of the National Conference on Social Work, Fifty-fourth Annual Session Held in Des Moines, Iowa, May 11, 1927,* p. 551.

3. Paul S. Taylor, *An American-Mexican Frontier,* p. 167.

4. Paul Livingston Warnshius, "Crime and Criminal Justice among the Mexicans in Illinois," in *Report on Crime and Criminal Justice in Relation to the Foreign Born,* ed. Abbott, p. 267.

5. Ibid., pp. 122–139; F. Arturo Rosales, "Mexicans, Interethnic Violence, and Crime in Chicago Area during the 1920s and 1930s," in *Perspectives in Mexican American Studies,* vol. 2, ed. Juan García, pp. 59–97.

6. *La Opinión,* February 24, 1928.

7. Arthur Pettit, *Images of the Mexican American in Fiction and Film,* p. 85; Emory Bogardus, *Immigrants and Race Attitudes,* passim; Mark Reisler, *By the Sweat of Their Brow,* p. 128.

8. "Report of Frank Buckley of the Bureau of Prohibition," in United States, 71st Congress, 3d Session, *Enforcement of the Prohibition Laws: Official Records of the National Commission on Law Observance and Enforcement,* vol. 4, p. 924.

9. Deutsch, *No Separate Refuge,* p. 152.

10. Escobar, "Race and Law Enforcement," pp. 134–135.

11. *Los Angeles Times,* November 12, 1919; T. Earle Sallenger, "The Mexican Population of Omaha," *Sociology and Social Research* 24 (May–June 1924): 263; Alida C. Bowler, "Recent Statistics on Crime and the Foreign Born," in *Report on Crime and Criminal Justice in Relation to the Foreign Born,* ed. Abbott, pp. 100–102.

12. United States Bureau of the Census, *Fifteenth Census of the United States Taken in the Year 1930, General Report of Statistics by Subjects,* vol. 2, pp. 247, 362, 609, 638, 642; also pp. 115–131, 724–805, 852–949; Warnshius, "Crime and Criminal Justice among the Mexicans in Illinois," pp. 279–281; Taylor, "Crime and the Foreign Born," pp. 204–207; Bowler, "Recent Statistics on Crime and the Foreign Born," pp. 100–102.

13. Taylor, "Crime and the Foreign Born," p. 2; Max Sylvius Handman, "Preliminary Report on Nationality and Delinquency: The Mexican in Texas," in *Report on Crime and Criminal Justice in Relation to the Foreign Born,* ed. Abbott, pp. 245, 258; Paul S. Taylor, *Mexican Labor in the United States: Dimmit County, Winter Garden District, South Texas,* p. 232; Treviño, "Prensa y Patria," pp. 451–472.

14. United States Bureau of the Census, *Fifteenth Census of the United States Taken in the Year 1930,* vol. 3, *Population, Part II,* p. 116; Taylor, "Crime and the Foreign Born," pp. 229, 237.

15. Handman, "Preliminary Report on Nationality and Delinquency," pp. 245, 258; Taylor, *Mexican Labor in the United States: Dimmit County, Winter Garden District, South Texas,* p. 230; Treviño, "Prensa y Patria," pp. 451–472.

16. See Vargas, *Proletarians of the North,* pp. 86–123; Montejano, *Anglos and Mexicans in the Making of Texas,* passim; Valdés, *Al Norte,* pp. 8–29; Romo, *East Los Angeles,* pp. 112–128.

17. Taylor, "Crime and the Foreign Born," p. 218.

18. Montejano, *Anglos and Mexicans in the Making of Texas,* pp. 197–120.

19. C. L. Bouvé, agent of the United States, to Dan Moody, governor of Texas,

September 24, 1927, TSA, RG 301, Box 56; Manuel Payno, consul in Phoenix, to SRE, November 21, 1929, AHSRE, IV-107-26.

20. J. Corzine, J. Creed, and L. Corzine, "Black Concentration and Lynching in the South: Testing Blalock's Power-Threat Hypothesis," *Social Forces* 63 (1983): 774–796.

21. Taylor, *An American-Mexican Frontier,* p. 172.

22. F. Arturo Rosales, "The Mexican Immigrant Experience in Chicago, Houston, and Tucson," in *Houston: A Twentieth Century Urban Frontier,* ed. Rosales and Barry J. Kaplan, pp. 58–77; F. Arturo Rosales, "The Regional Origins of Mexicano Immigrants to Chicago during the 1920s," *Aztlán* 7 (Summer 1976): 187–201; Sheridan, *Los Tucsonenses,* pp. 89–90.

23. Treviño, "Prensa y Patria," pp. 451–472; Carlos Vélez-Ibáñez, *Border Visions,* pp. 40–47; Alvarez, *La Familia,* pp. 118–150; Rosales, "The Mexican Immigrant Experience in Chicago, Houston, and Tucson," pp. 58–77.

24. Ramón Prida, "La criminalidad en Mexico en los últimos años," p. 726; United States Bureau of the Census, *Fifteenth Census of the United States Taken in the Year 1930, Appendix on Families,* "Statistics of Mexican, Indian, Chinese, and Japanese Families," pp. 200–215.

25. Handman, "Preliminary Report on Nationality and Delinquency," pp. 250, 260.

26. For community studies demonstrating this kind of support levels, see Alvarez, *La Familia;* Rosales, "The Mexican Immigrant Experience in Chicago, Houston, and Tucson."

27. Taylor, "Crime and the Foreign Born," pp. 204–207; Bowler, "Recent Statistics on Crime and the Foreign Born," pp. 131–132.

28. Taylor, "Crime and the Foreign Born," p. 211; Escobar, "Race and Law Enforcement," passim.

29. José Anguiano, interview.

30. Knight, *The Mexican Revolution,* vol. 2, p. 520.

31. Knight, *The Mexican Revolution,* vol. 2, p. 395; Prida, "La criminalidad en México en los últimos años," pp. 708–709; José Anguiano, interview; Hilario Silva, interview.

32. O. H. Kleinderg, "The Causes of Violence," in *Violence and Its Causes,* ed. Jean Marie Domenach, p. 87.

33. Luis González, *San José de Gracia,* pp. 142–143.

34. Paul Friedrich, *The Princes of Naranja,* p. 274.

35. Prida, "La criminalidad en México en los últimos años," p. 713.

36. Ibid., p. 718.

37. Erich Fromm and Michael Maccoby, *Social Character in a Mexican Village,* p. 167.

38. Octavio Paz, *The Labyrinth of Solitude,* pp. 65–88; Samuel Ramos, *Profile of Man and Culture in Mexico,* passim; Eric R. Wolf, *Sons of the Shaking Earth,* pp. 238–255.

39. Wolf, *Sons of the Shaking Earth,* p. 33.

40. Frantz Fanon, *The Wretched of the Earth,* passim.

41. González, *San José de Gracia,* p. 143.

42. William B. Taylor, *Drinking, Homicide, and Rebellion in Colonial Mexican*

Villages, passim; Mary Frances Berry and John W. Blassingame, *Long Memories,* pp. 227–260.

43. Friedrich, *The Princes of Naranja,* pp. 274.

44. Taylor, "Crime and the Foreign Born," p. 240.

45. *El Cosmopolita,* June 21, 1919.

46. E. E. Cota, Phoenix consul, to SRE, September 28, 1932, AHSRE, IV-5-7.

47. *Hispano América,* July 7, 1923.

48. Smith, "Mexicans in Kansas City," pp. 29–58.

49. Ibid., pp. 28–31.

50. F. Arturo Rosales and Daniel T. Simon, "Mexican Immigration to the Urban Midwest: East Chicago, Indiana, 1919–1945," *Indiana Magazine of History* 77 (December 1981): 333–357; Ciro Sepúlveda, "Research Note: Una Colonia de Obreros," *Aztlán* 7 (Summer 1976): 237–336.

51. *South Chicago Daily Calumet,* February 22, 1927.

52. *Calumet News,* February 7, June 23, October 3, 14, and 31, 1931.

53. Daniel T. Simon, "Mexican Repatriation in East Chicago, Indiana," *Journal of Mexican American History* 2 (Summer 1974): 11–23; Neil Betten and Raymond Mohl, "From Discrimination to Repatriation: Mexican Life in Gary, Indiana, during the Great Depression," *Pacific Historical Review* 42 (August 1973): 270–388; my survey of the *Calumet News* from 1932 to 1935 yielded only three stories of Mexican violence.

54. Chicago Police Department Homicide Logs, 1921–1930, Illinois Historical Society Archives (henceforth cited as IHSA).

55. *Mexicans in California, Report of Governor C. C. Young's Mexican Fact-Finding Committee,* p. 203.

56. *Arizona Republican,* January 1, 2, 5, 1910.

57. See this notion in a story in *La Lucha,* March 10, 1934, CFLPS.

58. Bowler, "Recent Statistics on Crime and the Foreign Born," pp. 189–194.

59. Smith, "Mexicans in Kansas City," p. 38.

60. "Informe de protección de mexicanos correspondiente al mes de marzo, 1930 en Pittsburgh, Pennsylvania," Consul Servando Barrera Guerra to SRE, AHSRE, IV-73-88.

61. *Arizona Sentinel,* October 17, 1907; see *Arizona Republican,* October 6, 1909, and January 13 and 15, 1910, for other examples.

62. Gamio, *The Life Story of the Mexican Immigrant,* pp. 102–103; José Rocha, interview, April 10, 1927, Gamio Papers, Box 2, File 14.

63. *Calumet News,* July 2, 1926; *El Correo Mexicano,* June 12, 1931.

64. Taylor, "Crime and the Foreign Born," pp. 201–211.

65. Detroit Consul to Consul General in El Paso, June 15, 1931, AHSRE, IV-132-39.

66. Dávila, "The Mexican Migration Problem"; "Informe de protección . . . en Pittsburgh, Pennsylvania," Barrera Guerra, consul, AHSRE, IV-73-88.

67. *Mexicans in California, Report of Governor C. C. Young's Mexican Fact-Finding Committee,* p. 200.

68. Warnshius, "Crime and Criminal Justice among the Mexicans in Illinois," pp. 78–79; *Calumet News,* February 24, 1929, March 7, 1930.

69. Julia Kirk Blackwelder, *Women of the Depression,* pp. 160–161.

70. Mary F. Odom, *Delinquent Daughters,* pp. 145–146; *Mexicans in California, Report of Governor C. C. Young's Mexican Fact-Finding Committee,* p. 200.

71. Blackwelder, *Women of the Depression,* pp. 156–158; García, *Desert Immigrants,* p. 147; Gamio, *The Life Story of the Mexican Immigrant,* pp. 78–79.

72. Luis Castro to SRE, January 22, 1931, AHSRE, IV-73-7.

73. Eduardo Peralta, interview.

74. *Houston Chronicle,* June 13, 1910; *El Imparcial de Texas,* February 27, 1919.

75. Mauricio Mazón, *The Zoot-Suit Riots,* pp. 1–14, 105; Juan Gómez Quiñones, "On Culture," *Revista Chicano Riqueña* 5 (Spring 1977): 29–47.

76. *New York Times,* April 3, 1920.

77. Sub-Secretario to Secretario, Secretaría de Industria, Comercio, y Trabajo, June 5, 1923, Ramo Trabajo, AGN, 704-26.

78. Ibid.

79. *La Patria,* November 15, 1921; September 6, 1923; Reisler, *By the Sweat of Their Brow,* pp. 24–48; Cardoso, *Mexican Emigration to the United States, 1897–1931,* pp. 119–143.

80. *New York Times,* September 8, October 25, and December 24, 1925; January 20, 1926; *La Opinión,* November 8, 1926; James J. Davis, secretary of labor, to Frank Kellogg, secretary of state, April 6, 1925, NA, RG 59, 711.129.

81. H. H. Leonard, U.S. vice consulate in Matamoros, to secretary of state, April 15, 1925, RG 59, 711.12.

82. Clipping in TSA, RG 301, Box 80; *La Prensa,* July 4, 1928; Clifford Alan Perkins, *Border Patrol,* pp. 108, 110.

83. Andrés Morán, interview, March 8, 1927, Gamio Papers, Box 2, File 11; José Anguiano, interview.

84. *La Patria,* November 8, 1921; David Gutiérrez, "Border Patrol," in *Voices of Pimería Alta,* pp. 152–157.

85. *El Imparcial de Texas,* April 8, 1920.

86. Andrés Morán interview, March 8, 1927, Gamio Papers, Box 2, File 11.

87. "Report of Frank Buckley of the Bureau of Prohibition," p. 942.

88. *Memoria de Relaciones Exteriores en el Estados Unidos y Guatemala,* p. 27.

89. García, *Desert Immigrants,* p. 205.

90. *La Opinión,* April 30, 1928; "Listas de algunos mexicanos que fueron muertos en los Estados Unidos de Norte America durante los años de 1911–1919, compilados por el consul en El Paso," January 1920 (henceforth cited as "Listas"), Ramírez y un mexicano desconocido, August 6, 1919, AHSRE, 11/19/24; *El Imparcial de Texas,* April 1, 1921.

91. Pedro Silva interview, March 16, 1927, Gamio Papers, Box 1, File 3.

92. F. Burelach to John D. Works, U.S. senator, July 10, 1913, NA, RG 59, 812.114.

93. John W. Dye, U.S. consul, to the Department of State, "The Narcotic Curse in Ciudad Juárez, Confidential Memorandum," February 24, 1923, NA, RG 59, 812.144.

94. *La Patria,* November 8, 1921; Robert Buffington, "Prohibition in the Borderlands," *Pacific Historical Review* 63 (February 1994): 19–38.

95. Duncan Aikman, "Hell along the Border," p. 17; Charles E. Vermylia to

Frank Kellogg, "Recommendations from the Commission on International and Interracial Factors Adopted by the El Paso Conference, December 11–16," January 11, 1926, NA, RG 59, 711.12/861.

96. George W. P. Hunt, governor of Arizona, to President Warren G. Harding, May 7, 1923, NA, RG 59 711.129; Charles E. Hughes to U.S. commissioners in Mexico City, NA, RG 59 711.129; *New York Times,* February 17, April 3 and 9, 1924; *Houston Chronicle,* March 22, 1924.

97. Felipe Seijar, president, and Isidro A. Torres, secretary, of the Comité Pro-Juárez to governor of the State of Chihuahua, March 17, 1925, NA, RG 59 711.129; *New York Times,* September 21, 1924.

98. "Smuggling on the border between the U.S. and Mexico, Ciudad Juárez Consular District in Mexico," April 23, 1925, NA, RG 59, 711.129.

99. Drew Linard, consul in Piedras Negras, to Secretary of State, April 15, 1925, NA, RG 59 711.12.

5. POLICE TREATMENT OF MEXICAN IMMIGRANTS

1. Micaela Tafolla and Anni Clo Watson, *From Mañana to Ahorita,* p. 1.

2. Warnshius, "Crime and Criminal Justice among the Mexicans in Illinois," pp. 279–280.

3. Antonio Ríos Bustamante, "'Guilty as Hell,' Copper Mines, Mexican Miners, and Community, 1920–1950," manuscript, Chicano Collection, Hayden Library, Arizona State University, Tempe, pp. 1–3.

4. Escobar, "Race and Law Enforcement," p. 31.

5. Ibid., p. 25.

6. *Colton Chronicle,* February 4, 1910, AHSRE, 8/10/144; *San Bernardino Daily Sun,* September 11, 1910, AHSRE, 8/10/144.

7. Taylor, *An American Mexican Frontier,* p. 167.

8. Eliodoso Pérez, Morelia, Michoacán, to Dan Moody, governor of Texas, August 22, 1927, and Moody to C. M. Chambers, state attorney general, August 28, 1927, TSA, RG 301, Box 80.

9. Frank L. Polk, Department of State, to Eliseo Arredondo, confidential agent in Washington, D.C., August 9, 1916; Juan Burns, consul in Galveston, Texas, to Chief of Consular Service, September 8, 1916; Chief of Consular Service to Burns, September 23, 1916; Chief of Consular Service to Ignacio Bonilla, Mexican ambassador, September 23, 1916; all in AHSRE, 12/7/110.

10. Smith, "Mexicans in Kansas City," pp. 38–39.

11. *Wickersham Commission Reports,* no. 14, *Report on the Police,* pp. 61–63.

12. R. E. Johnson, mayor of Marble Falls, to William J. Bryan, secretary of state, September 10, 1913, NA, RG 59, 311.122, Johnson.

13. *La Prensa,,* January 6, 1928; *La Opinión,* March 13, 1928.

14. Montejano, *Anglos and Mexicans in the Making of Texas,* p. 205.

15. *El Imparcial de Texas,* March 24, 1921.

16. Sánchez, *Becoming Mexican American,* pp. 209–226.

17. *La Opinión,* February 14, 1928.

18. "Listas," Manuel Cantú, June 6, 1912.

19. García, *Desert Immigrants,* p. 147.

20. *El Cosmopolita,* January 8, 1916; June 1, 1918.

21. *El Correo Mexicano,* September 30, 1926, and January 7, 1931, CFLPS; quoted in Taylor, "Crime and the Foreign Born," pp. 231–232.

22. Taylor, "Crime and the Foreign Born," p. 299.

23. Escobar, in "Race and Law Enforcement," references no such hostility provoked by ethnic rivalry in Los Angeles.

24. Gamio, *The Life Story of the Mexican Immigrant,* p. 138.

25. Sheridan, *Los Tucsonenses,* p. 215.

26. "Listas," Francisco Rubio, July 30, 1911.

27. Luis Castro, consul in Phoenix, to SRE, January 22, 1931, AHSRE, IV-73-7; Ríos Bustamante, "Guilty as Hell," p. 42.

28. Klondike J. Todd, "Crazed Killer 'Shoots It Out'—48 Shots Fired in Gun Battle on Street," *Arizona Peace Officers' Magazine* 1 (April 1937): 4.

29. Manuel Payno, Mexican consul, Phoenix, to Mexican Ambassador, January 29, 1929, *Arizona Republican,* January 24, 1929, AHSRE, IV/92/15.

30. Andrés García, Mexican consul in El Paso, to Tom Bell, deputy labor commissioner for Texas, June 12, 1918, Bell to T. C. Jennings, state labor commissioner, June 8, 1918, and Jennings to García, June 12, 1918, Ramo Trabajo, AGN, 137-12-11.

31. Téllez to Department of State, March 23, 1922, and Department of State, to Téllez, April 4, 1922, NA, RG 59, 311.1213.G131.

32. C. L. Bouvé, agent of the United States, general and special claims commissions, United States and Mexico, to Governor of Texas, September 24, 1927, TSA, RG 301, Box 56.

33. Téllez to Tanis, May 11, 1923, NA, RG 59, 311.1213, Quintanilla, Alejo; Bouvé to Moody, September 24, 1927, TSA, RG 301, Box 56.

34. Gamio, *The Life Story of the Mexican Immigrant,* p. 157.

35. "Listas," Pablo Ramos, September 16, 1911.

36. Chicago Police Homicide Log, 1921–1930, IHSA.

37. *El Universal,* June 26, 1931.

38. National Commission on Law Observance and Enforcement, *Report on Lawlessness in Law Enforcement,* p. 159.

39. William Fellows, "The Need for Mexicans to Americanize in Arizona," *Latino Americano* 1 (April 1934): 6.

40. National Commission on Law Observance and Enforcement, *Report on Lawlessness in Law Enforcement,* p. 71.

41. *El Tucsonense,* April 9, 1915.

42. *El Tucsonense,* April 24 and 28, May 1, 1915; *El Cosmopolita,* February 17, 1917.

43. Zach Lamar Cobb, chief customs inspector, El Paso to Robert Lansing, January 28, 1916, NA, RG 59, 311.122.

44. Perkins, *Border Patrol,* p. 109.

45. Ibid., pp. 102–103.

46. "Report of Frank Buckley of the Bureau of Prohibition," "Civilians Killed by Customs Officers," pp. 220–221.

47. *El Tucsonense,* July 4, 1931.

48. *El Tucsonense,* July 7 and 11, 1931; *Arizona Republic,* July 3, 1931.

49. Walter Prescott Webb, *The Texas Rangers,* passim.

50. *New York Times,* March 15, 1914. For anti-Ranger polemics, see Mirandé, *Gringo Justice,* pp. 66–69; Acuña, *Occupied America,* pp. 19–20; Julián Samora, *Gunpowder Justice,* passim; Américo Paredes, *With a Pistol in His Hand,* passim. More analytic are Sandos, *Rebellion in the Borderlands,* passim, and Montejano, *Anglos and Mexicans in the Making of Texas,* passim. For a recent, more balanced view, albeit bordering on the apologetic, see Harold J. Weiss, Jr., "The Texas Rangers Revisited: Old Themes and New Viewpoints," *Southwestern Historical Quarterly* 97 (April 1914): 620–640.

51. Américo Paredes, *Uncle Remus con chile,* pp. 19–20.

52. Martínez, *Fragments of the Mexican Revolution,* p. 164; *New York Times,* March 16, 1914.

53. *New York Times,* May 22, 1915.

54. "Listas," Juan Tovar, May 1915.

55. P. C. Alamía to Moody, November 15, 1927, TSA, RG 301, Box 2.

56. Juan Rodríguez, Encargado del Despacho, to Eliseo Arredondo, November 4, 1915; Report of Leoncio G. Reveles, consul, Rio Grande City, September 17, 1915; Encargado del Despacho, Mexican Embassy, Washington, D.C., to Reveles, November 4, 1915; Encargado del Despacho to Eliseo Arredondo, Mexican chargé d'affaires, Mexican Embassy, December 10, 1915; all in AHSRE, 12/7/84.

57. García, *Desert Immigrants,* p. 92.

58. *El Imparcial de Texas,* January 3, 1918.

59. Alvin A. Adee, sub-secretary, Department of State, to Henry Wilson, March 9, 1918, NA, RG 59, File 711.12/68a; Gonzalo de la Mata, consul in San Antonio, to Salvador Diego Fernández, oficial mayor, encargado de relaciones exteriores (month and day missing), 1919, AHSRE, 14-19-38.

60. Gonzalo de la Mata, consul in San Antonio, to Salvador Diego Fernández, oficial mayor, encargado de relaciones exteriores, October 9, 1919, AHSRE, 14-19-38.

61. Martínez, *Fragments of the Mexican Revolution,* pp. 164–171; García to Bell, June 12, 1918, Ramo Trabajo, AGN, 137-12-11. See *El Imparcial de Texas,* February 13, 1919, for a thorough account of these hearings.

62. Howard C. Hopkins, Memorandum for the Inspector General, Department of Labor, "Obtaining Mexican Labor," July 2, 1918, NA, RG 85, Box 243, 54261/202B.

63. Carlos Larralde, "J. T. Canales and the Texas Rangers," *Journal of South Texas History* 10 (1997): 38–68, reveals how Texas Rangers attempted to intimidate the legislator into ceasing his investigation.

64. *Hispano América,* August 16, 1919.

65. Armando Morales, *Ando Sagrando: A Study of Mexican American–Police Conflict,* p. 13.

66. James Horn, "U.S. Diplomacy and the 'Specter of Bolshevism,'" *The Americas* 32 (July 1975): 31–45.

67. "Memory of a Man," pp. 345–346.

68. Carl M. Rathbun, "Keeping Peace along the Mexican Border: The Unceasing Task of the Arizona Rangers," *Harper's Weekly* 5 (November 17, 1906): 1633–1634.

69. "Memory of a Man," pp. 283–284, 346–347.

70. Newspaper clippings regarding the Gregorio Cortez incident in Texas sent by M. Zapata Vera, SRE, to SRE Sub-Secretario, June 28, 1901, AHSRE, 15-9-43; Robert J. Rosenbaum, *Mexicano Resistance in the Southwest,* pp. 45–49.

71. P. Ornelas, consul in San Antonio, to Manuel Azpiroz, Mexican Embassy, October 9, 1901, and Sección de Justicia e Instrucción Pública, Veracruz Gobierno, to SRE, September 27, 1901, AHSRE, 15-9-43.

72. *Mason County News,* July 5, 1901, AHSRE, 15-9-43.

73. Escobar, "Race and Law Enforcement," pp. 108–112.

74. Taylor, *Mexican Labor in the United States: Chicago and the Calumet Region,* p. 150.

75. *Arizona Republican,* November 25, 1913.

76. Menchaca, *The Mexican Outsiders,* p. 33.

77. *New York Times,* August 21, 1914; Philip J. Mellinger, "'The Men Have Become Labor Organizers': Labor Conflict and Unionization in the Mexican Mining Towns of Arizona, 1900–1915," *Western Historical Quarterly* 23 (August 1992): 337.

78. *New York Times,* August 19, 1914; *Arizona Republican,* August 15, 1913.

79. *New York Times,* September 13, 1922.

80. Escobar, "Race and Law Enforcement," p. 17; *Chicago Daily Tribune,* December 7, 1926.

81. Phillip Sonnichsen, *Texas Mexican Border Music,* vols. 2 and 3, Corridos, Parts 1 and 2.

82. Ibid.

83. Rafael de la Colina, Los Angeles Mexican consul, to Mexican Ambassador, September 24, 1930; Rafael de la Colina to Departamento de Consular, SRE, December 16, 1930; SRE to de la Colina, December 17, 1930; A. Lubbert, Mexican consul in San Francisco, to SRE, May 7, 1931; *El Tucsonense,* May 12, 1931; all in AHSRE, IV/320/17.

84. *México,* January 30, 1930, CFLPS.

85. *México,* February 22, 1930, CFLPS.

86. *México,* February 18, 1930, CFLPS.

87. *México,* March 6 and 8, May 6 and 10, 1930, CFLPS.

88. Raat, *Revoltosos,* p. 259.

89. Cardoso de Oliveira, Brazilian Embassy, to William S. Bryan, secretary of state, January 25, 1915, NA, RG 59, 311.1221, R16; Zamora, *The World of the Mexican Worker in Texas,* pp. 142–143.

90. *Houston Chronicle,* January 16 and February 3, 1908; Perkins, *Border Patrol,* p. 108.

91. Perkins, *Border Patrol,* pp. 65–71.

92. Ibid.

93. Ibid.; David Gutierrez, "Border Patrol," pp. 152–157.

94. Ramón J. Sesma to Plutarco Elías Calles, president of Mexico, n.d., AHSRE, IV/94/34; *Tucson Citizen,* April 24 and 26, August 22, 1926; *Arizona Republican,* May 30, 1926.

95. *El Tucsonense,* March 17 and 29, April 5, and December 17, 1927; J. E. Anchondo, Tucson consul, to Enrique Liekens, El Paso consul, October 30, 1928,

C. Palacios Roji, Nogales, Arizona, consul, to Anchondo, September 14, 1926, and Liekens to SRE, January 4, 1928, AHSRE, IV/94/34; *Grijalva vs. State,* 260 P 188 (Supreme Court of Arizona, 1927).

6. Civilian Violence against Mexican Immigrants

1. See Montejano, *Anglos and Mexicans in the Making of Texas,* pp. 106–155.

2. Susan Olzak, *The Dynamics of Ethnic Competition and Conflict,* p. 32.

3. See Arnoldo De León, *They Called Them Greasers,* passim, for the array of causes creating anti-Mexican antipathy in Texas.

4. See Richard Maxwell Brown, *No Duty to Retreat.*

5. David Garson and Gail O'Brien, "Collective Violence in the Reconstruction South," in *Violence in America: Historical and Comparative Perspectives,* ed. Hugh D. Graham, p. 134.

6. Olzak, *The Dynamics of Ethnic Competition and Conflict,* pp. 64–86.

7. Richard Maxwell Brown, *Strain of Violence,* p. 45.

8. Perkins, *Border Patrol,* p. 183.

9. Taylor, "Crime and the Foreign Born," p. 241. Taylor relates other incidents of this kind in this essay.

10. William Z. Foster, *Pages from a Worker's Life,* p. 26.

11. W. R. Jones, district attorney, Brownsville, Texas, to Pat Neff, governor of Texas, July 15, 1921, NA, RG 59, 311.1213 Sa 8.

12. Governor Pat Neff to Charles E. Hughes, secretary of state, July 21, 1921, and Chargé d'Affaires Manuel Téllez to Hughes, January 13, 1923, NA, RG 59, 311.1213 Sa 8.

13. Ambassador Manuel Téllez to Secretary of State Charles E. Hughes, June 23, 1924, NA, RG 59, 311.1213, Rivas.

14. Ibid.

15. Ibid.

16. Ibid.

17. "Listas," Raúl Mendoza, June 10, 1914; Jesús Arias, January 12, 1913; Tomas Soto, November 12, 1912.

18. L. A. Navarro, Phoenix consul, to SRE, June 30, 1900, AHSRE, 12-7-238.

19. I scanned various issues of *La Voz del Pueblo* in Las Vegas, New Mexico, looking for such incidents. Deutsch, in *No Separate Refuge,* does not give the impression that anti-Mexican attacks existed to the same degree in New Mexico and Colorado as in other areas of the Southwest.

20. "Buzo de Amézquita, Claim against the United States of Cecilia Buzo de Amézquita for the Wrongful Death of Luis Amézquita Gomar," typescript in Otto Kerner, attorney general, to Henry Horner, governor of Illinois, March 12, 1935, IHSA, RS101.30, Henry Horner Correspondence.

21. Ramón Prida, *Datos y observaciones sobre los Estados Unidos de América,* p. 165.

22. M. N. Morales, Kansas City consul, to Servicio Consular Mexicano, July 25, 1917, AHSRE, 12-7-12. See F. Castillo Nájera, Mexican ambassador, to Cordell Hull, secretary of state, December 30, 1935, and Roy D. Jackson, district attorney, El Paso, to James Allred, governor of Texas, January 14, 1936, NA, RG59, 311.1213, Artalejo, for discussion of violence between Mexicans and civilians in El Paso.

23. Manuel Téllez to Frank B. Kellogg, June 9, 1926, NA, RG 59, 311.1213, Aguilar; "Listas," Carmen Salazar, February 25, 1917; typescript dated October 25, 1926, Gamio Papers, Box 3, no. 10.

24. F. Arturo Rosales, *Chicano*, p. 118.

25. José Martínez to Alvaro Obregón, August 23, 1924, Ramo Presidentes, AGN, Obregón-Calles, 104-T-10.

26. "Listas," Jesús Navarrete, January 15, 1919; Ignacio Bonilla, Mexican ambassador, to Frank Polk, Department of State, February 6, 1919, W. P. Hobby, governor of Texas, to Polk, March 13, 1919, Bonilla to Polk, April 19, 1919, and Hobby to Polk, May 2, 1919, NA, RG 59, 311.121 N22.

27. Foster, *Pages from a Worker's Life*, pp. 27–28.

28. See Jonathan C. Brown, "Foreign and Native Workers in Porfirian Mexico," *American Historical Review* 98 (June 1993): 786–818, for the relationship between Anglo American foremen and Mexican workers in Mexico itself.

29. Manuel Téllez to Charles E. Hughes, May 19, 1921, and Governor Pat Neff to Hughes, June 6, 1921, NA, RG 59, 311.121, 8 C15.

30. Raymond Brooks, secretary to Governor W. P. Hobby, to Colby, September 14, 1920, NA, RG 59, 311.1213 R14.

31. "Listas," José Castro, May 9, 1912; Ignacio Bonilla, Mexican ambassador, to Robert Lansing, secretary of state, October 28, 1919, and Lansing to Bonilla, January 18, 1920, NA, RG 59, 311.1221 R94.

32. Edmundo L. Aragón, Caléxico Consul, to San Francisco Consul, May 20, 1932, AHSRE IV/187/21.

33. Edmundo L. Aragón to A. R. Underwood, Imperial County coroner, May 13, 1932; M. F. Alatora, SRE, oficial mayor, to Joel Quiñones, acting consul general, San Francisco, June 6, 1932; Quiñones to Aragón, June 14, 1932; Quiñones to Aragón, June 16, 1932; all in AHSRE, IV/187/21.

34. Elmer W. Heald to Edmundo L. Aragón, May 24, 1932; unidentified typescript in Aragón to A. Lubbert, consul general, San Francisco, July 21, 1932; Joel Quiñones to SRE, September 1, 1932; Rafael de la Colina, secretary, SRE, to Lubbert, November 11, 1932; Oscar Duplán, P.O. del Secretario of SRE, to Lubbert, August 16, 1932; Lubbert to la Colina, n.d.; all in AHSRE, IV/187/21.

35. *La Prensa*, January 27, 1913.

36. See Zamora, *The World of the Mexican Worker in Texas*, pp. 66–70. In a humorous novel by Daniel Venegas from the 1920s, the author shows the immigrant protagonist Don Chipote quitting one disagreeable job after another. See Daniel Venegas, *Las aventuras de Don Chipote o cuando los pericos mamen*.

37. Jesús Valle, interview, May 18, 1927, Gamio Papers, Bancroft Library, File 2, Box 1.

38. Basil Pacheco, interview, East Chicago, 1975.

39. *El Cosmopolita*, March 29, 1919.

40. Vargas, *Proletarians of the North*, p. 111.

41. See Olzak, *The Dynamics of Ethnic Competition and Conflict*, pp. 64–86.

42. Luther Ellsworth, consul in Piedras Negras, to Philander C. Knox, secretary of state, September 1, 1910, NA, RG 59 812.00/402; *Tucson Citizen*, May 4, 1912.

43. Alberto Leal, consul, Rio Grande City, to F. Gamboa, sub-secretario, SRE,

March 15, 1910; Leal to SRE, March 20, 1910; *Washington Post,* March 15, 1910, March 14, 1910, and March 3, 1910; all in AHSRE, 15-26-11.

44. Rosales, "The Lynching of Antonio Rodríguez," unpublished manuscript.

45. F. W. Meyer to President William H. Taft, November 10, 1910, NA, RG 59, 311.122 R61.

46. Ellsworth to Philander C. Knox, secretary of state, November 15, 1910, NA, RG 59, 812.00.

47. Taylor, *Mexican Labor in the United States: Dimwit County, Winter Garden District, South Texas,* pp. 27–48; Louise Año Nuevo Kerr, "The Chicano Experience in Chicago, 1920–1970," pp. 11–27; Rosales and Simon, "The Mexican Immigrant Experience in the Urban Midwest," pp. 335–336; "Informe general del mes de junio, 1917, Chicago," AHSRE, IV/1064.1 (72:73)/1; United States Department of Labor Circular, submitted by S. L. Alatriste, commercial agent in Chicago for the Secretaría de Industria, Comercio y Trabajo, June 19, 1919, Ramo Trabajo, AGN, 177-6-2.

48. William M. Tuttle, Jr., *Race Riot,* pp. 156–183. "Blanco Report," August 10, 1919; R. Ruíz, consul general, New York City, to SRE, August 19, 1919; José L. Sepúlveda, Chicago consul, to SRE, September 13, 1919; Ramón de Negri, consul general, New York City, to SRE, September 19, 1919; all in AHSRE, 24/25/23.

49. *The Ferguson Forum,* December 16, 1920, clipping in Ramo Presidentes, Obregón-Calles, AGN, 104-T-10.

50. *Houston Chronicle,* February 6, 1921.

51. *New York Times,* February 17, 1921; *Houston Chronicle,* February 18, 1921; *La Prensa,* February 18, 1921; *El Tucsonense,* February 22, 1921.

52. *La Prensa,* February 18, 1921.

53. *La Prensa,* February 20, 1921.

54. *La Prensa,* February 25, 1921.

55. Arnold Shankman, "The Image of Mexico and the Mexican American in the Black Press," *Journal of Ethnic Studies* 3 (Summer 1975): 43–56.

56. Reisler, *By the Sweat of Their Brow,* pp. 51–52.

57. *La Prensa,* March 10, 1921.

58. *La Prensa,* March 9, 1921.

59. *Houston Chronicle,* May 15 and 24, 1921.

60. *New York Times,* November 11, 1922.

61. *La Prensa,* January 25, 1923; Menchaca, *The Mexican Outsiders,* pp. 52–53; *Hispano América,* September 8, 1923.

62. *Chicago Daily Tribune,* June 23, 24, and 26, 1922.

63. Typescript, October 5, 1926, Gamio Papers, Box 3, File 2.

64. Taylor, *Mexican Labor in the United States: Chicago and the Calumet Region,* p. 151.

65. Manuel Téllez to Frank B. Kellogg, September 11, 1925, NA, RG 59, 311.1213, Kansas City.

66. Eduardo Peralta, interview, 1974; *Chicago Daily Tribune,* July 8 and 9, 1931.

67. *San Angelo Evening Standard,* June 13, 1931.

68. Juan E. Achondo, Dallas consul, to Lorenzo Lupián, consul general, San Antonio, May 20, 1931, *Dallas Dispatch,* clipping, n.d., AHSRE, IV-325-68.

69. Juan E. Achondo to Lorenzo Lupián, May 20, 1931; Lupián to SRE, May 20, 1931; Juan C. Torres to Anchondo, May 20, 1931; Achondo to Lupián, May 22, 1931;

San Antonio Evening News, clipping, May 20, 1931; *El Mundo,* clippings both dated May 22, 1931; all in AHSRE, IV-325-68.

70. Lorenzo Lupián to SRE, May 3, 1931; Alatora, SRE, oficial mayor, to Lupián, June 1, 1931; *La Marina* and *El Mundo* clippings, both dated May 22, 1931; all in AHSRE, IV-325-68.

71. Fernando I. Delgado and J. E. Rojas, officers of the Unión General de Trabajadores Mexicanos en Los Estados Unidos de America, Dallas, Texas, to Pascual Ortiz Rubio, president of Mexico, May 25, 1931; Lorenzo Lupián to SRE, May 30, 1931; Atalora to Lupián, June 10, 1931; Juan E. Achondo to Sheriff C. C. Pharris, Malankoff, June 12, 1931; Lupián to Mexican Embassy, Washington, D.C., June 30, 1931; all in AHSRE, IV-325-68.

72. Rómulo Vargas, P.O. de cónsul general, San Antonio, to SRE, July 9, 1931, AHSRE IV/186/51.

73. G. C. Martin, chief of police, Newport, Arkansas, in Joaquín Amador, Oklahoma City consul, to Lupián, Report, July 21, 1931, AHSRE IV/186/51.

74. *El Nacional,* May 20, 1931, CFLPS.

75. List of California Lynchings compiled by Clare "Bud" McKanna, University of Nebraska, Lincoln; David Lawrence Abney, "Capital Punishment in Arizona: 1863–1963" (Master's thesis, Arizona State University, 1988), p. 198.

76. *People v Valenzuela,* 147 P 97 (2nd District of California, 1915).

77. *New York Times,* September 13 and 15, 1919; *Hispano América,* December 11, 1920; see Harry Farrell, *Swift Justice.*

78. David L. Chapman, "Lynching in Texas" (Master's thesis, Texas Tech University, 1973), pp. 55–57.

79. Acuña, *Occupied America,* p. 161; "Listas," Antonio Gómez, July 19, 1911, AHSRE, 11/19/24.

80. *Houston Chronicle,* December 30, 1914; *New York Times,* December 24, 1915.

81. *El Imparcial de Texas,* March 10, 1922; *New York Times,* November 11, 1922.

82. Reisler, *By the Sweat of Their Brow,* pp. 142–143.

7. Mexicans and Justice in the Courtroom

1. González, *San José de Gracia,* pp. 87–89; Knight, *The Mexican Revolution,* vol. 2, p. 405.

2. Paul J. Vanderwood, *Disorder and Progress,* demonstrates that throughout the late Porfiriato, jurisdictional and local conditions made for law enforcement inconsistency.

3. Escobar, "Race and Law Enforcement," pp. 18–19; Subsecretario de Gobierno to Secretario de Fomento, October 3, 1913, AGN, Trabajo, 8-3; *El Cosmopolita,* March 11, 1916.

4. Warnshius, "Crime and Criminal Justice among the Mexicans in Illinois," p. 325.

5. Ibid., pp. 291–293.

6. *San Francisco Call,* January 12, 1921.

7. *Chicago Daily Tribune,* November 4, 1923; *Daily Calumet,* December 1 and 3, 1923; "Bernardo Roa, Reclamación no. 3475," AHSRE, VI/454/1. The scant records of the trial suggest Lupián's allegations were correct. See Gregorio Rizo, File 34003, Robbery, 1924, Robert Tórrez, Bernardo Roa, Gregorio Rizo File 32281, Murder, all in Cook County, Circuit Court Criminal Records.

8. Lorenzo Lupián, Mexican consul in Chicago, to SRE, October 31, 1924, AHSRE, VI/454/1.

9. Pedro Gama y Uriquien, Mexican consul in Douglas, Arizona, to SRE Secretario, September 19, 1910, AHSRE, 18-25-102.

10. Sub-Secretario de Gobierno to Secretario de Fomento, October 3, 1913, AGN, Trabajo, 8-3.

11. Gustavo G. Hernández, Mexican consul in Globe, Arizona, to SRE, January 30, 1918, AHSRE, 217-10-73.

12. E. A. McEahern, Miami, Arizona, justice of the peace, to Gustavo G. Hernández, December 20, 1918, AHSRE, 217-10-73.

13. Gustavo G. Hernández to SRE, January 30, 1918, AHSRE, 217-10-73.

14. Taylor, *Mexican Labor in the United States: Chicago and the Calumet Region,* p. 154; Warnshius, "Crime and Criminal Justice among the Mexicans in Illinois," pp. 204–304.

15. Escobar, "Race and Law Enforcement," p. 53.

16. *El Universal,* May 23, 1929.

17. Sub-Secretario, SRE, to Enrique Ferreira, Mexican consul in San Diego, May 23, 1929, Ferreira to SRE, August 5, 1929, and *San Diego Union,* August 8, 1929, AHSRE, IV/78/32.

18. Buffington, "Prohibition in the Borderlands," p. 30. Sub-Secretario Enrique Ferreira to SRE, September 9, 1929; SRE to Ambassador Manuel Téllez; SRE to G. Lubbert, consul general, San Francisco, November 18, 1929; Téllez to Henry L. Stimson, secretary of state, December 30, 1929; Acting Secretary of State to Pablo Campos Ortiz, Mexican chargé d'affaires, Mexican Embassy, March 13, 1930; all in AHSRE, IV/78/32.

19. Paul Kelly to William P. Doak, secretary of labor, March 4, 1932, American Legion Repatriation File, East Chicago Historical Society, East Chicago, Indiana, Library.

20. *Calumet News,* March 21, 1930.

21. F. Arturo Rosales, "Shifting Self-Perceptions and Ethnic Consciousness among Mexicans in Houston, 1908–1946," p. 83; Patrick Lukens, "The Timoteo Andrade Citizenship Case" (History seminar paper, Arizona State University, 1993).

22. Lukens, "The Timoteo Andrade Citizenship Case," p. 12.

23. María Elena Andrade, telephone interview, 1987.

24. Eduardo Peralta, interview, South Chicago, 1974.

25. *Chicago Daily Tribune,* July 8, 1931.

26. Ambassador Manuel Téllez to W. R. Castle, acting secretary of state, July 8, 1931, in United States, Department of State, *Papers Relating to the Foreign Relations of the United States,* 1931, vol. 2, pp. 727–728.

27. *Chicago Daily Tribune,* July 8, 1931.

28. Louis L. Emmerson, governor of Illinois, to Castle, July 9, 1931, and Castle to Ambassador Manuel Téllez, July 10, 1931, in United States, Department of State, *Papers Relating to the Foreign Relations of the United States,* 1931, vol. 2, pp. 728–729; *Chicago Daily Tribune,* July 9, 10, and 11, 1931.

29. S. Diego Fernández, Mexican Embassy, to Bainbridge Colby, secretary of state, May 3, 1920, and Colby to the governor of Texas, May 15, 1920, NA, RG 59, 311.1213 F661.

30. Griswold del Castillo, *The Los Angeles Barrios, 1850–1890*, p. 116.

31. *El País,* October 23, 1910.

32. John O. Baxter, "The Villista Murder Trials: Deming, New Mexico, 1916–1921," *La Gaceta* 7 (1983): 11.

33. *Hispano América,* November 8 and 14, 1924; *El Tucsonense,* November 13, 1924; Hernández, *Mutual Aid for Survival,* p. 81.

34. Warnshius, "Crime and Criminal Justice among the Mexicans in Illinois," p. 286.

35. Taylor, "Crime and the Foreign Born," p. 280.

36. Ibid., p. 233.

37. Warnshius, "Crime and Criminal Justice among the Mexicans in Illinois," p. 295.

38. *El Amigo de Hogar,* January 17, 1926.

39. *El Nacional,* December 19, 1931, CFLPS.

40. *San Francisco Call,* January 12, 1921; *San Francisco Post,* January 12, 1921; *Hispano América,* January 15, 1921.

41. *El Nacional,* April 29, 1930, CFLPS; *United States ex rel Velasco v Ragen,* 158 F2d 87 (1946); M. Jesús Gallo, secretary to Manuel Avila Camacho, president of Mexico, Presidentes, Camacho, AGN, 575.1/87; *Chicago Sun Times,* n.d., AGN, 575.1/87; *New York Times,* July 19, 1950.

42. *El Cosmopolita,* January 15, March 25, 1916; *El Nacional,* August 29, 1931, CFLPS; *New York Times,* June 14, 1927; *Joliet Evening Herald,* March 12–17, 1927.

43. Copy of Declaration given before Notary Public, E. B. Devine, in Pinal County by Manuel Martínez, May 24, 1923, Presidentes, Obregón-Calles, AGN, 8ll-A-70.

44. *New York Times,* January 13 and 26, 1921; *La Prensa,* January 6, 1921.

45. Hernández, *Mutual Aid for Survival,* p. 81; *Hispano América,* October 16, 1926.

46. Rafael de la Colina, consul of Mexico, Los Angeles, to Ambassador Manuel Téllez, August 27, 1930, AHSRE, IV/320/17.

47. *El Amigo del Hogar,* February 6, 1926.

48. José Anguiano, interview, East Chicago, 1974.

49. See García, *Mexican Americans,* passim, for discussion on Manuel González; *El Universal,* June 26, 1931.

50. *El Imparcial de Texas,* August 7, 1919; clipping in Latin American Club file, Houston Metropolitan Research Center Houston Metropolitan Research Center (henceforth cited as HMRC); *Houston Post,* June 4, 1937; De León, *Ethnicity in the Sunbelt,* pp. 62–63.

51. *La Prensa,* March 10, 13, and 14, 1928.

52. *El Tucsonense,* June 8, 1926; *Arizona Republican,* June 8, 1926.

53. *El Tucsonense,* June 15, 1926; March 17 and 29, April 5, and December 17, 1927.

8. CAPITAL PUNISHMENT AND MEXICANS IN THE UNITED STATES

1. Abney, "Capital Punishment in Arizona," pp. 179–218.

2. *El País,* October 23, 1910; Richard Sloane, governor of Arizona, to Philander P. Knox, secretary of state, October 22, 1910, NA, RG 59, 311.122 M34.

3. Luis Gaxiola to George P. Hunt, governor of Arizona, May 24, 1915, José M. Maytorena, governor of Sonora, to Hunt, May 24, 1915, and William Jennings Bryan, secretary of state, to Hunt, May 25, 1915, George P. Hunt Collection, Arizona Collection, Arizona State University Library; Abney, "Capital Punishment in Arizona," pp. 17–18.

4. *New York Times,* July 28 and 29, 1915.

5. Ives Levelier, consul in Douglas, Arizona, to SRE, May 23, 1916; *Douglas Daily Dispatch,* May 17, 1916; *Douglas Daily International,* May 17, 1916; all in AHSRE, 12/7/100; Abney, "Capital Punishment in Arizona," p. 197; "Executions in Arizona, 1910 to 1965," Arizona Department of Library, Archives and Public Records (henceforth cited as ADLAPR), RG 85, Box 1.

6. Abney, "Capital Punishment in Arizona," pp. 91–92.

7. Ibid., pp. 93–110; "Inmates Sentenced to Life Imprisonment or Given Death Sentences in Arizona from 1875 to January 1, 1967," ADLAPR, RG 85, Box 85.

8. *Justicia,* April 27, 1920.

9. *Arizona Republican,* August 11, 1923.

10. Ibid.; *El Tucsonense,* June 20, July 17 and 22, August 22 and 26, 1922.

11. Roberto Quiroz, Phoenix Mexican consul, to SRE, May 16, 1923, and Quiroz to Manuel Téllez, Mexican ambassador, May 18, 22, 1923, AGN, Presidentes, Obregón-Calles 811-A-70.

12. Roberto Quiroz to Comisiones Honoríficas Mexicanas, Flagstaff, Williams, Ashfork, Clarksdale, Hayden, Sonora, Miami, Globe, and Jerome, Arizona, May 23 and 25, 1923, AGN, Presidentes, Obregón-Calles, 811-A-70.

13. Roberto Quiroz to Manuel Téllez, Mexican ambassador, May 28, 1923, Alvaro Obregón, president of Mexico, to Quiroz, June 8, 1923, and Obregón to Alejandro Martínez, Phoenix consul, August 10, 1923, AGN, Presidentes, Obregón-Calles, 811-A-70; *Arizona Republican,* August 11, 1923.

14. *El Tucsonense,* June 2 and 6, 1933; June 14, 1935.

15. Rosenbaum, *Mexicano Resistance in the Southwest,* pp. 60, 134; Carlos C. de Baca, *Vicente Silva,* pp. 38–48; M. Watt Espy and John Ortiz Smykla, "Executions in the United States, 1608–1987: The Espy File" (Ann Arbor: Inter-University Consortium for Political and Social Research, machine readable data file 8541).

16. Baxter, "The Villista Murder Trials," pp. 1–24.

17. Ibid.

18. Ibid.; Espy and Ortiz Smykla, "Executions in the United States."

19. *El Cosmopolita,* July 7, 1917; E. F. Harrell, warden of Texas Prison System, to Moody, January 1, 1930, TSA, RG 301, Box 41.

20. L. C. Martínez to de la Barra, August 3, 1911, NA, RG 59, 311.122 M36; *El Paso Times,* November 4, 1911.

21. *Ex Parte Martinez,* 66 Tex Crim 45 (Court of Criminal Appeals, 1912); *El Paso Times,* November 4, 1911.

22. Huntington Wilson, acting secretary of state, to León Cárdenas Martínez, Sr., September 18, 1911; Colquitt to Woodrow Wilson, president of the United States, February 12, 1912; Jesse C. Gakins, assistant attorney general, to J. B. Moore, counselor, Department of State, October 15, 1913; all in NA, RG 59, 311.122 M36; *Houston Chronicle,* April 19 and 21, May 11, 1914.

23. A. S. García et al. to William H. Taft, president of the United States, July 9, 1911; Dr. Vicente Osolla et al. to Taft, September 15–16, 1911; Juan Paz et al. to

Woodrow Wilson, president of the United States, April 19, 1914; all in NA, RG 59, 311.122 M36.

24. Juan Raino, ambassador of Spain, to William Jennings Bryan, secretary of state, May 8, 1914, NA, RG 59, 311.122 M36. Another teenager, Federico Sánchez, was hanged in 1915 for the murder of Henry Hinton, a jailer at the Live Oak County jail, in spite of vigorous Mexican government and immigrant efforts to save him. See Sillman to Bryan, March 9, 1915, NA, RG 59, 311.1221, Sa.

25. *El Tucsonense,* February 27, 1923; Apolinar, "Hablando de Clemente Apolinar, colgado 1923," *Caracol* 1 (December 1974): 4–7.

26. Quoted in Gamio, *Mexican Immigration to the United States,* pp. 102–103.

27. *La Prensa,* January 5 and February 13, 1928.

28. "Night Warden Return after Execution," Huntsville, State Prison, September 7, 1928, TSA RG 301, Box 40.

29. *El Defensor,* August 15, 1930; June 19, July 10, and October 11, 1931.

30. *Hispano América,* January 8, 1921; Manuel Mata to Adolfo de la Huerta, president of Mexico, June 17, 1920, AHSRE, 17/13/25.

31. *San Francisco Hispano América,* January 8, 1921.

32. *La Prensa,* April 1 and 19, 1928; "Governor Moody Records on Convict Actions," TSA, RG301, Box 42.

33. *La Prensa,* January 5, February 13, and March 4, 1928; Dan Moody, governor of Texas, to M. L. Speer, Huntsville warden, March 10, 1928, TSA, RG 301, Box 42.

34. *La Prensa,* March 13 and 14, April 1 and 19, 1928; E. H. Harrell, warden in Huntsville, to Moody, August 29, 1928, and October 19, 1928, TSA, RG 301, Box 41. At age seventy-three, in 1965, Vargas sued the state for false imprisonment and received a twenty-thousand-dollar settlement. See James Marquart, Sheldon Ekland-Olson, and Jonathan R. Sorensen, *The Rope, The Chair, and the Needle,* pp. 111–112.

35. James Allred, governor of Texas, to Cordell Hull, secretary of state, December 15, 1935; Hull to Allred, December 23, 1935; Allred to Hull and Hull to Allred, January 21, 1936; all in NA, RG 59 311.1221; Hay to Allred, March 31, 1936, AHSRE IV/742/2.

36. Espy and Ortiz Smykla, "Executions in the United States."

37. "Informe de las gestiones del Consulado General [Alberto Mascarenas] de México en San Francisco California, E.A.U., a favor del ciudadano mexicano Simón Ruíz, February 11, 1921" (henceforth cited as "Informe"), AHSRE, 17-12-98.

38. *San Francisco Call,* January 12, 1921.

39. "Informe," AHSRE, 17-12-98; *Hispano América,* December 24, 1920; January 1, 1921.

40. *Hispano América,* January 8, 1921; "Informe," AHSRE, 17-12-98.

41. "Informe," AHSRE, 17-12-98; *Hispano América,* January 15, 1921.

42. *San Francisco Call,* January 14, 1921; *San Francisco Chronicle,* January 13 and 14, 1921; *San Francisco Post,* January 15, 1921; "Informe," AHSRE, 17-12-98.

43. "Informe," AHSRE, 17-12-98.

44. Antonio Orfila to Garza Zertuche, consul general of Mexico, July 13, 1921, AHSRE, 17-12-98; *Hispano América,* March 12, 19, and 26 and April 9, 1921.

45. Quoted in José Gutiérrez, "La inolvidable peregrina," in *Mexico: Nuestra Gran Historia,* pp. 312–316. See also Antoinette May, *Passionate Pilgrim.*

46. *Hispano América,* January 27 and March 3, 1923.

47. *El Tucsonense,* April 5, 1923; *Los Angeles Times,* October 20, 1922; *People v Pompa,* 192 Cal Reptr 412 (2nd District, 1923).

48. *El Tucsonense,* January 5, 1924.

49. Reprinted in *El Tucsonense,* April 3, 1923.

50. *El Tucsonense,* March 29, 1923; Alvaro Obregón, president of Mexico, to F. W. Richardson, governor of California, January 7, 1924, AGN, Ramo Presidentes, Obregón-Calles, 811-P-64.

51. *El Tucsonense,* March 15, 1924; Elena de la Llata to Alvaro Obregón, president of Mexico, March 8, 1924, and Obregón to de la Llata, March 8, 1924, AGN, Ramo Presidentes, Obregón-Calles, 811-P-64.

52. *La Opinión,* October 3, 1926; Antonio Castro Leal, Mexican Embassy, to Frank B. Kellogg, secretary of state, October 16, 1926, NA, RG 59, 311.1221, Trinidad, Mauricio.

53. *Hispano América,* October 30, 1926.

54. Nancy Ann Nichols, *San Quentin inside the Walls,* p. 7.

55. Fernando González Roa, Mexican ambassador, to Cordell Hull, secretary of state, July 30, 1934, NA, RG 59, 311.1221, Campos Apolonio.

56. Cordell Hull, secretary of state, to Frank F. Merriman, governor of California, August 1, 1934, NA, RG 59, 311.1221, Campos Apolonio.

57. Espy and Ortiz Smykla, "Executions in the United States"; *New York Times,* January 28, 1921.

58. *New York Times,* January 28, 1921.

59. Salvador Diego Fernández, Mexican chargé d'affaires, to Bainbridge Colby, secretary of state, April 28, 1920, and Alfred Smith, governor of New York, to Colby, April 30, 1920, NA, RG 59, 311.1221 G16.

60. *New York Times,* December 19, 1920; Manuel Téllez, Mexican ambassador, to Bainbridge Colby, secretary of state, December 10, 1920, and Ramón P. de Negri, New York City consul, to Alvaro Obregón, president of Mexico, December 15, 1920, NA, RG 59, 311.1221 G16.

61. *New York Times,* January 13 and 15, 1921; *La Prensa,* January 6, 1921.

62. Manuel Téllez, Mexican ambassador, to Bainbridge Colby, secretary of state, January 14, 1921, NA, RG 59, 311.1221 G16.

63. *New York Times,* January 26, 1921.

64. Ramón P. de Negri, New York consul general, to Alvaro Obregón, president of Mexico, December 15, 1920, AGN, Presidentes, Obregón-Calles 811-S-2; *Hispano América,* January 1, 1921; *La Prensa,* December 26, 27, and 31, 1920.

65. *El Imparcial de Texas,* December 23, 1920.

66. *Hispano América,* December 10, 1920. All these petitions, which were sent as early as July 1920 to President Woodrow Wilson, are in NA, RG 59, 311.1212 Sa.

67. Alvaro Obregón, president of Mexico, to Ramón de Negri, New York consul general, December 13, 1920, AGN, Presidentes, Obregón-Calles, 811-S-2.

68. Francisca L. Vda. de Sánchez to Alvaro Obregón, president of Mexico, December 14, 1920, and Eduardo B. Sánchez to Obregón, January 10, 1921, AGN, Presidentes, Obregón-Calles, 811-S-2.

69. E. Martínez, secretario general del Comité Central, CROM, to Alvaro Obregón, president of Mexico, December 16, 1920, Genaro Gómez, Secretario del Sindicato de Obreros Panaderos, to Obregón, December 20, 1920, and Eduardo B. Sánchez to Obregón, January 10, 1921, AGN, Presidentes, Obregón-Calles, 811-S-2.

70. Alvaro Obregón, president of Mexico, to W. P. Hobby, governor of Texas, December 20, 1920; Obregón to Octaviano A. Larrazola, governor of New Mexico, December 20, 1920; Obregón to Thomas E. Campbell, governor of Arizona, December 20, 1920; Larrazola to Obregón, December 29, 1920; all in AGN, Presidentes, Obregón-Calles, 811-S-2.

71. *New York Times,* January 26 and 28, 1921.

72. *El Imparcial de Texas,* January 20 and February 3, 1921.

73. *Joliet Evening Herald News,* June 16 and 20, 1927; *New York Times,* June 14 and 16, 1927; *Chicago Daily Tribune,* June 16, 1927.

74. *Joliet Evening Herald News,* June 17 and 20, 1927; *Daily Calumet,* June 17, 1927; Martín Blanco, interview, Chicago, 1974; José Anguiano, interviews, East Chicago, 1974, 1975, and 1987.

9. DOING TIME FOR MEXICANS IN THE UNITED STATES

1. See, for example, *Mexicans in California: Report of Governor C. C. Young's Mexican Fact-Finding Committee,* pp. 197–200.

2. Warnshius, "Crime and Criminal Justice among the Mexicans in Illinois," pp. 300–307.

3. Roberto Martínez spent three years in the George West County jail (Texas) before he saw a judge. See Enrique Santibáñez, *Ensayo acerca de la inmigración mexicana en los Estados Unidos,* p. 52.

4. Dulben Oppenheimer, *The Administration of Deportation Laws of the United States,* pp. 30–31; *El Defensor,* January 16, 1930; Servicio Consular Mexicano, Hidalgo, Texas, "Informe sobre visitas del suscrito a las carceles, conforme al artículo 262 del reglamento consular vigente, February 1930," AHSRE, IV/78/26.

5. Unidentified person from Giddings, Texas, to Consul General in San Antonio, March 22, 1914, and R. A. Esteban Ruíz, SRE, to Mexican Consul, San Antonio, April 14, 1914, AHSRE, 12-7-135.

6. Ruíz to Mexican Consul, San Antonio, April 14, 1914, AHSRE, 12-7-135.

7. García, *Desert Immigrants,* p. 148; Oscar J. Martínez, *Fragments of the Mexican Revolution,* p. 141; Mexican Embassy in the U.S.A. to Cándido Aguilar, SRE, February 1, 1917, AHSRE, 11/19/24.

8. Allen J. Clark, "Yuma Territorial Prison," Ray Davis, Seminar Class Papers, pp. 78–80, MS 539, AHSA, Tucson; Allen Gene Patraz, "The Transfer of Arizona's Territorial Prison from Yuma to Florence" (Master's thesis, Arizona State University, 1982), p. 119; "Statistics on 2,000 Inmates of Arizona State Prison for the Period May 8, 1911 to April 7, 1920," ADLAPR, RG 85, Prison, Box 1.

9. Warnshius, "Crime and Criminal Justice among the Mexicans in Illinois," p. 312.

10. See Chapter 3 for demographic profile in the 1930s. Secretaría de Relaciones Exteriores, *Memoria de la Secretaría de Relaciones Exteriores de Agosto de 1928 a Julio 1929,* p. 32; "Los Hermanos Hernández," *El Latino Americano* 1 (August 1934): 14.

11. "Criminal Record Office, Distribution of Forces," February 25, 1926, TSA, RG 301, Box 42; *La Prensa,* April 19, 1928; *Houston Post,* July 17, 1930.

12. California State Senate, "Report of the Committee Relative to the Condition and Management of the State Prison," Document no. 25, Session 1855, California State Library Archives, Sacramento; *Hispano América,* March 8, 1919; Departa-

mento Consular Washington, D.C., to Consul General, San Francisco, December 31, 1929, AHSRE IV-94-28.

13. Warnshius, "Crime and Criminal Justice among the Mexicans in Illinois," pp. 312–313, 320–322; *Proceedings of the Sixty-second Annual Congress of the American Prison Association, Indianapolis, Indiana, October 3rd to 7th,* pp. 400–403; Joaquín Terrazas, Mexican consul in Detroit, to Bartolomé Carbajal y Rosas, Mexican Embassy, March 15, 1927, AHSRE, 17/04/9; Austin H. MacCormick and Paul W. Garrett, eds., *Handbook of American Prisons, 1926,* pp. 231, 290; Margaret Werner Cahalan, *Historical Corrections Statistics in the United States, 1850–1894,* pp. 29, 37.

14. Secretaría de Relaciones Exteriores, *Memoria de la Secretaría de Relaciones Exteriores de Agosto de 1928 a Julio 1929,* p. 32.

15. Manuel Payno, Phoenix consul, to SRE, December 4, 1928, AHSRE, IV-92-14.

16. "Inmates Sentenced to Life Imprisonment or Given Death Sentences in Arizona from 1875–1965," typescript, ADLAPR, RG 85, Prisons, Box 1.

17. E. F. Harrell, warden, Texas Prison System, to Dan Moody, governor of Texas, January 1, 1930, TSA, RG 301, Box 42; *Houston Post,* July 17, 1930.

18. *Hispano América,* March 8, 1919.

19. Taylor, "Crime and the Foreign Born," pp. 204–207.

20. Warnshius, "Crime and Criminal Justice among the Mexicans in Illinois," pp. 312–313; Terrazas, to Bartolomé Carbajal y Rosas, March 15, 1927, AHSRE, 17-04-96; *Proceedings of the Sixty-second Annual Congress of the American Prison Association,* pp. 400–403. Statistics on the reasons for imprisonment were not available for San Quentin in California, which held the majority of Mexican prisoners in the state.

21. Warnshius, "Crime and Criminal Justice among the Mexicans in Illinois," pp. 276–278; Handman, "Preliminary Report on Nationality and Delinquency," pp. 259–261.

22. For prison conditions in this period, see MacCormick and Garrett, eds., *Handbook of American Prisons, 1926;* Abbott, ed., *Report on Crime and Criminal Justice in Relation to the Foreign Born,* passim; Gladys A. Erickson, *Warden Ragen of Joliet;* James B. Jacobs, *Statesville;* Kenneth Lamott, *Chronicles of San Quentin;* Shelly Bookspan, *A Germ of Goodness;* Steve J. Martin and Sheldon Ekland-Olson, *Texas Prisons; Wickersham Commission Reports,* no. 9.

23. *El Imparcial de Texas,* December 27, 1917.

24. *La Prensa,* February 22 and 25, 1921.

25. Stephen Love, Chicago attorney, to Dan Moody, governor of Texas, November 27, 1927, and Moody to Love, November 29, 1927, TSA, RG 301, Box 42.

26. Lamott, *Chronicles of San Quentin,* pp. 198–199.

27. *Ballad of an Unsung Hero,* film.

28. Mike Shortell, "Riot and Reform: The Arizona Territorial Prison, 1876–1909," *New Mexico Lawman* 37 (August 1971): 20–31.

29. Dayton Moses to Dan Moody, governor of Texas, November 13, 1928, and Russ Daniel to Moody, March 15, 1927, TSA, RG 301, Box 42; see Martin and Ekland-Olson, *Texas Prisons,* pp. 9–15, on corruption and influence peddling in the Texas prison system. On rare occasions non-Mexicans intervened on behalf of Mexican prisoners, according to documents in the TSA.

30. Jacobs, *Statesville,* pp. 19–27.

31. Erickson, *Warden Ragen of Joliet,* passim.

32. Charles S. Wharton, *The House of Whispering Hate.*

33. Lamott, *Chronicles of San Quentin,* pp. 153–161; Harrell to Moody, January 1, 1930, TSA, RG 301, Box 42; *Houston Post,* July 17, 1930; "Research of Arizona State Prison, 1940," typescript, Arizona Historical Foundation, Hayden Library, Arizona State University (henceforth cited as AHF).

34. *Hispano América,* February 28, 1925.

35. Wharton, *The House of Whispering Hate,* pp. 206–207.

36. *La Prensa,* April 7, 1921.

37. Dan Moody, governor of Texas, to Henry L. Stimson, secretary of state, December 7, 1929, George Summerlin, Department of State, to Secretary of State, December 8, 1929, and Pat Dougherty, secretary to Moody, to Secretary of State, December 10, 1929, NA, RG 59, File 311.1221.

38. Sheridan, *Los Tucsonenses,* p. 90.

39. "Los Hermanos Hernández," p. 14.

40. Warnshius, "Crime and Criminal Justice among the Mexicans in Illinois," p. 323.

41. Joaquín Terrazas, Mexican consul, Detroit, to Bartolomé Carbajal y Rosas, Mexican Embassy, AHSRE, 17-04-96.

42. *El Cosmopolita,* May 20, 1916.

43. Paul Knepper, "Southern-Style Punitive Repression: Ethnic Stratification, Economic Inequality, and Imprisonment in Territorial Arizona," *Social Justice* 16, no. 4 (Winter 1989): 132–149; Patraz, "The Transfer of Arizona's Territorial Prison from Yuma to Florence," pp. 111–119; "Convict Labor in Arizona," typescript, AHF.

44. September 14, c. 1927, Gamio Papers, Box 3, File 10.

45. Ibid.

46. *El Imparcial de Texas,* January 9, 1919.

47. *Hispano América,* March 8, 1919.

48. *La Opinión,* September 14, 1928.

49. Warnshius, "Crime and Criminal Justice among the Mexicans in Illinois," pp. 309, 320–322, 325; *El Cosmopolita,* July 21, 1917.

50. *El Cosmopolita,* June 29, 1916.

51. Quoted in Taylor, "Crime and the Foreign Born," p. 203.

52. Warnshius, "Crime and Criminal Justice among the Mexicans in Illinois," pp. 309, 320–322.

53. M. Jesús Gallo to Manuel Avila Camacho, president of Mexico, n.d., *Chicago Sun Times,* n.d., AGN, Presidentes, Camacho, 575.1/87; *El Nacional,* April 29, 1930, CFLPS.

54. See R. Theodore Davidson, *Chicano Prisoners,* pp. 81–101, on Chicano prisoner solidarity during the 1960s.

55. In March 1932, Joliet whites murdered convict Joseph Carrasco in what appeared to be a racially motivated killing. *El Nacional,* March 12, 1932, CFLPS.

56. Lamott, *Chronicles of San Quentin,* p. 197.

57. *Hispano América,* February 21, 1925.

58. Smith to Department of State, May 6, 1925, and Smith to Friend W. Richardson, governor of California, May 23, 1925, NA, RG 59, 312.11/San Quentin; *Hispano América,* May 2, 1925; Lamott, *Chronicles of San Quentin,* pp. 198–199.

59. Harrell to Dan Moody, governor of Texas, January 1, 1930, TSA, RG 301,

Box 42; *Houston Post,* July 17, 1930; "Convict Labor in Arizona," c. 1930, typescript, AFC; September 14, c. 1927, Gamio Papers, Box 3, File 10. See also Martin and Ekland-Olson, *Texas Prisons,* p. 15.

60. J. W. Denton, chief clerk, Texas Prison System, to Pat Dougherty, secretary to Moody, May 27, 1930, TSA, RG 301, Box 62; *Hispano América,* April 3, 1926.

61. "Inmates Sentenced to Life Imprisonment or Given Death Sentences in Arizona from 1875–1965," typescript, RG 85, Prisons, Box 1, ADLAPR.

62. T. Gorrel, Dallas lawyer, to Dr. Ira P. Hildebrand, professor, Southern Methodist University, April 6, 1929, TSA, RG 301, Box 44; *El Imparcial de Texas,* January 27, 1921; *New York Times,* January 23, 1921.

63. Assistant Secretary to Texas Governor Dan Moody to Jordan, February 11, 1929, RG 301, Box 42. In Illinois where parole eligibility was determined by a point system, no one bothered to explain the system to Mexicans who did not speak English. See Warnshius, "Crime and Criminal Justice among the Mexicans in Illinois," p. 309.

64. Manuel González Abalardo to Barry Miller, assistant to Texas Governor Dan Moody, January 7, 1927, and J. D. Hall, assistant secretary to Moody, to A. P. Carrillo, consul in San Antonio, April 14, 1927, TSA, RG 301, Box 80. At times, hardship cases allowed Mexicans to temporarily leave prison. See Moody to J. R. Jordan, prison clerk, Huntsville, March 31, 1927, TSA, RG 301, Box 40.

65. "Informes sobre protección" (henceforth cited as "Informes"), Consulado de San Diego, California, por Enrique Ferreira 1929, AHSRE, IV/73/13.

66. "Informes," Consulado de Mexico en Kansas City, por Alfredo C. Vásquez, 1929–1931, AHSRE, IV/70/75. In October 1930, Vásquez ignored a request from Francisco Moreno because of three previous robbery convictions.

67. Manuel Payno, Phoenix consul, to SRE, December 4, 1928, and Payno to SRE, June 29, 1929, AHSRE, IV-92-14.

68. Juan E. Achondo to George W. K. Hunt, governor of Arizona, May 19, 1929, AHSRE, IV/94/34; *El Tucsonense,* May 20, 1929.

69. L. Medina Barrón, consul general, El Paso, to H. P. Frazier, acting governor of Arizona, July 23, 1930, AHSRE, IV/94/34.

70. *El Tucsonense,* March 10, 1933; June 14, 1935; "Inmates Sentenced to Life Imprisonment or Given Death Sentences in Arizona from 1875 to January 1, 1967," ADLAPR, RG 85, Prison, Box 1.

71. A. Spears, Cisco, Texas, to Dan Moody, governor of Texas, April 3, 1928, TSA, RG 301, Box 42.

72. Jordan to Wardens and Farm Managers, Memorandum, April 6, 1927, TSA, RG 301, Box 40; "Prison Escapees Captured Prior to June 26, 1929," J. S. Denton, clerk, Texas Prison System, to Wardens and Farm Managers, Memorandum, November 28, 1929, TSA, RG 301, Box 44.

73. *Houston Chronicle,* February 27 and 28 and March 9, 1924; H. Walker Sayle, chairman of the Board of Prison Commissioners, to J. D. Hall, secretary to Texas Governor Dan Moody, May 23, 1926, TSA, RG 301, Box 42.

74. "Lista de presos mexicanos en la Penitenciera de Florence, Arizona, en el 11 de Abril, 1929" and "Inmates Sentenced to Life Imprisonment or Given Death Sentences in Arizona from 1875 to January 1, 1967," ADLAPR, RG 85, Prison; *Winslow Mail,* September 28, 1934.

75. *Chicago Daily Tribune,* November 4, 1923; "Bernardo Roa, Reclamación no. 475," AHSRE; Lorenzo Lupián to SRE, August 10, 1924, NA, RG 59, 411.12; *Daily Calumet,* December 1 and 3, 1923; *New York Times,* March 8, 1927.

76. *New York Times,* May 6 and 7, 1926; *Chicago Herald Examiner,* May 6 and 7, 1926; *Chicago Tribune,* May 6 and 7, 1926; Erickson, *Warden Ragen of Joliet,* p. 127.

77. José Anguiano, interview, East Chicago, September 14, 1974; Martín Blanco and Eduardo Peralta, interviews, South Chicago, February 1975; Victor Torres, interview, South Chicago, December 1975; Hovar Rodríguez, interview, Joliet, 1987; *New York Times,* May 7, 1926; *Chicago Daily Tribune,* May 6, 1926; *Joliet Evening Herald News,* May 6, 1926.

78. *Chicago Daily Tribune,* November 27, 1926; March 14, 1927; Hovar Rodríguez, interview, Joliet, 1987; Mary Belle Spencer to Hjalmar J. Rehn, Will County attorney, September 27, 1926, Will County Circuit Court Records, File 8023.

79. *Joliet Evening Herald News,* March 14 and 15, 1927; *New York Times,* March 13 and 16, 1927; *El Amigo del Hogar,* March 15, 1927; *Chicago Daily News,* March 27, 1927.

80. *Joliet Evening Herald News,* June 13, 14, 15, and 20, 1927; *New York Times,* June 14 and 16, 1927; *Chicago Daily Tribune,* June 13, 14, 15, and 16, 1927.

81. Raat, *Revoltosos,* p. 261.

82. Martha M. McElroy, "William H. Laustauneau: Menace or Martyr," typescript, Arizona Special Collections; *Prescott Courier,* August 8, 1906; Philip J. Mellinger, *Race and Labor in Western Copper,* pp. 42–48.

83. Martin and Ekland-Olson, *Texas Prisons,* p. 10.

84. Assistant Secretary to Texas Governor Dan Moody to Jordan, February 11, 1929, and B. K. Ross, manager, tubercular unit, to H. W. Sayle, general manager at Huntsville, December 3, 1927, TSA, RG 301, Box 42. Some of the Mexican notables who died from illnesses in prison were Laustauneau at the Yuma Territorial Prison on August 20, 1906; Victoriano Huerta at Fort Bliss on January 31, 1916; and Ricardo Flores Magón at Fort Leavenworth on November 21, 1922.

85. Phillip Sonnichsen, *Texas Mexican Border Music,* vols. 2 and 3, *Corridos,* Parts 1 and 2 (recordings).

86. A. Lubbert, San Francisco consul, to SRE, May 7, 1931, AHSRE, IV/320/17.

87. R. Cervantes Torres, Secretario General para el Comité Central de CROM, May 28, 1931, to SRE, AHSRE, IV/320/17.

88. Petra Reyna to Rafael de la Colina, consul of Mexico, Los Angeles, May 11, 1931, and de la Colina to A. Lubbert, consul general, San Francisco, May 11, 1931, AHSRE, IV/320/17.

10. Extradition between Mexico and the United States

1. See *Ex Parte McCabe,* 46 F 363 (W.D. Texas, Austin Div, 1891).

2. Zorrilla, *Relaciones políticas, económicas y sociales de México en el extranjero,* vol. 3, pp. 10–11.

3. Honorable Richard Coke of Texas, "Mexican Outrages in the Texas Border," Speech in the Senate of the United States, November 14, 1911, Huntington Library.

4. *Correspondencia diplómatica relativa a las invasiones del territorio mexicano por*

fuerzas de los Estados Unidos, 1873–1877, pp. 1–12. See also Ethan A. Nadelmann, Cops across the Border, pp. 60–65.

5. Richard Coke, governor of Texas, "Mexican Outrages in the Texas Border," p. 15. For specifics on extradition arrangements with Mexico, see I. I. Kavass and A. Sprudzs, Extradition Laws and Treaties, United States.

6. "Reminiscences of Edward Samuel McEuen as told to Mrs. George F. Kitt, November 2, 1938," typescript, MS14-2, AHSA.

7. See, for example, Olga Cárdenas and Rubén Pliego, Guía de archivos de la embajada de México en los Estados Unidos, 1910–1912, pp. 142–144.

8. Hart, Revolutionary Mexico, p. 255; Philander C. Knox, secretary of state, to Henry Lane Wilson, ambassador to Mexico, September 19, 1912, NA, RG 59, 812.0144.

9. Ignacio Bonillas to Robert Lansing, secretary of state, October 31, 1919, and Lansing to Bonillas, NA, RG 59, 311.12221. Much of the information in the draft was deleted in the letter, which was ultimately sent to Bonillas on November 24, 1919; "Listas," Hermenigildo Domínguez, April 2, 1919.

10. Dominguez v State, 90 Tex Crim 92 (Court of Criminal Appeals, 1914).

11. Bonillas to Robert Lansing, secretary of state, October 31, 1919, NA, RG 59, 311.12221.

12. Robert Lansing, secretary of state, to Bonillas, November 2, 1919, NA, RG 59, 311.12221.

13. Baxter, "The Villista Murder Trials," p. 2.

14. Cárdenas and Pliego, Guía de archivos de la embajada de México en los Estados Unidos, 1910–1912, pp. 142–144.

15. Department of State to Frank B. Kellogg, secretary of state, Memorandum from the Mexican Division, January 5, 1926, NA, RG 59, 711.12/839.

16. Carl White, immigration officer, Department of Labor, to Department of State, April 16, 1924, and Joseph Crew, under secretary of state, to James J. Davis, secretary of labor, April 24, 1924, NA, RG 59, 311.1221.

17. La Patria, November 26, 1921.

18. Juan C. Valadés, Historia general de la revolución mexicana, vol. 7, pp. 222–227.

19. Los Angeles Examiner, November 17, 1904; Robert Bacon, acting secretary of state, to Mexican Embassy, June 25, 1906, AHSRE, 15-12-29. See M. Cherif Bassiouni, International Extradition, pp. 238–240.

20. James Grafton Rogers, acting secretary of state, to Mexican Embassy, April 15, 1932, AHSRE, III-189-2.

21. A. M. Sánchez, Mexican consul, Nogales, Arizona, to Francis J. Dyer, U.S. consul, Nogales, Sonora, January 13, 1922, and Dyer to Secretary of State, February 14 and 18, 1922, NA, RG 59, 812.04511.

22. E. E. Cola, consul in Phoenix, to SRE, September 28, 1932, A. Alanís Fuentes, sub-secretario, Poder Ejecutivo Federal, to SRE, August 23, 1933, and Cola to SRE, June 23, 1933, AHSRE, IV-551-7.

23. El Universal, February 11, 1935.

24. Ibid.

25. La Prensa (Mexico City), February 13 and October 16, 1941; El Nacional (Mexico City), February 18, 1941; January 21, 1942; El Universal, February 19, 1941.

26. The most recent and famous example is the kidnapping of Dr. Machain-Alvarez from his Guadalajara home during 1990 by agents paid by the U.S. Drug

Enforcement Agency. The Mexican physician was accused of helping to keep DEA agent Enrique Camarena (who was assigned to Mexico) alive while drug traffickers tortured and murdered him. See Bassiouni, *International Extradition,* pp. 241–246.

27. Erickson, *Warden Ragen of Joliet,* p. 126.

28. Rafael Matos Escobedo, Office of the Attorney General, to SRE, March 15, 1948, AHSRE, 41/21/32; Jesús Roa, interview, León, Guanajuato, 1988; Elodia Ramos de Roa, interview, León, Guanajuato, 1988.

29. Jesús Roa, interview.

30. Joseph Rehn, telephone interview, Joliet, Illinois, 1981.

31. Hurbert S. Bursley, American consul, Guaymas, Sonora, to Hjalmar J. Rehn, Will County state attorney, October 30, 1928, and J. Reuben Clark, Jr., U.S. Embassy in Mexico, to Bursley, November 27, 1928, NA, RG 59, 212.11, Roa.

32. Dudley G. Dwyre, United States consul, Mexico City, to W. R. Castle, Jr., acting secretary of state, June 9, 1932, and Hjalmar Rehn to F. L. Abbey, secretary to Illinois Governor Emmerson, June 23, 1932, NA, RG 59, 212.11, Roa; United States Embassy to SRE, July 5, 1932, AHSRE 41/21/32.

33. Manuel C. Téllez, secretary of SRE, to J. Reuben Clark, U.S. ambassador to Mexico, July 7, 1932, NA, RG 59, 212.11, Roa; D. S. Frueba to Police Chief, Mexico City, July 13, 1932, Manuel J. Sierra to Mexican attorney general, September 12, 1932, and Clark to Téllez, September 23, 1932, AHSRE, 41/21/32.

34. Agent, Mexican Attorney General's Office to SRE, February 11, 1933, AHSRE, 41/21/32; E. Jiménez D., SRE, to Josephus Daniels, U.S. ambassador to Mexico, December 28, 1933; William Phillips, acting secretary of state, to Henry Horner, governor of Illinois, January 16, 1934; Daniels to Secretary of State, January 16, 1934; Horner to Secretary of State, January 20, 1934; F. Torreblanca to Daniels, March 13, 1934; Stanley Hawks, second secretary of embassy, to José Manuel Puig Casuranc, March 20, 1934; all in NA, RG 59, 212.11, Roa.

35. Thomas D. Bowman, U.S. Embassy, Mexico City, to Secretary of State, November 5, 1935, and Josephus Daniels, ambassador, to Secretary of State, November 7, 1935, NA, RG 59, 212.11, Roa.

36. Ibid., pp. 126–127.

37. Cordell Hull, secretary of state, to Henry Horner, governor of Illinois, November 2, 1935, NA, RG 59, 212.11, Roa; Hull to U.S. Embassy, Mexico City, November 30, 1935, R. Henry Norweb, counselor of Embassy, to Hall, December 4, 1935, and Teniente Coronel Ignacio Sánchez Anaya to SRE, November 29, 1935, AHSRE, 41/21/32; Erickson, *Warden Ragen of Joliet,* p. 125.

38. Erickson, *Warden Ragen of Joliet,* p. 125.

39. *El Excelsior,* January 12, 1936.

40. R. Henry Norwebb to Cordell Hull, secretary of state, January 14, 1936; R. Walton Moore to Daniels, January 23, 1936; John H. MacVeah, U.S. Embassy, to Eduardo Hay, secretary, SRE, March 13, 1936; Daniels to Hull, December 11, 1936; John E. Cassidy, Illinois attorney general, to Henry Horner, governor of Illinois, January 24, 1939; all in NA, RG 59, 212.11, Roa; Luis G. García, federal agent, to SRE, October 1, 1936, AHSRE, 41/21/32; Erickson, *Warden Ragen of Joliet,* p. 125.

41. Otto Kerner, Illinois attorney general, to Cordell Hull, secretary of state, September 14, 1938, and Green H. Hackworth, legal advisor for the Secretary of State, to Kerner, September 21, 1938, NA, RG 59, 212.11, Roa.

42. United States Embassy to Hay, October 2, 1938, and Eduardo Rincón

Gallardo, chief of police, Mexico City, to Hay, November 16, 1938, AHSRE, 41/21/32; see Nadelmann, *Cops across the Border,* pp. 81–102, for a discussion of transnational cooperation between United States and foreign police.

43. James B. Stewart, American consul general, Mexico City, to Cordell Hull, secretary of state, October 14, 1938, J. Ignacio Delgadillo to George P. Shaw, American consul, Mexico City, October 3, 1938, and R. Walton Moore to Josephus Daniels, U.S. ambassador to Mexico, October 20, 1938, NA, RG 59, 212.11, Roa.

44. Josephus Daniels, U.S. ambassador to Mexico, to Secretary of State, October 26, 1938; Henry Horner, governor of Illinois, to Cordell Hull, secretary of state, October 31, 1938; Daniels to Hull, November 17, 1938; R. Beteta, SRE, to Daniels, November 11, 1938; all in NA, RG 59, 212.11, Roa; Genaro V. Vásquez, attorney general, Mexico, to Hay, November 11, 1938, Luis G. García to Rincón Gallardo, November 18, 1938, and Armando Flores to Mexico attorney general, November 24, 1938, AHSRE, 41/21/32.

45. Hay to Josephus Daniels, U.S. ambassador to Mexico, November 24, 1938, Daniels to Cordell Hull, secretary of state, December 1, 1938, and R. Walton Moore to Henry Horner, governor of Illinois, December 9, 1938, NA, RG 59, 212.11, Roa; Erickson, *Warden Ragen of Joliet,* p. 125.

46. Cordell Hull, secretary of state, to U.S. Embassy, Mexico, January 28, 1939; Henry Horner, governor of Illinois, to Hull, February 1, 1939; Ramón Beteta, secretary of the Foreign Ministry, to Josephus Daniels, U.S. ambassador to Mexico, February 6, 1939; Daniels to Hull, February 10 and 16, 1939; all in NA, RG 59, 212.11, Roa; Daniels to Hay, January 30, 1939, and Romeo León Orantes to SRE, February 11, 1939, AHSRE, 41/21/32.

47. J. Jesús Morales to President Franklin D. Roosevelt, December 3, 1940, and Morales to Roosevelt, February 12, 1941, NA, RG 59, 212.-11, Roa.

48. Cordell Hull, secretary of state, to Dwight H. Green, governor of Illinois, February 19, 1941, and Sumner Welles, acting secretary of state, to Josephus Daniels, U.S. ambassador to Mexico, March 22, 1941, NA, RG 59, 212.-11, Roa; Enrique Monterrulio, SRE, to Office of the Attorney General, Mexico, April 10, 1941, and Daniels to Ezequiel Padilla, minister of SRE, March 25, 1941, AHSRE 41/21/32.

49. Green H. Hackworth, legal advisor for the Secretary of State, to George F. Barrett, Illinois attorney general, May 13, 1944, NA, RG 59, 212.11, Roa; R. T. Piper, superintendent, Illinois Bureau of Criminal Identification & Investigation, to Barrett, April 20, 1944, George Messersmith to Ezequiel Padilla, Ministry of SRE, May 16, July 3, 1944, AHSRE 41-21-32.

50. Josephus Daniels, U.S. ambassador to Mexico, to Cordell Hull, secretary of state, March 9, 1948, NA, RG 59, 212.11, Roa; George C. Marshall, secretary of state, to Dwight A. Green, governor of Illinois, March 10, 1948, Rafael Matos Escobedo, Office of Mexico Attorney General, to Ezequiel Padilla, Ministry of SRE, March 15, 1948, and Oscar Treviño Ruíz, SRE, to Federal Public Ministry, Guanajuato, March 16, 1948, AHSRE 41/21/32.

51. Joseph E. Ragen, warden, Illinois State Penitentiary, to George C. Marshall, secretary of state, March 10, 1948; Dwight H. Green, governor of Illinois, to Marshall, March 17, 1948; Charles M. Robson, assistant state attorney, Illinois, to Marshall, March 17, 1948; R. W. Flournoy, assistant legal advisor, Department of State, to George F. Barrett, Illinois attorney general, March 23, 1948; Acting Secretary of State to Josephus Daniels, U.S. ambassador to Mexico, April 6, 1948; R. W.

Flournoy, Department of State, to Walter Thurston, American ambassador, Mexico, April 13, 1948; all in NA, RG 59, 212.11, Roa.

52. Bernardo Roa Berber to Miguel Alemán, president of Mexico, March 10, 1948, Rafael Araiza Romero, general secretariat, Guanajuato, to Roberto Amoros, first secretary to Alemán, March 5, 1948, and Amoros to Roa, March 16, 1948, Ramo Presidentes-Alemán, AGN 103-5a.

53. Jack B. Tate, for the Secretary of State, to Walter Thurston, U.S. ambassador to Mexico, April 14, 1949; George F. Barrett, Illinois attorney general, to Cordell Hull, secretary of state, May 11, 1944; Ernest A. Gross to Thurston, May 27, 1948; Taylor G. Belcher, Embassy official, Mexico, to George C. Marshall, secretary of state, July 15, 1948; all in NA, RG 59, 212.11, Roa.

54. See George C. Marshall, secretary of state, to SRE, April 22, 1948, and Marshall to SRE, October 4, 1949, AHSRE 41-21-32.

55. Taylor G. Belcher, Embassy official, Mexico, to George C. Marshall, secretary of state, August 1, 1949, NA, RG 59, 212.11, Roa.

56. Luis F. Canudas Orezza, SRE, to Attorney General Office, Mexico, August 29, 1952, AHSRE 41-21-32, encloses legal opinion written by Rafael Vejas Cervantes.

57. SRE to U.S. Embassy, Mexico, November 21, 1952; U.S. Embassy to SRE, February 13, 1951; U.S. Embassy, Mexico, to SRE, June 21, 1951; U.S. Embassy, Mexico, to SRE, July 31, 1952; all in AHSRE 41-21-32.

58. Three previous quotations from Erickson, *Warden Ragen of Joliet*, p. 126.

59. "Penitentiary Murderers Are to Hang," *Criminal Justice Journal of the Chicago Crime Commission* 53 (July–August 1927): 11–12; Erickson, *Warden Ragen of Joliet*, pp. 126–127.

60. Erickson, *Warden Ragen of Joliet*, p. 126.

61. Interviews with retired ejidatarios in Veredas, Guanajuato, April 18, 1996.

62. Last two quotations from José Anguiano, interview, East Chicago, Indiana, 1987.

63. Jesús Roa and Elodia Ramos de Roa, interview, León, Guanajuato, 1988.

CONCLUSION

1. Quoted in Reisler, *By the Sweat of Their Brow*, p. 159.

2. Raat, *Revoltosos*, p. 265.

3. *New York Times*, November 4, 1926.

4. Vargas, *Proletarians of the North*, p. 84; *Hispano América*, July 30, 1923; Walker, "Mexican Immigrants and Citizenship," pp. 450–456.

5. Quoted in Romo, *East Los Angeles*, p. 155.

6. For numerous sources on the Immigrant Protective League and Mexicans, see *Daily Calumet* files in East Chicago Historical Society.

7. *Houston Chronicle*, December 30, 1914; *New York Times*, December 24, 1915.

8. Martínez, *Fragments of the Mexican Revolution*, p. 165.

9. Ernesto Hidalgo, *La Protección de mexicanos en el los Estados Unidos*, p. 53.

10. Ibid., passim.

11. *El Tucsonense*, July 10, 1934 (emphasis added).

12. In 1928, Governor C. C. Young's commission on Mexicans explained that fewer Mexicans were in Folsom than at San Quentin because Mexicans had arrived in this country more recently than other immigrant groups. See Taylor, "Crime and the Foreign Born," p. 203.

BIBLIOGRAPHY

ARCHIVAL AND MANUSCRIPT COLLECTIONS

Archivo General de la Nación (AGN), Ramos Presidentes y Secretaría de Industria, Comercio y Trabajo. Mexico City.

Archivo Histórico de la Secretaría de Relaciones Exteriores (AHSRE), Consular Records. Mexico City.

Arizona Department of Library, Archives and Public Records (ADLAPR). Phoenix.

Arizona Historical Foundation (AHF), Hayden Library, Arizona State University. Tempe.

Arizona Historical Society Archives (AHSA). Tucson.

Arizona Special Collections (ASC), Hayden Library, Arizona State University. Tempe.

Biblioteca Estatal de Guanajuato.

California State Library, Archives and Documents. Sacramento.

Chicago Historical Society, Chicago Foreign Language Press Survey (CFLPS).

Chicano Collection, Hayden Library, Arizona State University. Tempe.

Colección Porfirio Díaz (CPD), Hemeroteca, Universidad Ibero Americana. Mexico City.

East Chicago, Indiana, Historical Society.

Espy, M. Watt, and John Ortiz Smykla. "Executions in the United States, 1608–1987: The Espy File." Ann Arbor: Inter-University Consortium for Political and Social Research, 1990, machine readable data file 8541.

Gamio, Manuel. Papers. Bancroft Library, University of California. Berkeley.

Gobierno del Estado de Sonora, Archivo Histórico, Hermosillo.

Hayden Collection, Hayden Library, Arizona State University. Tempe.

Hemeroteca de la Biblioteca Estatal de Jalisco. Guadalajara.

Hemeroteca Miguel Lerdo de Tejada. Mexico City.

Hemeroteca Municipal de León de Aldamas. Guanajuato.

Houston Metropolitan Research Center (HMRC). Houston.

Huntington Library. San Marino, California.

Illinois Historical Society Archives (IHSA). Springfield.

McKanna, Clare "Bud." Personal collection. "List of California Lynchings."

McWilliams, Carey. Papers. Federal Writer's Project Collection. Special Collections, University of California, Los Angeles.

National Archives (NA), Record Group (RG) 59, Department of State. Washington, D.C.

Texas State Archives (TSA), Texas State Library. Austin.

NEWSPAPERS

Arizona Republican (Phoenix)
Arizona Sentinel (Prescott)
Calumet News (East Chicago, Indiana)
Chicago Daily Tribune
Chicago Herald Examiner
Chicago Sun Times
Colton Chronicle (Colton, California)
Daily Calumet (South Chicago)
Dallas Dispatch
Diario Oficial (Mexico City)
Douglas Daily Dispatch (Douglas, Arizona)
Douglas Daily International (Douglas, Arizona)
El Amigo del Hogar (East Chicago, Indiana)
El Anunciador (Trinidad, Colorado)
El Correo Mexicano (CFLPS)
El Cosmopolita (Kansas City)
El Cronista del Valle (Brownsville, Texas)
El Defensor (Edinburg, Texas)
El Excelsior (Mexico City)
El Imparcial de Texas (San Antonio)
El Mosquito (Tucson)
El Mundo (Mexico City)
El Nacional (CFLPS)
El Observador Mexicano (Phoenix)
El Ocasional (Phoenix)
El País (Mexico City)
El Paso Times
El Tucsonense (Tucson)
El Universal (Mexico City)
The Ferguson Forum (Temple, Texas)
Hispano América (San Francisco)
Houston Chronicle
Houston Post
Joliet Evening Herald News (Illinois)
Justicia (Phoenix)
La Defensa (CFLPS)
La Gaceta de Jalisco (Guadalajara)
La Gaceta Mexicana (Houston)
La Lucha (CFLPS)
La Opinión (Los Angeles)
La Patria (El Paso)
La Prensa (San Antonio)
La Raza (Los Angeles)
Latino Americano (Phoenix)
Los Angeles Times
Mason County News (Texas)

México (CFLPS)
New York Times
The Oasis (Nogales, Arizona)
Prescott Courier (Arizona)
Revolt (El Paso)
San Angelo Evening Standard (Texas)
San Antonio Evening News
San Bernardino Daily Sun (California)
San Diego Union
San Francisco Call
San Francisco Post
Washington Post
Winslow Mail (Arizona)

INTERVIEWS

Andrade, María Elena. Telephone interview, Buffalo, N.Y., 1987.
Anguiano, José. East Chicago, Ind., September 14, 1974.
Blanco, Martín. South Chicago, Ill., 1975.
Cruz, José. Houston, March 21, 1976.
García dc Rosales, Mercedes. Tucson, October 15, 1991.
Navarro de Garza, Ana. Schererville, Ind., 1975.
Pacheco, Basil. East Chicago, Ind., 1975.
Peralta, Eduardo. South Chicago, Ill., February 1975.
Ramos de Roa, Elodia. León, Guanajuato, May 1988; July 1994.
Roa, Jesús. León, Guanajuato, May 1988; July 1994.
Rodríguez, Hovar. Joliet, Ill., 1987.
Rosales, Rodrigo. Tucson, 1982.
Rosales de Dalton, Refugio. Tucson, October 15, 1991.
Silva, Hilario. East Chicago, Ind., March 1975.
Torres, Victor. South Chicago, Ill., December 1974.
Yañez, Jovita. Houston, March 29, 1976.

COURT APPEALS

Castro v State of Indiana, 147 NE 321 (Supreme Court of Indiana, April 25, 1925).
Dominguez v State of Texas, 90 Tex Crim 92 (Court of Criminal Appeals, June 24, 1914).
Ex Parte Martinez, 66 Tex Crim 1 (Court of Criminal Appeals, March 27, 1912).
Ex Parte McCabe, 46 F 363 (W.D. Texas, Austin Div, April 2, 1891).
Grijalva v State of Arizona, 260 P 188 (Supreme Court of Arizona, October 17, 1927).
People v Corona, 300 SW 80 (Court of Criminal Appeals of Texas, November 30, 1927).
People v Gonzalez, 164 P 1131 (2nd District of California, March 28, 1917).
People v Herrera, 163 P 880 (2nd District of California, January 27, 1917).
People v Pompa, 192 Cal Reptr 412 (2nd District of California, November 12, 1923).
People v Valenzuela, 147 P 97 (2nd District of California, January 26, 1915).
United States ex rel Velasco v Ragen, 158 F2d 87 (7th Cir, November 5, 1946).

ARTICLES, BOOKS, PRINTED DOCUMENTS, AND UNPUBLISHED WORKS

Abbott, Edith, ed. *Report on Crime and Criminal Justice in Relation to the Foreign Born, for the National Commission on Law Observance and Enforcement,* no. 10. Washington, D.C.: Government Printing Office, 1931.

Abney, David Lawrence. "Capital Punishment in Arizona: 1863–1963." Master's thesis, Arizona State University, 1988.

Acuña, Rodolfo. *Occupied America: A History of Chicanos.* 3d ed. New York: Harper and Row, 1988.

Aikman, Duncan, "Hell along the Border." *American Mercury* 5 (May 1925): 17.

Alvarez, Roberto R., Jr. *La Familia: Migration and Adaptation in Baja and Alta California, 1800–1975.* Berkeley: University of California Press, 1987.

Año Nuevo Kerr, Louise. "The Chicano Experience in Chicago, 1920–1970." Ph.D. dissertation, University of Illinois, 1976.

Apolinar, Armando. "Hablando de Clemente Apolinar, colgado 1923." *Caracol* 1 (December 1974): 4–7.

Balderrama, Francisco E. *In Defense of La Raza: The Los Angeles Mexican Consulate and the Mexican Community, 1929–1936.* Tucson: University of Arizona Press, 1982.

Balderrama, Francisco E., and Raymond Rodríguez. *Decade of Betrayal: Mexican Repatriation in the 1930s.* Albuquerque: University of New Mexico Press, 1995.

Baldwin, Deborah J. *Protestants and the Mexican Revolution: Missionaries, Ministers, and Social Change.* Albuquerque: University of New Mexico Press, 1994.

Bassiouni, M. Cherif. *International Extradition: United States Law and Practice.* 3d ed. Dobbs Ferry, N.Y.: Oceana Publications, 1996.

Baxter, John O. "The Villista Murder Trials: Deming, New Mexico, 1916–1921." *La Gaceta* 7 (1983): 11–21.

Berry, Mary Frances, and John W. Blassingame. *Long Memories: The Black Experience in America.* New York: Oxford University Press, 1982.

Betten, Neil, and Raymond Mohl. "From Discrimination to Repatriation: Mexican Life in Gary, Indiana, during the Great Depression." *Pacific Historical Review* 42 (August 1973): 270–388.

Blackwelder, Julia Kirk. *Women of the Depression: Caste and Culture in San Antonio, 1929–1939.* College Station: Texas A&M University Press, 1984.

Bogardus, Emory. *Immigrants and Race Relations.* Boston: D. C. Heath and Company, 1928.

Bookspan, Shelly. *A Germ of Goodness: The California State Prison, 1851–1944.* Lincoln: University of Nebraska Press, 1991.

Bowers, William J. *Legal Homicide: Death as Punishment in America, 1894–1982.* Boston: Northeastern University Press, 1984.

Bowler, Alida C. "Recent Statistics on Crime and the Foreign Born." In *Report on Crime and Criminal Justice in Relation to the Foreign Born, for the National Commission on Law Observance and Enforcement,* no. 10, edited by Edith Abbott, pp. 83–194. Washington, D.C.: Government Printing Office, 1931.

Brown, Jonathan C. "Foreign and Native Workers in Porfirian Mexico." *American Historical Review* 98 (June 1993): 786–818.

Brown, Richard Maxwell. *No Duty to Retreat: Violence and Values in American History and Society.* New York: Oxford University Press, 1991.

——. *Strain of Violence: Historical Studies of American Violence and Vigilantism.* New York: Oxford University Press, 1975.

Buffington, Robert. "Prohibition in the Borderlands: National Government–Border Community Relations." *Pacific Historical Review* 63 (February 1994): 19–38.

Cahalan, Margaret Werner. *Historical Corrections Statistics in the United States, 1850–1894.* Washington, D.C.: U.S. Department of Justice, Bureau of Justice Statistics, 1986.

Camarillo, Albert. *Chicanos in a Changing Society: From Mexican Pueblos to American Barrios in Santa Barbara and Southern California, 1848–1930.* Cambridge: Harvard University Press, 1979.

Campa, Arthur. *Hispanic Culture in the Southwest.* Norman: University of Oklahoma Press, 1979.

Cárdenas, Olga, and García Pliego. *Guía de archivos de la embajada de México en los Estados Unidos, 1910–1912.* Mexico City: Secretaría de Relaciones Exteriores, 1994.

Cardoso, Lawrence. "Labor Emigration to the Southwest, 1911–1920: Mexican Attitudes and Policy." *Southwestern Historical Quarterly* 84 (April 1973): 400–416.

——. *Mexican Emigration to the United States, 1897–1931.* Tucson: University of Arizona Press, 1980.

Chapman, David L. "Lynching in Texas." Master's thesis, Texas Tech University, 1973.

Chávez, John. *The Lost Land: The Chicano Image of the Southwest.* Albuquerque: University of New Mexico Press, 1984.

Christian, Carole. "Joining the American Mainstream: Texas's Mexican Americans during World War I." *Southwestern Historical Quarterly* 92 (April 1989): 559–595.

Coerver, Don M. A., and Linda B. Hall. *Texas and the Mexican Revolution: Study in State and National Border Policy, 1910–1920.* San Antonio: Trinity University Press, 1984.

Correspondencia diplómatica relativa a las invasiones del territorio mexicano por fuerzas de los Estados Unidos, 1873–1877. Mexico City: Imprenta Ignacio Cumplido, 1888.

Corzine, J., J. Creed, and L. Corzine. "Black Concentration and Lynching in the South: Testing Blalock's Power-Threat Hypothesis." *Social Forces* 63 (1983): 774–796.

Cumberland, Charles. *The Mexican Revolution: The Constitutionalist Years.* Austin: University of Texas Press, 1972.

Davidson, R. Theodore. *Chicano Prisoners: The Key to San Quentin.* Prospect Heights, Ill.: Waveland Press, 1974.

Dávila, José. "The Mexican Migration Problem." Address delivered at the Friends of Mexico Conference, Claremont, Calif., January 1928. Photocopy in author's files.

De Baca, Carlos C. *Vicente Silva: The Terror of Las Vegas.* Las Truchas, N.M.: Tate Gallery Publications, 1968.

De León, Arnoldo. *Ethnicity in the Sunbelt: A History of Mexican Americans in*

Houston. Mexican American Studies Monograph Series, no. 7. Houston: University of Houston, 1989.

———. *Mexican Americans in Texas: A Brief History.* Arlington Heights, Ill.: Harlan Davidson, 1993.

———. *The Tejano Community, 1836–1900.* Albuquerque: University of New Mexico Press, 1982.

———. *They Called Them Greasers: Anglo Attitudes toward Mexicans in Texas, 1821–1900.* Austin: University of Texas Press, 1983.

De León, Arnoldo, and Kenneth Stewart. *Not Room Enough: Mexicans, Anglos and Socioeconomic Change in Texas, 1850–1900.* Albuquerque: University of New Mexico Press, 1993.

Deutsch, Sarah. *No Separate Refuge: Culture, Class, and Gender on the Anglo-Hispanic Frontier in the American Southwest, 1880–1940.* New York: Oxford University Press, 1987.

Erickson, Gladys A. *Warden Ragen of Joliet.* New York: E. P. Dutton & Co., 1957.

Escobar, Edward J. "Race and Law Enforcement: Relations between Chicanos and the Los Angeles Police Department, 1900–1945." Manuscript in author's files.

Esposito, Matthew Donald. "From Cuauhtémoc to Juárez: Monuments, Myth, and Culture in Porfirian Mexico, 1876–1900." Master's thesis, Arizona State University, 1993.

Fanon, Frantz. *The Wretched of the Earth.* New York: Grove Press, 1968.

Farrell, Harry. *Swift Justice: Murder and Vengeance in a California Town.* New York: St. Martin's Press, 1996.

Fellows, William. "The Need for Mexicans to Americanize in Arizona." *Latino Americano* 1 (April 1934): 6.

Foley, Neil. "Mexican Migrant and Tenant Labor in Central Texas Cotton Counties, 1880–1930: Transformation in a Multicultural Society." *Wooster Review* 9 (Spring 1989): 95–99.

Foster, William Z. *Pages from a Worker's Life.* New York: International Publishers Co., 1939.

Franco, Jesús. *El alma de la raza: Narraciones históricas.* Reprint, with different pagination. El Paso, Tex.: Compañía Editora "La Patria," 1923.

Friedrich, Paul. *The Princes of Naranja: An Essay in Anthrohistorical Method.* Austin: University of Texas Press, 1986.

Fromm, Erich, and Michael Maccoby. *Social Character in a Mexican Village: A Sociopsychoanalytic Study.* Englewood, N.J.: Prentice-Hall, 1970.

Gambino, Richard. *Vendetta: A True Story of the Worst Lynching in America, the Mass Murder of Italian Americans in New Orleans, 1891, the Vicious Motivations behind It and the Tragic Repercussions That Linger to This Day.* Garden City, N.J.: Doubleday and Company, 1977.

Gamio, Manuel. *The Life Story of the Mexican Immigrant: Autobiographical Documents Collected by Manuel Gamio.* New York: Dover Publications, 1970.

———. *Mexican Immigration to the United States: A Study of Human Immigration and Adjustment.* New York: Dover Publications, 1971.

García, David Ray. "The Romo Decision and Desegregation in Tempe." Senior thesis, Arizona State University, 1993.

García, Mario T. *Desert Immigrants: The Mexicans of El Paso, 1880–1920*. New Haven: Yale University Press, 1981.

———. "La Frontera: The Border as Symbol and Reality in Mexican American Thought." *Mexican Studies/Estudios Mexicanos* 1 (Summer 1985): 195–225.

———. *Mexican Americans: Leadership Ideology and Identity, 1930–1960*. New Haven: Yale University Press, 1990.

———. "Porfirian Diplomacy and the Administration of Justice in Texas, 1877–1900." *Aztlán* 16 (1985): 1–26.

Garson, David, and Gail O'Brien. "Collective Violence in the Reconstruction South." In *Violence in America: Historical and Comparative Perspectives*, edited by Hugh D. Graham, pp. 134–142. Beverly Hills: Sage Publications, 1979.

Gledhill, John. *Casi Nada: A Study of Agrarian Reform in the Homeland of Cardenismo*. Albany: Institute for Mesoamerican Society, State University of New York at Albany, 1989.

Gómez Quiñones, Juan. "On Culture." *Revista Chicano Riqueña* 5 (Spring 1977): 29–47.

———. "Piedras contra la luna: México en *Aztlán* y *Aztlán* en México: Chicano-Mexican Relations and the Mexican Consulates, 1900–1920." In *Contemporary Mexico: Papers of the IV International Congress of Mexican History*, edited by James Wilkie, pp. 494–527. Mexico City: El Colegio de Mexico and UCLA Latin American Studies Center, 1975.

González, Gilbert G. *Chicano Education in the Era of Segregation*. Philadelphia: Balch Institute Press, 1990.

———. "Labor and Community: The Camps of Mexican Citrus Pickers in Southern California." *Western Historical Quarterly* 22 (August 1991): 290–312.

González, Gilbert G., and Raúl Fernández. "Chicano History: Transcending Cultural Models." *Pacific Historical Review* 58 (November 1994): 469–498.

González, Luis. *San José de Gracia: A Mexican Town in Transition*. Austin: University of Texas Press, 1972.

Greenberg, James. *Blood Ties: Life and Violence in Rural Mexico*. Tucson: University of Arizona Press, 1989.

Griswold del Castillo, Richard. *The Los Angeles Barrios, 1850–1890: A Social History*. Berkeley: University of California Press, 1980.

Gutierrez, David. "Border Patrol." In *Voices of Pimería Alta*, pp. 152–160. Nogales, Ariz.: Pimería Alta Historical Society, 1991.

Gutiérrez, David G. *Walls and Mirrors: Mexican Americans, Mexican Immigrants and the Politics of Ethnicity*. Berkeley: University of California Press, 1995.

Gutiérrez, José. *"La inolvidable peregrina,"* Mexico: *Nuestra Gran Historia*. Mexico City: Selecciones de Reader's Digest, 1973.

Handman, Max Sylvius. "Preliminary Report on Nativity and Delinquency: The Mexican in Texas." In *Report on Crime and Criminal Justice in Relation to the Foreign Born, for the National Commission on Law Observance and Enforcement*, no. 10, edited by Edith Abbott, pp. 245–264. Washington, D.C.: Government Printing Office, 1931.

Harris, Charles H., III, and Louis Sadler. "The 1911 Reyes Conspiracy: The Texas

Side." In *Border Revolution,* edited by Harris and Sadler, pp. 27–52. Las Cruces, N.M.: Center for Latin American Studies/Joint Border Research Institute, New Mexico State University, 1988.

————. "The Plan de San Diego and the Mexican–United States War Crisis of 1916: A Reexamination." In *Border Revolution,* edited by Harris and Sadler, pp. 1–100. Las Cruces, N.M.: Center for Latin American Studies/Joint Border Research Institute, New Mexico State University, 1988.

Hart, John M. *Revolutionary Mexico: The Coming and Process of the Mexican Revolution.* Berkeley: University of California Press, 1987.

Haynes, Suzanne. "A Quarrel among Mexicans: A Study of Aggression in the Colonia of Kansas City." Unpublished manuscript in author's files.

Hernández, José Amaro. *Mutual Aid for Survival: The Case of the Mexican American.* Malabar, Fla.: Robert E. Krieger Publishing Company, 1983.

Hertzog, Peter. *Legal Hangings.* Santa Fe: Press of the Territorian, 1961.

Heyman, Josiah McConnell. *Life and Labor on the Border: Working People of Northern Mexico, 1886–1986.* Tucson: University of Arizona Press, 1991.

Hidalgo, Ernesto. *La Protección de mexicanos en los Estados Unidos: Defensores de oficios anexes a los consulados.* Mexico City: Talleres Gráficos de la Nación, 1940.

Higham, John. *Strangers in the Land: Patterns of American Nativism, 1860–1925.* New York: Atheneum, 1966.

Horn, James. "U.S. Diplomacy and the 'Specter of Bolshevism' in Mexico, 1924–1927." *The Americas* 32 (July 1975): 31–45.

Horsman, Reginald. *Race and Manifest Destiny: The Origins of American Racial Anglo-Saxonism.* Cambridge: Harvard University Press, 1981.

Ichioka, Yuji. "Ameyuki-san: Japanese Prostitutes in Nineteenth-Century America." *Amerasia* 4 (Spring 1978): 1–21.

Jacobs, James B. *Statesville.* Chicago: University of Chicago Press, 1977.

Justice, Glenn. *Revolution on the Rio Grande: Mexican Raids and Army Pursuits, 1916–1919.* El Paso: Texas Western Press, 1992.

Kanellos, Nicolás. *A History of Hispanic Theatre in the United States: Origins to 1940.* Austin: University of Texas Press, 1990.

Kavass, I. I., and A. Sprudzs. *Extradition Laws and Treaties, United States.* Buffalo: W. S. Hein, 1979.

Kleinderg, O. H. "The Causes of Violence: A Psychological Approach." In *Violence and Its Causes,* edited by Jean Marie Domenach, pp. 86–92. Paris: UNESCO, 1981.

Knepper, Paul. "Southern-Style Punitive Repression: Ethnic Stratification, Economic Inequality, and Imprisonment in Territorial Arizona." *Social Justice* 16, no. 4 (Winter 1989): 132–149.

Knight, Alan. *The Mexican Revolution.* 2 vols. London: Cambridge University Press, 1986.

————. "Popular Culture and the Revolutionary State in Mexico, 1910–1940." *Hispanic American Historical Review* 74 (Fall 1994): 393–444.

Kreneck, Thomas H. "The Letter from Chapultepec." *Houston Review* 3 (Summer 1981): 268–271.

Laird, Judith Fincher. "Argentine Kansas: The Evolution of a Mexican American Community, 1905–1940." Ph.D. dissertation, University of Kansas, 1975.

La Migración y Protección del Mexicano en el Extranjero. Mexico City: Imprenta de la Secretaría de Relaciones Exteriores, 1928.

Lamott, Kenneth. *Chronicles of San Quentin: The Biography of a Prison.* New York: David McKay Company, 1961.

Larralde, Carlos. "J. T. Canales and the Texas Rangers." *Journal of South Texas History* 10 (1997): 38–68.

Leopold, Nathan. *Life Plus 99 Years.* New York: Doubleday, 1957.

Lescochier, Don D. "The Vital Problem, Mexican Immigration." In *Proceedings of the National Conference on Social Work, Fifty-fourth Annual Session Held in Des Moines, Iowa, May 11, 1927,* pp. 551–560. Chicago: University of Chicago Press, 1927.

"Los Hermanos Hernández." *El Latino Americano* 1 (August 1934): 14.

Lukens, Patrick. "The Timoteo Andrade Citizenship Case." History seminar paper, Arizona State University, 1993.

MacCormick, Austin H., and Paul W. Garrett, eds. *Handbook of American Prisons, 1926.* New York: G. P. Putman's Sons, 1926.

Marquart, James, Sheldon Ekland-Olson, and Jonathan R. Sorensen. *The Rope, The Chair, and the Needle: Capital Punishment in Texas, 1923–1990.* Austin: University of Texas Press, 1994.

Martin, Steve J., and Sheldon Ekland-Olson. *Texas Prisons: The Walls Came Tumbling Down.* Austin: Texas Monthly Press, 1987.

Martínez, John. *Mexican Emigration to the United States, 1910–1930.* San Francisco: Arno Press, 1971.

Martínez, Oscar J. *Border People: Life and Society in the U.S.-Mexico Borderlands.* Tucson: University of Arizona Press, 1994.

———. *Fragments of the Mexican Revolution: Personal Accounts from the Border.* Albuquerque: University of New Mexico Press, 1983.

———. "Prohibition Depression in Ciudad Juárez–El Paso." In *U.S.-Mexico Borderlands: Historical and Contemporary Perspectives,* edited by Oscar J. Martínez, pp. 151–161. Wilmington, Del.: Scholarly Resources, 1996.

———. *Troublesome Border.* Tucson: University of Arizona Press, 1988.

May, Antoinette. *Passionate Pilgrim: The Extraordinary Life of Alma Reed.* New York: Paragon House, 1993.

Mazón, Mauricio. *The Zoot-Suit Riots: The Psychology of Symbolic Annihilation.* Austin: University of Texas Press, 1984.

McBride, James D. "The Liga Protectora Latina: A Mexican American Benevolent Society in Arizona." *Journal of the West* 14 (October 1975): 82–90.

McWilliams, Carey. *Factories in the Fields: The Story of Migratory Labor in California.* Santa Barbara: Peregrine Press, 1971.

Mellinger, Philip J. "'The Men Have Become Labor Organizers': Labor Conflict and Unionization in the Mexican Mining Towns of Arizona, 1900–1915." *Western Historical Quarterly* 23 (August 1992): 323–348.

———. *Race and Labor in Western Copper: The Fight for Equality.* Tucson: University of Arizona Press, 1995.

Memoria de Relaciones Exteriores en el Estados Unidos y Guatemala. Mexico City: Secretaría de Relaciones Exteriores, 1928.

Menchaca, Martha. *The Mexican Outsiders: A Community History of Marginalization and Discrimination in California.* University of Texas Press, 1995.

Mexicans in California: Report of Governor C. C. Young's Mexican Fact-Finding Committee. San Francisco: State Building, October 1930.

Miller, Kerby. *Emigrants and Exiles: Ireland and the Irish Exodus to North America.* New York: Oxford University Press, 1985.

Mirandé, Alfredo. *Gringo Justice.* Notre Dame: University of Notre Dame, 1987.

Montejano, David. *Anglos and Mexicans in the Making of Texas 1836–1896.* Austin: University of Texas Press, 1987.

Morales, Armando. *Ando Sagrando: A Study of Mexican American–Police Conflict.* Los Angeles: Perspectiva Publications, 1972.

Nadelmann, Ethan A. *Cops across the Border: The Internationalization of U.S. Criminal Law Enforcement.* University Park: Pennsylvania State University Press, 1993.

National Commission on Law Observance and Enforcement. *Report on Lawlessness in Law Enforcement, for the National Commission on Law Observance and Enforcement*, no. 11. Washington, D.C.: Government Printing Office, 1931.

Nichols, Nancy Ann. *San Quentin inside the Walls.* San Quentin, Calif.: San Quentin Museum Press, 1991.

Odom, Mary E. *Delinquent Daughters: Protecting Female Sexuality in the United States, 1885–1920.* Chapel Hill: University of North Carolina Press, 1995.

Olson, James Stuart. *The Ethnic Dimension in American History.* New York: St. Martin's Press, 1979.

Olzak, Susan. *The Dynamics of Ethnic Competition and Conflict.* Stanford: Stanford University Press, 1992.

Oppenheimer, Dulben. *The Administration of Deportation Laws of the United States: Report to the National Commission on Law Observance and Enforcement.* Washington, D.C.: Government Printing Office, 1931.

Paredes, Américo. *A Texas-Mexican Cancionero: Folksongs of the Lower Border.* Austin: University of Texas Press, 1995.

———. *Uncle Remus con chile.* Houston: Arte Público Press, 1993.

———. *With a Pistol in His Hand: A Border Ballad and Its Hero.* Austin: University of Texas Press, 1958.

Patraz, Allen Gene. "The Transfer of Arizona's Territorial Prison from Yuma to Florence." Master's thesis, Arizona State University, 1982.

Paz, Octavio. *The Labyrinth of Solitude: Life and Thought in Mexico.* New York: Grove Press, 1961.

"Penitentiary Murderers Are to Hang." *Criminal Justice Journal of the Chicago Crime Commission* 53 (July–August 1927): 11–12.

Perkins, Clifford Alan. *Border Patrol: With the U.S. Immigration Service on the Mexican Boundary, 1910–54.* El Paso: Texas Western Press, University of El Paso, 1978.

Pettit, Arthur. *Images of the Mexican American in Fiction and Film.* College Station: Texas A&M University Press, 1980.

Phelan, John Leddy. "México y lo mexicano." *Hispanic American Historical Review* 36 (August 1956): 309–318.

Pletcher, David. *Rails, Mines, and Progress: Seven American Pioneers in Mexico, 1867–1911.* Ithaca: Cornell University Press, 1958.

Powell, Phillip Wayne. *Tree of Hate: Propaganda and Prejudices Affecting United States Relations with the Hispanic World.* New York: Basic Books, 1971.

Prida, Ramón. *Datos y observaciones sobre los Estados Unidos de América.* Mexico City: Librería de Mauricio Guillot, 1923.

———. "La criminalidad en Mexico en los últimos años." *Primer Centenario de la Sociedad Mexicana de Geografía y Estadística* 2 (1933): 721–734.

"Prison Reforms in Arizona." *Charities and the Commons* 1907: 333.

Proceedings of the Sixty-second Annual Congress of the American Prison Association, Indianapolis, Indiana, October 3rd to 7th. New York City, 1932.

Raat, W. Dirk. *Revoltosos: Mexico's Rebels in the United States.* College Station: Texas A&M University Press, 1981.

Ramos, Samuel. *Profile of Man and Culture in Mexico.* Austin: University of Texas Press, 1972.

Rathbun, Carl M. "Keeping Peace along the Mexican Border: The Unceasing Task of the Arizona Rangers." *Harper's Weekly* 5 (November 17, 1906): 1633–1634.

Reisler, Mark. *By the Sweat of Their Brow: Mexican Immigrant Labor in the United States: 1900–1940.* Westport, Conn.: Greenwood Press, 1976.

"Report of Frank Buckley of the Bureau of Prohibition, Treasury Department, Submitting Detailed Information Relative to a Survey of Prohibition Enforcement in the State of Texas." In United States, 71st Congress, 3d Session, *Enforcement of the Prohibition Laws: Official Records of the National Commission on Law Observance and Enforcement,* vol. 4, pp. 923–970. Washington, D.C.: Government Printing Office, 1931.

Rice, Harvey. "The Lynching of Antonio Rodríguez." Master's thesis, University of Texas, 1990.

Richmond, Douglas W. "Mexican Immigration and Border Strategy during the Revolution, 1910–1920." *New Mexico Historical Review* 57 (July 1982): 279–287.

———. *Venustiano Carranza's Nationalist Struggle, 1893–1920.* Lincoln: University of Nebraska Press, 1983.

Ríos Bustamante, Antonio. "'Guilty as Hell,' Copper Mines, Mexican Miners, and Community, 1920–1950: The Spatial and Social Consequences of Mining Town Industry in Arizona." Chicano Collection, Hayden Library, Arizona State University. Tempe. Manuscript.

Rocha, Rudolfo. "The Influence of the Mexican Revolution on the Mexico-Texas Border, 1910–1916." Ph.D. dissertation, Texas Tech University, 1981.

Rodríguez, Juan. *Crónicas diabólicas de "Jorge Ulica"/Julio G. Arce.* San Diego: Maize Press, 1982.

Romanucci-Ross, Lola. *Conflict, Violence, and Morality in a Mexican Village.* Palo Alto: National Press Books, 1973.

Romo, Ricardo. *East Los Angeles: History of a Barrio.* Austin: University of Texas Press, 1983.

Rosales, F. Arturo. *Chicano: A History of the Mexican American Civil Rights Movement.* Houston: Arte Público Press, 1996.

———. "The Lynching of Antonio Rodríguez: An Historical Reassessment." Manuscript in author's files.

———. "The Mexican Immigrant Experience in Chicago, Houston, and Tucson: Comparisons and Contrasts." In *Houston: A Twentieth Century Urban Frontier,* edited by Rosales and Barry J. Kaplan, pp. 58–77, 192–194. Port Washington, N.Y.: Associated Faculty Press, 1983.

———. "Mexicans, Interethnic Violence, and Crime in the Chicago Area during the 1920s and 1930s: The Struggle to Achieve Ethnic Consciousness." In *Perspectives in Mexican American Studies,* vol. 2, edited by Juan García, pp. 59–97. Tucson: Mexican American Studies Center and Research Center, University of Arizona, 1989.

———. "Mexicans in Houston: The Struggle to Survive, 1808–1975." *Houston Review* 3 (Summer 1981): 224–248.

———. "The Regional Origins of Mexicano Immigrants to Chicago during the 1920s." *Aztlán* 7 (Summer 1976): 187–201.

———. "Shifting Self-Perceptions and Ethnic Consciousness among Mexicans in Houston, 1908–1946." *Aztlán* 16 (Double issue, 1985): 71–94.

Rosales, F. Arturo, and Daniel T. Simon. "Mexican Immigration to the Urban Midwest: East Chicago, Indiana, 1919–1945." *Indiana Magazine of History* 77 (December 1981): 333–357.

Rosenbaum, Robert J. *Mexicano Resistance in the Southwest: "The Sacred Right of Self-Preservation."* Austin: University of Texas Press, 1981.

Ross, Stanley R. "Dwight Morrow and the Mexican Revolution." *Hispanic American Historical Review* 38 (November 1958): 506–527.

Sallenger, T. Earl. "The Mexican Population of Omaha." *Sociology and Social Research* 24 (May–June 1924): 263.

Samora, Julián. *Gunpowder Justice: A Reassessment of the Texas Rangers.* Notre Dame, Ind.: University of Notre Dame Press, 1979.

Sánchez, George J. *Becoming Mexican American: Ethnicity, Culture, and Identity in Chicano Los Angeles, 1900–1945.* New York: Oxford University Press, 1993.

Sandos, James A. *Rebellion in the Borderlands: Anarchism and the Plan of San Diego, 1904–1923.* Norman: University of Oklahoma Press, 1992.

San Miguel, Guadalupe. *"Let All of Them Take Heed": Mexican Americans and the Campaign for Educational Equality in Texas, 1910–1981.* Austin: University of Texas Press, 1987.

Santibáñez, Enrique. *Ensayo acerca de la inmigración mexicana en los Estados Unidos.* San Antonio: Clegg Co., 1930.

Secretaría del Relaciones Exteriores. *Memoria de la Secretaría de Relaciones Exteriores de Agosto de 1928 a Julio 1929.* Mexico City: Secretaría de Relaciones Exteriores, 1930.

Sepúlveda, Ciro. "Research Note: Una Colonia de Obreros: East Chicago, Indiana." *Aztlán* 7 (Summer 1976): 237–336.

Shankman, Arnold. "The Image of Mexico and the Mexican American Black Press, 1980–1935." *Journal of Ethnic Studies* 3 (Summer 1975): 43–56.

Sheridan, Thomas E. *Los Tucsonenses: The Mexican Community in Tucson, 1854–1941.* Tucson: University of Arizona Press, 1986.

Shortell, Mike. "Riot and Reform: The Arizona Territorial Prison, 1876–1909." *New Mexico Lawman* 37 (August 1971): 20–31.

Simon, Daniel T. "Mexican Repatriation in East Chicago, Indiana." *Journal of Mexican American History* 2 (Summer 1974): 11–23.

Skerry, Peter. *Mexican Americans: The Ambivalent Minority.* New York: Free Press, 1993.

Smith, Michael M. "Mexicans in Kansas City: The First Generation, 1900–1920." *Perspectives in Mexican American Studies* 2 (1989): 29–58.

Solliday, Scott W. "The Journey to Rio Salado: Hispanic Migrations to Tempe, Arizona." Master's thesis, Arizona State University, 1993.

Tafolla, Micaela, and Anni Clo Watson. *From Mañana to Ahorita.* Reprinted for the Department of Immigration and Foreign Communities, National Board YMCA. New York: Woman's Press Club, 1929.

Taylor, Paul S. *An American-Mexican Frontier: Nueces County, Texas.* Chapel Hill: University of North Carolina, 1934.

———. "Crime and the Foreign Born: The Problem of the Mexican." In *Report on Crime and Criminal Justice in Relation to the Foreign Born, for the National Commission on Law Observance and Enforcement,* no. 10, edited by Edith Abbott, pp. 199–244. Washington, D.C.: Government Printing Office, 1931.

———. *Mexican Labor in the United States: Chicago and the Calumet Region.* Berkeley: University of California Press, 1931.

———. *Mexican Labor in the United States: Dimmit County, Winter Garden District, South Texas.* Berkeley: University of California Press, 1930.

———. *Mexican Labor in the United States: Valley of the South Platte, Colorado.* Berkeley: University of California, 1929.

———. *A Spanish-Mexican Peasant Community: Arandas in Jalisco, Mexico.* Berkeley: University of California Press, 1933.

Taylor, William B. *Drinking, Homicide, and Rebellion in Colonial Mexican Villages.* Stanford: Stanford University Press, 1979.

Todd, Klondike J. "Crazed Killer 'Shoots It Out'— 48 Shots Fired in Gun Battle on Street." *Arizona Peace Officers' Magazine* 1 (April 1937): 4–6.

Treviño, Roberto, "Prensa y Patria: The Spanish Language Press and the Biculturalization of the Tejano Middle Class, 1920–1940," *Western Historical Quarterly* 22 (November 1991): 451–472.

Tuttle, William M., Jr. *Race Riot: Chicago in the Red Summer of 1919.* New York: Athenaeum, 1970.

Ulloa, Berta. *Revolución intervenida: Relaciones diplomáticos entre México y Estados Unidos, 1910–1914.* Mexico City: El Colegio de México, 1971.

United States Bureau of the Census. *Fifteenth Census of the United States Taken in the Year 1930, General Report of Statistics by Subjects,* vol. 2. Washington, D.C.: Government Printing Office, 1933.

———. *Fifteenth Census of the United States Taken in the Year 1930: Population,* vol. 3, part 2. Washington, D.C.: Government Printing Office, 1933.

———. *Fifteenth Census of the United States Taken in the Year 1930, Appendix on*

Families: Statistics of Mexican, Indian, Chinese, and Japanese Families. Washington, D.C.: Government Printing Office, 1933.

United States Department of State. *Papers Relating to the Foreign Relations of the United States, 1919,* vol. 2. Washington, D.C.: Government Printing Office, 1934.

———. *Papers Relating to the Foreign Relations of the United States, 1931,* vol. 2. Washington, D.C.: Government Printing Office, 1946.

Valadés, Juan C. *Historia general de la revolución mexicana,* vol. 7. Cuernavaca, Morelia: Manuel Quesada Brandi, 1967.

Valdés, Dennis Nodín. Al Norte: Agricultural Workers in the Great Lakes Region, 1917–1970. Austin: University of Texas Press, 1991.

Vanderwood, Paul J. *Disorder and Progress: Bandits, Police, and Mexican Development.* Wilmington, Del.: SR Books, 1992.

Vargas, Zaragoza. *Proletarians of the North: A History of Mexican Industrial Workers in Detroit and the Midwest, 1917–1933.* Berkeley: University of California Press, 1993.

Vélez-Ibáñez, Carlos. *Border Visions: Mexican Cultures of the Southwest United States.* Tucson: University of Arizona Press, 1996.

Venegas, Daniel. *Las aventuras de don Chipote, o cuando los pericos mamen.* Mexico City: Secretaría de Educación Pública, 1984.

Walker, Helen. "Mexican Immigrants and Citizenship." *Sociology and Social Research* 8 (1929): 450–456.

Warnshius, Paul Livingston. "Crime and Criminal Justice among the Mexicans in Illinois." In *Report on Crime and Criminal Justice in Relation to the Foreign Born, for the National Commission on Law Observance and Enforcement,* no. 10, edited by Edith Abbott, pp. 265–332. Washington, D.C.: Government Printing Office, 1931.

Webb, Walter Prescott. *The Texas Rangers: A Century of Frontier Defense.* Boston: Houghton Mifflin, 1935.

Weeks, O. Douglas. "The League of United Latin American Citizens: A Texas Mexican Civic Organization." *Southwestern Social Science Quarterly* 10 (December 1929): 257–278.

Weiss, Harold J., Jr. "The Texas Rangers Revisited: Old Themes and New Viewpoints." *Southwestern Historical Quarterly* 97 (April 1914): 620–640.

Wharton, Charles S. *The House of Whispering Hate.* Chicago: Madelaine Mendelsohn, 1932.

Wickersham Commission Reports, no. 9, *Report on Penal Institutions, Probation and Parole.* Montclair, N.J.: Patterson Smith, 1968.

———, no. 14, *Report on the Police.* Montclair, N.J.: Patterson Smith, 1968.

Winkler, Karen J. "Scholars Say Chicano Studies Field 'Revolutionized' by Issues of Diversity." *Academe Today: Chronicle Archive.* Reprint from *Chronicle of Higher Education,* September 26, 1990.

Wolf, Eric R. *Sons of the Shaking Earth.* Chicago: University of Chicago Press, 1959.

Zamora, Emilio. *The World of the Mexican Worker in Texas.* College Station: Texas A&M University Press, 1993.

Zorrilla, Luis G. *Relaciones políticas, económicas, y sociales de Mexico en el extranjero,* vol. 3. Mexico City: Luis G. Zorrilla, 1995.

FILMS

Ballad of an Unsung Hero. San Diego: Cinewest/KPBS, 1983.

RECORDINGS

Sonnichsen, Phillip. *Texas Mexican Border Music,* Long-Play Recordings and Text, vols. 2 and 3, *Corridos,* Parts 1 and 2. Arhoolie Records, 1974.

Index

Index compiled by Beth Luey and the Scholarly Publishing Program at Arizona State University.

Abbott, Edith, 49
abuse, of immigrants, 1, 4–5. *See also* violence
Achondo, Juan E., 116
Acosta, Francisco G., 13
activism. *See* legal aid societies
age comparisons of immigrants, 58, 159–160
agriculture, labor control in, 76, 106–107, 109
Agrupación Protectora Mexicana (San Antonio), 27
Aguacaliente Casino: robbery of couriers, 126
Aguirre, Martin and Joseph, 165
Aguirre Manjarrez, Raúl, 48
Aikman, Duncan, 73
alcohol, 32–33, 60–61, 66–67, 71–72, 195–196
Alemán, Miguel, 190
Algodones, attack on, 11–12
Alguin, "Little Phil," 94
Alianza Hispano Americana (Tucson), 27, 135
Alianza Liberal Mexicana (San Antonio), 29
Allred, James, 147
Alvarez, Tomás, 152
Americanization, 5, 36, 42, 44
American Latin League (Los Angeles), 36

Amigo del Hogar (Indiana), 25, 46
Andrade, Timoteo, 127–128
Andrews, J. N., 126
Anglo American Chamber of Commerce (Mexico City), 153–154
Anguiano, José, 59, 61, 71, 192
anti-Americanism, 3, 5, 10–11, 12, 13
Apolinar Partida, Clemente, 144
Arango, Rodolfo, 32, 45
Arce, José Antonio, 17
Arce, Julio, 29–32, 35–36, 148–149, 165
Arizona: activism in, 27; arrest rates in, 52; capital punishment in, 136–141, 199–200; civilian violence in, 103–104; clemency movement in, 32; courts in, 130; internecine crime in, 61–62; labor control in, 75, 76, 107; lynchings in, 118; police in, 80–82; prisons in, 159–160, 164, 166, 167, 172–173; sentencing in, 161–162; third degree in, 85–86. *See also* Bisbee; Clifton; Miami; Phoenix; Ray; Tucson; Yuma
Arizona Rangers, 91–93
Arizona Republican, 14
Arizona Sentinel, 167
Arizona Territorial Legislature, 91
Arkansas, mob violence in, 117
arms embargo, in Mexican Revolution, 12, 17, 20
Arredondo, Eliseo, 39
arrest rates, 4, 49, 51–58, 156
arrests, 26, 80–85
Asamblea General (Bisbee, Ariz.), 23
Asamblea Mexicana (Houston), 27–28

Ashurst, Henry, 23
assimilation, 5, 36, 42, 44
Avila, Andrés, 22

Baca, Elfego, 142
Baize, C. C., 77
Ballad of an Unsung Hero, 164
bandido, as stereotype, 50
banditry, 2, 10–11, 89, 178–180
Bernard, Sam, 82
Bernhart, Theodore, 144
Beteta, Ramón, 188
Big Bend (Texas), 16, 89–90
Bisbee, Ariz., 23
"Black Legend," 9
blacks, 25–26, 113, 160
Blackwelder, Julia, 67–68
Blanco, José, 111
Blanco, Lucio, 181
Bogardus, Emory, 195
Bonilla, Ignacio, 40
bootlegging, 66–67, 68, 71–72
border agents, 50, 70, 86–87, 97–98
border: control of, 9, 17, 73; crime on, 2, 9, 64, 68, 91, 96–97, 110–111; raids along, 16, 17–20, 141–142
Borrego, José, 126
Box, John C., 44, 193
Brindley, Verne, 95–96
Brite Ranch, attack on, 18–19, 89–90, 179
Brooklyn courthouse bombing, 46–47, 133
Brown, Richard Maxwell, 99–101
"Brown Scare," 3, 10–11, 101
Bryan, William Jennings, 144
Bucareli Agreement, 43
Buckley, Frank, 50
Burelach, Father F., 72
Burns, Juan T., 20
Bustamante, Leo, 81–82

Caballo, León, 88
Cadena, Frank, 144–145
Cadena, Joaquín, 135
Calexico, Calif., KKK in, 73
California: arrest rates in, 53; capital punishment in, 147–152, 200; civilian killings in, 104; courts in, 131, 132; employer abuse in, 107–108; immigration to, 54; internecine violence in, 62; Ku Klux Klan in, 25, 73; lynchings in, 119; in Mexican Revolution, 13–14; prisons in, 160–161, 164, 169; segregation in, 25–26; sentencing in, 162, 163. *See also* Colton; Lemon Grove; Los Angeles; San Diego; San Francisco; Santa Paula
California Civic League, 149
California Law 263, 47
Calles, Plutarco Elías, 44, 181
Calumet News, 63
Campbell, Jack, 146
Campos, Apolonio, 152
Canales, José T., 88, 91, 120, 197–198
Canales, Servando, 34
Cananea Strike, 92
Cano, Pedro, 130–131
capital punishment: activism against, 30–32, 200; in Arizona, 136–141, 199–200; in California, 147–152, 200; decline of, 199–200; in Midwest, 152, 154–155; in New Mexico, 141–142; in New York, 152–154; patterns of, 134, 135, 146–147; in Texas, 142–147, 200
Cárdenas, Lázaro, 48, 147, 184
Cárdenas Martínez, León, 38, 143–144
Carranza, Venustiano, 17, 20, 35–36, 39–41
Carrillo Puerto, Felipe, 149
Carrizal, conflict at, 17, 89
Catholic Church, 5, 44, 62
Centro Radical Mexicano, 27, 80–81
Cerda, Jesús María, 17
Chacel, Arturo, 28
Chapa, Francisco, 23, 30, 145–146, 153
Chapman, David, 119
Chávez, Arcadio, 183
Chávez, Gregorio, 149–150
Chávez, N. B., 138–139
Chicago: Anglo attitudes in, 49; arrests in, 45, 52–53, 57–58; courts in, 123–124, 125, 131; crime in, 32, 65; immigrant community in, 28, 56, 58; inter-

necine violence in, 58–59, 63–64, 213–217; legal aid in, 28, 33; México Lindo in, 6; mob violence in, 115, 117; police in, 79–80, 84, 95, 96; sentencing in, 156; unemployment in, 57
Chicago Tribune, 23–24
chicanada (Mexican folk), 109
Chinese, smuggling of, 70
Círculo de Santa Teresa, 153
citizenship, judges' role in, 127–128
City Drug Store (Phoenix), burglary of, 81–82
Ciudad Juárez, 12, 68
civilian violence, 100–104. *See also* violence
civil rights groups. *See* legal aid societies
class: and Anglo attitudes, 2, 3; divisiveness of, 32, 33; and violence, 59, 84–85
"clemency movement," 32
Clifton, Ariz.: mining strike in, 40–41, 91, 174
Club Chapultepec, 151
Club Social Mexicano (Phoenix), 34
cocaine, 71
Coke, Richard, 177–178
Colorado, 50, 78, 118–119
Colquitt, Oscar B., 11, 12, 14, 88, 144
Colton, Calif., police abuses in, 76
Columbus, N.M., border raid in, 16, 141–142
Comisiones Honoríficas Mexicanas, 24, 42, 108, 114, 140, 151
Comité de Defensa (Waco, Tex.), 144
Comité de Defensa de Mauricio Trinidad, 151
Comité Pro-Galván, 147
Comité Pro Grijalva, 98
Comité Pro-Juárez, 73
Committee Against Alcohol (Chicago), 33
Confederación de Sociedades Mexicanas, 28, 133–134, 151
Confederación de Sociedades Mexicanas de los EUA (Chicago), 28
Congress of the Latin American Press, 30

consuls: and desegregation, 44–45; and espionage, 34–36, 44, 45; and extradition, 184; immigrant opinions of, 40–41, 45–48; and immigrant protection, 37, 39–40, 132–134, 170–171, 195; and México Lindo, 5, 34; reform of, 37, 40
Conventionalist Government, 36
conviction rates, 125
Cook, J. Willis, 46
Corpus Christi, Tex.: Villista plot in, 16
Correo Mexicano (Chicago), 6, 79
corruption, 72, 77–78, 92–93, 173
Cortés-Rubio, Emilio and Salvador, 84–85
Cortez, Gregorio, 93
Cortina, Juan Nepucemo, 177
Cosmopolita, El (Kansas City), 35, 36, 79
Coss, Francisco, 44
Cota Robles, Amado, 36
courts, 2, 31, 122–125, 130–132. *See also* capital punishment; sentencing
coyotes, 69–71
crime: on border, 2, 9, 64, 68, 91, 96–97, 110–111; causes of, 59–60, 195–196; internecine, 32, 58–64; nature of, 4, 6–7, 32–33, 64–66, 142, 144–145, 161–163; perceptions of, 49; regional differences in, 49, 53
Cristero Rebellion, 44, 45, 91, 194
Crites, Maurice E., 127
Crosby, Cecil, 84–85
cross burnings, 114
customs agents, 13, 147

Dancinger, Jack, 35, 39, 123
Dávila, D. R., 143
Dávila, Francisco, 5
Dávila, José M., 67
defamation, 23–24
defense funds. *See* legal aid societies
defense lawyers, 132–134, 199
Defensor, El, 195
de la Barra, Francisco León, 37, 137
de la Colina, Rafael, 45
de la Lama, Pedro, 29, 30
de la Peña, Horacio, 167–168

de la Rosa, Luis, 16, 88
del Hoyo, Julián, 46
de los Santos, Isabel, 17
del Río, Nivardo, 45
del Valle, Reginald, 36
Demócrata, El (Phoenix), 104
de Negri, Ramón P., 35–36, 153–154, 161
Denver, mass arrests in, 78
deportation, 16, 170. *See also* extradition; repatriation
desegregation, 44–45, 133
Detroit, 28, 54, 57
Deutsch, Sarah, 50
Día de San Juan festival: banning of, 104
Díaz, Máximo, 103
Díaz, Norberto, 77–78
Díaz, Porfirio, 10, 34–35, 37
Dillinger, John, 134
Dimmit County, Tex., 53
diplomatic immunity, 47, 128–129
disorderly conduct laws, 75
Domínguez, Adolfo, 47, 128–129
Domínguez, Hermenegildo, 179, 180
draft registration, 39
dragnets, 75, 78–80
drugs, smuggling of, 71–72
Dúran, Mónico, 165
Dye, John W., 72

Elías, Arturo, 35, 46
Elko, Nev., 26
El Paso, Tex.: border tension in, 13, 16, 73; crime in, 68, 72; deportations from, 16; jail fire in, 158; police killings in, 42, 86; third degree used in, 85
El Polvo Ranch, 19
escapes: from prison, 172–174, 178
Escobar, Edward, 76
Escobar, Ramón, 135
Estill, Robert G., 134
Estrada, Rafael, 166
ethnocentrism, Anglo, 50
evictions of immigrants, 13
expatriates, American, in Mexico, 10
extradition: agreements on, 177–178; illegal, 139–140, 147, 178–182, 184,

201–202; refused, 183–184; resistance to, 201; of Roa, 184–192

Fall, Albert Bacon, 12, 19–20
family ties: and crime, 55
Fanon, Frantz, 60
farm workers, 76, 106–107, 109
Félix, Antonio, 182
Ferguson, James E., 23, 111–112
Ferguson, Miriam "Ma," 29
Fern, Victor, 46
Fernández, Eugenio, 46
Fernández, J. A., 13, 38
Ferreira, Enrique, 171
fiestas patrias, 5, 42, 104, 110
films, 23, 50, 164
Flores Magón brothers, 10, 34–35, 174
Forbes, Thomas, 85–86
Foreign Miners Tax, 37
Foster, William Z., 102, 106
Fox, J. M., 90
Fraesier, M. F., 81–82
Franco, Jesús, 30, 42, 140
Friedrich, Paul, 60, 61
Friendly Settlement House (Phoenix), 42
Fromm, Erich, 60
Fronterizo, El, 5

Gallegos, Rudolfo, 13–14
Galván, Raúl Ramiro, 147
García, Agustín, 79
García, Enrique, 152–154
García, Gregorio, 135
García, Mario, 81
García, Max, 96
García, Ramón, 167
García Gómez, Manuel, 84–85
García Treviño, Eliud, 33
García y Alva, Francisco, 29
Garson, David, 101
Garza, Agustín, 88
Garza, Catarino, 34
Garza, María Ester, 32
gender ratios and crime, 55–56, 57
Germany: Mexican support of, 20, 40–41
Gibler, Frank, 27–28

Gómez, Antonio, 27, 37, 119
Gómez, Victor, 107–108
González, Jesús, 77
González, José, 118
González, Luis, 60, 61
González, Manuel, 134–135
González, Sevariano, 123
González Abalardo, Manuel, 170
Gram, Sam, 102–103
Great Depression, 116–117, 127. *See also* unemployment
Green, Thomas, 128–129
Grijalva, Alfredo, 98, 135, 171
Guadalupe, Our Lady of, 5
Guess, William E., 84–85
guilty pleas, 125
gunrunning, 69
guns, ownership of, 33, 47, 61, 94

Hall, Raymond, 132–133
Hamilton, Grace, 133, 153
Harley, James, 90
Harper's Weekly, 92
Hatfield, Joseph Robert, 107–108
Heraldo de México, 151
Heras, Jesús, 150
Heras, Juan de, 30
Hernández, Fred and Manuel, 140–141
Hernández, Gustavo G., 40, 125
"Hispanic," defined, 8
Hispano América (San Francisco), 25, 150, 151, 154, 169
Hobby, W. P., 23
Home Mission Council, 73
home ownership, 56
Hoover, J. Edgar, 47, 187
Horta, Juvenciano, 47, 132
Houston, self-defense groups in, 27–28
Huerta, Victoriano, 12–13, 20, 35, 38–39, 174
Hunt, George W. P., 138–139, 166, 171

Idar, Nicasio, 27, 37
Illinois, sentencing in, 154–155, 162–163. *See also* Chicago
Illinois Superior Court, 131
Immigrant Protective League, 127

immigration: laws on, 9, 30, 69, 70; Mexican government and, 42; responses to, 1; as temporary exile, 5; undocumented, 69–71, 157
Immigration Act of 1917, 69;
Immigration Border Patrol, 86–87
Immigration Quota Act of 1924, 70
Imparcial de Texas (San Antonio), 23, 30, 170
Imperial County, Calif., 53
Imperial Valley Immigration Committee, 108
Indiana, internecine violence in, 62–63
Indiana Harbor Welfare Committee, 127
indigenismo, 5
industrialization, 2–3
Industrial Workers of the World, 125–126, 144
insanity: and capital punishment, 144, 155
intermarriage, 120
interpreters, 31, 123. *See also* language problems

jails, local, 156–158. *See also* prisons
Jim Crow laws, 4, 115
Johnstown, Penn.: Mexicans expelled from, 95
journalists, activism of, 30. *See also* newspapers
Juárez, Benito, 5, 34, 177
Juárez (city), 12, 68
judges, 124–129
juntas patrióticas, 34, 36
justices of the peace, 125

Kansas, 25, 84, 161
Kansas City: class divisions in, 32, 33; internecine violence in, 62; legal aid in, 26; muggings in, 66; partisans in, 35; police misconduct in, 77, 79; weapons laws in, 61
Kidder, Jeff, 92
Klein, Peter M., 173, 184–192
Knight, John, 127–128
Kondall, Hugh K., 82
Ku Klux Klan, 25, 72–73, 91, 112, 114, 115

labor: abuse of, 107, 169–170; competition for, 7, 99–101, 111–115, 118–119, 120: control of, 2, 3, 24, 28, 54, 75–76, 78, 105–109, 157: disputes, 27, 39–41, 81, 91, 94, 174: employer need for, 90, 113; in prisons, 166–167; stratification of, 22;

land reform, 59–60

language, retention of, 5. *See also* Americanization

language problems: and arrest rates, 52; in court system, 2, 31, 122–124, 129–130, 131–132; in prison, 168–169

Laredo, Tex., 17, 27, 72, 73

Las Casas, Bartolomé de, 9

Las Norias Ranch, 88–89

Latin American Club, 135

Laustauneau, William "Wenceslao," 174, 175

lawyers, 2, 85, 129–135, 199

League of United Latin American Citizens, 44–45, 134

legal aid societies: in capital punishment cases, 138–139, 140, 143, 144, 145, 147, 151–152; in Los Angeles, 36, 37, 133–134, 145, 151; role of, 26–29, 30, 34

Lemon Grove, Calif., 25, 55, 133

Leonard, H. H., 70

León brothers, 85–86

León de la Barra, Francisco, 37, 137

Levelier, Ives, 40, 139

Liekens, Enrique, 154

Liga Protectora de Refugiados (Phoenix), 29

Liga Protectora Latina (Phoenix), 27, 28, 29, 138–139

Liga Protectora Mexicana (Los Angeles), 133–134, 145, 151

Lira, Vicente, 17

literacy: and prison conditions, 168–169

livestock rustling, 88, 177–178

loitering. *See* vagrancy laws

Lomelí, Manuel, 80

López, Bernardo, 26

López, Juvencio, 119

Los Angeles: arrests in, 26, 53: judges in, 125–126; labor in, 24, 76, 125–126;

legal aid in, 28, 36, 37, 133–134, 145, 151; police in, 78–79, 80, 83–84, 95–96; prostitution in, 68; vagrancy enforcement in, 46, 50

Louisiana: illegal arrests in, 46

Lozano family, 30

Lupián, Lorenzo, 45, 124

lynchings: in Arizona, 118; in California, 119; Mexican responses to, 119–120; motives for, 198; prevention of, 26; in Southwest, 2; in Texas, 11, 27, 37, 103, 110–111, 114, 119–121, 143. *See also* mob violence

machismo, 60

Madero, Francisco I., 11–12, 35, 38

Magill, J. A., 76

Malakoff Fuel Company, 116–117

Manifest Destiny, 3, 9

marijuana, immigrant use of, 66–67

Márquez, Francisco, 130, 136–137

Marshall, George C., 190

Martínez, C. Emilio, 40–41

Martínez, Manuel, 133, 139–140, 181

Martínez, Paulino, 17

Martínez Palomares, F., 35

mártires de Texas, 29, 97

Marvin, George, 91

Mascarena, Alberto, 148–149

Masonic lodges, 149

Mata, Juan, 145

Matlock, N. W., 81

McEahern, E. A., 125

McLatchey, Alonso, 127

media. *See* newspapers

Medina, E., 23

Medreno, Mario, 46

Mefistófeles, 35–36

Menchaca, Martha, 94

Mercado, J. J., 27

"Mexican," defined, 7

"Mexican American," defined, 7

Mexican-American War, 9

"Mexican Hall" (Malakoff, Tex.), bombing of, 116–117

"Mexican Problem," 3–4

Mexican Protective Association (San Antonio), 143

Mexican Revolution: and American opinion, 7, 193–194; arms embargo in, 17, 20; border provocations in, 11–12; capital punishment during, 137–138; and court system in Mexico, 122; extradition during, 180; gunrunning in, 69; and immigration, 3–4; impact of, on U.S., 9–11; propaganda during, 34–36; prostitution during, 68
Mexico, violence in, 59–61
México (Chicago), 24, 96
México Libre (El Paso), 22
México Lindo, 5–6, 22–23, 34, 194–195
Meyer, F. W., 111
Miami, Ariz., 81
Midland, Tex., 77–78
Midwest: capital punishment in, 152, 154–155; civilian killings in, 104; immigration to, 55; internecine violence in, 62–64; legal aid in, 28; mob violence in, 111; police raids in, 79–80; prisons in, 161, 166, 173; trials in, 131–132. *See also* Chicago
military, U.S., killings by, 104–105
Miller, Kerby, 5
Miller, Nathan A., 153–154
mining communities: labor control in, 40–41, 75–76, 91, 174; police killings in, 81; prostitution in, 68; working conditions in, 40
miscegenation, 198
mob violence, 110–115, 117, 198–199. *See also* lynchings
Modesto, Calif., 25
Moeur, B. B., 166
Mondragón, A. L., 155
"mongrelization," 3
Monroy, Nemesio, 126
Montecristo Ranch: executions at, 89
Montejano, David, 99
Montes, Felipe, 66
Moody, Dan, 77, 164
Morán y Mariscal, Ignacio, 180
Morenci copper strike, 40–41, 91, 174
Morín, Colonel, 16
Morris, W. T., 93
Mosquito, El (Tucson), 23
Moss, Andrew, 73

mugging, 66
Muñoz, Nicandro, 145
murder. *See* violence
mutual aid societies, 26–29. *See also* legal aid societies

Nacional, El (Chicago), 26, 132
National Guard: on border, 17
nationalism, 10, 23, 24–25, 42. *See also* México Lindo
Native Americans, 15, 66, 177
naturalization, rates of, 195. *See also* Americanization
Navarrete, Jesús, 106
Navarro, León, 34
Navarro, Olivio, 66
Neff, Pat, 42, 170
neutrality laws, 10, 11, 13, 34
Neville Ranch, 19
New Mexico, 16, 104, 130, 141–142, 200
newspapers: and anti-Americanism, 11, 13, 22; on border raids, 12, 15; crime reporting in, 4, 50, 63–64; and moral reform, 32–33; on police brutality, 77; on prison conditions, 164; on race, 23–24
New York: capital punishment in, 152–154
New York Times, 87–88
Nogales, 15–16, 20
Noon, Fred, 133
norteños, 22, 55
Núñez, Hilario, 78

Oakville, Tex., 26
Obregón, Alvaro, 19–20, 41–48, 114, 146, 150–151, 154, 171
O'Brien, Gail, 101
Odom, Mary, 68
Ojo del Agua Ranch, 79
Oklahoma, 84–85, 108, 113–114
Older, Fremont, 148
Olzak, Susan, 99
Omaha, 52
Opinión, La (Los Angeles), 23, 24, 151
oppression, theories of, 1–2, 7
Orden Caballeros de Honor, 27
Orozco, Pascual, 12, 20, 174

Orozco y Jiménez, Francisco, 45
Ortega, Juan, 94
Ortiz, Salvador, 118
Ortiz Rubio, Pascual, 117; killing of nephew of, 128–129
Osorio, D. F., 35
Owls Fraternal Club, 114

Pacheco, Basil, 109
Pacheco, Luis and Juan, 200
Padilla, Miguel, 33
Palomares, F. Martínez, 35
Pan American Round Table (San Antonio), 153–154
pandering, 67
Pardo Zamora, Rubén C., 87
parole, 170–171
Partido Liberal Mexicano (PLM), 10, 29, 144
"pass system," 78
patria chica, 24
Payno, Manuel, 162, 171
Paz, Octavio, 60
peon, as stereotype, 50
Perales, Alonso L., 23
Peralta, Eduardo, 61
Peralta, Miguel, 138–139
Pereda, Francisco, 66
Pérez, Eduardo, 138–139
Perkins, Clifford A., 86, 97–98, 101
Pershing, John, 16, 17, 39
Pesquiera, Francisco A., 151
Pharris, C. G., 116
Phoenix: Americanization in, 42; crime in, 64, 68; legal aid societies in, 27–29, 34, 138–139; police in, 81–82, 104
Plan de San Diego, 15–17, 88–89, 119
Plan de San Luis Potosí, 11–12
Plaza Methodist-Episcopal Social Service Center (Los Angeles), 28
police: attitude of, 115; corruption among, 68, 77–78; ethnicity of, 2, 96–97; killing of, 137–138, 145, 197; Mexicans as, 80, 96–97; private, 82–83; protests against, 197; resistance to, 26, 93–97; violence of, 42, 75–77, 79–87, 143, 196–197

political prisoners, 29
Polvo Ranch, 19
Pompa, Aurelio, 30, 109, 150–151
Ponce, Victoria, 16
Porfiriato, 10, 34–35, 37
Porvenir massacre, 18–19, 90
poverty: and crime, 196
Preciat, C. Emilio Martínez, 40–41
Prensa, La (San Antonio), 45, 113, 144, 153
Price, James, 173, 191–192
Prida, Ramón, 59, 60, 105
Primer Congreso Mexicanista (Laredo), 27
prisons: art in, 167; conditions in, 163–165; deaths in, 174–176; escapes from, 172–174, 178; immigrant population of, 158–161; labor in, 166–167; language problems in, 168–169; violence in, 169–170; white inmates in, 164–165
Prohibition, 66, 71–72, 196
prosecutors, bias of, 129
prostitution, 67–69
Puebla, Juan, 181–182
Puig, Enrique, 78
Puig Casauranc, José, 47
"Punitive Expedition," 16, 17, 39

Quijano, José, 151
Quinney, Richard, 52
Quiñones, Joel, 46
Quintero, *el payaso*, 178
Quiroz, Roberto, 140

race: and capital punishment, 146–147
racism: Arce on, 31–32; historiography of, 1–2; and lynching, 119; in newspapers, 23–24; and perceptions of criminality, 3, 4, 49; and violence, 99–101, 109, 120–121, 198
Ragen, Joseph E., 184, 186–188, 189–191
railroads, 22, 27, 106
Ramírez, Alfonso, 44, 50
Ramos, Samuel, 60
Rangel, Jesús, 29, 96

rape, 64, 69, 105, 145
Ray, Ariz.: police/immigrant battle
in, 94
recession of 1921, 111–112
recession of 1926, 24
recidivism, 201
Redfield, Robert, 131
Redondo, Antonio, 32
Reed, Alma S., 148–149
Regeneración, 35
Rehn, Hjalmar, 184, 185–186
Reina, Francisco, 181
Rentería, Eusebio, 141–142
Rentería, Jesús, 179
repatriation: after Mexican War, 37; in
mining strike, 40–41; and unem-
ployment, 37, 42, 47–48, 66, 112, 114,
117, 127. *See also* deportation
Resíndez brothers, 114–115
Reveles, Leoncio, 88–89
Reyes, Alfonso, 96
Reyna, Anastasio, 166
Reyna, Juan, 95–96, 134, 175–176
Rice, Ben, 124
Richardson, F. W., 150–151
Rivas, Cenobio, 89
Rizo, Gregorio, 173–174
Roa, José Cristóbal, 46
Roa Berber, Bernardo, 155, 173–174,
184–192
Robles y Mendoza, Margarita, 44
Rodríguez, Antonio, 11, 37, 110
Rodríguez, Clemente, 145
Rodríguez, Francisco, 138–139
Rodríguez, Jesús, 135
Rodríguez, Raúl R., 36
Rodríguez, Victor, 145
Rodriguez v. Texas, 127
romanticization: of criminals, 50, 144–
145; of Rangers, 87–88, 92
Romero, Julian, 142
Romo, Ricardo, 3
Roque Estrada, Enrique, 29
Rosales family, wedding picture of, 56
"Rosita Alvarez" (ballad), 62
Ruffo, J. B., 29
Ruíz, D. Eduardo, 42, 43

Ruíz, Enrique, 165
Ruíz, Simón, 124, 132, 148–149

saboteurs, 34–35
Sacco-Vanzetti execution, 46
sadism: among police, 76–77
Sáenz, Moisés, 44
Salas, Fernando, 27–28
Salazar, Carmen, 105
Salt River Valley (Arizona), 14–15
San Antonio, Tex.: arrest rates in, 53–
54; immigrant community of, 5, 55,
56, 58; legal aid in, 27, 29, 143; prosti-
tution in, 68; smuggling in, 74
San Benito, Tex., 11
San Bernardino, Calif., 25
Sánchez, Agustín L., 152–154
Sánchez, Pedro, 146
San Diego, 126–127
San Diego Sun, 108
San Diego Union, 87
San Francisco, 25, 37, 53
San Francisco Call, 148–149
San Francisco Forum, 149
San Ignacio Army barracks, 17
Santa Paula, Calif., 47, 94
Santa Ysabel massacre, 86, 89, 105
Santibáñez, Enrique, 156–157
Sarabia, Manuel, 29
Saragoza, Alex, 1–2
Saucedo, Pedro, 102–103
Saucedo, Salvador, 120
Saylor, Anna, 149
Schroeder, Marie, 102, 120
Seen, E. M., 28
segregation, 25–26, 54, 114, 166–167, 169
self-defense, 69, 102, 103, 107, 150, 152–
154
self-defense groups. *See* legal aid soci-
eties
sentencing, 2, 54, 126, 156, 161–163. *See
also* capital punishment
Servín, Ezequiel, 145
Sheridan, Thomas, 32, 80–81
Silva, Jesús, 46
Silva, Pedro, 72
Silvas, Plácido, 133

Sloan, Richard P., 137
Small, Lee, 77
Smith, Alfred, 153–154
Smith, Michael, 62
smuggling: attitudes toward, 72–74; on border, 2, 64; of drugs and alcohol, 71–72; enforcement against, 9; of humans, 69–71; treaty on, 73; and violence, 72, 87, 97–98
social change: and violence, 59–60
Sociedad Cruz Azul Mexicana, 151
Sociedad Mutualista Benito Juárez (Kansas City), 33
Sociedad Mutualista de Obreros Mexicanos, 96
Sociedad Mutualista Guadalupana, 173
Sonnichsen, C. L., 101
Sonora: Arizona Rangers in, 91, 92
Southwest, 2, 9, 80, 118. *See also* Arizona; border; New Mexico; Texas
Spanish language, 42. *See also* Americanization; language problems
Spencer, Mary Lee, 133, 155
spying: in consulates, 34–36, 44, 45
Staleski, Walter, 155
Stephens, William D., 148–149
stereotypes, 24, 49, 60, 193–194
Stiles, Billy, 92–93
strikebreakers, violence against, 111, 114–115, 118–119
strikes, 39–41, 91, 174. *See also* labor
suicide: in prison, 175–176

Tafolla, Micaela, 75
Tampico, uprising in, 11
Taylor, Paul S., 54, 79–80, 102, 131, 162
Taylor, William B., 61
Tecate, post office robbery in, 14
Téllez, Manuel, 41–42, 43, 128–129, 153, 154
Texas: Anglo attitudes in, 49; capital punishment in, 142–147, 200; courts in, 124–125, 129; crime rates in, 56; labor control in, 54; legal aid societies in, 26–27, 144; lynchings in, 11, 27, 37, 103, 110–111, 114, 119–121, 143; Mexican rebels in, 11, 12, 13, 16; native Tejanos in, 26; parole in, 170–171;

police in, 54, 76–77, 79, 82–84; prisons in, 157–158, 160, 164–166, 169–170, 172; sentencing in, 162; unemployment in, 57; vagrancy laws in, 78; violence in, 101–103, 106–107, 112–113, 114, 116–117, 197–198, 213–217. *See also* El Paso; Houston; Laredo; San Antonio
Texas Rangers: in Border Patrol, 86–87; conduct of, 38, 72, 87–91; and Corpus Christi plotters, 16; killed in San Benito, 11; and Mexican Revolution, 12; in Mexico, 178; in Porvenir, 18–19; protect Mexicans, 91, 113, 116–117
Texas Rebellion, 9
Tijuana, 126
third degree, 75, 85–86
Torres, Simplicio, 139
Tórrez, Roberto, 133, 155, 173–174
torture, 85–86
Tovar, Juan, 89
Treaty of Guadalupe Hidalgo (1848), 127
Trejo, José I., 29
Treviño, Ricardo, 73
Treviño de García, María, 105
Trinidad, Mauricio, 131, 134, 151
Tucson, 5, 27, 55
Tucsonense, El, 5, 36, 200
Turner, Kenneth B., 113

Ulica, Jorge. *See* Arce, Julio
unemployment: and anti-Mexican activity, 42–44; and crime, 57, 63, 66, 67; and mass arrests, 78–79; and violence, 91, 95, 111, 112–113, 116–117
Unión de Obreros Mexicanos, 134
Universal, El (Mexico City), 46–47
Urbina, M. A. and J. A., 35
Uriburu, J. J., 36
Utah, 130–131
Utily, Ernest R., 108

vagrancy laws, 46, 50, 78–80, 157
Valdez, Santos, 135
Valle, Jesús, 109
Vargas, Anastasio, 147
Vasconcelos, José, 36
Vásquez, Alfredo C., 171

Velasco, Alberto, 47, 132, 168–169
Velasco, Carlos, 27
Velásquez, Euralio, 16
Vélez, Rudolph, 81–82
Venegas, Daniel, 32
Veracruz, invasion of, 39, 88, 144
vigilantes, 2, 18–19. *See also* lynchings
Villa, Francisco (Pancho), 13, 15–19, 89, 141–142
Villa, Hipólito, 20
Villalobos, Ramón, 138–139
Villarreal, Elías, 120
Villaseñor, David, 23
Villaseñor, Victor, 66
violence: by border officials, 86–87; civilian, 100–104, 203–211; and class, 59, 84–85; internecine, 32, 47, 58–64, 146–147, 213–217; and marijuana, 67; in Mexico, 59–61; by mobs, 110–115, 117, 198–199; in prison, 169–170; by private guards, 82–83; and racism, 99–101, 109, 120–121, 198; and smuggling, 72; and women, 64, 69, 105, 145; in workplace, 107–109, 197–198. *See also* police: violence of
Volstead Act, 71

Warnshius, Paul: on arrest tactics, 75; on courts, 123–124, 125, 131, 156; on

crime statistics, 49, 159, 161, 163; on prison, 166, 168
War Prohibited Act of 1918, 71
weapons, ownership of, 33, 47, 61, 94
Webb, Walter Prescott, 87
"web of control," 54, 75, 76–77
Welch, John, 81
Welch, Mitchell, 18
Welles, Sumner, 128
Wharton, Charles S., 165
Wickersham Commission, 49, 56
Wilson, Henry Lane, 11
Wilson, Woodrow, 12–13, 14, 15, 17
Wolf, Eric, 60
women: and crime, 62, 63, 64, 67–69, 105, 145
Women's Christian Temperance Union, 149
workers. *See* labor
World War I, 20, 39

Yaquis, 10, 15
Yripanga incident, 20
Yuma, Ariz., 11–12, 66

Zapata, Emiliano, 29
Zimmerman telegram, 20
Zorilla Flores, Juana, 90
Zuburán Capmany, Rafael, 35